FRO WHENCE WE CAME

THE BIBLICAL AGE OF WORLD ENLIGHTENMENT

ROBERT SOPER

[1]

First printing 2008. Second edition 2016
ISBN 978-1-326-64669-1

Pompacalie Publishing

Contact author on bobsoper@live.co.uk

Cover design and layout by Oscar J Soper ©
Line drawings Copyright Oscar J Soper ©

Dedicated to the memory of the late Rev Derek Shaw and his wife Christine of Bramham village in the County of Yorkshire, England, who surreptitiously put some of the ideas into my head.

Also by Robert Soper

Antiques and the Stately Homes, the story of Castle Fairs.

The Fairest Isle – The Foulest Deeds – a novel of the Slave Trade.

World Slavery – The Bigger Picture. The story of Slavery and the Slave trade from Ancient times to the 21st century.

The Bones of Cathy King and more tales from the other side. – A series of short stories about ghosts and other unexplained phenomena.

The Real Riviera. A light hearted romp through the South of France as some English thieves take on the French and Russian mafias.

The Wars of Patrick O'Grady, VC. The story of the struggle of a soldier severely wounded in Afghanistan as he comes to terms with life outside the army.

Whitewashed. 9/11, David Kelly, Princess Diana and other inquiries where the official verdict may not agree with the facts.

The Ugly Ducklings. Fun and games in the Deep South as two innocents abroad take on the might of the US mafia.

Donald Crumb, Tycoon. A story of life in Yorkshire for the Sixties generation of businessman. How they worked and played, not always by the rules.

The Lord Giveth...... How a man made catastrophe may provoke the third and final mass extinction on earth. Frightening and only too realistic.

The Dorset Sopers. The story of the family of the author and how they emerged from being illiterate farm labourers to successful professionals all over the world.

Motor Sport's Golden Age. The story of the involvement of the author in motor sport during '60s Yorkshire. Especially his involvement with the British Automobile Racing Club at the time.

The Battling Bickerdykes. How Len Bickerdyke, former Yorkshire miner and serial shirker eventually got the better of his scheming and devious wife.

All these books can be bought from your local book shop or on line from Amazon.com or direct from the printers, Lulu.com.

INDEX

[7]

Thomas Edison, when faced with a difficult problem, remarked, *'It is too difficult for a specialist to understand, better wait for some amateur to come along and solve it.'*

FOREWORD

THE BIBLE OR DARWIN? COULD THEY BOTH BE RIGHT?

When my father was a young man in the days of the silent movie, each Saturday morning he would to go to see the latest episode of an adventure series called *'The Perils of Pauline'*, starring a young lady named Pearl White. Miss White was a 'Femme Fatale' who got herself into the most impossible of scrapes, such as hanging over a precipice by her little finger, or being tied to a railway track with an express bearing down on her. There she would be left until the following week when the episode would begin with the phrase, *'With One Mighty Bound She Was Free'*.

This saved the writers much anguish in extricating her, leaving them free to get on with the story without having to explain some very difficult questions. And this, I always feel, is how much of the Bible and the ancient world is treated today. *"How did they build the pyramids?" "Obviously they dug up the blocks by hand." "How did they do that?" "Don't be difficult, how else could they have done it? Then they simply dragged them along for a mile or two and put them into position. Simple."* With one 'mighty bound' they were there. Ask what they were built for. *'Tombs of course, everyone knows that pyramids are tombs. Silly question. What else could they use them for?'* And it is the same with so many other awkward questions throughout history where the 'mighty bound' theory is the best answer. Or, even more convenient, the air brush. Then the story can emerge as being the one that the historian had intended it to be with the awkward questions put to one side to be forgotten by all.

I am that difficult person who refuses to do that and indeed, asks those very awkward questions. I ask the *'What else?'* question and try to answer it. The answers are not always there but they do take the reader down new paths and open doors that have remained firmly closed throughout time. It makes interesting reading.

Having been fascinated by the pyramids and Ancient Egypt all my life, as well as being a reluctant agnostic, I have avidly read much of the published literature over the years. From this I do not see how anyone can question, let alone dismiss, the *basic* theory of *'Natural Selection'* and *'The Survival of the Fittest'* as promulgated by Darwin. I cannot over-emphasize the word *'basic'.* Always bear that in mind when hearing the arguments for and against. There is simply too much evidence from Palaeontology to be able to raise much doubt. And the Genesis version of the Creation does take some swallowing. As do the theories, myths, legends or whatever else one wants to call them, of the, again, *basic* foundations of most of the great religions.

In this book is an interesting and different explanation of the Creation, as first suggested by no less an authority than Einstein himself. And then there is man himself who, as Homo sapiens, wandered the Earth from well before the last Ice Age, but who never progressed anywhere out of the Stone Age, only to suddenly emerge any time between twenty five thousand and ten thousand years ago as the builder of some of the world's greatest buildings. At that moment evolution as such stopped and man began to change it to suit himself. If the Virgin birth, the Resurrection and the ascent into Heaven are to believed, along with the teaching of Mohammed, then some form of spirit world must be accepted as possible, the extension to this being that some form of extra terrestrial activity, whether divine or secular, must be **considered.** This single item, merely a possibility at this stage, will be dismissed with equal contempt by main stream theologians and historians alike. Except, of course, when it suits them to explain the Ascensions of both Christ and Mohammed. It will immediately be dismissed as 'pseudo-science' by those doing the dismissing, they being careful to airbrush from history any inconvenient facts to the contrary.

How any historian can seriously believe in either Christianity or Islam yet categorically deny any prospect of other extra terrestrial activity is beyond me. This has always given me a problem but the more I read, the clearer it gets. And one of my first amazing conclusions, which may shock many in the Christian church, is that, apart from a few obvious mighty bounds, the Bible, especially the New Testament, may just about be true. By making this basic assumption, treating it as a history book, and following it logically through, some remarkable things emerge.

But the more I read on the subject, the more annoyed I get. Having done an amazing amount of research some other writers seldom come to a logical conclusion. All they seem to do is to identify the problem, describe and illustrate it and then finish with *'Why did they make this?'*, *'How can this be explained?'* or even *'What is it?'* Now this I find infuriating. That surely is their job. Raise the question and then research a credible explanation. I want an explanation that I can get my teeth into, that I can argue with, totally rebuff or accept as a possible solution. I do not want to be left with another question each time.

And that is the purpose of this book. I offer what I think are credible answers to a lot of these questions. To many of the questions there can be no answer at all. A lot of people may not like what I say, many will disagree, and I must confess that virtually all my original thoughts and explanations when I began, have gone by the board as further facts have emerged. There is no question of adjusting the facts to confirm a pet theory but, as the book unfolded, logical answers to simple questions like *'Why use so much granite in the Giza pyramids?'* which at first seem ludicrous, are suddenly made more believable. Especially when this is linked to the Biblical Ark of the Covenant. To my knowledge no one before has thought that the two may be somehow linked.

Whether you agree or not it will give you something to think about. I am certain that I am not 100% right on it all but my research does point other historians in possibly a different direction to accepted wisdom. And that can't be a bad thing.

The book is not to be considered an academic study of the times for I cannot claim degrees or doctorates in the subject. It is the story of those times, looked at through the eyes of a simple engineer, who has spent his life solving engineering problems from the only point of view an engineer understands. Logical common sense with everything worked out from *first principals.* I never went to university and, because of this, I am not governed, nor am I restricted, by any pre-existing theory or dogma handed down by theologians or Egyptologists. Nor am I by anthropologists or palaeontologists, and certainly not by the growing and intolerant atheist lobby. I am that rare breed of writers who approaches his subject with a very open mind, prepared to consider *every* point of view and to follow the story wherever it leads.

An engineer first identifies a problem or need and then sets about finding the easiest way to solve that problem. Given the same challenge, in the same location, today how would a competent civil engineer, mining engineer or mechanical one, or an architect, solve that problem? Then I look at, given the knowledge and equipment available at the time, how engineers so long ago solved the problems of, for instance, building the pyramids or Stonehenge, since it is undeniable by anyone that they exist and that they are manmade. As are many other ancient buildings. That is a question that so far no one seems to have answered with any conviction. I ask why they were built, how they were built, when they were built and, most of all, who actually built them. When we begin to make some sense of that we can look at the wording of the Old Testament and see whether there are any clues there. We may have to rattle a few cages in the process. We may tread on some sensitive toes in our search and we most certainly will look carefully at some very diverse and seemingly unconnected subjects, dispelling on the way some long cherished legends and theories. We may travel around the world a few times in the progress but, out there, there must be some answers. We shall see. Since the publication of the First Edition in 2008 I have done more research. Books that were out of print then have been reprinted which has given a better slant on some of my most outlandish ideas. Amazingly the conclusions I came to in 2008 were also the conclusions of other, much better qualified writers, of some time ago.

For my research I have used many sources including a great number of un-attributed works on the internet. I have read both the *'Holy Bible'* and the *'Holy Koran'*, *'The Bible Code'* by Michael Drosnin, *'Genesis Unveiled'* by Ian Lawton, *'The Gods of Eden'* by Andrew Collins, *'Fingerprints of the Gods'* by Graham Hancock, *'The Great Religions'* by Richard Cavendish, *'The Times Atlas of World History'*, Konemann's *'Egypt'*, *'The Holy Grail'* by the Fieberg Brothers, much information on Anthropolis, Crystalinks and Wikipedia, *'Vanishing Point'* by Stephen Goodfellow, *'Monument Creation'* by Tingley Monuments, *'The Plan of the Giza Pyramids'* by John A R Legon, much work by Flinders Petrie, Richard Holliday of the Gold Council helped, *'How the Egyptians built the Pyramids'* by Richard Koslow, *'Khufu –*

The secrets behind the building of the Great Pyramid' by Jean-Pierre Houdin, *'Tabletop Nuclear Devices'* by Physorg.com, *'Pyramids – Tapping Cosmic Energy'* from Life Positive, *'The Human Devolution'* and *'Forbidden Archaeology'* by Michael Cremo, *'The Handbook of Ancient Artefacts'* by William Corless, 'The *Origin of Species'* by Charles Darwin, *'Building the Great Stone Circles of the North'* by Colin Richards ,*'The Bicameral Mind'* by Julian James, the works of David Davidovitch, *'The Blue Nile'* and *'The White Nile'* by Alan Moorhead, *'The Chariots of the Gods'* by Eric von Daniken, *'Chiaracuso'* by Augustus John, *'The Secret Country'* by John and Janet Bird, *'Ancient Egyptian Masonry'* by Somers Clark, *'The Lost Book of Enki',* *'The Lost Realms'* and *'There Were Giants upon the Earth'* by Zecharia Sitchin, *'Map Makers of the Ancient World'* by Charles Hapgood, *'The Old Straight Track'* by Alfred Watkins, *'Handbook of the Geology of Great Britain'* by Dr J.W Adams and Dr C.J Stubblefield, *'The Giza Power Plant'* and *'Lost Technologies of Ancient Egypt'* by Christopher Dunn and many others. With most of these I merely comment on the work and from just a few I quote the copyright work direct. If I have missed an attribution, especially from the Internet, on the way, please forgive me. It is certainly not deliberate and details forwarded to my publishers will make sure that it is corrected in subsequent editions. In this edition I use a lot of pictures, some I have taken myself but others have been taken off the internet and I have no idea who owns the copyright. I have assumed that all I use are in the public domain. If I have inadvertently used anything that is not considered as being in the public domain then again, please contact either me or my publishers and I will put it right. I offer special thanks to my son, Oscar J Soper BA, MSc, who designed the cover and was responsible for all the line drawings and graphics in the book. I also thank my friend Tony Riall, BSc who is a Consulting Civil Engineer off whom I have bounced many thoughts on mining and minerals. Plus the many contributors on The Megalith Portal web site who have offered their thoughts.

One thing that I have deliberately done is to skip over areas that others cover in depth. It is pointless, just to fill pages, to rehash what others have spent years researching and cover in the smallest detail. I have tried as I go along to point out in whose book you will find the information, and I recommend that you read those books to give you a better depth for your study. My objects in the book are quite clear. I merely want to prove them as near as it is possible so to do.

There is one other apology that I must make. For such a big subject the book is relatively small and that is because my writing style precludes me from inserting pages of 'padding' just to fill the space. Having quoted that 'x' on expedition 'y' had dug up artefact 'z', I fail to see how filling the next six pages with how he then dug up similar pots 'a', 'b', 'c, etc., can advance the story. I point you in the direction of works with those six pages but you will not find them here. I also, as far as is possible refrain from quoting at length the supposed names of ancient peoples. I find it very confusing to have to try to remember who they are all supposed to be.

My object is to make what can be a very weighty and complicated subject interesting to everyone, not just a few academics. I want you to be able to read it and understand from where I am coming each time. To me, whatever the subject, in order to maintain reader interest, the book must flow and I find that having every other sentence interrupted by a source reference intensely irritating and, in most cases, totally irrelevant and unnecessary. If a writer claims to have referred to another work then let us accept it as such. Alan Moorhead is a great example of this method. As is Charles Hapgood. I for one have never ever read carefully through the hundred odd pages of references in any book and then gone to the unbelievable trouble of actually checking them out. Yet this is standard academic procedure in these days. Not in this book however. I give you a typical example of what I mean.

"*Of course Howes and Dobson [Blah, 1974, page 123] look at it from a more esoteric point of view to Smith and Jardine [Blah blah, 1961, pages 486, 487] but Jones and Malenkov [Blah blah, blah, 1993 page 978] disagree, offering a more pragmatic version that is the complete opposite to that of White and Blackey [Blah, blah...etc, etc...].*"

All interspersed with reference notes which, if you can be bothered merely state *ibid,* in which case you must search for earlier references and so on and so on. By which time you have lost all threads of the plot, you have no idea what the writer is trying to prove and put the book down.

If this is known, or thought to be, sound scholarship, then so be it. You will not find it here. I am one of Edison's '*amateurs*' and am writing it for you, the average man or woman in the street, because it is very much about you and me, all our friends, our neighbours, our families, our [in many cases] common ancestors of long ago and our descendents as yet unborn. It is our story - that of Earth's people. How we all began and from whence we came. I hope you enjoy it.

PART 1

IN THE BEGINNING

1

THE BEGINNING

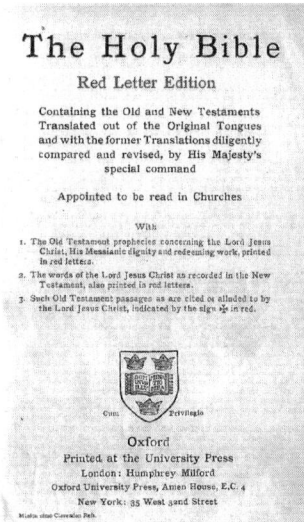

The Holy Bible

Red Letter Edition

Containing the Old and New Testaments
Translated out of the Original Tongues
and with the former Translations diligently
compared and revised, by His Majesty's
special command

Appointed to be read in Churches

With

1. The Old Testament prophecies concerning the Lord Jesus
Christ, His Messianic dignity and redeeming work, printed
in red letters.

2. The words of the Lord Jesus Christ as recorded in the New
Testament, also printed in red letters.

3. Such Old Testament passages as are cited or alluded to by
the Lord Jesus Christ, indicated by the sign ✠ in red.

Oxford
Printed at the University Press
London: Humphrey Milford
Oxford University Press, Amen House, E.C. 4
New York: 35 West 32nd Street

My grandmother's copy of the Holy Bible. So many questions; so many answers.
All we need do is to look for them.

It is very difficult for any trained scientist or engineer to accept that the wording of the Bible, particularly the books of Genesis and Exodus, could in any way represent the real truth. It directly contradicts the more or less irrefutable evidence of natural evolution. Similarly any Jewish, Christian or Islamic believer has a problem accepting that Darwin says we all must have a direct line back over billions of years to an amoeba. If Darwin is right we all began so many millions of years ago, but the Old Testament says that it was only in the last 4 to 5 thousand years that mankind, as such, began walking the earth.

But could they both actually be correct? Is it possible to accept Darwin one minute and the next to say that it is possible to

2

not only make sense of, but to actually believe in one of the great religions? Which one of them is for the reader to decide? It is my contention that this is the case and this book sets out to give the reasons, if not the absolute scientific proof. Many scientists agree, being leaders in fields that contradict all religions yet being committed Christians, Jews, Muslims or followers of a host of other religions.

Theology is not in any way an exact science, but a science it must be, since it relies on the careful analysis of documents written many years ago, much of which has been based on stories handed down by word of mouth over many millennia. These documents are then interpreted in different ways by the different sects, each of which has thrown up its fair share of prophets. The prophets such as Christ and Mohammed then have their own followers which again are divided into other groups giving different interpretations - all of which are, to them, the only true version. It is then difficult to know whether any of them are correct.

In Christianity we have the Catholics, ruled from Rome by an all powerful Pontiff, who have a different doctrine to the Anglican and Episcopal churches of Britain and America. These really got their doctrines to suit the current marital problems of an English King. Then there are the various Non Conformist movements such as the Baptists and Methodists and the harder line Lutheran church on the continent. They were the original 'Protestants' who protested against the excesses of the Roman church, in particular the clergy. There are the myriad of spin offs in America with the Latter Day Saints being the biggest. Not forgetting the Eastern Orthodox versions and the Copts of Egypt and Ethiopia.

Islam has thrown up the Shi'ites and the Sunnis, both of which are convinced that they have got it right. Each has its own version of the Koran and so hates the other accordingly. Their differences are based on who should have been the true successor to the prophet. The Shi'ites declared that it must be from his family but the Sunnis insisted that it came from the tribal elders. Because of this the hatred between the two has gained an appalling

3

momentum and, as this revision is being written in 2016, the entire Middle East is embroiled in a huge war between the two factions with atrocities being committed worse than anything since the Middle Ages.

St Peter's Rome

The Dome of the Rock, Jerusalem

The Sun City Synagogue, Florida

Three Temples to the same God. All have totally different interpretations of the same book.

The Jews vary from the strictly orthodox to various more liberal sects, again believing that they and only they are right.

What is more, all of them, no matter which religion they belong to, are perfectly happy to go to war and kill the other side just to prove it. Jew will kill Jew; Muslim kill Muslim and Christians kill Christians, all in the name of God. Which is why, behind every conflict, somewhere down the line, religion is the justification for the most unspeakable barbarity that has gone on since time began. And still goes on to this day.

Catholics do not believe in divorce, contraception, homosexuality or the marriage of the priesthood but are perfectly relaxed about having a drink of alcohol. Anglicans accept divorce, contraceptives, marriage in the priesthood and drink, and will now re-marry divorced people and same sex couples in church. The Non-Conformists are perfectly happy to re-marry divorced people but are struck with horror at the thought of a drink. Muslims are very relaxed about divorce but a glass of wine can be a capital offence. As is homosexuality and possession of a Christian Bible. They also have the appalling idea that killing someone of another faith, or even a different version of their own will somehow give them martyrdom if they kill themselves in the process. They are supposed to go straight to Heaven where 70 virgins await them. This is an attractive proposition for a spotted youth who has difficulty attracting a girl friend. Seldom do you find a Cleric or one of his family put this to the test, it usually being an impressionable youngster from a poor family to whom they tie the suicide bomb. Very often it is just a child to whom the suicide bomb is attached and all justified by a twisted version of Islam, reinforced by rigid Sharia Law which brings back memories of the atrocities committed in Nazi Germany.

And what about the Jews? No race of people throughout history has been the subject of such sustained and bitter hatred and persecution, beginning in Egypt well before Christ and carrying on in the Middle East today. They, of course, are supposed to be 'God's Chosen Race' which gives some of their more orthodox members a problem when trying to see the point of view of the average Muslim Arab, or Christian for that matter. They believe that they are descended from Abraham (as do the Christians and Muslims) but are still waiting for their Messiah to come in the future. Christians and Muslims believe that Jesus Christ and Mohammed respectively are their Messiahs. To Islam, Christ was just another prophet. The Jew shares with the Muslim a hatred of the pig, thinking it to be unclean, but the Christian thrives on pork and bacon.

And this all comes from the one book - *The Old Testament of the Holy Bible* - which is common to all three basic religions. The wording is the same and it is actually in writing, not still merely word of mouth, but it is still incredible that so many people manage to put such different interpretations into those words. The only thing that they all hold in common is the belief in the one God from whom all mankind are descended.

Were the Eastern religions involved in all this? We must include the Hindus here because their ideas come from a creative rather than philosophical ideology but at least we can put a realistic time scale on the rest since they each were founded by a mortal man during a known period between two and three thousand years ago. The followers of these religions take their beliefs from the teachings of the Buddha, Confucius, Lao Tzu and others and the only real impact they have on the story is that each of these prophets was born into a time and place of great and continuing strife and war in the region. I will return to this point later on in the book. They are more of a philosophy rather an unswerving belief.

So the only religions that have a real problem with Darwin are those that believe that God was responsible for the entire creation of the Earth and everything about it, including mankind, in those seven short days. This is, as any scientist will tell you, nonsense since the evidence of geology and palaeontology is overwhelming. Who could possibly dispute the existence of the dinosaurs and the various periods of early man from the first to stand upright down to the present? But if not, you must dismiss

Genesis as rubbish, and if that is not true, then what is? This is a dilemma that has taxed scholars for generations.

Could the answer lie in those words of Genesis covering an enormous period of time during which little was written down? We all know about 'Chinese Whispers' where someone tells another a story in confidence. That person repeats it to another who in turn does the same, so that a week later when it gets back to the originator, it has changed completely. The early books of the bible are 'Chinese Whispers' which lasted many thousands of years. Much of it will be true or, at best, based on the existence of a person or event that either existed or happened, but some will be the victim of exaggeration. I would not dispute that many, if not most, events and people did actually exist. What I do dispute is the interpretation put on those events. But, open to the most careful scrutiny, must be the time scales involved during this period.

Go back in the UK to just over one hundred and fifty years ago into the 19th century and the Victorian age and you will find that there was little mobility in the population. The great economic migrations from country to industrial city had taken place and now the only migrations were abroad to the new colonies of the Empire. There was no TV or radio, no Internet but there were newspapers for those who could read. There were railways, but little in the way of roads since most road transport was still by horse and carriage. People tended to grow up, work, marry and bring up families in the immediate area where they lived. My grandfather lived in Leeds all his life but never went to London, and he was the norm. He had little knowledge or interest in what was out of his sight.

Now go back a thousand years and all you have is a few small towns, some villages and some rough tracks between. Many people in those days never even visited the next village, few could read if there was something to actually read and so their knowledge of the outer world was down to zero. The Bible was in Latin and the 'educated' classes spoke a form of French. The native British spoke different languages and dialects throughout the country. Throughout the world since time began, the ruling classes have preferred to keep the proletariat ignorant, especially of any

7

knowledge of the outside world. Not to imply that the proletariat did not have intelligence, just that there was no escape from the daily grind and so no outlet for that intelligence.

From this if we go further back many thousands of years to the days of the Bible and the Ancient World, just what interpretation would the average goat herd put on some extra terrestrial, but perfectly natural, happening? Such as with the appearance of a comet, an eclipse, or the aftermath of the eruption of a distant volcano. Even a drought or a flood? It only takes one person who may be their leader to tell them that there is a 'God' up there and that he is not happy with them and said goat herd will believe it. He knows nothing else. How can he? Apart from passing the time of day with neighbouring tribesmen, he only has his own little community with whom to discuss things.

And this is the time when the Bible story began. I feel that something dramatic did happen to provoke the story of Adam and Eve but the biggest mystery here is not whether it happened or how it happened, but when it happened?

Following the theory of Evolution and The Survival of the Fittest promulgated by Darwin in the 19th century, I think it is fair to say that from the end of the Neanderthal period about 35,000 years ago when Homo sapiens or modern man, having replaced Homo erectus (1.8m - 200k BC) in Africa and Europe, was beginning the massive exodus out of Africa, mankind across the world evolved at more or less the same rate. Those who had gradually migrated into lands now cut off by water evolved both physically and mentally at comparative speeds, give or take the odd 1000 years. Depending on local conditions and climate they evolved in different skin colours, different bone structures and different physiques but intellectually, put them all together, and they will only be a few hundred years apart. They all discovered flint as a cutting tool about the same time as they did with fire and the need for clothing and shelter. So that a native American of 150,000 years ago, if there was such a creature, may have developed a different colour and bone structure to that of a native African or an ancient Briton but, gather them together for an intelligence or initiative test and there would be little to choose between them.

In fact to survive at all, from a very early age, man the world over must have been a very intelligent creature indeed. And this includes the other two species of Neanderthal and Homo erectus as well. He would have to have been because that was all he had. Physically he was then, as he is now, inferior to most of the other animals. He could run but nowhere near as fast as most animals, he could swim but all fish and most mammals could easily beat him, he could climb but so could other primates, many bears and the big cats, and in face to face unarmed combat, animals very much smaller would be his match. In comparison with the animal world he was puny and weak.

Not for him the razor like teeth, the claws to sink into flesh, the powerful loins and arms to outrun or fight an enemy. He didn't even have the physical means of digging without tools as had the rodents. Even the very tiny ones were better equipped. No, all he had was a superior intellect to outwit his enemies. He needed shelter, that he must build, against the elements and fire to keep him warm and yet, not only did he survive against overwhelming odds, he survived so many of his more powerful enemies whilst domesticating many of the rest. He emerged eventually as the dominant species on the world that he was destined to rule. To do this all over that world, more or less simultaneously, meant that he had something special.

But survive he did, and then for many millennia everywhere his sole pre-occupation was to satisfy the basic needs. These were to provide enough food, clothing, shelter, heat and, the most basic of all animal needs, the need to breed and so maintain the species into another generation. Time went on into the Upper Palaeolithic age which lasted for about 90,000 years up to 10,000 BC. And in all that time, for 190,000 years, mankind everywhere had only progressed from using flint tools to now slightly more sophisticated stone ones, plus some bows and arrows with bone being fashioned for the arrows. This I find astonishing. We are talking here of at least 9,500 generations, possibly more, during which time our ancestors, Homo sapiens, walked upright and had to find the necessary skills to eat, breed and provide shelter. Homo erectus lasted longer as did the Neanderthal with no better skills and without any of the necessary survival tools enjoyed by the animal kingdom. And no, they didn't all live in caves since there were very few caves about, in the same way that there are few caves about today, suitable to use as homes. They had to build homes and means of protection against the elements, as well as those predators, but no one during this enormous period of time, anywhere in the world, was able to progress further than the use of flints, bones and stones as their only tools and weapons. They were no better than the animal kingdom around them.

At the end of that time period the northern areas of Europe, including Britain, plus North America and parts of Siberia were gradually emerging from the last Ice Age - the Pleistocene Age which began the European Stone Age. The most favourable areas for mankind to live were across Greece and Turkey, through the Middle East and into Persia and, in Africa, south down the Nile Valley into the Rift Valley of Middle Africa. Present day Kenya, Uganda and Tanzania. The Sahara was in the process of becoming the desert that it is today.

We are now approaching the period of recorded history and we see that by 7,500BC sheep and goats were being domesticated in the Near East; pigs, cattle and horses were tamed in Europe and experiments were being made with agrarian agriculture.

And all this was being repeated in China, North and Central America and the Andes and Amazon regions of South America.

Copper was discovered in Africa about 4,000 BC, Bronze 1,000 years later and iron another 1,000 years further on. Actual writing began in 3,000 BC with the Pictographs of Mesopotamia followed by the Cuneiform and then the Hieroglyphics of Ancient Egypt. It took a staggering 200,000 years before 'intelligent' man arrived at a method of communication other than by word of mouth. And that was, in fact, a mere 5,500 years ago.

So here we are, 3,500 years before the arrival of Jesus Christ, still using basic cutting tools of stone. That was all they had. Using only whatever stone or flint that was available, timber must be cut to fashion weapons and tools, and for construction work. I cannot over emphasise how important it is to realize that, according to all accepted thought, this was the only way that they could hunt, kill, build and farm. There was nothing else. It was some two thousand years later that bronze became available and that increased the scope and range of work possible. Copper, along with gold, was the first to be identified but, being so soft, it was quite useless as a building tool. And this takes us right up to the period when they built some of the greatest buildings of all time which had to be done using only stone, accompanied by some artefacts made from bronze and copper, and just communicating through the ancient languages. We are still 3.5 thousand years away from the first printing press with mankind all over the world now emerging from the basic Stone Ages. Except, that is, for the tiny area ranging from the north of the east coast of the Mediterranean Sea, across to the Tigris and Euphrates in the east and south along the Nile Valley to the first Cataract at Aswan. China still slept, or at least kept to itself. Similar stirrings were happening in the Americas.

Somehow into this area, and during the period beginning 25,000BC, up to the time of Christ, we have to slot in the Old Testament of the Bible plus the incredible happenings that were the Golden Age of Egypt. Just what happened to justify the stories in the Bible and to account for the construction of some of the most amazing edifices of all time? How could people just discovering iron have perfected the art of the jeweller and goldsmith to be able to create the wonders of the tomb of Tutankhamen? How did they know that the basically useless soft metals, copper, gold and silver, were actually the most valuable of all? How could they have a very good working knowledge of not only precious stones, but how to cut, polish and then set them, when all they had to work with was either softer or more brittle? From where, how and why did they learn the art of enamelling which was then used extensively throughout history?

11

Where did the skills to build the city of Jericho in 8,000BC come from, and who maintained those skills for 5,500 years until the time came to build the pyramids? With nothing in the way of tools and equipment other than small pieces of flint, and no method of writing, how was it possible to design and build a great city that would stand for thousands of years? Looking at it logically, nothing really adds up, but the buildings are there and someone built them. Who did, when they were built and how they built them, we are going to try to find out.

2

THE MYTHS OF THE CREATION

The Old Testament of the Holy Bible is quite specific about The Creation. Genesis 1 (1-31) begins with "*In the beginning God created the heaven and the earth.*" *But the earth was without form and void and darkness was upon the deep. He said "Let there be light and there was light". It was good. He split the light from the darkness to give day and night. He then created Heaven from the waters and separated the waters from the land. So, after three days we had heaven, land and seas.*

On the fourth day he brought grass, herbs and fruit trees then said "*Let there be lights in heaven to divide the day from the night and let them be for signs and for seasons and for days and for years. And let the lights of heaven give light to earth. On the fifth day the waters gave forth life in the form of whales......* (Whales???? Why are they specific about this species, which is not indigenous to the Eastern Mediterranean, or The Red Sea? It is an ocean animal to be seen in the Atlantic [and Pacific] beyond the Pillars of Hercules, only occasionally in the Western Mediterranean. How could people living in Palestine be aware of one species living so far away? Furthermore, how did they know it was not a fish?) *......fish and on land cattle, beasts and creeping things. And the fowls that flew and multiplied before, on the sixth day, he created man. Man in his image after his likeness to have dominion over the fish of the sea, the fowls of the air and over the cattle, the earth and all creeping things. God blessed them, told them to go forth and multiply and saw them. And what He saw, He thought was all very good".* In actual fact the Guttenberg Bible when translated from the Latin does not mention 'Whales' as such. It says 'Sea Monsters' and so the whales must have been added during the translation for the King James edition. The fact that they were not fish then appears in later editions during the twentieth century when this fact was known.

This is the basis of Christianity, Judaism and Islam and it is difficult to believe in anything further if you in any way question the above. If you do think the above is a load of rubbish, at what point in the Old Testament, the New Testament or the Koran do you think that the truth is being told? You cannot have it both ways. You believe in all, as is, or none.

Or is this a convenient myth handed down over many thousands of years by word of mouth to justify the irrefutable fact that mankind did in fact exist and that he was able to tame animals? Where else could he possibly have come from and, if there was a God up there, let us give him the credit just to be on the safe side. Maybe this is so, but this story came from a tiny piece of the earth now known as Israel, Palestine, Jordan and Syria, and was promulgated by wandering Semitic tribes of herdsmen.

What about the rest of the world? They also had their Gods and their myths, but not everyone was necessarily obsessed by idea of the creation. Some just accepted that man had always been there. Let us compare what they thought.

We have to start with the pre-historic Pagan period which began way back in time to a period before or during the last Ice Age. This was the time of basic Homo sapiens, and there was little difference either physically or mentally between them, wherever they lived in our now scattered and isolated world. Continents had drifted apart so that the physical make up of the world was more or less as it is today. Ices were melting in the north, so filling up the seas. This cancelled out the land barriers of the Barents Sea and submerged the Continental Shelf that joined Britain to Europe and further separated Ireland from the mainland of England and Wales.

Now the Indians of North America could wander the Great Plains, evolving totally independent of the Indians who had made their way further south to become the indigenous inhabitants of Central America, the Aztecs and the Mayans. Those who inhabited the islands became the Caribs and the Arawaks, and those who made their way to the Andes, the Incas. Off shoots of these would hide away in the rain forest only to meet the modern world in the 19th and 20th centuries AD. Australia was cut off from the world and her indigenous peoples remained more or less in the Stone Age until the arrival of Europe in the 18th Century. Polynesia and Micronesia were populated by hordes of westward travelling people from South America meeting eastward travelling peoples from Asia, leaving diverse cultures in the myriad of Pacific islands. They worshipped convenient and dramatic Gods who could be represented by a pole carving. A Totem Pole (as did the native North American Indians). As time went on, more and more Gods needed more and more totems leaving the rich and varied heritage we see today. But the big Asia/Europe land mass gave the greatest scope for emigrating masses to travel unhindered by physical boundaries. This was the pre-historic Pagan world.

So what did they believe in and, more to the point, why should they believe in anything at all?

The one thing that was to separate Homo sapiens from the animal world was that we buried our dead. A dead monkey or lion or elephant, was left by it's fellows to be food for the scavengers, but not a human. From the dawn of time humanity both revered and feared it's dead. They believed in the supernatural and justified all unexplained phenomena to be the work of mythical divinities, or dead ancestors, come back to haunt them. In some areas of France, the bodies were trussed at death before Rigor Mortis could set in, to prevent the dead leaving the grave and returning to haunt and torment the living. They believed in an after life. In tombs in France there is evidence of tools and food for the afterlife being buried with the dead. It was thought that illness and drought were brought on by the evil spirits of the dead.

There is ample evidence in cave painting throughout Europe that they hunted with stones and bows and arrows. There is no evidence of cooking or cultivation and certainly, by the end of this era which is about 10,000 BC, there was no evidence of any God or Divine person. Evolution across the world was fairly constant and so as dawn arose in 10,000BC this was the state of play.

Chipped, but not polished, stones used for hunting and domestic use. Where available, flint was used.

No agriculture but possibly some domesticated cattle.

Death both revered and feared but, in any case, buried.

Some stone carvings in caves.

No evidence of marriage but some of the family unit.

Hunted wild animals for food but not necessarily cooked the meat.

No evidence of actual permanent dwellings. Most, if not all were nomadic.

Jungle giving way to desert in North Africa. Beginning of Sahara Desert in Egypt.

Ice Age in north coming to an end.

Adam and Eve????

The Biblical Creation?????

The next six to seven thousand years are a grey area all over the world. The northern lands were gradually recovering from the Ice Age which, as it receded, left vast areas of steaming, impenetrable bogs with forests emerging on the higher ground. In this world the Celts and Teutonic races fought for a bare existence but still had time to bury and revere their dead. In Ireland for instance, in the valley of the River Boyne, are a multitude of crude mounds covering stone burial places and these emerged around 3500BC. They had only the very basic tools of stone, flint and bone but still managed to create some formidable mounds. These mounds were the result of the labours of many people in moving lots of earth from one place to another. They were muck shifters rather than builders for the simple reason that they had neither the tools nor the ability to build other than the crudest structures. They appear to have worshipped the trees which gave them shelter.

Whilst the earliest known burial mounds date from around 3500BC, little is known of most of the northern races until the final millennium before Christ. As they emerged from Stone, through Bronze to the Age of Iron, life got better. They grew crops and domesticated animals. And they were able to think of higher things including the eternal question of where we all came from. The

Icelandic creation began with a cloud covering the great abyss. A fountain arose out of the abyss, which formed twelve glacial rivers, to the south of which lay the land of fire. From the south flowed hot rivers of bitter water which set forming land. The cool waters from the north caused a hoar frost but the warm southerly air made the ice melt and from the tepid drops emerged a giant in human form - Ymir.

The Gods were all giants and heaven, where they had their palaces, was over the bridge made by the rainbow.

They made crude jewellery and pottery and identified gold as a special metal. Their spear heads were crude iron and they used as the emblem of one of their Gods - Thor - the swastika which was also just appearing in China.

An interesting parallel with the New Testament and the book of Revelations written hundreds of years later is that, in Teutonic myth, is the anticipation of Armageddon when the Gods all fell out. As in Wagner's 'Twighlight of the Gods', they killed each other until there was no one left and all was over.

Then a new world appeared, born again from the wreckage. The sun shone again, new Gods appeared and mankind was reborn but this time with no giants.

Moving south to the Middle East, the Babylonians described the Creation on seven tablets dating from around 1000BC but based on much older scripts. Here water is the prime element with all beings, beginning with the Gods, emerging from the fusion of sweet and salt water. The first to be born were serpents who left the swamps and from whom mankind gradually emerged.

Little is known about Persia pre-1000BC. Zoroaster (660 - 583) taught that the world was of 12000 years duration divided into four distinct periods of three thousand years.

1st Three thousand. Emergence from the dark.

2nd Three thousand. Creation of all beings by man and the demon.
3rd Three thousand. Up to the time of Zoroaster who describes the vicissitudes of man.
4th and final three thousand ends with the last judgement.

By this period they had mastered very accurate stone work and could carve out bas reliefs of some size even though they still only had primitive tools.

The first evidence of man in India is between 3000 and 1500BC. The first Brahmins were the warrior class of about 1400BC and they believed in reincarnation. Their theory of Creation was that in the beginning was a dark watery chaos. A germ of life developed heat which became a Primordial Giant, a cosmic man 'Purusha'. The different parts of the world are his wings. A golden egg from the primordial waters gave birth to the supreme God 'Brahma'. In this egg were the continents, oceans, mountains, planets, Gods, demons and humanity. At the end of a thousand years the egg opened and Brahma began the work of creation. Seeing that the world was still submerged under water, he assumed the aspect of a wild boar, dived in and lifted it out with his tusks.

Like most of the rest of the world, there is little evidence of other than nomadic and warrior tribesmen in either China or Japan much before 1000BC. There are no early written details of the American Indians; all Oceania was folk law with nothing written down except for the crude but enormous statues on Easter Island. The only interesting thing in North America was that the Luiseno Indians of Southern California say that a flood covered the highest mountains and destroyed most of mankind. Only a few were saved. In Haiti they believe a flood drowned all the women and turned the men into trees. In fact, most of the mythology of Central and South America talks about a flood, even those perched on top of the Andes.

In Central and South America there were the great civilizations of the Maya, Aztec and Inca. These supposedly came much later in the last millennium before Christ, and were at their height during that time and to well after His death. But they still had ideas about the Creation. The Aztecs thought that the pious Coatlicue was the mother of the God of War as well as of a daughter and other sons. One day, as she was praying, a crown of feathers fell from heaven onto her breast. She became pregnant and gave birth to Huitzilopochtli, the God of War, who emerged covered in armour and fully armed. He killed his sister and all who plotted against his mother, so becoming the protector of the Aztecs. They had literally hundreds of similar deities but no obvious theory of creation.

The Mayas, however, believed in a God of Creation, benefactor of the world and who was constantly at war with an evil deity, the enemy of mankind. The Mayas of Guatemala believed that everything was under water in the beginning and above these hovered two Gods - the givers of life. They said "Earth" and immediately earth was created. Mountains rose out of the waters and the earth was covered with vegetation. They gave the earth animals that could not speak and so could pay no homage to the Gods. Eventually the Gods decided to punish them by having them killed and eaten after which they created four men and four women who became ancestors of man.

In Honduras a 'White Woman' came down from heaven. She built a palace and remained a virgin yet gave birth to three sons. In old age she had her bed carried to the highest point of the palace from where she ascended to heaven in the form of a beautiful bird.

The Nicaraguan Gods of the Niquirans lived in heaven and were immortal. They were the creators of every living thing on earth. After death, souls departed either to heaven or to the fiery underworld.

In Central America and the Andes regions cultivation began about 7000BC. By 1500BC maize was the basis of life. Farmers now lived in permanent villages which grew into large towns after 1000BC. They had discovered luxury materials, precious stones and the rare metals which they imported over large distances. There were the rich and the poor, leaders and the led and they were prolific builders, not merely movers of earth.

In the classical Mayan period from 1000BC onwards they could write using hieroglyphics and their astronomers had calculated the exact length of the solar year and lunar month. They could predict eclipses and were able to lay out cities in a very precise grid. They also built pyramids.

And so to Egypt, the land that has posed so many questions over the years and, no doubt, will provide some answers, if only we know where to look. The known, or recorded, history of this tiny strip of land that stretched from the Mediterranean Sea to as far south as the first cataract of the Nile, began with the First Dynasty of Kings - the Pharaohs - who began their rule in 3022BC. Before that is a story of wandering tribes. From the start of the 1st Dynasty in 3022BC until the end of the New Kingdom and the 20th Dynasty in 1069BC there were 199 individual Pharaohs. In 1953 years each reigned an average of only 9.81 years yet between them they created cities, incredible gold work and jewellery unsurpassed by anything in Renaissance Europe, enormous tombs, the Sphinx, the huge temples at Luxor and, of course, the pyramids. Or did they?

Whilst there is archaeological evidence of life well before the First Dynasty - they were making first class pottery items in the Sudan c.7500BC - there is no hint of what they believed in. After the emergence of the first Pharaoh, he became their divine God. They worshipped local Gods, 'Lords of the City', as well as the sky, the earth, sun, moon and the Nile. The God Atum, who was unmarried, was supposed to have fathered the first divine one without a wife (the exact opposite of Christ), and this son was considered the ancestor of the human race. He was Ra.

Ra, in turn, created twins without a woman. One of them, Geb was the father of Osiris and he eventually ascended into heaven. In those days the Egyptian calendar had 360 days but the vizier, Thoth, played a game with the moon and won another 5 days to give 365. A figure deduced in Central America many years

20

later. Thoth was the creator of the world from the sound of his lips. His incantations of magic were to resurrect the dead Osiris. Thoth was endowed with complete knowledge and wisdom. He invented the arts, arithmetic, surveying, geometry, astronomy, medicine, surgery, music and writing the hieroglyphics. And he ascended into heaven.

Osiris reigned for 28 years before he was killed overseas. His wife, Isis found his body cut into fourteen pieces and returned it to life. His son, Horus, was magically inseminated from the corpse of his dead father and it was Horus who was considered to be the ancestor of the Pharaohs. Osiris, Isis and Horus were the main Trinity of Egypt. Osiris became the God of the Dead and gave his devotees the hope of eternal life in a land ruled by a good and just king or God. Eventually he departed by ascension to retire to the 'Elysian Fields' where he welcomed the souls of the just and reigned over the dead.

Hathor, wife of Horus, is the first mention of holding the long ladder that the deserving could climb to heaven. The judgement of the dead was before Osiris with Thoth at his side, weighing the heart to see if it was wanting. This was known as the 'Weighing of the Souls'. If the deceased was found to be pure he would pass to a life of Eternal Happiness in the Kingdom of Osiris. Even today the Egyptians revere the dead. In Cairo is the famous 'City of the Dead' where the remains of ancestors are kept in tombs so big that in many cases they are better than the actual homes of the living.

By the time we get to Greece and Rome it is too late for their mythology to have emerged from, as it were, a virgin origin. They were too near to the much older Middle Eastern areas whilst wandering tribesmen from the north could influence their thinking. They had access to the library at Alexandria as well. For this reason I have discounted them (for the time being) from this period. And so, by the time the modern world emerged in about 3500BC in Europe and the Near East, and two thousand years later in the Americas, we can see how man had guessed at the creation whilst finding himself some convenient Gods in the process.

What is interesting is that so many describe the primordial swamp, as did Darwin many years later, and that those in the Americas mention the flood, but not the Egyptians nor their neighbours. But the Bible does. Another thing that emerges is the ascension to heaven by either ladder or flying and the presence of Giants in the form of white men. In Nicaragua, which is in Central America, they had the same ideas of a 'heaven' and a fiery 'Hell', exactly the same as the Middle Eastern religions. There is no mention in any mythology anywhere in the world of an ability to build anything other than ships in Egypt. What I find most interesting is that so many peoples of this ancient world had come to the same ideas and conclusions as had others from far away, and of whom they should have had no knowledge at all.

From here we must now look at the Bible and what the prophets had to say about it all.

3

THE PROPHETS

The prophets, and here I include Christ, Mohammad, The Buddha, Confucius and Lao Tzu, have the one thing in common and that is that they all preached that mankind should live in harmony. Mankind should love its fellow men. I see no evidence in the New Testament of Christ encouraging his followers to make permanent war on the others. Nor do I find this in the Koran. The contrary is the case. It was the same for the Far Eastern prophets. All preach peace and understanding. Only when we get to the works of such evil men as Marx, Hitler or Mao Tse-Tung do we find a call to arms to crush and destroy all who oppose. In the 21st century the only peoples who preach this doctrine are the militant fundamental Muslims who seek to impose strict Sharia Law on the rest of mankind. It may be controversial, racist even, to suggest that they, in fact, are no better than the Stalinists, Maoists or even the Nazis who were also dedicated to imposing their own doctrines on mankind. If that is the case, then so be it.

Another thing that they have in common with the Old Testament ones is their promise of hell and damnation to those who failed to do this, the ultimate sanction being Armageddon or the end of the world. But they all needed an arbitrator who would decide that the others were transgressing, and who better than God himself?

Going back again to the dawn of time, legend has it that some Semitic tribesmen settled in Egypt where they increased in number, only to be enslaved by the rulers who treated them very badly. They appealed to their own God who set them free and delivered them to their 'promised land' of Canaan, a land flowing with milk and honey. These Semitic people were the tribes of Hebrews and it is from this legend that has given them the firm belief of the power of 'their God', that they are His chosen people, and that the land of Canaan was (and still is) their God given homeland. This legend is written in the Bible as the Exodus and placed in time around that of Rameses 11 between 1450 and 1250 BC. In actual fact it could have happened at any time during the preceding two thousand years but, for this exercise, I will go along with the accepted wisdom and accept that there is probably more of a grain of truth in the story, further accepting the salient points as having happened.

It was, of course, led by Moses who was another of the great Biblical prophets, and introduces into the story both The Ark of the Covenant and the mysterious food known as 'Manna', which appeared every day and fulfilled the dietary needs of all the tribes for forty years. The time they wandered in the wilderness.

To become a fully fledged prophet in Judea one had to have had a face to face meeting with either God himself – usually in a dream – and so become God's spokesman on earth. Or, at least contact with the Angel Gabriel. The Moses encounter is well documented since it resulted in the Ten Commandments by which all mankind must live. These are:-

1. *Thou shall not kill.*
2. *Thou shall not commit adultery.*
3. *Thou shall not steal.*
4. *Thou shall not bear false witness against thy neighbour.*
5. *Thou shall not covet thy neighbour's house; thou shall not covet thy neighbour's wife, nor his manservant, nor his maid servant, nor his ox, nor his ass, nor anything that is thy neighbours.*
6. *Honour thy father and thy mother.*
7. *Thou shall not take the name of the Lord thy God in vain.*
8. *Remember the Sabbath Day and keep it Holy. Six days may you labour but the seventh is the Sabbath of the Lord thy God. In it thou shall do no work.*
9. *Thou shall have no other Gods before me.*
10. *Thou shall not make unto thee any graven image, or any likeness of anything that is in heaven above or that*

is in the earth beneath or that in the waters under the earth.

This is the model, dictated by the Lord God to Moses on Mount Sinai and then set in stone on the ten tablets, safely stored in the Ark of the Covenant, by which the Hebrews now set out on their journey to the Promised Land, should live. And a better start in life is difficult to imagine. There was nothing in there to say that, once established in the Land of Milk and Honey, they should assemble an army to knock seven bells out of all the neighbours.

But the next chapter of Exodus shows the Lord God giving Moses further instructions which do rather contradict these commandments. Here he promulgates the 'Eye for an Eye' theory which rather neuters the 'Thou shall not kill' commandment. There are in fact now large numbers of perfectly good reasons to kill someone. Murder is top of the list that includes *'smiting thy father and thy mother'* – even cursing thy father or thy mother – 'selling another man (presumably into slavery) with a firm instruction in Exodus 22(18) (King James Version) *'Thou shall not suffer a witch to live'*. But it gives no proper definition of an actual witch. That has given subsequent religious bigots through the ages a very convenient scapegoat for doing away with anyone with whom they had fallen out.

The problem with the Ten Commandments is that they are both obvious and benign. If you live by them you are a good person but what happens if you do not? History tells us that genuinely good people were fairly thin on the ground. Most people throughout the world did, and still do, covet their neighbour's house, many their neighbour's wife (or husband), few have not cursed their parents at some time or another and it will be a very brave and boring person who, on Judgement Day, can put hand on heart and truthfully say they have never broken any commandment.

So for God to be more than a guiding light in our lives, he needed beefing up. He needed an enemy, almost as powerful, who would equally embrace us all, but with the only one being able to defeat him being God himself. That enemy is the Devil or Satan.

You now could believe in either God who could save you or Satan who would destroy you. If you were Pagan and worshipped the sun that brought prosperity and harvests, then your God's enemy was tempest, floods, locusts and drought.

The more enemies God had, the more powerful he became so now the Jew became enemy of anyone who did not believe, including the Gentiles. The Jewish kings all believed this but the prophets did not. Whether they were people with a vision or merely wise men who rebelled against sin and immorality, we do not know. The prophet Micah says that all God wants is that man be good, do justice, love and kindness and walk humbly with Him. But he was a lone voice. With their people firmly settled in the Promised Land and now backed by their own all powerful God, the Israelites could fight whom they pleased and, for years ever since, the area has been the number one hot bed of war and disturbance. Right up to the present day. Not that the Jews were all to blame. That was far from the case. Egypt was just as culpable as were first Alexander to be followed by Rome and Carthage. The fact does remain however that the Middle East has _never_ known a long and lasting peace.

Isaiah and Ezekiel both sent warnings of hellfire and brimstone if mankind did not behave. Isaiah in 53(3) tells of the coming of a Messiah some 800 years before Christ. 53(4) '*He is despised and rejected of men, a man of sorrows and acquainted with grief*'. 53(5) '*Surely he has borne our grief and our sorrows*' ....'*but he was wounded for our transgressions*'. You will note that this person, to be sent in the very long distant future, was merely going to resurrect the Ten Commandments, not the massive hero who would lead them into battle. Yet, since the time of the prophet right up to the arrival of Christ, the area was at war whilst the rest of the world enjoyed relative peace.

But the warnings persisted including for the eventual and ultimate catastrophe – Armageddon, the end of the world as we know it and all because mankind would not behave.

So let us consider briefly Armageddon as they could envisage it between two and three thousand years ago. Not as we know it now where we actually have the means by which it could so easily be achieved.

Go back just the two thousand years to the time of Christ and let us see what mankind as a whole has got. This is the known world of the Middle East and the Eastern Mediterranean, nothing to do with the Americas, China, Western Europe nor the rest of Africa. They could now harden iron to make a form of steel out of

The prophet Isaiah as envisage by an illustration published in 1904 by the Providence Lithograph Company.

which they made swords and shields, they had wheels and were able to carve stone and wood for buildings and roads. The Greeks and Romans had become net builders rather than being mere muck shifters and were constructing some incredible buildings all over the known world at the time. Armageddon is a man made catastrophe, rather than a natural disaster over which no man has ever had any control. Therefore, it is difficult to see just what the equipment of a Roman, Greek, Egyptian, Persian, Hebrew or Sumerian warrior could do to cause the calamity. Disease could, and there was plenty of that going round, and there was always the chance of Etna, Stromboli or Vesuvius going off causing tidal waves or dust storms. Santorini was now a very distant memory or legend. Locusts were an eternal problem, but just what could man

27

do that would replicate any of these disasters or, for that matter, avoid them? The answer is simple. Nothing. Not one thing could man do to bring about the total annihilation of the world and of civilization. We could now, but just why did all those prophets so long ago keep banging on about this when they knew it could not happen? That is, unless of course, they had incredibly accurate foresight.

Then along comes Christ whose existence and story I do not doubt. He was born into meagre circumstances, but to an enormous fanfare, which takes some explaining since in those days communication was limited, to say the least. How did the three kings, the wise men and the shepherds get to know about it well in advance so that they could so conveniently turn up soon after the birth? Who could have told them and why? And what about that star? Astronomers can find no obvious one that would have shone so bright while remaining stationery for so long over one spot. So was it a genuine star or could it have been something else? And, if something else, just what? This is difficult but very interesting.

Then, after brief mentions of his youth in the Gospels, he vanishes from history only to reappear some thirty years later for the last few months of his life. This is the period that forms the basis of Christianity. Although I have never seen the actual proof, I am prepared to unconditionally accept that the child born that day in Bethlehem and the man crucified at Calvary were one and the same person. By arguing this fact, it opens a can of worms that has little to do with this book. Yes, even I am prepared to accept this one 'Mighty Bound'.

The story of Christ is well documented elsewhere even though the story was written in the Gospels many years after his death and some forty years before Paul, who never met him, had his Damascene conversion. Therefore we must accept the Chinese whispers theory that some exaggeration may be involved. Be that as it may, he comes into this work after the Resurrection and Ascension into Heaven, only to reappear to St John the Divine on the island of Patmos. Here he dictated his Revelation of the future of mankind and this is what he predicted.

The Lord appeared to St John some 50 years after the Crucifixion as an old man with bright staring eyes. He said *'I am Alpha and Omega ... the first and the last....'* And then gave John instructions to write down what was said and send them to the seven churches of Asia. He said *'I am he that liveth and was dead and behold, I am alive for evermore, Amen. I have the keys of hell and of death.'*

He was not happy, for each church had transgressed in such a short time, and to each he sent a dire warning. Either they ceased, or repented, or serious consequences would result. However, those that did repent were promised rich rewards including power over all nations that were to be ruled with a rod of iron. Not exactly my idea of peace and tranquillity for all men. Only for God's chosen people.

This, basically, is the message given to St John who then went on to have a further vision of heaven. He saw all creatures including the strongest trying to open the sealed book. The book was then easily opened by the lamb so setting loose the seven spirits of God. The lamb opened the Seven Seals which revealed, amongst other things, the forthcoming apocalypse. Here he describes a great earthquake, the sun becoming black accompanied by a mighty wind. Mountains shook and rocks fell but the only ones saved were 12,000 from each of the twelve tribes of the children of Israel - 144,000 in total.

On the opening of the seventh seal, seven trumpeters appear and, as each sounded his trumpet, a great mountain burning with fire was cast into the sea leaving a third of all creatures dead and a third of all ships lost. A great star then fell from heaven contaminating a third of all rivers. Many died because of the bitter water and the sun and the moon were blotted out. Is it coincidence that this star should be called, of all things *'Wormwood'* which word, when translated into Russian, becomes *'Chernobyl'*? Another star will fall leaving the bottomless pit and the fall of Babylon. This is Judgement Day for all nations and out of all this chaos eventually a New Jerusalem will arise.

Now this is all stirring stuff that should frighten the life out of a wayward monk back in the first century AD. He is effectively saying (to all mankind or just the Jews????) *'Behave yourselves or you will all suffer a terrible death.'* And He is implying that these, basically natural disasters, which may or may not happen in the future, are His to command. Could he in fact, be aware of both time and place when and where they would happen somewhere in the distant future?

St John on Patmos writing the Revelations of Christ as envisaged by Hieronymus Bosch

And the Christian church, particularly that of Rome but including all the alternatives, have cherry picked parts of these teachings and used them for their own ends. Not least in the treatment of supposed 'witches'. Throughout the entire Middle Ages anyone with an idea that was new and with which the clergy could not understand, must be a witch for whom unspeakable punishments were in store. Scientists, including Newton and Galileo, were included here. There was even a Pope who had welcomed some radical thinking.

Throughout history church and state have battled for control, the church using carefully chosen phrases to justify its behaviour. In the UK these resulted in the magnificent monasteries where the clergy lived off the fat of the land entirely at the expense of the poor. Henry V111 brought them down to size but not for that reason. He also lived off the fat of the land at the expense of the peasantry. In pure Catholic countries today it is worse. A year or two ago I visited a small Italian fishing village that quite obviously was not, and never had been, prosperous. Yet the church displayed in vulgar opulence a myriad collection of huge and expensive paintings and marble sculptures – all paid for in the end by generations of poor fishermen. And all in direct contravention of the graven image commandment.

We are back to the church needing enemies in order to become rich and powerful. The more 'enemies', as in the Inquisition, the more power needed to fight the all embracing 'devil', or 'Satan' who was behind it all. If you don't follow our line then you must be possessed with Satan. A good flogging will help as would a ducking in the pond. If you die you are innocent, if you live you must be guilty and so die in an even more barbaric way. Is this really what Jesus had in mind?????

But not only had the church the need for enemies. Politicians need them more than ever. Away from their own borders and so safe from reprisals these days, but sworn enemies none the less. Hitler rose to power on the back of the wealthy middle class Jew. Without him to envy and blame, Hitler's task would have been much harder. In later years Blair and Bush hung on to power as they demonised the evil Islamic enemy of 'Al Quieda' on whom they could safely put the blame for the 9/11 attacks on New York. They then, for the flimsiest and most fraudulent reasons, proceeded to invade the stable, evil but secular land of Iraq. This was even more anti-Al Quieda but they managed to topple the regime of Saddam Hussein, creating in the process, yet another unstable area of conflict in the Middle East. By so doing they succeeded in exacerbating the everlasting dispute between Israel and its Arab neighbours. But overshadowing even that was the swift rise of the barbaric medieval state of ISIS that straddled both Iraq and Syria. That was a state ruled entirely by Sharia law and funded by supposed pro-western neighbouring countries. And this was begun by supposed devout Christians in

31

the name of Christ who must now be ringing His hands in despair. The entire region was left a complete mess and all was created in the name of one or other of the great religions.

So we return to our wayward monk, pulling up his pants after having his evil way with the carpenter's daughter, before returning to his little cave where he ekes out his miserable first century existence. He sees nothing but catastrophe unless he defends his faith against somebody. But against whom should he defend it? Rome was now Christian and his fellow villagers minded their own business, so he might as well start with the Israelites who were not Christians at all. Our monk, if he knew where it was, could go to Israel and tell them what was in store unless they joined the fold. But what would he tell them? Just what was (and still is) in store as told to St John the Divine? Is he describing a man made holocaust as perpetrated by Hitler and Stalin (which surely Divine intervention could have prevented?)? No. Is this the result of a nuclear conflagration where mankind will one day destroy itself? If I say *'possibly'* it opens up a very big can of worms indeed, but I do, as I explain later. Is it the inevitable result of global warming because of man made pollution? No. So what does he predict?

Described here is possibly a NATURAL catastrophe of global proportions. There is a massive earthquake, followed by a volcano that blows a mountain into the sea. This is followed by not one, but two meteorites falling onto the land and into the sea. There is no indication whether these events were to be simultaneous or spread over a long period of time. The description of these consequences is quite accurate, but let us first consider what the knowledge of this type of thing would have been to the man in the street in AD 80.

The one thing that is for certain is that, fortunately, this type of natural catastrophe is very rare indeed and there would be no contemporary account of any of it happening in living memory. They may have heard of the eruption of Vesuvius which buried Pompeii and Herculaneum. This will have sent a dust cloud over the Middle East which may have been recorded. But that was it.

We don't know when Santorin went up and the resulting tsunami will have been relegated to the distant past, possibly causing the supposed parting of the Red Sea and the numerous plagues in the area at the time. But that is all. There is nothing else. They would listen with incredulity at the stories of the dinosaurs if they were remotely aware of their existence, as they would the various theories of their ultimate extinction. In Biblical terms, it is only very recently that a giant meteorite has been thought to be a possible cause. There is no possible way, unless there was an ancient script in the Alexandria library [like the one on which the Pirie Re'is map was based] that could put the idea into someone's head. How could anyone so accurately predict what the certain outcome of a large stone falling from the sky would be? What gave them the idea in the first place that both it could happen and, when it did, the appalling consequences were tantamount to Judgement Day?

On what evidence could anyone predict, again so accurately, the results of an undersea volcano blowing the side of a mountain into the sea? There is no suitable mountain in the Mediterranean Sea. Krakatoa and Martinique were both nearly two thousand years and vast oceans away in the future. Still to happen is the very big one when the island of La Palma in the Canaries goes up which will give the predicted results on the eastern seaboards of North and South America. We had to wait until 2004 for the first of the predictions to take place in modern times with the devastating earthquake in the Indian Ocean, decimating coasts as far away as Africa.

So we go back to the Rhetorical Question again. How could anyone possibly predict these things which were so far beyond any scientific or geographical knowledge both at the time and for over a thousand years to come????

From the first page of Genesis to the closing lines of the Revelations, the Bible throws up totally unanswerable questions, leaving room for much doubt, plenty of debate and the subsequent plethora of explanations.

1. How can anyone possibly believe the Biblical account of the Creation in the face of such overwhelming Darwinian, anthropological and geological evidence? But Darwin himself comes under fire from other Eastern sources.

2. Genesis Chapter 5 gives the genealogy of the Jewish Patriarchs showing them living to prodigious old ages. Adam lived 130 years, his son Seth 105 years, Jared 162, Lamech 182 and Noah was 950 years old when he died. He was 600 when he built the Ark. How do we account for this when, at the same time in Egypt – not all that far away – from the beginning of the First Kingdom to the eventual decline, the average reign of a Pharaoh was under ten years? No Pharaoh lived anywhere near as long as did these people.

3. Why is the otherwise totally useless metal, other than for jewellery, gold, the first to be said to be plentiful?

4. Who were the giants amongst men who bred with the indigenous peoples, also described independently as far apart as Iceland and the Americas? What became of their offspring?

5. A flood that would have carried the Ark so far inland would have had to be of an enormous depth. Since it would have had to maintain a constant level across the world, it would have drowned the whole of North Africa, the Middle East, Europe and the British Isles. But it didn't. There was no flood in Egypt and only localised flooding is reported in places like the Caribbean and Western America. Could these have been tsunamis, in which case how did Noah get sufficient notice to build his boat?

6. Why would Isaiah feel the need to prophesy the arrival of a Messiah some 800 years in advance? How could he possibly guess at the state of things so far into the future?

7. And then the questions on which the Christian faith is based. Was a virgin birth feasible given our present knowledge of obstetrics? How did the shepherds and the kings get so much prior warning of the birth? What

was the star? Was Lazarus actually raised from the dead or was he merely unconscious? How can modern science account for the other supposed miracles? Was Jesus in fact dead when they took Him down from the cross, or just unconscious? Could He have come round and then lived another forty days before finally dying? After all, Joseph of Aramathea used the supposed 'Holy Grail' to collect Christ's blood as he was being laid out. Dead men don't bleed! If He did return to life from being actually physically and brain dead, how was this possible? What were the actual circumstances of the ascension to heaven? Did He just vanish into thin air or was there a vehicle of some sort awaiting him? What exactly was the Holy Ghost?

It does make life a lot easier just to take a 'mighty bound' and accept it all without question but, when you think about it, there can be no definite answer to any of the above. In particular, the one about forthcoming natural disasters if we rely on nothing but the accepted wisdom of today. Present thought and learning preclude any logical answers to the above. The answers just cannot be found. Unless we challenge present thought, think the unthinkable, explore what has been merely Science Fiction up to now and delve into the unknown, the answers can never be found.

Whether this comes up with logical answers, we must wait and see.

4

DARWIN OR THE CREATION?

From this – or??????

Before we begin this section there are a few 'words' that must be considered since they affect most of that which follows. The first word is *'THEORY'*. A theory is just that, a theory. An idea that may, or may not be, proved correct over the passage of time. As has been pointed out to me by others, theories put forward by academics are based on exhaustive research, the facts of which are beyond dispute. Theories put forward by others, 'amateurs' like me, are, at best, put down as 'conspiracy theories', or 'pseudo-science', which makes everything else in this book invalid. Most of the following theories, that have been proposed by some of the most eminent scientists of all time, have proved to be sometimes nearly correct. But not necessarily 100% correct. Others are far from being so but until all are proved beyond any doubt whatsoever, theories they remain and, as such, are open to question.

Charles Hapgood was the author of *'Maps of the Ancient Sea Kings'* who had a growing contempt of 'experts'. He was a professor of the history of science at Keene State College in Massachusetts in the '20s and '30s and this is what he had to say. I quote verbatim from his book.

'The investigation [into the Piri Re'is map] was undertaken in connection with my classes at the college, and the students from the beginning took an active part in it. It has been my habit to try to interest them in problems on the frontier of knowledge, for I believe that unsolved problems provide a better stimulation for their intelligence and imagination than do already solved problems taken from text books. I have also found that the amateur has a much more important role in science than is usually recognised. I teach the history of science, and have been aware of the extent to which most radical discoveries [sometimes called 'breakthroughs'] have been opposed by the experts in the affected fields. It is a fact, obviously, that every scientist is an amateur to start with. Copernicus, Newton, Darwin were all amateurs when they made their

Charles Darwin in 1854 before the publication of 'The Origin of Species'.

principal discoveries. Through the course of long years of work they became specialists in the fields that they created. However the specialist who starts out by learning what everyone else has done before him is not likely to initiate anything very new. An *expert is a man who knows everything, or nearly everything, and usually thinks he knows everything important in his field. If he doesn't think he knows everything, at least he knows that other people know less and that amateurs know nothing. And so he has an unwise contempt for amateurs, despite the fact that it is to the amateurs that innumerable important discoveries in all fields of science have been due. It is for these reasons I did not hesitate to present the problem of the Piri Re'is Map to my students.'*

'Ouch!!!!' I like Hapgood already.

I include in my list of theories which may not hold too much water Darwin's theory of evolution, the 'Big Bang' theory, how, why and when they built the pyramids and the various interpretations of The Holy Bible. Not forgetting, of course, The Holy Koran. I am perfectly happy to go along with most theories until I sense a flaw at which I like to investigate. What follows in this book are the results of my logical investigations together with my own alternative theories. I am also one of Hapgood's amateurs. All are put forward following years of similar exhaustive research but mine have been arrived at with no pre-determined agenda to follow. As this is being written in 2014, I have been watching a series of programmes on television about this very subject. It now appears that the 'Big Bang' theory is no longer such. It is fact and a more or less accurate date has been arrived at. Good, but I still don't agree. I believe in the steady state idea and nothing I've read or heard convinces me otherwise.

I say repeatedly in this text that Darwin is irrefutable. Not so, according to the Creationist lobby. They give many reasons for this and quote at length the evidence of palaeontology, which is the study of fossils. I have looked carefully at both arguments and still remain in the Darwin camp. But only just. As I look at the evidence that emerges in this book my thoughts change. As we will see, much of Darwin's work was a very big 'Mighty Bound'. There are some very profound questions to be asked, for which Darwin [if he had thought of them – he probably did] has no answer, and neither have I. So far I have heard of no one else who has, even if they had thought to ask those same questions.

Let us go back to the very beginning again. The Earth began like all the other planets and moons as a spinning cloud of rocks and gases, thought by most to have come from an explosion on the Sun. With that I do not argue. Over an eternal length of time this mass became a solid molten sphere that, after yet another eternity, gradually cooled and became a still very hot and arid land mass. Yes, again I must and do accept that unconditionally as well. But the obvious first question must be how all this dust and rock remained molten and extremely hot during its journey through space? Which it did not, and could not have done, since outer space is extremely cold indeed. If it was a mass of individual rocks and gases that took billions of years to join together to become a planet, surely all that heat from the sun would have dissipated? Yet the core is molten and always has been. Is this logical? No, it is not. Could a mass of cold rocks join together to become so hot and remain in that state into eternity? Hmmm!! The idea that they may have remained hot while travelling through space is soon quashed by the fact that asteroids today only heat to those temperatures on contact with the stratosphere, and there was no atmosphere of any kind until the seas came. That was after the planet had cooled. Only long, continuous, chemical reactions over an immense period of time could result in so much heat building up in the core of our planet.

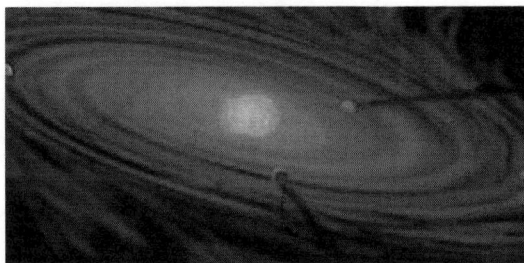

An artist's impression of a Solar Nebula consisting of a spinning mass of Inter Stella dust which combined with Hydrogen and Helium came together to form our planets. I contend that our moon came in the same way rather than by the accepted theory of being the result of a collision sending a large lump of Earth out as a satellite.

It is indisputable that comets fly through space with a trail of ice behind them. The logical progression of this is that if, for argument's sake, four huge comets joined together to become one spinning mass, that mass would consist of rocks and ice joined together, not an arid mass with an incredibly hot core making up most of that mass. The answer, I feel sure lies in the theory of gravity. From the spinning clouds, the heavier minerals must have been attracted by simple magnetism towards the core that was growing and warming up as the forces became stronger. Again we must suggest that surely the heavier elements would remain at the outer edge of the spinning rocks, not at the centre? This would be due to centrifugal forces. All this happened over billions of years until we ended up as we are today. However, this aspect of our past is a digression from the ideas to follow. I leave it for others to explain. I can't even begin to.

Be that as it may, one would have thought that on the final cooling, Earth would be a relatively smooth land mass, similar to the moon, in which case just where did all the water come from? All astronomers and geologists agree that the initial gases for all the planets were, in the main, hydrogen and helium, of which only the hydrogen was a main constituent of water.

Fiji in the South Pacific is a mere dot in the vast expanse of the Pacific Ocean. No one has the faintest idea where all that water came from.

Water is the product of burning hydrogen in oxygen which means that the Earth must have been incredibly hot with an enormous supply of both elements. There was from the beginning adequate hydrogen, but to make water – H_2O – half as much again of oxygen was needed. Just where did this come from? If it did at all. In fact there was none and so this idea is fatuous. It is generally considered that the oxygen we take for granted today comes from the water and from plants.

This makes things very difficult. As the water was formed, had it done so as the Earth cooled, it would have instantly vaporised, thus accelerating the overall cooling until enough condensed to settle in the seas and the lakes. But the seas and lakes contain 330 million cubic miles of water, all of which would have had the necessary cooling effect to halt the burning of the hydrogen and so curtail any future manufacture of more water. That is assuming that that had been how the seas formed. With all this I have a problem since there must have been a finite moment when the process began and an equally finite one when it all ended. Otherwise the water would have risen inexorably until it drowned everything. So far I have been unable to find any geological evidence of exactly how this all happened, or when. Reviewing this some eight years later for a second edition, no new credible theories have emerged. One I heard on the British BBC4 television channel, given by an astronomer with a PhD, was that on cooling a heavy dew formed which, on lifting, condensed to form the seas. Now that is a 'Mighty Bound' if ever I heard one. This remains the one big enigma that must be explained before many of present thoughts and theories can be confirmed or dismissed.

Every reference book I have consulted, including the Old Testament, seems to take a 'Mighty Bound' from the point when the crust began to cool to the fact that an enormous amount of water suddenly appeared. Logic would suggest that the source of heat to burn the hydrogen would come from the molten core so that, as it burned, the residue would be water. But that does not happen. When a volcano erupts it sends massive clouds of dust into the atmosphere, not water so I ask again, from where did the water come?

I am told that it could only have come from the tails of comets, or a huge comet, crashing into the earth. Let us think

41

about that. Comets are not very big in themselves but they do have enormous tails that contain a mixture of rocks and ice. A comet a mile across would have a tail a million miles long. This comet, if it landed on the earth at all, would have an impact that could shatter the earth's crust and end up in the mantle, possibly destroying much of it as well. The question to ask is what would happen if the million mile tail landed across the surface of the earth? Let us now consider what could happen next.

The comet has split the crust which means that lava in enormous quantities would pour out over the damaged crust. Hurtling into this crater would come a torrent of rocks and ice. Slowly the ice would melt as the shattered earth continued to spin, and over the barren earth it would leave a trail of rocks and ice. The tail would contain at least fifty percent rocks. This means that half a million cubic miles of water would end up on earth. But there are those 330 million cubic miles in the seas alone. And so over a very short period of geological time, 660 at least, similar comets must have landed with the same result. All must have missed our moon and none landed on Mars. All safely negotiated the asteroid belt and made a straight line for Earth and then, having left just the right amount of water, they stopped – for all time! Even after all this time there should be evidence somewhere of plates that were once in small and scattered pieces, some piled on top of one another, plus huge mountains of solid granite. And out there still, visible to the naked eye or through giant telescopes, are hundreds, even thousands, more that will orbit throughout our galaxy into eternity without ever hitting a planet.

Comets travel through space at incredible speeds with nothing to slow them down. They travel at anything between 40 and 350 km/second. Let us look at one that is one mile square [or equivalent sized round] that has a tail that million mile long and it in turn composes of 50/50 ice and rocks. It scores a direct hit on Earth bang on the Equator before there was any water on the planet. Let us assume that it is travelling at 200 km/second. So we have an enormous impact as the comet itself makes landfall. 200km/second equates to 720,000km/hour, and so at that speed it will not take very long for the one million mile or 1.6m km of tail to land. About two hours in fact during which time the Earth will have spun two thousand miles and show a similar two thousand mile long fissure. Into that fissure will have poured 500,000 cubic miles of rock and a similar quantity of water. The water will run off leaving a ridge of 250 cubic miles of rock across every mile on the trajectory. Obviously it will be spread out over a huge distance but, even so, it must leave some enormous mountain ranges behind. For all the seas to have come from this source we need 660 minimum similar impacts leaving a similar 660 massive mountain ranges. It is patently obvious that this just has not happened as even this simplistic example shows. Few could argue that our mountain ranges came from the shifting of the plates or volcanic outbursts. In gorges in the Alps are huge folds in the strata showing exactly how it actually did happen. Not theory, fact. The same astronomer who told about the theory of the dew also said that the Moon was littered with water filled craters following comet strikes. Conveniently they all seem to be on the far side out of our vision. Hmmmmmm?

It just doesn't add up and so I ask again, just where did it all come from?

Hopefully someone will help me on this one or could it be a major plus for the 'Creationist' lobby? However, geographers have come across one possible mountain of granite that could have come from this source. As we all know, mountain ranges come either from ice in massive quantities pushing land out of place, or the plates colliding and pushing the land out of the way. All the big mountains were formed that way, except those that came from volcanic action, as along the African Rift Valley or California's Sierra Nevada. None so far have been identified as having derived from a descending comet.

But recently a big mountain range has been discovered under the Antarctic ice that most certainly cannot have come from plates colliding. This is because the Antarctic sits comfortably on its own plate out of harm's way. I cannot find out just what the basic minerals are since research is still going on and the mountain range, the size of the Alps, is a long way under the ice sheet. We must wait and see.

If the water has an extra terrestrial source, one must then ask the obvious question of where it was originally formed, and how it got into the tails of the comets. As with all these questions from the 'Big Bang' onwards, there must always be asked what was there before that happened? With the Big Bang, there had to be something to set it off. What was that? Was it an atom that went off? Or even something smaller as has been suggested, and if so, where did that come from? How long had it been there waiting to go off? Most of all, why did it go pop? Is there even another one waiting to repeat the exercise and, if so, where did it come from and why has it not exploded before? If it does, will it blow us all to smithereens? With the ice in the tails of the comets, just where did such enormous quantities come from in the first place? I can accept the rocks as from space debris as in the 'Asteroid Belt', but water? Logic would suggest that in that belt there should be some large lumps of ice as well. And this takes us to life itself. Where did that come from?

We can create the tiniest and most complicated electronic devices but so far cannot create the simplest of flowers or animals. Yes, we can create some nasty viruses for germ warfare but we have never bridged the gap from virus to anything useful. Life must have come from somewhere a long time ago but, if this arrived on the back of a comet or meteorite, where did it come from originally, and how did it get onto its host vehicle? And so on and so on, *ad infinitum*. Do I accept that it was an accidental result of a chemical reaction in some sludge that created the right conditions? I do not know, but my argument is that any microbe that formed in this way could not have survived over billions of years. So a steady stream of similar chemical reactions must have formed over those billions years. Realistic? Again, I do not know but would very much doubt it.

Astronomers have suggested that large areas of Mars show evidence of dried up rivers and equally dried up former seas. If this can be proved to be the case, which at the time of writing has not

44

been, then we must ask not one question, but two. First, where did all _that_ water come from and second, even more importantly, where did it all go? As this was being written, the latest space vehicle to investigate Mars had just entered its orbit to find out where the water went. I want to know where it came from please???? Later on after the probe had landed – a remarkable feat of engineering – there was still no absolute proof of water on the planet. There have been a few sensational revelations but all have proved to be just that, sensational without really moving things forward. I wait with interest but don't hold my breath.

The outer shell of our earth solidified but the centre remained extremely hot and molten which it does to this day. The solidified outer shell fractured in many places to provide the 'Plates' that float relatively freely on the molten centre - The 'Mantle'. Where these plates meet we get the earthquakes and volcanoes of today.

Again, over an immense period of time the plates floated, some separating and others crashing into each other, pushing land masses vertically to form the mountain ranges, and eventually to leave the continental structure more or less as we have it today. During these enormous periods at the beginning, life existed as can be easily seen in the huge bands of limestone exposed in gorges in the Alps and other mountain ranges. But, in an earlier era as the Earth cooled, at some point in time, and from somewhere of which we have no knowledge, a spark of a living organism either settled or emerged on this planet. _'Emerged'_ is a much used word in the history of our world. It enables a whole series of 'Mighty Bounds' to take place.

Looking at this logically it can only have come from one of two sources. The first is that it came from an unknown source far away, having survived an enormous journey from its host planet through the incredibly hostile environment of outer space. It then landed without burning up as it entered our atmosphere amongst the hundred odd tons of outer space debris that has landed on our planet every day since. Most burns out in the Stratosphere but some gets through as witnessed by the many shooting stars we see

45

in the night sky. Of course, at the time there was little in the way of an atmosphere, that coming after the water. Accepted wisdom suggests that it came in the frozen tail of a passing comet and this would, to a certain extent, answer the question of how it survived the enormous journey through space and time.

The second option is that it was a Divine Creation placed on earth by 'God' Himself in order to eventually create the human race. I am inclined to believe the first scenario. I cannot see any 'God' placing life on any planet and then waiting billions of years for it to evolve. That is the basis of the Darwinist argument. They say that he didn't, it just happened and we are the end result. But the Creationists ask 'Why not just start with intelligent mankind?' Which, of course, is what they believe. If that same 'God' did put the life on the planet, in what form did it take and when did it happen? The Creationists will tell me that to 'God', time is eternal, and therefore this line of argument irrelevant. Another hmmmm!!

And so, according to Darwin, this organism divided into multiple cells, after 2 billion years as a single cell, to reproduce itself and then, over periods of time impossible for us to even contemplate, it gradually evolved into small crustaceans of which there are numerous fossils as proof. These became fish which eventually developed legs and lungs to walk on the land so becoming the reptiles. These reptiles then mutated to become the dinosaurs which dominated the entire planet for around 250 million years. Again there is much fossil evidence to support this theory. It is well known that the dinosaurs were all wiped out more or less simultaneously over a relatively brief period of time. This is now thought to be because of a sudden cooling of the entire planet, probably because of a large meteorite creating a huge dust storm that obliterated the sun. Or a comet giving the same result. There is much evidence to support the meteorite theory with a very large crater in Mexico. Or even a huge natural movement of the plates that could have created a similar volcanic winter. Who knows for certain? The answer is that nobody does. It is all conjecture.

The survivors of this period were the simple warm blooded mammals which then spread over the entire planet, evolving

46

through 'Natural Selection' or the 'Survival of the Fittest' to become the animals we have today. Darwin's fittest were those most able to adapt to changing surroundings, not necessarily the strongest or, for that matter, the most intelligent. Homo sapiens became the dominant species and has remained so ever since. It did however take a great deal of time for Homo sapiens to emerge as a branch of the ape family and to eventually walk upright. From then for a few hundred thousand years we gradually became modern man, evolving at more or less the same rate, give or take the odd thousand years, all over the world. Cut off from each other we developed our colours, bone structures and physical attributes according to local conditions and local needs.

That would be the logical progression according to Darwin, but later theories discount it as being not true. They suggest that man did not evolve separately over an immense period of time, but remained in Africa until very late in the evolutionary process. I dispute this totally as I show later on in the book.

The major flaw in this thinking is back with the fossils. During these billions of years animals were born and eventually died. The vertebrates, they are those with a backbone, and the crustaceans that lived in shells, died and were soon buried under rotting vegetation, this vegetation becoming compacted in layers leaving in many cases the fossilised remains of those animals. The vegetation itself became coal, natural gas and the oil we take for granted today. And so today we can date with reasonable accuracy most fossils from the bedrock in which they are embedded. Put simply, anything found embedded in a lump of rock can only have been put there when that rock was forming. And here we get into difficulty, especially when we look at some of the 'Awkward Questions' later on in the book.

The earliest fossils are the simple curved ammonites and then we get large gaps of millions of years before the next ones. There should be earlier ones as well, since the simple microscopic multi cell beings had to mutate into something tiny first, before 'emerging' as the much bigger ammonites. It is not unreasonable to suggest that during that period there would be lots of mutations as species gradually changed, but so far no fossilised evidence of this is available. It is as though the giant reptiles suddenly 'emerged' overnight as fully developed creatures; as though the early mammals suddenly appeared as did many fishes and the birds in the sky. So far there is no scientific evidence of these enormous leaps in evolution other than the irrefutable fact that they did, in fact, happen. Darwin recognised this and hoped that future palaeontologists would make the discoveries that would prove his theory. So far no one has succeeded. Yes, there are a few examples that, by stretching the imagination, may be considered to be 'transitory' but not sufficient for competent scientists to be able to say anything for definite.

The Darwinists all agree that life on earth began when that single cell having arrived, possibly from outer space, split into more than one cell, so beginning the long road towards the animal kingdom. I hesitate to argue with that, but the obvious follow up question has to be, that if that simple amoeba went on to become all the animals, did it also produce the necessary 'seeds', for want of a better word, that also produced the plant kingdom?

Without wishing to labour the point I feel that this argument needs further examination. As above, it is the accepted wisdom that possibly just one tiny organism started it all off. Fine, let us cling to that one. But if it did arrive on the tail of a comet or impacted into a meteorite, is it not reasonable to suggest that out there in space are other similar organisms all looking for a host planet on which to develop? Other organisms, that can only have come from another planet, somewhere out there in the cosmos that could support life. In which case where did that life come from? And so on, again, *ad infinitum*. Could there be others in the debris entering the atmospheres of all the planets? Without the necessary water to develop, as on Mars, Venus, our Moon etc, they presumably would simply either die or remain dormant forever. But some should arrive here on earth. I know of one eminent astronomer who is trying to actually prove that this is in fact still happening.

If they do, and have been doing so over the ages, then surely there should be similar ammonite type fossils but of totally different date? These later organisms should surely have produced similar creatures that evolved in different ways. And at different times as well. Then, over the millennia, we would see evidence of this happening. We do not see this as far as I am aware. There should be a long series of different ammonite type creatures that have evolved in a similar way over the life of the planet. There should be similar organisms landing right now that are beginning the whole process over and over again if there is a stream of organisms landing now. So far my astronomer friend has found none and he has people checking across the globe. The fossils should show similar creatures but millions of years apart. Do they? I cannot say for certain.

And this is where I get into difficulties. I must ask what the exceptional circumstances were all those millions of years ago that persuaded a fish that it must adapt into an amphibian, that are much different to the circumstances 100 million years later or, in fact, to the present day? And then leave the rest of the fish to swim about as before, totally unaware of this need. What were the reasons for an ape that was perfectly happy in the tree tops, to need to adapt into a feeble animal of little more intelligence whose only attribute was to begin to walk upright? Why did it do so then, nearly half a million years ago and not be doing the same today?

So in what form would one of these organisms evolve if it landed today? First we would have to find a piece of rock that had come from outer space and this would be difficult. A piece of granite that was not there the day before, lying in a limestone valley would be a good place to start. A careful forensic examination should tell whether said bug is actually there or not and, if it is, it must be put in careful quarantine. It may, and here I emphasise the word 'may', actually be a rather nasty virus against which we have no antidote. Another AIDS perhaps? Or ebola? Is that where they suddenly came from not all that long ago? Some experts think so.

Could it develop and evolve into new plant species? Animal species, or other nasty viruses? So far there is no proven evidence that this has ever happened. This leaves us with the single amoeba, billions of years ago, theory and the eternal question of where it came from.

There is another problem that causes me to ask more questions. All will agree that, in order to sustain life on any planet, various important criteria must be met. These are an ambient temperature, adequate but not too much, sunshine, adequate quantities of water, oxygen to breathe plus the most important of all and that is top spoil to grow plants in. Without the plants we would run out of oxygen very quickly. So where does this come from, and how long does it take to make?

The fertile areas of Earth are covered in a miniscule thickness – compared to the size of the planet – of fine soil, full of the necessary nutrients to sustain plant life in quantity. In low lying areas, flooding rivers deposit fresh silt to replenish the land, but what about higher ground? Surprisingly, in geological terms of time, it takes a very short period to provide a suitable covering. Until 12,000BC, much of Britain, Scandinavia and Canada, was covered in ice. This will have scraped every last vestige of soil off the bedrock, yet now all the lower hills and the sides of even the highest mountains are covered in a more or less even layer of fertile soil. There is enough to maintain massive forests and provide a carpet of green grass. Where did this all come from? Obviously not flooding rivers, but in a short period of time everywhere was covered in that same even layer that never gets thicker but which quickly washes or blows away if vegetation is removed. Looking at it logically the grass and the soil must therefore have arrived together, but where from? Did it simply 'emerge'? Another tick in the Creationist box? Probably not.

In the Mediterranean areas much of the coast is subject to severe forest fires in summer and these are combated with planes known as 'Canadairs' which scoop up a few tons of water from the sea. They then fly to the affected parts and deposit the lot in one go, on just one part that is on fire. They run in relays of three or four and do a very good job. But their drawback is that once the hold is open, it all comes out at once rather than as a heavy spray over a bigger area.

There are, however, other things that do just that and those are our clouds. The average cumulus thunder cloud holds a hundred or even a thousand times more water than does a Canadair but it does not drop it all at once. Instead it falls as rain, ice or snow in a steady, even way over a huge area, and this in itself is quite remarkable. But, like the sea, we just take it for granted. Let us look a little closer into the phenomenon.

Clouds are formed from the evaporation of water out of the sea or from lakes or wet land. The bigger they get the more water, and ice particles, they hold, until it reaches a point where the individual droplets in the cloud gather together and gravity takes over. It starts to rain. In a tropical storm or hurricane situation, the clouds hold millions, sometimes billions, of tons of water, and it would not be unreasonable to think that a point would be reached where the weight could no longer be sustained, and that a colossal amount would fall at one time. Those underneath would think that they lived under Niagara Falls. Yes, in a tropical storm the precipitation is very heavy but not to that degree and, as the storm moves relentlessly on, it continues to deposit the same even layer over a very wide area.

Let there be no doubt about this, without clouds and their eschewing rainfall, life on any planet could not exist. Life in any country depends on a year round steady fall of rain over most of the land, filling the reservoirs and the rivers, so that crops will grow and animals can be fed. Too much and there are floods, too little and a drought soon turns all into a desert and the top soil simply blows away. And it all conveniently falls evenly over the ground. During Hurricane Ike in 2008 the storm was 900 miles wide as it crossed the Mid West of America. It contained millions of gallons of water which it proceeded to deposit, not in one go, but evenly as though it was coming from an enormous sprinkler system. And it did so for days on end, spreading its life giving water over a massive area of America, before petering out over the North Atlantic.

The way that clouds form is not in dispute, it is the way that they then ration out the rain that I find most remarkable. Is this another tick in the Creationist box? Again, maybe not.

And this is the argument of the Creationist lobby. They argue that it was a Divine being that was responsible, citing this lack of scientific evidence as proof that they must be right. They insist that the human genome is so complex that only a Divine presence could have created it. They say that man cannot change this genome no matter how he breeds and it is passed down intact through the generations.

It is my feeling that of the two, Darwin will emerge as being nearest to the truth, and one of the purposes of this book is to explain why. I think that there are flaws in his argument, as there must be with any theory that was breaking new ground one hundred and fifty years ago. But, as in any scientific experiment, there

Warm Mediterranean air rises as huge cumulous rain clouds on hitting the colder Alps.

must always be what is known as a 'Control'. Scientists will take one hundred people with the same problem, give 50 of them the new wonder drug and the other 50 a placebo which is an inert pill. They are the control. No one knows who has the drug except the scientists and so, after the given time of the research, they can measure the difference between the two groups. That is the purpose of the 'Control'.

Unknown to Darwin, or maybe he never thought about it, perhaps he did, there was and always has been, one massive 'Control' available to those studying this subject. From this control we can accurately measure the relative progress of mankind, picking out obvious sudden changes on the way. This book shows that there were dramatic changes in the evolutionary process in comparatively recent years and these can in no way be attributed to anything put out by Darwin. But do they prove or not the Creationist theory? We must wait and see.

My problem with the Creationist theory is that the Divine had no need to bother with the entire Dinosaur period at all. To them it all began in 4,004 BC which conveniently takes a very big 'Mighty Bound' over it all. That, of course, is assuming that the whole object was to eventually end up with one dominant species with all the animals in a lower capacity. This is the theory thrown up by theologians everywhere. Here we have 250 million wasted years, for few would argue that the presence of such creatures would have been a welcome benefit at the time. It simply did not happen! Good, let us get on with it then. But we can't, because it did happen as must be obvious by now.

The only real benefit from the entire period has been that their rotting bodies and vegetation eventually produced the fossil fuels that made the Industrial Revolution and modern sciences happen. If we are to believe that this was a pre-ordained Divine phenomenon, with the same Divine authority deciding that enough was enough before killing them all off, then I fear we are entering the realms of sensational science fiction. Taking it one stage further and looking at Homo sapiens, we must ask the obvious question of why so many different races were placed on earth at

53

the same time, and were then left for 200,000 years, never anywhere in the world to take that one massive step out of the Stone Age? That is assuming that they were spread across the world from Day One, which is not now thought to be the case. Surely at least one group would have been created, or would 'emerge', that could make this step? As it happened in the real world, one such group did suddenly emerge from nowhere some twenty thousand years ago and it is another purpose of this book to try to explain how that may have come about.

Now that we can analyse the human genome so carefully, scientists from the University of New Mexico are saying that they have new evidence that Neanderthal man did breed with early Homo sapiens leaving Neanderthal genes in us all. This is interesting because according to the basic laws of evolution, man should have come from the Neanderthals, or Homo erectus, anyway, and so we must share a very large proportion of their genes. But if this is not so and we were a completely different species, where did those species come from and from what did they emerge? From what did they evolve? We are supposed to come from Africa, they came from more northerly climes where there is no obvious evidence of earlier apes or primates from which to evolve.

If we accept that some 1.8 million years ago Homo erectus was evolving all over the world, 300,000 years ago the Neanderthals were evolving in Europe and Western Asia and, at approximately 100,000 years later Homo sapiens were evolving in Africa, where they remained until around 50 to 40,000 years BP, is this in itself not remarkable? That the Neanderthals and Homo erectus should become extinct at around the same time that Homo sapiens were leaving Africa is a remarkable coincidence. Both species were far more powerful and would have had very little less brain power than early man. As far as is known Neanderthal man remained just the one skin colour and one race over a period of 300,000 years yet we, Homo sapiens, evolved in many different colours and with many different facial characteristics over, effectively no more than 50,000 years. But we only differ by those skin colours and facial characteristics. With everything else we are more or less identical. Logically it should be thought that groups living in the rain forests would develop longer and stronger arms to climb trees. The Native Americans on the Great Plains should have enormous and strong legs to chase animals; those living in colder climes must evolve with thick coats of fur for warmth as did the animals. But they did not. They did not evolve to improve their chances of survival at all. Anatomically an Indian living in the Amazon rain forest is more or less identical to an African, European, Inuit or an Australian Aborigine. I wonder why? And apart from the skin colour and facial differences, we are all very much the same.

An interesting theory based on the works of Einstein, and since expanded by a Canadian Astrophysicist named Dr Hugo Ross, gives a remarkable explanation to the seven days of creation. Einstein believed that since the Universe is still rapidly expanding, it could never have been in a 'Steady State'. The analogy is to pulling out the pin on a grenade. When you do so, matter is sent flying in all directions, completely at random. He said that the Universe began with a 'Big Bang' many billions of years ago, and that the being to pull out the pin and so start it off, was a vastly superior intellect, namely 'God'. At this moment 'Time' began and before then all was a void.

Developing the argument Ross claims that the seven days were in fact a metaphoric seven days, rather than the Earth based seven days of Genesis, so that 'In the beginning etc' was the moment of the Big Bang. The subsequent days were when he created everything else in the order given, but each metaphoric day was spread over millions, if not billions of years. Now we are in the last of the days which is the day of rest and the explanation for this is that, quite truthfully, since Homo sapiens first walked the Earth no other new species is known to have evolved. New species have been discovered but none has been seen to evolve or be in the process of evolving. Many have become extinct. Now the superior intellect is at rest. Different versions of known species are constantly being found but no completely new actual creatures have simply 'emerged'.

As do I in this work, Ross expands on the incredibly narrow parameters that allow life to exist on this planet and, according to him, on this planet alone. He remarks about the speed of rotation of Earth and how it set out at a supposed 20 hour period [others say sixteen, but who knows?] during which time life would have been difficult because of storms and hurricanes. I would have thought that the extra centrifugal force would make everything lighter as well. Could it have suddenly slowed during the dinosaur period making them all too heavy to move about? Probably not. He thinks that it is slowing down and will eventually take 26 to 28 hours. If it does he thinks that life will not be possible because during the day it will be 170 degrees Fahrenheit and at night minus 100. That I feel may not be true, since we already have our seasons where the periods of night and day away from the Equator certainly vary by more than plus or minus two hours.

Because life is so incredibly finely balanced on the Earth he believes that only a superior intelligence could have designed and created it, that intelligence being 'God' himself. Therefore there was a 'Big Bang' and the Creation lobby wins.

I feel that much of this argument is very much one of having a good theory and then finding the facts to prove it. Another 'Mighty Bound' in fact but as with it all, I am perfectly happy to be proved wrong.

A further thought being floated since the first edition of this book   is that modern science has more or less stopped the Darwinian theory in its tracks. Evolution has, if not stopped then has certainly slowed down. Medicines and chemicals have stopped the weakest making way for the strong. The sick are no longer allowed to die and that includes the animals and plants. Man made mutations – the so called 'Frankenstein Foods' – have changed the way that plants grow and we have cross bred our animals to produce more food. Because of this change to 'Natural Selection' people live longer but there is insufficient room for them to live. Because they seek a better life they emigrate to the more prosperous regions where there is no longer room for them. Because they live longer, infant mortality has been reduced to a fraction of previous years. More and more people need the finite resources of the planet and the sheer weight of numbers is becoming unsustainable. The very existence of so many people, and now domestic animals for food, is causing a slow and gradual rise in the temperature of the planet that will eventually make the tropical regions uninhabitable. Then what?????

We also meddle with Natural Selection by not allowing species that can no longer cope with changing circumstances to simply die out. Vast resources are expended to protect endangered species that, according to Darwin's theory should be just allowed to become extinct. Should we be doing this even when it is not necessarily due to the progress of mankind that has endangered them? It is an emotive subject that can cause extreme reactions but I just raise it as part of our story.

5

THE CHICKEN OR THE EGG?

In its simplest form, Darwin's theory says that we all began with a simple single cell organism. This split into more cells and so life on earth began. These cells became simple crustaceans as we see in the many fossils around the world, the crustaceans became fish, the fish became amphibians, the amphibians became reptiles, some of the reptiles learned to fly and became birds, other reptiles became mammals and the mammals became man.

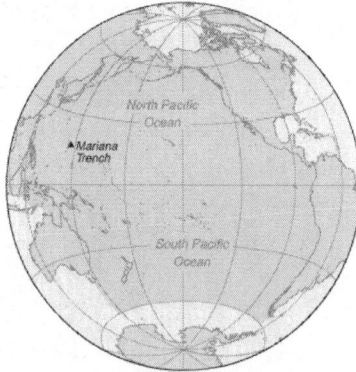

The Pacific Ocean alone has an area of 63.8 million square miles at an average depth of 2.5 miles. The total world land mass is 58 million square miles.

Fine, so is that it? Or, may it just be that tiny bit too simplistic? Let us go back to the beginning again. I have already mentioned that there is no explanation available, as I write this in 2010, and revised in 2014 and going to press in 2016, for the presence of the sea. Since the publication of the first edition in 2008, I have scoured every scientific paper possible and no new credible theories have come up. Producing it by burning hydrogen in oxygen is a ludicrous idea. That it came on the tail of a comet is also just as ludicrous but, nevertheless, it is the favourite one.

However, simple logic rules this idea out for the reason that there is too much of it. 330 million cubic miles too much. Throughout this work I illustrate how basic, simple arithmetic destroys so many cherished and much researched theories. Put this into context. The entire land mass of our planet is 58 million square miles; the area of the Pacific alone is 63.8 million square miles and the average depth is around the 2.5 miles region. Do your maths on that one before we do some simple arithmetic for comets.

The biggest comets have tails of around one million miles long, but those tails are no more than a square mile in thickness. They are by no means all full of ice, containing a large proportion of rocks as well and so there would have had to be over a thousand of these at least hitting the surface of our planet to produce so much water. They would also have left behind at least 500 million cubic miles of rocks as well, of which there would still be evidence today. These, if <u>evenly</u> spread, would result in a layer 2.58 miles thick over the entire planet, including in the sea itself!!!!! Water finds its own level, rocks do not.

The crust of the earth that floats on the mantle varies from four to twenty two miles thick – as much as fifty to eighty under some mountain ranges - and so this would have made a very significant difference in parts. There should be evidence of this, undisturbed on the sea bed, possibly in the Southern Ocean around Australia which was not subject to much plate movement. If it all arrived on the tails of hundreds of comets, the geological evidence would be there in our mountains where the strata would not be even. There would be enough geological evidence left somewhere on the planet to show this amount of debris arriving, over a relatively short period of time, from outer space. But there is not.

The favourite explanation that I have found so far is that around 4.1 billion years ago the oceans and the atmosphere began to develop. How? Take a Mighty Bound instead. Hmmm.

But the water is there for all to see and it must have come first. Without it that first cell would have perished on the arid earth, as it would equally had it landed on our moon. And so, some 3.8 billion years ago, there must have been water in abundance on our planet which enabled the first cell to take hold and to, eventually i.e., 2 billion years later, become more cells. But is it unreasonable to suggest that if one small cell arrived from outer space, there must have been many more in a continuous stream over the next 2 billion years? It is always thought that the cell came on the tail of a comet, but this is unlikely because it again would have needed millions, if not billions of these over the same time scale, all coming from the same life supporting source and miraculously all landing on earth. Hundreds, thousands, even millions and billions, of them, in various stages of development that were then spread evenly across a large area of the globe. These would have had far more chance of getting a foothold than just one. Most would die but enough did not and so it all began. And this must have been a continuous process over at least those 2 billion years. Or, what is most likely, for the first 3.8 billion years of our planet there was in fact no life at all. Nothing landed that took hold. This gives the sea a far greater time to appear, but from where?

Accepted modern theory suggests that these single cell beings inhabited the planet for two billion years before the first multi cell ones began. Think about that. It would be impossible for one cell to last that long but, if it was only a single cell, it could not split into two. Single cells do not breed as such, they merely multiply on their own as with the simplest bacteria of today. They grow by clinging to rocks, gathering on the seabed or floating in the atmosphere but, most of all, they need water and, but not necessarily, air to survive. Today they exist in deep sludge at the bottom of still ponds where there is little movement of the water. Therefore, if accepted science is correct, for two billion years our planet must have either been showered with these cells or they simply hung on since time began. Does this still continue today or was it all shut off when multi cell ones emerged? No, we still do have plenty of single cell organisms about but surely, throughout the entire existence of our planet, similar life forms would have arrived from outer space?

We have to ask the obvious question that no one can offer any answer to, and that is, where was the planet in outer space that provided the life form in the first place? So far, no one has been able to manufacture a similar one artificially. Therefore, how did it become a living thing? Or did the multi cell embryos simply 'emerge' on Earth from nowhere? I don't know and nor does anyone else.

One school of thought goes down the path of pure chemistry by assembling the basic elements of life into the correct order. These produce the correct amino acids which in turn are the building blocks of DNA and life itself. They think that this all happened by accident so kick starting the whole process. This is a good idea but is flawed by the need for the process to last those enormous periods of time, plus the fact that in none of the modern advanced laboratories across the globe has anyone been able to replicate the process. Could it have happened randomly by accident? And then keep on repeating that random selection over a billion years? No. I discuss this in Part 2. If it had done so, what kept those first cells alive for such an impossibly long period of time? Or did the accidental creation of those cells carry on for billions of years, only to shut off some 500m years ago when things had got hold and the process was well under way? Or could it all have begun much, much later? Be that as it may, according to the theory of evolution, these minute organisms eventually became fish, as is universally accepted, and so it all progressed at a very slow pace. But let us stop right there and jump forward to the present day.

Let us now look briefly at life as it is on this planet today. Life is made up of small microbes; the insects such as wasps and flies; the invertebrates which include jelly fish, squid and octopus; the crustaceans such as crabs, shrimps and lobster; the fish from the tiniest Angel Fish to the huge Great White Sharks; the reptiles from the tiniest gecko to the salt water crocodiles; the birds in the air and the mammals on land to include Homo sapiens. Add to that the plant kingdom which includes everything from simple grass to the tallest trees and you have hardly scratched the surface.

61

Again very briefly, so that we do not get embroiled too much in the minute details of these things, we will look at the physiology of these creatures. Forget for a moment the invertebrates as we look at the fish. These vary in size, shape and colour but all have the same basic make up of a solid backbone attached to which are smaller bones, or ribs, that radiate out to form the skeleton. Attached to the skeleton is flesh that is covered by skin, into which are some moveable fins. Most fish live by eating smaller fish in a constant food chain, the food being taken through the mouth where it is either swallowed whole, or bitten by teeth. Other fish live on plankton and krill. These are minute crustaceans absorbed by filters in the mouth. They breathe through gills and breed by depositing clouds of eggs that are fertilised by similar clouds of male eggs. In a situation such as on coral reefs, where there are thousands of different species, only eggs of individual species fertilise each other. For instance an egg from an angel fish never mates with one from a moray eel. For defence they use speed and the safety of a large shoal. They have some method of identifying predators and communicating the fact between themselves. It should go without saying that they live all the time in water and cannot exist for long out of it.

Discount for the moment the snakes as we consider the reptiles. Like the fish they have the same back bone, complete with ribs, and that is all they share with fish apart from being cold blooded. Nothing else. The fish from the very beginning must have had fins but on the reptiles, and the amphibians, there are none. Fins are not connected to the skeleton in any way.

The reptiles have legs, four of them, on which they walk around. These are physically connected to the skeleton and to the flesh. Small lizards have legs to help them move quickly, a salt water crocodile has short legs on which it too can move quickly but only for a short period of time. Prey is caught either in the jaws, or by the use of a long tongue, which flicks out to catch an insect. They all have powerful jaws, sharp teeth and claws, a powerful tail and, most of all, they are cold blooded. This means that their body temperature varies with the ambient temperature of the air or water. If it gets too cold their blood could simply freeze, which is why most reptiles live in tropical or sub tropical areas, rather than in northern Europe or southern Australia. They breed by laying fertilised eggs which hatch after which the young must fend for themselves. There is no maternal instinct and the newly hatched young are as likely to be eaten by their parents as anything else. The young are incubated in the eggs and emerge with no help from the parents. All are carnivorous in that they only eat meat.

For defence and survival they have speed of movement, powerful jaws, sharp claws and a very powerful and agile tail.

Again for this exercise I am leaving the birds [and the insects] to one side and moving on to the mammals, as in the animal kingdom. What have these in common with the reptiles? Again more or less the same skeleton but now the arms and legs are more important and the tail very much less so. The four legs are primarily used for walking, some that are vegetarian only have cloven hoofs on their feet as with horses and cattle, others have claws to catch and kill their food, such as the cats and the bears. The digestive system of the vegetarian animals means that they only eat grass, leaves and plants but not any form of meat. The carnivores eat meat alone and their digestive systems rely only on a supply of lesser animals for food. Having said that, some bears eat grass and flowers, together with salmon and other smaller animals and fish. And so a massive cow, horse, elephant or giraffe gets by on just the nutrients in simple grass or leaves and equally a huge lion or tiger only needs a plentiful supply of fresh meat for all its vitamins and calories.

These creatures are all warm blooded in that body temperature remains more or less constant whatever the ambient temperature of the air around them. And so a lion, bred on the plains of tropical Africa, can cope perfectly well outside in a zoo in New York. And a dog from north Europe will survive in the tropics. They breed by the male penetrating the female when she is in season and at very often the same time of the year so that the young are born in the spring. The embryo grows in the body of the mother and after a suitable gestation period the young and helpless offspring is born. It is then weaned by the female, using milk produced in the mammary glands, until it is old enough and strong enough to eat either grass or meat. Generally the more powerful the creature such as a lion, the more helpless is its young. A newly born calf will be walking within minutes of being born but a lion is blind for a few days. Maturity is achieved within one to two years for the bigger animals, a few months for smaller ones.

The vegetarians have powerful teeth to grind up the vegetation that is taken by mouth only, but the carnivores use powerful claws on their front legs to hold their food. This is then torn apart by the very powerful teeth and jaws. For defence some of the vegetarians have horns on their head, they have very powerful legs with which to kick and the smaller ones have speed to outrun an enemy. The carnivores have the same sharp claws used for hunting, they have the same powerful jaws and sharp teeth, and they too have high speed to outrun a more powerful enemy.

Many of the smaller reptiles can easily climb trees as can most of the cat family and many species of bear, and this is an additional aid to self preservation. The other things that all have in common, and here I include the entire animal kingdom, are that their sole reason to be around is to eat, sleep and breed. They will all eventually end up as part of the food chain where even the biggest, and most powerful of animals, will eventually die and be eaten by a younger and fitter one. None can reason, they cannot speak and have no creative knowledge or ability. There is no question of them ever breeding with a member of the reptile family. That would be a physical impossibility.

What about the primates such as monkeys and chimpanzees? They are warm blooded and usually vegetarian, finding their food in the trees. Physically they are the same as the other mammals except that they have powerful legs and tails that enable them to leap from tree to tree over some big distances. And they have very long arms for the same reason. They use speed for defence and have powerful jaws and very sharp teeth. They have sharp claws and, to a certain extent, they are capable of a basic reasoning that can enable them to outwit a far more powerful big cat. The largest of the primates, the gorillas, have powerful arms, legs and teeth and a thick coating of fur. They walk on all four feet.

The one thing that every other species on the planet has in common is that they vary in size. Look just at the mammals. The cat family varies from the smallest wild mountain cat to the huge tigers. Dogs, descended from wolves, go to similar extremes as do all the primates which vary from the tiniest monkey to huge gorillas. Another thing is that they tend to look more or less alike. Few people can tell the difference between cows in a herd, individual dogs of the same breed or sheep in the field. Man, on the other hand, hardly varies in size and every single one of us looks different.

The entire theory of Evolution and the 'Survival of the Fittest' is that first the fish evolved into the reptiles, the reptiles into mammals, and then the mammals into primates, from which the ultimate all powerful, species of them all – Homo sapiens – emerged. That was us.

So what about early man? He who evolved from all those powerful beasts. What had he got that they hadn't? What made him need to change in order to survive and outwit all these other creatures? How did he adapt to meet the changing conditions? He stood upright for one thing and, like the big cats, he could use the arms or forelegs to help him eat. But he didn't have any claws, his jaw was not very strong and his teeth not sharp. He didn't have the strength to climb very far up trees and his legs were only strong enough to support himself, walk and run, not very quickly, but for no more than a few hundred metres at speed before tiring. His body strength was so weak that other animals that were much smaller could easily overpower and kill him. Any fish could swim faster and the bigger ones could catch and kill him with ease, as could the bigger reptiles. Also he had shed all covering hair that kept him warm, the only animal so to do. So what physically had he brought with him in this stage of the evolutionary process that was superior to the members of the animal kingdom from which he had evolved? What did he bring to the table that would prove beyond doubt the theory of 'The Survival of the Fittest'? The survival of only the strongest, leaving the rest to perish into extinction. The ultimate species that was able to adapt to changing circumstances where others could not. What made him such an immediate and massive success? After all, his predecessors in the evolutionary journey were perfectly content as slugs, snails, fish, lizards, rodents, monkeys, et al. Thousands of those species had felt no need to change into something else over time, so why had Homo sapiens felt the need to do so whilst living in the same environment? With what was he endowed that would make him into a towering success in such a relatively short period of time?

Nothing. Not one single thing that was of any use for gathering food or escaping an enemy had he inherited from his animal ancestors. Including all the other primates. Every single thing that they needed for survival, man had rejected. Other ways that he differed was that he was able to ingest both meat and vegetables, but the most important was in the time that it took his young to mature. A helpless blind lion cub is almost fully grown after a year, as is a baby chimpanzee or gorilla, but a baby Homo sapiens is dependent on its adults until around eight or nine years which, in the early days, was for about a third of its life. It was not sexually mature until at least thirteen which, again, was nearly half of its life. Most other small animals were at the end of their lives by fifteen.

All he had, which did not evolve from anywhere else, was a marginally superior brain that enabled him to use fire for warmth and to build a crude shelter away from the elements. All he could use for defence were staves from trees that he had pulled down, and perhaps rocks to throw, but that was all. For nearly two hundred thousand years, possibly much more, he did not develop enough creative mentality to devise other than the simplest of stone tools. It took him 120,000 years to work out the bow and arrow rather than simply throwing stones. He certainly could not chop down a tree. It was as though evolution had gone back a billion years and said *"This is not good enough, start again."* Homo erectus, Homo sapiens and the Neanderthals were little further advanced than any other animal on the planet. And they were physically by far the weakest of all. With Homo sapiens being the very weakest of the three.

Let us look at the chronology of man himself. The first homids recorded have been dated at around 10mBP. [Before the present]. 6 million years later he began walking on two legs rather than four. Around 1.7mBP the first humanoid traits began and Homo erectus roamed the world. He was a brutal figure, a wanderer gatherer who ate meat. He discovered how to sharpen a stone to cut meat but that is about all. He was around until the eruption of Mount Toba around 68,000BP caused so many species to go into extinction. Around 350,000BP Neanderthal man emerged, from where no one knows. This is because there were no other primates from which he could have evolved known to be living in Europe or northern Asia. He was around until about 35,000BP. Overlapping this was modern man as we know him today who first emerged around 200,000BP in Africa but it was not until 180,000 years later that his new and much larger brain emerged at between 20 and 10,000BC. We co-habited the planet with Homo erectus for 130,000 years and Neanderthal for 150,000 years. We did not cause their extinctions and neither did they hinder our advancement. You will note the continuous use of the word 'emerge'.

It is a common myth that as soon as we left Africa, we made war on the much bigger Neanderthal and so caused their extinction. Let us look at the facts. Neanderthal had been roaming Europe and Asia for 300,000 years before Homo sapiens began to leave Africa and this, according to accepted theory, would have been 40,000BP. Since the last mass extinction, Homo sapiens in Africa would not have increased in numbers by a huge amount, and so those entering Europe and Western Asia would not have been numerous. I understand that present [2014] academic thought is that it was less than 10,000. With this I do have a problem. Now Europe and Western Asia is spread over a massive area and over that area, south of the glaciations line, would be a still significant but declining population of Neanderthals. Why were they declining? Disease perhaps? Contracted from Homo sapiens? Again a possibility but no one can know for certain.

10,000 as a maximum would consist of around 3,000 breeding pairs, plus their offspring, and this is no more than the population of a small market town in the UK. I would contend that this number, roaming in groups of around 10 to 20 families, could not have spread far enough in the short period of time between Homo sapiens entering Europe and the final extinction of the Neanderthal. Generations of each species would never have come anywhere near each other and so I would suggest that there must be another explanation for the extinction. This number of Homo sapiens, had they made frequent contact with the Neanderthal, would have been easily picked off, one group at a time. They would have caused our extinction, not the other way round. Could it possibly have been some sort of disease, to which they had no resistance, and possibly brought from Africa by us, that caused the problem? A form of ebola or some other nasty tropical disease easily transmitted by man. As I say, no one knows.

And so, some 3.5 to 3 billion years ago, that first speck of life is assumed to have arrived on our planet to begin the process that ends with us here today. It remained a single cell according to accepted science for nearly two billion years before it became a multi cellular creature. It took another 400 million years before the first simple animals in the form of grubs appeared, after another 70 million years the first complex animals appeared in the form of fish. Twenty five million years later plant life began, to be followed seventy five million years later by insects and seeds. This takes us up to 400 million years ago.

So the state of play 400 million years ago was that on earth there were ferns, mosses, fungi and algae and some insects such as spiders and millipedes [from what did they all evolve???] and in the waters the first primitive fish with teeth. It took 3.4 billion years to get this far and so all the rest took place during the following 400 million years. During the next 120 million years the big explosion of life happened. Those simple fish became great sharks, millions of other species of fish emerged and on land the first amphibians grew into the massive dinosaurs that would dominate the earth for another two hundred million years. They, of course, were cold blooded reptiles. Concurrent with this the first simple warm blooded mammals appeared. Then around 65.5 million years ago, something happened that wiped out half the animal kingdom including all the dinosaurs. Just what it was is still a mystery but there are theories. This is mine.

It was at this time that some of the great land and sea upheavals were taking place. The African plate was pushing against the European one to form the Alps. The Rockies and Himalayas were also being formed by upheavals that are impossible to imagine. This would have caused enormous earthquakes and tsunamis all over the world. There must have been many volcanoes all sending ash into the air and if, as it is inevitable that it must have been the case, they were spread all over the world, they would have created enormous dust clouds, so giving the volcanic winter that killed off so many species. Not a single meteorite as is the accepted unproven theory, but many natural eruptions across the Earth over a long period of time.

During the next sixty five million years every bird, fish, insect and animal now on the planet evolved. Neanderthal man emerged around 350,000 years ago and roamed the planet for 315,000 years, which is between 10 and 12,000 generations, and he was little different to any other mammal in that his sole reason for existence was to eat, sleep and breed. His creative achievements were restricted to a few crude stone tools. He added nothing more to civilization at all. His predecessor and then contemporary, Homo erectus, was no different. Just another animal species that wandered the earth for no other purpose than to eat, sleep and breed. And the same must be said about his successor, modern man, who first appeared around 200,000 years ago. For 180,000 of those years he was just the same in that he created nothing but merely existed alongside all the other animals. Then just ten to twenty thousand years ago, he underwent a massive change into a creature that could build a great city like Jericho out of stone, using tools he had made himself. And Mohenjo Daro in Pakistan. Both big, seemingly impossible, complexes for Stone Age man.

The entire evolutionary process and theory is that there was at some point a mutation of sorts for the better that would enable the mutant to either replace its predecessor, or live alongside it. The survival of the fittest, leaving the rest to perish. The mutated species has become aware of a new necessity that will enable it to proceed further. It adapts to the new circumstances and becomes a new species in its own right. This means that at some finite point all those years ago, a simple invertebrate began to grow a shell and, very much later, that creature in its shell began to discard it to enable it to swim rather than crawl along the sea bed. Again, when this process was complete and the fish had its back bone, gills and fins, at some finite moment something told it that it needed to begin to grow feet and legs and to find some way of breathing air other than through gills.

Before going any further let us look again at this without recourse to the 'Mighty Bound' theory. From being a lifeless planet, albeit full of water, it took 90% of it's time to get to the first simple beings other than cells. The next almost full 10% saw everything including the arrival and subsequent extinction of the dinosaurs leading up to the arrival during the last twenty five million years of many, if not most, of the animal species we see today including pigs, giraffe, deer, dogs and cats. Nearly two million years ago our kinsman, Homo erectus arrived and survived for over 65,000 generations without evolving into anything else, merely existing as a species. Over half way through the last million years, Neanderthal man arrived, survived 13,000 generations before fizzling out and then modern man took another 7,500 generations before he did anything constructive. Everything that has created civilization as we know it has come in just 200 generations or less. That is if we agree that it all began in Egypt in 3022BC. I use an arbitrary figure of 40 generations per 1000 years but this may be generous. I can trace my family back to the mid 17th century and we have 33 generations per 1000 years. The pre Norman kings of England averaged just under 34 generations per 1000 years and the post Norman ones show the number rising to 37. If my own family are typical there have been only 185 generations since 3022BC for mankind to become civilized and mobile.

With this time scale I do not argue. Enough work has been done by competent geologists and palaeontologists who have examined fossils and arrived at this graph. But, what puzzles me is the idea that it is all supposed to be based on the survival of the fittest, and that at some point in time species changed into other ones. With this, I have a problem. Another thing that gives me a problem is that when said species mutated into another it simply stopped and just died out. So that when those first fish found their way onto land, no others followed. Surely over the millions of years that followed other fish would be following suit, right up to today? There should be in the waters many fish, such as the Coelacanth, with legs and tails in various stages of evolution. There should be frogs that are half lizard, lizards that are warm blooded and so on. But there are none. As each evolutionary step has been taken, what has gone before has been discarded except that we are left with fishes, lizards, mammals and monkeys that are locked in to their present state and that over time have never found the need to mutate into something else. To my knowledge there are no birds, fish, reptiles or mammals alive today that are half way between one generic species and another. I would further say that the physiology of a reptile, over no matter how many mutations, could never result in it becoming a warm blooded mammal.

I use an analogy of a school. A child enters school a baby at four or five years old. Each year he gets older and moves up into the next class, and he does this until he leaves as a man at eighteen. Behind him in every class year are others, following on in an endless stream of children growing up. If this first child emulated the theory of evolution as promulgated, there would be no one following in his footsteps. As he got one year older, those behind would simply perish into extinction or remain as babies or tiny children, never growing up. Surely in the natural world there should be at least a few species at the in between stages, but it seems that there are not. Or none that I am aware of.

If it is all down to the survival of only the fittest, from where, and why, did the Neanderthals emerge? There were no other primates in northern Europe or Asia. They were amongst the weakest of all creatures as were the other homids. As are rabbits and field mice, neither of which have any real means of defence, any more than does a cow or a sheep, even ancient, wild versions of them. On the plains of Africa are deer and other animals with no means other than some speed for defence. They have neither evolved nor adapted with speed or defences to escape the clutches of their predators. It is as though these creatures have evolved solely to provide easy food for the predator carnivores. Under no circumstances can any of these, including man himself, be considered to be amongst the strongest members of the animal kingdom. So where do they fit into the bigger picture?

6

SCIENTIFIC FACT OR A MIGHTY BOUND?

Geology is very nearly an exact science. Rocks are there to be seen and it is a relatively simple exercise to be able to identify them, what is above and what is below. From this a date can be established, which will be not far from the correct one, given the enormous time scales involved. Palaeontology, on the other hand, is not quite so easy. The palaeontologist discovers his fossils and deduces the age of them by comparing them to the neighbouring rock. And so he, or she, finds a dinosaur footprint in some limestone, compares it with others that are similar, and then puts out the theory that 'x' dinosaur was walking about at that place at that time. Fine, until a footprint appears that is dated well before said dinosaur was supposed to be about, in which case all previous theories must be reconsidered. Unfortunately, this happens all the time, and virtually the entire time line of life on earth is bound up in theories from various academics. And as new facts appear, so do the new theories alongside them. Little comes from actual undisputable fact.

Since their's are merely theories, I throw in my hat with theories of my own, most of which academia will not like at all. But why should I be wrong and they right? No, I do not wander the earth with a little hammer and a microscope, I just use common sense and simple logic. And mine are formed after many hours, days and years of painstaking research. Decide for yourself.

According to accepted theory, which I do not dispute, the earth was formed some 4.8 – 4.5 billion years ago and that is our starting point. Let us go on from there.

1. 4.54 billion years BP the earth began as a spinning cloud of dust and rocks.

2. 3.8 billion years BP the earth was a solid formation with hot centre but cool crust. From somewhere single cell creatures arrived on earth. The sea formed.

3 1.8 billion years BP multi cell creatures arrive from outer space, simply emerge or evolve from the single ones.

4. 230 million years BP Dinosaurs appear.

5. 68 million years BP Dinosaurs vanish. The first mass extinction.

6. 350,000 years BP. Neanderthals in Europe.

7. 200,000 years BP Homo sapiens appears in Africa. Neanderthals and Homo Erectus in Europe.

8. 70,000 years BP. Homo sapiens approaches present state of physical maturity. Second mass extinction, including Homo Erectus, leaving approximately between 2,000 and 20,000 only Homo sapiens on the earth. From these everyone on earth is descended.

9. 40,000 years BP. Homo sapiens begins to leave Africa.

10.. 35,000 years BP. Neanderthals extinct.

11. 20,000 years BP. Possible date for Sphynx.

12. 10,000 years BP. 8,000BC Jericho built. Mohejo Daru.

13. 1800AD, Industrial Revolution and modern age begins.

And so from this it can be seen that it took 2 billion years for the first single cell creatures to evolve into multi cell ones. It then took another 1.77 billion years for those simple multi cell ones to eventually evolve into the dinosaurs which, over the next 160 million years, evolved/mutated into herbivores, carnivores, flying beings, and those that lived in water. They were suddenly made extinct over a very short period of time, leaving only the water based crocodiles and alligators we see today.

Some time towards the end of this period, the early mammals appeared and these took 66 million years before Homo erectus emerged and 67.4 million years before the Neanderthals appeared in Europe only. These were an upright walking animal very closely related to Homo sapiens – us. It is thought that a version of modern man was around in Ethiopia around 160 – 200,000 years BP. He then vanished. In South West Africa, on the border of present day Angola and Namibia, true modern man first appeared around 180,000 years BP but he didn't achieve maturity until around 70 – 50,000 years ago, after the second mass extinction, by which time he had begun to leave Africa.

There was, however, an event at around 68,000 years BP that changed everything. Mount Toba in Sumatra erupted in one of the biggest volcanic eruptions of all time. During recorded history, the biggest eruption was Mount Tambo in Indonesia in 1816 and that dwarfed those of Santorin and Krakatau. Toba was well over twice the magnitude of Tambo and it triggered a volcanic winter that lasted for between 6 and 10 years. There is ample geological evidence of this. It is also thought to have triggered the last major glaciations. It left a layer of toxic volcanic dust 15 centimetres thick over much of the planet and wiped out thousands of plant and animal species, almost killing off our own. The reason for this was that the toxic ash killed the plants, leaving animals with no food, and so the food chain was destroyed. When earth recovered from this at around 60,000BC, as we have seen, the accepted theory is that there were only between 1 and 10,000 breeding pairs of Homo sapiens in the entire world. It is interesting that the Neanderthals survived this intact which would indicate that most of the dust must have fallen in the Equatorial regions. Even so, they all died out during the next 25,000 years. Why would that happen? It certainly was not because of Homo sapiens since they were only just out of Africa and still very much primitive Stone Age beings. Plus that there were not many of them. Unless they carried a deadly transmittable disease that only affected our rivals. Sorry but hmmmmm again.

Let us just dwell on this for a moment, because it is at this point that the whole 'Survival of the Fittest' and Evolutionary theories begin to waver. In 60,000BC there were at the most, according to contemporary accepted academic theories, 20,000 human beings on earth in total, all in Africa and all, presumably of one skin colour. This would probably be black. [I do not go along with this theory but, be that as it may, let us just be indulgent right now.]It has taken 140,000 years of evolution from the first Homo sapiens to get to this state. That would equate to around 6,000 generations. These 20,000 people obviously bred and the population increased until they began to leave Africa, presumably with the same colour skin and physical attributes with which they began. For 800 generations they hung about in Africa, spreading across the continent as black people to become the Bantu, pygmies, Ebo, Ethiopians and Nubians etc, etc. No native African tribes were white or had oriental features and it is very important to realise this. All native Africans had a black pigment to their skins. They entered Europe, presumably down the Nile valley or by way of the Red Sea, or wherever, with still the same skin pigments at around 40,000BC just as the Neanderthals were facing extinction and, it is thought, that some of these people, or creatures, interbred. So, at around the 30 – 40,000BC period in Europe, there would be some mixed specie people about. At around 14,500BC they arrived in the Americas. By this time we are looking at the beginning of actual civilization. Jericho is dated at around 8,000BC which is 10,000 years ago or between 330 and 400 generations.

And it is this that gives me a massive problem because most of this just could not have happened as previously thought. Just looking at Homo sapiens alone, they 'appeared' or 'emerged' around 200,000 years ago but took 140,000 years to become remotely like modern man. That is 6,000 generations allowing for four generations per century. But it only took 2,400 generations for those 20,000 equally primitive people to evolve from being black Africans [or brown or white Africans, it doesn't matter] into white skinned Europeans, blond Nordics, brown Indians, Asiatics with their individual eyes, Aborigine Australians, native Americans, brown skinned South American Indians and brown or black skinned Polynesians. Were the Aborigine still black skinned on entering Australia or did the native Australians revert to the original African pigments once they were established, but with a totally different bone structure? The same in the Americas. According to this theory, if they only arrived in the Americas by way of the Bering Straight [which did not freeze over during the glaciations] at around 14,500BC, they subsequently 'evolved' into American Indians, Aztecs, Incas, Caribs, the myriad of small tribes in the rain forest of South America, and many others. Subsequently some of them made their way west across the Pacific to become the

Polynesians, Fijians and Maoris of Micronesia. And all this happened in under 600 generations.

What racial characteristics did those first intrepid Stone Age travellers show on crossing the Bering Strait in 14,500BC? What made those people who then made their way north to the frozen wastes change into different looking people to the ones who settled on the Great Plains? And those who travelled further south changed again, and again to become the various indigenous races we see today. Those who then ventured west on Kon Tiki type rafts changed again on settling on the myriad of islands of the Pacific, many reverting back to the black skin pigment but not the African bone structure. Those who went into China, Japan and South East Asia developed a different facial feature that, as they made their way further east to meet the émigrés from the Americas, changed into the black pigment of the Africans again. Those crossing into Australia also discarded the paler skin and oriental face to become black again.

But we know for certain that civilization began in Egypt at least 220 generations ago, and that the only thing to change in us since then has been in the use of our brain. Yes, we are physically bigger but that is only down to diet. The cranial cavity of an Egyptian pharaoh was little different to that of a 21st century AD Egyptian. Anatomically we were identical to 21st century man. All improvements since then can only be put down to a slightly better diet that enabled us to live marginally longer. At the start of the twentieth century life expectancy was still very low in the 'civilized' part of the world such as Europe and North America. If this can be said to be 'evolutionary', then so be it.

In just 1600 generations, man 'evolved' from those 20,000 common ancestors into the myriad of different racial characteristics we see today, yet it took 5,200 generations for him just to reach some sort of maturity. The Neanderthal lived through 12,600 generations without changing.

If, as popular academic thought would have us believe, this is what actually did happen, then the changes must have come thick and fast. Two black people breeding must have produced a white child at some point. Another white child must have emerged to begin the European races of the north. And this should be happening right now, but it is not. Since 3,000BC, or 200 generations it has not done so which is remarkable. 1400 generations and every different race and colour of Homo sapiens appears simultaneously across the globe only to stop dead, and then during the next 200

Could we all have evolved into all these different racial groups in just 1,600 generations? If we only began to leave Africa c 40,000BCE we had to have done. This somewhat stereotype picture from the 1930s illustrates exactly what I mean.

generations there is nothing. As said earlier, for the Americas it is even more incredible since there have been less than 600 generations from the moment the first humans are supposed to have crossed the Bering Straight up to the present day. During this time everyone from the Intuits in the north, the Caribs in the east, the Polynesians in the west and the Indians on Tierra del Fuego in the south had to develop their own individual colours, bone structures and physiques. That takes some believing and an awful lot of explaining. Since the tribes of the Americas were well established by around 1,500AD, that leaves even less time for them all to have evolved.

Leaving aside the occasional Albino child, no two pure bred Africans living in Africa have produced a fair skinned blond Caucasian child. Neither have they produced one with Native American features, a Chinese child or an Aborigine. Nor has a pure white Aryan couple produced a pure Chinese child. It is a physical impossibility for this to happen, especially over such a ludicrously short period time.

For this theory to have any credence it would be the norm for a Chinese couple to produce a black baby with Afro features, a black couple to produce a blond one and a Polynesian couple to come up with a Native American. This, of course, does not happen unless there has been a mixed race union sometime in the recent past. That is during the previous 10 to 20 generations. It should also be the norm to find an indigenous tribe in the jungles of South America, untouched by modern civilization, that bears very closely the racial characteristics of a people on another continent. The wandering people from Africa must have scattered across Asia on their way north east and so there should be some people in, for argument's sake, the Caucuses who have a remarkable likeness for that tribe in South America. If that is the case, then my argument folds. If it is not the case then it should be difficult to argue with my thoughts.

So how did those 10,000 black Africans, it doesn't really matter how many, evolve so quickly into such diverse races in just 1,400 generations? Or, more likely, far less? Those 1,400 generations that also had to find their way across Asia and up into the distant corner of the Barents Sea to cross into the Americas, whilst others spread into China, Japan, the Philippines, Indonesia and Australia. Some of those going to the Americas had to build substantial boats to sail across the Pacific and so populate Oceania. We are not talking about rafts here, we are talking about lots of sea going craft to transport hundreds of men, women and children plus their livestock and tools across a massive ocean to a totally unknown destination. And yet it took all of 7,000 generations before he even began to use his only asset, namely his superior brain power, to make the simplest and crudest of tools and weapons from stone? And only the simplest of boats that would have had difficulty crossing an ocean as the Kon Tiki experiment proved. By the time that it did strike land it was water logged and sinking. What could have happened to change this wandering primitive species into one that could build great monuments like the Sphinx and Jericho just 400 generations ago?

From this it would appear that, rather than the 'Survival of the Fittest', it has actually been the 'Survival of the Weakest'. In the wild today most of our endangered species, and not necessarily from the acts of man, are the very strongest animals. The lions, tigers and gorillas are at risk as are the crocodiles, but anyone who has visited the areas where they live would question that. In the wild, the creatures that survive are the rodents, including the defenceless rabbit, and the insects. A new theory, being suggested by academia, is that the reason that these animals survive is that they have had more space to do so, but so have the big cats in Africa. I do not agree with this hypothesis.

What about the crocodiles and alligators that have survived since the days of the dinosaurs? Across the globe they have remained as they were then, with none feeling the need to 'evolve' into something else. Surely over such an immense period of time there should be some that only live on land or only swim in the deep ocean but no, everywhere they remain the same as their fossilized remains show them to have been all those years ago.

And those defenceless creatures, such as the rabbit, the chicken, the cow, the sheep and the horse? The pheasant that can only fly short distances and the fish like the trout and the salmon? What else have they in common? Just the one thing, they are part of, mainly the human, food chain. Yes, I know that for the last five thousand years, many of these have been taken from the wild and carefully bred to give the docile animals that we see today. Much care has gone into the breeding but, over the years, not one of them has been born as a slightly different species to its parents. We have been giving evolution a huge push over thousands of years but have achieved nothing, and this has been going on since the animals were first domesticated. Modern attempts to do so produce what are called 'Frankenstein Foods' but, if you think about it, everything must go back to being a 'Frankenstein being or plant' if present day thought is to be accepted.

And so the big question, to add to the one of where the sea came from, is how did those twenty thousand black Africans change into all the other races in the world in just 1,400 generations, when it took 7,000 to become basic Stone Age man? Another is how, presumably the same peoples with the same physical and mental characteristics, and with enough enterprise to find the Bering Strait and cross it, and then spread out across the vast empty spaces of the Americas, then diverge into so many different types of people? Some of whom then decided to give it all up, revert to the Stone Age and hide in places like the extremely hostile Amazon basin. Since they were all well established at the time of the Conquistadores this must have all taken place during no more than 540 generations. No more 'Mighty Bounds' please.

A third big question is how did these new species simply 'emerge' or 'appear'? All work on the subject says that dinosaurs first 'appeared' at such and such a date. How is this defined? Surely if the science is correct it should be possible to say that 'the first mammal came from a mutating frog or caterpillar' not that it just simply 'appeared'. Saying that it just 'appeared' or 'emerged' is a very big 'Mighty Bound' indeed.

Of course, if we suggest that there may not be any element of truth in the above, it opens a can of worms when we ask about the alternatives. Supposing that man emigrated from Africa, not around 60,000BP, but very much earlier? Like another hundred thousand years earlier. Or very, very much earlier still, going back not thousands but millions of years? This gives more than another

4,000 generations to evolve into the different racial groups we see today. That is slightly more realistic as it becomes when we go back very much earlier still, before the continents divided and caused the mass extinctions. Yes, could they have been left isolated in Australia, Asia, the Americas etc, etc, far, far earlier? Again, when we consider the 'Awkward questions', this must be considered.

Some 200million years ago all the continents were joined into one big one named *'Pangea'* by geologists which allowed the dinosaurs to roam freely and this is proven by the presence of their remains across the globe. 135 million years ago Africa was still firmly joined to the Americas, Europe and Asia but 65 million years ago the continents were more or less as they are today. It is my contention that man could **only** have evolved into so many different races, breeds and colours if he had been about very much earlier and had settled on the individual continents when they were joined together i.e., not later than around 100million BP. He needed not hundreds of generations but thousands and thousands so to do. If I am right, and why should I not be, then the entire time line is thrown completely out? I contend that it would have been a physical impossibility for man to leave Africa as a black person and wander Asia for less than 1000 generations during which time he became Asiatic and then cross the Bering Straight and in another 550 generations become all the other races of the Americas and Polynesia.

What is even more amazing is that as mankind developed across the globe over no matter how many generations, it was at exactly the same pace, give or take the odd 20 to 40 generations. As I said earlier, this is the 'Control' against which any sudden change in development must be measured.

It would have been a very primitive form of being that made its way across into the other continents first. Because he was so primitive he could not have had the skill and basic reasoning powers to construct any craft that would have crossed the Atlantic or Pacific in such numbers to be able to breed and settle. And why should he? The Americas were uninhabited but perfectly habitable and he could have had no idea at all what lay beyond the horizon.

He can only have spread across the land masses on foot. Again, assuming that all were black in the first place, those remaining in the Middle East must have gradually lost their black pigment and facial features to become the fairer skinned Semitic races we see today. Those that went north and east became the Slavonic peoples, some of whom we are told bred with the Neanderthals. But were they around that much earlier? Those who went further east developed different eyes and facial features, but this was not shared by those peoples who found themselves in the very cold regions of the Arctic, before deciding to cross the not inconsiderable distance [in those days] across the Bering Strait. Or, of course, the peoples of Indonesia and the Australian Aboriginees. Those peoples did not feel the need to re-grow the warming covering of fur as enjoyed by seals and polar bears, remaining as naked as the inhabitants of the rain forest.

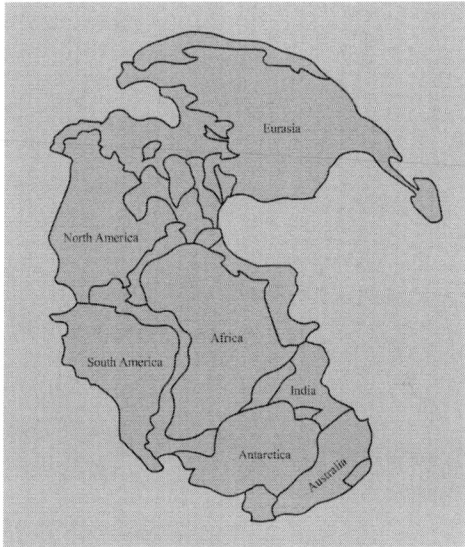

'Pangea', the super-continent where all the land mass was one. 65 million years ago these had separated to form the layout as it is today. Is it realistic to think that humanoid beings could have roamed the earth then, evolving into the races we see today?

Consider the Bering Strait. During the last Ice Age from 20,000 to 8,000BC, sea levels dropped at the most by 390 feet.

The depth of the sea at the Bering Strait is between 98 and 160 feet and so for a long period it would have been possible to walk from Russia to America. The Strait itself did not freeze over. But for the next 12,000 years the ice melted so raising the level of the sea. At the period under discussion i.e., 15,000BC, the sea level will have risen 230 feet, still well below present levels, but 5,000 years later it would have been a sea again as the ice continued to melt. So, if this migration did take place, it had to be between 20 and 12,000BC. That is between 800 and 480 generations ago. It could not have happened later because there was never any means of transporting large numbers of people across an unknown ocean from one treeless wilderness to another. The width is 53 miles with the Diomede Islands more or less in the middle. Visually it was just as impossible to estimate the distance to the next land as it would be from China or Australia. They could have been setting out to just across the horizon or across several thousand miles and there is, and was, no suitable material to build an ocean going craft, nor is there anything to make the tools necessary for the construction.

It would appear that all the Native American peoples, from the Intuits in the north to the Indians on Tierra del Fuego in the south, had a maximum of just 800 generations [if they crossed in 20,000BC] to 'evolve' into their different facial and bone structures. Those who became the various Polynesian races of the South Pacific had considerably less. To me, this time scale is impossible. During recorded history there have been 200 generations during which time all present racial characteristics have remained constant, as far as can be ascertained. Paintings in Egypt, going back that far, all show the same features as on modern day Egyptians. This is confirmed by mummies and death masks. If they didn't change, how could all the others?

This would suggest that man 'emerged', for want of a better word, very much earlier all over the globe and not necessarily from the same basic stock either. From where? Who knows? A mixture of Neanderthal, Homo erectus and/or something else? After all, all the different races have different blood groups, yet more or less all the same genes, something they should only have if they all descended from the same basic stock. But if this is the case, as I said earlier, then the thing that I find most remarkable of all is that they all progressed, not evolved, at more or less the same pace everywhere. And they were more or less the same size. That I find amazing. Only the Pygmies of West Africa were different. There was no race of giants, strong men, fast runners or people of creative ability. They found stone to make tools at the same time, they discovered copper and tin and the ability to make bronze, they discovered iron and, most of all, found and coveted the useless metals of gold and silver, together with many of our precious stones. And all at more or less the same time in history, give or take the odd thousand years. They also discovered, and were able to identify, extract and use, granite and diorite extensively. These were just as useless to them as was gold but they went to enormous lengths to obtain, prepare and install them both. Not just in Egypt either. Again I wonder why? Why was mankind, virtually from Day One, obsessed with minerals that had no possible utility for them when simple survival was the paramount problem of the day? Even the Bible mentions gold before it gets to Adam and Eve.

And now, as this is being written in 2016 comes the news that a skull discovered in Georgia on the Black Sea has been dated to at least 2mBP. It is of a primitive Homo sapiens with only a tiny brain cavity and not surprisingly has thrown all previous theories out of the window. If he was a simple creature wandering in the Caucuses so long ago, all my thinking as described above suddenly becomes credible. The report of a human femur in Chile, carbon dated to 17,000 BC, asks the same questions.

The alternative, of course, is the Creation.

7

ARMAGEDDON

The world of religion is obsessed with the concept of 'Armageddon'. The end of the world as we know it. After which we must go before our appropriate 'God' to repent our sins, and then be sent into eternity, either into paradise or down to the eternal fires of hell. The Day of Judgement, when our sins on earth are counted, our souls weighed or whatever. By obeying the teachings of the appropriate priest and going by the doctrines of how that particular religion interpreted things, you could get away with murder and still go into paradise. But, if you believed that being taught, or worshiped, in that mosque, or church over the road, or in a different version of your own faith, then nothing could be more certain than eternity in hell.

How very convenient.

So good Catholics, for hundreds of years, could happily burn at the stake or commit unspeakable torture on any non-believers or witches. [Which the Bible insists must die - Exodus 22/18. In actual fact this is not true. The Gutenberg Bible, from which the King James edition was edited, said 'poisoners', not witches, but the King insisted on the change, since he felt that he was being persecuted by witches, who had tried to drown him in a sinking ship.] They could torture their enemies or, for that matter, anyone whom they wanted rid of [by a suitable denouncement], and still expect automatic entry into the Kingdom of Heaven. Following the domestic difficulties of King Henry V111[th] and the incumbent Pope being reluctant to vary church teachings on divorce, we had forced onto us the Anglican Church. Then, since Henry conveniently made himself head of the new church, banning Catholicism, he in turn, was able to commit the self same unspeakable brutalities on anyone remaining true to the original faith. Or, whom he wanted rid of. Of course now only Henry's followers in Britain could go to heaven.

Down to the present day this still goes on. The struggle in Ireland was always a mixture of religious bigotry intermingled with highly organised crime. The terrible atrocities now being committed in the Middle East are very much doctrinal with Jew fighting Muslim and Muslim of Sect [1] fighting Muslim of Sect [2]. Then Muslims as a whole being incited to murder random targets in the west by a foolhardy 'Kamikaze' theory that every non Muslim, because they are non Muslim, must be an enemy of Islam which they are trying to destroy. They are involved in a 'Jihad', a Holy War all of their own with the promise, that by so dying, of going straight to paradise with all its accompanying benefits. This of course is rubbish on all fronts. The secular world accepts and respects all faiths equally, particularly the right of anyone to worship his or her faith openly without fear of either violence or State intervention.

It is, and has been through history, only the fundamental religious states where worship of other faiths has been banned, that religious bigotry has resulted in continuous strife with its subsequent mass loss of life. What is interesting is that eventually all the oppressive regimes, and here I include the ideological dictatorships, have eventually succumbed, with only the world of Fundamental Islam left to fight on alone. How long before they join the 21st century? It is also interesting here to go forward to the chapter about the 'Bulge'. Here we see that through the latter part of the second millennium and into the third, the whole world is stretching ahead with economic growth, coupled with an almost universal acceptance of basic human rights. That is except in the Middle East which, despite its enormous riches of oil, remains firmly in the Middle Ages. And this is the world of Islam. And in Latin America, where Catholicism reigns supreme, we have a similar zero advancement of enlightenment.

As we have already discussed, the mightier the external enemy, the more powerful will the country's leader become. Hitler rose to power on the myths of his Jewish enemies, Churchill came to power against Hitler but, as soon as the Hitler threat vanished, he was out. The all powerful Spanish Catholic Church maintained its power terrorising the population through the Inquisition. French Catholics drove out the Huguenots who then sort refuge in Britain. Fundamental Protestants made their way to the New World to enjoy religious freedom and then promptly burned as witches anyone who disagreed with them. But it was the leaders, be they national or local, who enforced it all, who were to become in turn more powerful and, more important, very much richer in the process. You only have to see the incredible wealth that the monasteries enjoyed compared to the ordinary people around them living in squalor and poverty. And the money flowed from those in poverty into the coffers of the church and the rich landowners, never the other way round. As it does in the Middle East today, with the few wealthy families enjoying the lot, propped up by an all powerful religious fraternity inflicting terror on those who disbelieve or oppose.

The inevitable march of education of the masses has resulted in much of the progress made in the last two hundred years, so that people can make up their own minds and see through the hypocrisy for what it is. Sooner or later Fundamental Islam will be forced to accept the emancipation and education of women as a basic human right, as it must accept the right of others to worship whomsoever they wish, wherever they wish without fear of either interruption or punishment. In some Middle Eastern countries today the possession of the Holy Bible can result in a public flogging of 80 lashes. Hardly the best method of proving that only the Koran, [which accepts the Old Testament as being part of Islam], is true. Surely only a convincing argument can do that and, sadly, that is something that Islam refuses to put to the test. Only then will that religion have any chance of emerging as the one leading true religion over all others. But that will only be when people can choose freely for themselves. Free converts are the zealous ones, never those on whom the ideology has been forced. It will never come by mass breeding of Muslim immigrants into Western countries, until they are a majority, and so can enforce their ideas on the indigenous, mainly Christian population.

The biggest threat handed down by religious leaders from the earliest times, in order to bring the population to order, has always been the catastrophic ending of the world, namely Armageddon. This, as we have seen, appears in Teutonic myth right up to the early days of the Bible. Behave yourselves; do as your God tells you or it will all end in tears. Apart from the obvious one of giving the local priest some much needed extra power over his generally illiterate flock, what could possibly be the reasons with this obsession with the ending of the world?

Let us suppose, for argument's sake, that in this book I am promulgating a theory for the very first time. I am saying that unless there is peace in the Middle East, unless India and Pakistan get together, the Taliban begin to behave themselves, until there is true peace in Ireland, Sri Lanka, fundamental Islam accepts that others have a right of life, especially in the Middle East and every other trouble spot on earth, there is going to be a big bang and all will be over. In order to prevent this, my good friend Gabriel here will bring to the centre of most of the troubles, a leader to guide you all out of the mess. But it won't be for at least 800 years and, what is more, that new leader will not be an all powerful warrior, but a gentle person of peace, who will teach you all the word of ....let's say, 'God', which I am trying to do now. But there will be a twist in the tale and to give people something to cling on to, you will reject him and kill him dramatically. Gabriel will be there to sort things out, bring him back to life briefly, before he goes up to 'heaven', after which he will return some forty years later to repeat the message to a chap named John on a Greek island. There he will reveal just what is going to happen and it isn't nice. If you don't all rally round this chap – and I'll give you six hundred odd years so to do – then I'll send Gabriel back again to find someone else. Unfortunately this new one won't be able to read, so poor old Gabriel must make him learn it all by heart and get others to write it down, and this will take the poor chap's entire lifetime. Gabriel must return time after time to give the chap his instructions then you will be equipped with not one, but two religions, each showing a parallel way to peace without strife on this earth. I will then, with my good friend Gabriel, who is getting a little tired by now, give you another fifteen hundred years by which time, if you are no better, I'll blow the lot of you up. And I'll call it Armageddon.

'What a load of rubbish', I hear you say but, before you dismiss it as such, read it again and see if you can find a parallel story somewhere. It shouldn't take long.

It is actually a fact that this threat has been hanging over mankind more or less since time began, so [a] why has it not happened – things have been black enough, often enough, to justify some divine intervention, and [b] in what force could it happen, either as a man made manifestation, or natural catastrophe. More to the point why, when we have had the aforesaid Inquisitions, plus the Holocaust murdering the supposed 'God's Chosen People', in their millions, and the Stalinist purges in Russia, was there no divine intervention? And now, in 2016, with the forces of Islam fighting itself to the death in the Middle East, whilst seeking to impose itself on everyone else, why is there no 'divine' intervention to stop it happening? Surely to those caught up in those dreadful pogroms and the horrors of ethnic cleansing it was Armageddon for real? Not all can have been wicked and undeserving, so just why was it allowed to happen?

If we accept for the moment that modern 'civilized' man has been about since around 10,000 BC, throughout the years just what has he controlled that would make the advent of a man generated Armageddon a realistic possibility? The answer is that it is very little indeed. From that emergence in the Nile valley all they had to fight with were stones and sticks followed by the discovery of metals giving them swords, spears and bows and arrows. None of these could in any way threaten an enemy more than a hundred yards away and no matter how vicious the butchery, it could never have any remote effect on tribes in North Europe, the Americas or the Far East. Only after 8,000 years did the Chinese discover gunpowder but, again, that was only useful against someone very close. Even the suicide bombers of today rely on densely populated targets to make an impact. Blowing themselves up in the middle of the desert would be only slightly more stupid than what they do today. No, gunpowder merely extended the range at which war could be conducted, but it could never, on its own, ever instigate Armageddon. And this was the state of play up to the end of the

Second World War. But should we consider natural disasters? In what way could they bring things about?

Going back into history it would seem that we have already had at least one Armageddon that wiped the dinosaurs off the map. Every large cold blooded animal perished over a very small period of time having dominated the earth for millions of years, and that can only have happened for one reason, namely a catastrophic drop in temperature simultaneously across the globe. This would have a devastating effect on the metabolism of the animals as well as on the eco systems around them. Plant life must have died and so interrupted the food chain, leaving only a handful of marine creatures, including the crocodiles, remaining plus a few of the now emerging mammals which included the ancestors of man. The only things that could have caused this would have been the eruption of a huge volcano caused by the shifting of the plates that formed the

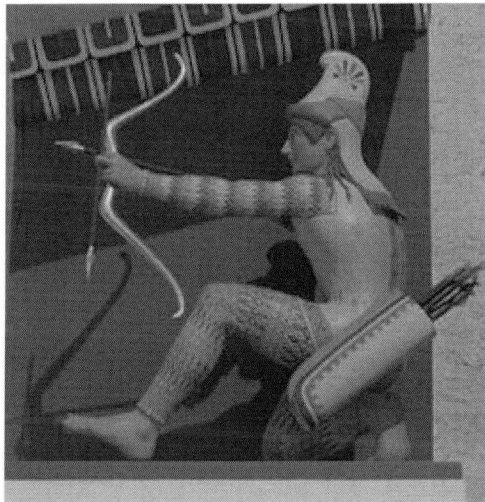

A Greek model of an archer c 450BC. Until the arrival of the rifle and cannon, throughout recorded history this was as near to Armageddon that mankind could get.

Alps or other mountain ranges. It could even be that the earth was hit by a massive object from outer space but that is unlikely. In a giant meteor storm there would have to be more than one object falling on different parts of the world. These would have needed to generate an enormous cloud that blotted out the sun thus lowering the temperature enough to kill the dinosaurs. The one in Mexico was certainly big but could it have done so? Some think it likely, I'm not so sure.

A second 'Armageddon' happened around 68,000BC with the eruption of Mt Tuba but that did not kill everything. It would need a much bigger bang to do that. Both of these mass extinctions happened well before recorded history began and so could have had no effect on thinking when the Bible was being written.

But now geologists have suggested that there was another enormous natural catastrophe around 10,000BC. Here, in many distant parts of the globe they have found a thin line of ash in the relatively recent rock that is consistent everywhere. The thickness indicates that it fell over several years during which time it would have blotted out the sun causing world temperatures to fall, crops to fail and massive loss of life – both human and animal. The source of the eruption may have been in Indonesia as a vast, previously undiscovered, volcanic crater shows, or in the Gulf of Mexico which is the favourite with the 'Flood School' of thinking. Who knows? But there is no evidence anywhere else of this happening. The latest theory is that a meteor hit the earth to cause this. It should have caused a temporary halt in the melting of the ice but it did not. I find it a mystery that nothing more has emerged to confirm that this actually happened.

So there could have been a foretaste of 'Armageddon' back in Biblical times. Could this have been the cause? Obviously no one in the Middle East at the time could have the slightest idea why, or from where it came. This enormous cloud that blotted out the sun would have simply occurred, dropped its ash and then slowly gone away. Could it have been Santorin going off? They would have been aware of that. Why should their superstitious minds not assume that it was not man made, but a warning sent by their 'God' to behave or else?

What else in those distant times could possibly cause universal, rather than local, Armageddon? As we have seen with weapons, nothing. Right up to the Second World War, the greatest distance a gun would fire was only about 20 miles whilst the V2 rockets had a range of fewer than 200. What about disease of which there has never been a shortage? Yes, this could decimate populations but, so far, none has killed everybody. From every epidemic of smallpox, diphtheria, bubonic plague and the myriad of tropical diseases, a fair proportion of the population has always survived. None were capable of jumping oceans to infect those in far distant lands. Most diseases are carried by insects, but those transmitted by man remained local until the voyages of discovery. From the fifteenth century onwards, they took nasty European diseases to infect, and so wipe out, many indigenous island populations that had no natural immunity. But even then, people survived. I think it is fair to say that, until that fateful day in 1945 in the New Mexico desert, mankind could never have provoked Armageddon. So why have religious leaders promulgated the theory for 3000 years? Unless they knew that, so far into the future, it would become a possibility. Who would know? Was it God perhaps, the Angel Gabriel or someone else?

The day we exploded that first bomb in New Mexico, that was to lead to the ending of the greatest conflict the world has known, man has indeed possessed the power and equipment to end it all. At the height of the Cold War in the fifties, Russia and America had enough fire power aimed at each other that would easily carpet the entire planet in a radioactive layer that would have literally killed off 99% of all the world's living things. Anything left would be a grotesque mutation to begin again years later.

That would not have been very clever, when you think about it. Because everyone knew that this was not merely a possibility, but an absolute certainty, reason prevailed and nothing happened. The threat remains but it is now no longer from the big powers. A zealous hothead could trigger the lot off by wrapping a small nuclear device around himself and blowing up a big western city. The people to do this now have the means and it remains the biggest threat that mankind has ever faced. For all their posturing, Khrushchev and Kennedy would never really have done anything so stupid, knowing that by pressing that button, they were sealing their own fate as well. But now someone who is stupid will be only too happy to seal his own fate. I only hope that the big powers have a contingency that does not include launching rockets everywhere in retaliation.

So is that it? What else can trigger Armageddon in modern times? It is unlikely that there will be a big enough volcano to do it. We know with modern science exactly where they all are and the likely effect of them going off. It is doubtful whether Krakatau will go off again in the

The mushroom cloud over Nagasaki in 1945 showed for all to see that we finally had the means of our own Armageddon.

foreseeable future, but the one in the Canaries most certainly will, and will have devastating consequences to the Atlantic seaboard of the Americas and much of Europe. Its dust cloud will take a long time to clear but it will not wipe out the human race. Santorin may go off again if the build up of magna under it continues. There is always the possibility of a large meteorite from outer space hitting us but it would have to be a very big one hitting dry land to blot out the sun significantly. If it landed in the ocean then there would be devastating Tsunamis, but it would need to be a mighty big one to kill us all off.

But now we have electricity that does not rely on the sun to heat us, give us light to see and to grow our food.

Ironically, it is our number one possible cause, namely Nuclear Fission that will provide our number one certain antidote, namely Nuclear Power Stations which we should all be building as fast as possible. Again, our man made objects of mass destruction in the form of Inter Continental Ballistic Weapons, with nuclear war heads, would be used to intercept and destroy in outer space any large meteorite that appeared on our radar screens. Unless we are incredibly careless in the future, this threat will remain a distinctly remote one.

What about disease? In the twenty first century, despite the billions spent in research all over the world, we are no nearer finding a cure, not to mention a vaccine against the three biggest killers – cancer, heart disease and AIDS. I tend to be a bit of a cynic about these things and wonder whether we ever will. After all, the research industry into these diseases is now enormous, all of which would stop if someone discovered a simple antidote. Not unlike the way that every petrol substitute in the past has been bought up and suppressed by the oil industry. These three are all killers, cancer and heart disease being ones that occur naturally. AIDS is thought to come from a mutating virus [or as a bug from outer space??], but it is of very recent origin. In the past it was not unknown for someone to die of a seizure or brain haemorrhage, consumption or infectious disease, but how many great men or leaders of the past succumbed to cancer or heart disease? I have difficulty thinking of one but, of course, they may have done with no proper diagnosis to identify the problem. Essentially they are twentieth century diseases possibly caused by stress, air pollution, food pollution [and here I mean additives to make food last longer.

I wonder what they put into cut loaves to keep them all week when a healthy French baguette is off in hours?], noise and light pollution plus, the totally unknown long term effects of the trillions of new radio waves that bombard us every minute of every day. Another possible cause is the Western obsession with cleanliness. Again, what goes into all those cleaning materials that kill all known bugs? Could much of it be doing us more harm than good? By being obsessed with having everything so clean, we lose a lot of our natural immunity from many complaints so that we leave ourselves wide open to infections. Most cancer victims I have known have come from scrupulously clean households, seldom from those living in the slums.

AIDS is a different thing all together. It is a virus passed blood to blood that never goes away. It is indisputable that in the West it was mainly spread through the gay community as a sexually transmitted disease, and therefore to a large effect, a self inflicted and avoidable phenomenon. In Africa it is a different story with babies being infected in the womb by their mother, most of whom were similarly infected themselves. It is spread from man to man and man to wife, and vice versa, during normal sexual activity and so far has shown no sign of slowing down its inexorable spread across the Continent. As vaccines are prepared it mutates into a different strain, carrying on immune from a cure.

And this, I fear, is where Armageddon – if it is to come at all – will come from. Not from Aids but from a similar virus that is air born. An extremely deadly virus that has a three to five day incubation period, that is new and possibly man made but with no, or little available, antidote, could sweep the world within a few days. Now we have the means. A small group of infected people in London could board mighty jets to carry them to the far corners of the world before they became aware of their infection. They infect others in New York, Moscow, Beijing and Capetown. Those now infected fly to Europe, South America, India and America's West coast. All before the first victim is stricken and dies. Soon the doctors and nurses are infected whilst the limited numbers of vaccines are reserved for top politicians. Before long the dead pile up since we can no longer bury them. They must be burned in huge pyres, holocaust fashion, but it doesn't take long before that is no longer an option. Soon the dead outnumber the living and we have our Armageddon, but it will not kill off everyone. No, there will be a limited number who will survive and from them the new human race will begin. We enter the realms of science fiction if we now speculate what happens from then on.

Do not think that the above is a whimsical scenario from a fertile imagination. In Porton Down in the UK, and similar research facilities in America and Russia, not to mention the possibility of more in China, Japan, Germany and the Middle East, stocks are held of a myriad of the most ghastly man made germs, all with no known antidote. Just why in the 21st century we actually need these is beyond me. One of them could kill us all, so why can we not now simply destroy them, together with remaining stocks of Smallpox, Bubonic Plague and other eradicated diseases? Do this safely in laboratory conditions and the world will be a safer place. Do not take comfort that these laboratories are impregnable from attack or accident. They are not. Nowhere is safe these days. In the good old days when we fought our world wars we knew exactly who the enemy was. If he was the Hun, he wore a German uniform. If he was a Jap, he had on a Japanese uniform so it was perfectly alright to go out and shoot him. If he wore no uniform he could be a spy but most likely he would be a civilian and we did not make war on civilians then.

Now we are back to the Middle Eastern fanatics who only make war on defenceless civilians, killing themselves in the process. Who are these people? Can we spot them in the street and have them arrested? Sadly, the answer must be no. Invariably they have been born in the host country that they wish to destroy and act as 'sleepers'. These are people who live normal peaceful lives until called either by their religious leaders or a hostile government to commit just one act of unspeakable barbarity, killing themselves in the process. One of these could spend twenty years as a respected senior scientist at one of the research facilities and then, when he heard the call and it was his time to act, could smuggle a lethal dose into the outside world and release it in a densely occupied area like Heathrow or a tube at rush hour. It is possible to make very small nuclear devices that could be strapped to a person but which, on detonation, would have catastrophic consequences. A so called 'dirty bomb' would not destroy much of the surrounding infrastructure but it would kill people and render the area uninhabitable for decades, centuries even. What would be the effect of one of these being detonated near or in Porton Down? Or a full scale bomb wiping the place out, from the inside, possibly doing the same to the stocks but not for a 100% certainty. Now farmers use drones to spray crops and those self same drones, that are readily available on line everywhere, could so easily be used to spray any type of poison gas, nuclear waste or disease bearing microbes over an entire city. That makes us all feel uneasy, especially when there is an enemy out there quite prepared to use them. But that still leaves all the rest. Sorry, but this is from whence we will find Armageddon. That is unless, of course, it is a natural disaster that was the root cause.

There is however, one other simple answer. We may all just die out with no nuclear winters, no global warming and no rampant disease. Is this a possibility? Yes, it is and this is the reason why.

When living in France, one of my favourite pastimes was to sit at a pavement café, with a beer or glass of wine in hand, and just watch the people go by. I also observe with interest what I see, and one thing that is becoming increasingly obvious is the growing gap between the numbers of boy children to the girls. If it is busy near the shops and markets, many young families will pass, and it is simple just to count mentally how many of each – say up to mid teens – go by. Over the last few years, in both France and the UK, no matter how big or small the sample, the average always, and by that I mean every time, comes out in the region of two girls for every boy. In Brazil it is becoming a crisis.

I am informed that a reason for this is the excessive use in the medical profession of the feminine hormone, oestrogen, which is prescribed for many ills. This passes through the body and ends up in the waters which are flushed away into the sewage system, reprocessed through the filter beds to return as drinking water again. The problem is that the oestrogen, being a natural substance, remains in the water supply to be consumed by both men and women. This is causing severe problems with such things as the male erection [why do you think that Viagra is such a big seller?] and the growing tendency to conceive girls. It could also explain the rise in homosexuality which is further depleting the breeding stock. Many fish in our rivers are turning out to be hermaphrodite, thus limiting their breeding potential. If this trend continues, I can see the females outnumbering the males by a far greater degree, with the social and economic problems so caused being fairly obvious. This is something we can do something about, so why don't we? Taking the argument further, now that so much of our water supply is recycled, is it possible that those with heart disease and cancer could be flushing traces of their illness into the sewers which then remain in our 'fresh' water supply out of the tap? Has any research been done based on diseases in areas dependent on recycled water compared to places where it comes fresh from the earth? It may make interesting reading.

8

THE BULGE

If we consider that mankind entered what we must call the dawn of civilization at around 10,000BC, and we allot an arbitrary number of points for each significant invention or contribution to that civilization over the years, then it is possible to put these figures on a graph. The graph should show the difference between what we now know as the collective 'West', the collective 'Far East', Latin America and the collective 'Middle East'.

This graph shows that, according to accepted wisdom, for seven thousand years there was little to choose between them. Then, in the millennium of 3-2,000BC the Middle East has a bulge that sends the graph vertically off the chart, returning to the status quo some time after the era of Christ. For Central America it is the same but a thousand or so years later. The other two shadow each other until about 1,000BC when each begins a slow climb. By 1,000AD the Middle East has a sharp rise into the lead after which the West takes off until it becomes a more or less vertical line into the 21st century. The rise of China continued until the 19th century after which it took a sharp dive to be followed by another nearly vertical line into the 21st century. But the Middle East shows a permanent decline, so that since about 1,600AD they have made an almost zero contribution to world civilization. After its bulge, Latin America also quickly returned to zero where it has remained ever since.

Now if we were to overlap onto this graph and using the same scales, the major world conflicts at the time, it becomes even more interesting. For the first 8-9,000 years there were little in the way of major conflicts, but then they began in earnest, through the time of Christ and into the period where we see the emergence of the prophet Mohammed and the birth of Islam.

For the next seven hundred years until 1,800 when war began to be global, the West easily outstripped them all with the

Far East a distant second and the Middle East dropping to insignificant third. The western warring nations carried the fight into Latin America which succumbed with little resistance.

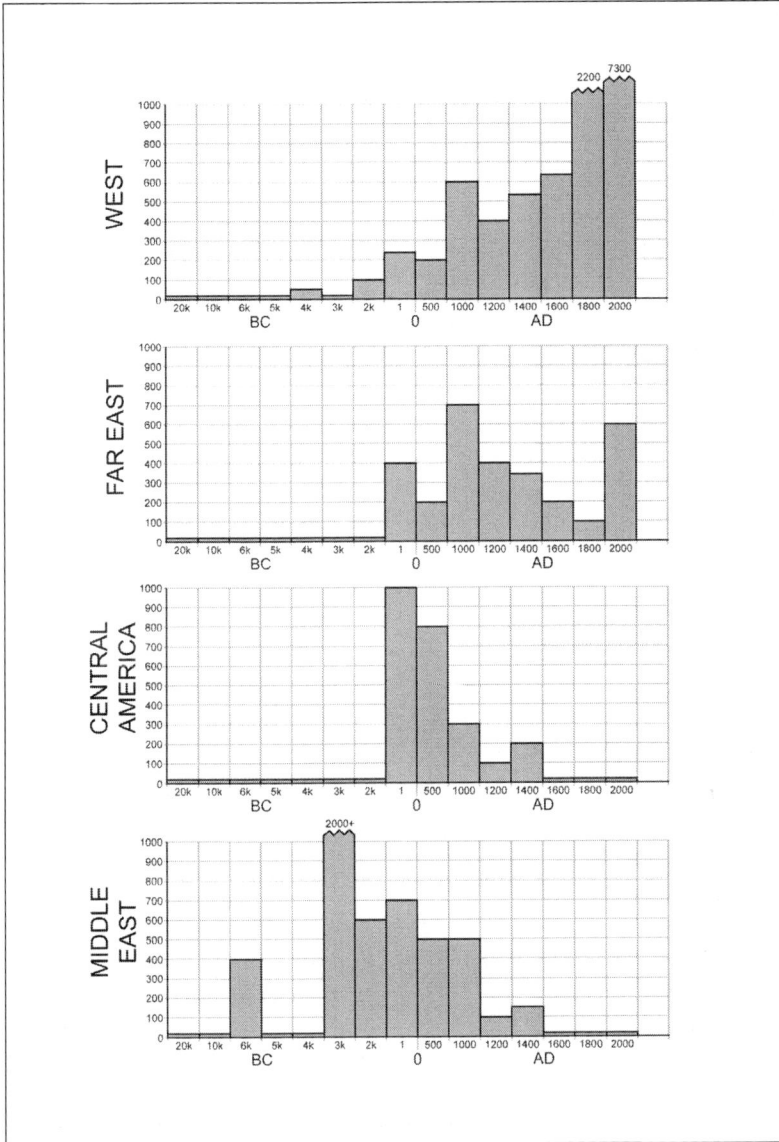

The Bulge according to accepted academic theories in 2008/2016.

Combining the graphs it can be seen that the economic and civilizing ways of the West were matched with parallel graphs of the periods at war. And similar graphs for the other three regions shows the same result. The more the war, the greater did civilization advance. But there is this one enormous anomaly that just cannot be ignored. It is the bulges that cannot have peaked later than about 2,500BC in Egypt and 1,500BC in Latin America.

Plus, of course, the not inconsiderable blip around 8,000BC when they built Jericho. There were no wars of any consequence at the time to accelerate science yet, in that relatively short period of our history, prodigious strides were made by, apparently, peoples who had contributed little to humanity beforehand and an equal amount since.

Think for a moment about Jericho. Now here is a period of history, well before any of the Biblical figures and stories, where virtually the entire world was still very much in the Stone Age as it slowly evolved according to Darwin. Out of nowhere, these Stone Age wandering people suddenly acquired sufficient knowledge and skills to build a complete city with protecting walls.

And they did it. There for all to see was the walled city of Jericho. The walls of the city were random stones but the dwellings were built from perfectly cut stones and mud bricks. After which there was nothing. They then reverted to their mud huts, tents and herds of goats for 5,500 years until someone else in Egypt decided to build for himself not a city, nor even a house, but a grave in the form of a pyramid. Again it is there for all to see. Now 5,500 years is a prodigious period of time. I will try to put it into some sort of context. Supposing in the UK, as the Ice Age receded and Britain was little more than a primeval swamp, a group of still Stone Age people had built a city on the site of London that was walled with roofed houses etc. The rest of the population would be still living in caves or whatever. They built nothing else, they let it all fall down and they themselves reverted to their Stone Age past. Then over the next five thousand years they remained firmly in the Stone and Bronze Ages with no advancement of any sort whatsoever.

Suddenly, out of the blue, someone with only flints and small copper tools decides to build a perfect skyscraper of Empire State Building proportions in Birmingham. And then goes ahead and does it. Makes you think, doesn't it? Whilst this book was just a few thoughts buzzing around in my mind, one of the first things I did was to sketch out the graph of the 'Bulge', exactly as it is, using as my sources all the accepted academic expert knowledge that was available. At the time I thought that only Egypt and Mexico had pyramids, the others obviously having been airbrushed from history. What an eye opener that turned out to be! I hesitated to contradict what throughout my life had been proven historical fact. But when all these 'facts' began to disintegrate around me, and the whole thing tumbled like a house of cards, my conscience was left clear to put down on paper all that then emerged. Everything that I had believed to be true had been the logical progression of a whole series on 'Mighty Bounds' and the generous use of the airbrush. In 1980 a book was published in America by Dr Julian James entitled *'The Origin of Consciousness in the Breakdown of the Bicameral Mind'*. Here Jaynes argues that there are two parts to the brain. One is the 'Bicameral' or unconscious one, the other being the conscious one.

The unconscious mind is devoid of awareness and merely repeats what has been done before. It has nothing to do with being in a coma, just that it accepts the status quo and has no ambition to change. As with the feet and hands it controls all our natural functions and becomes automatic. Everything from eating and sleeping through to swimming, riding a cycle or driving a car, as soon as they are learned, they are consigned to memory leaving our conscious mind to concentrate on something else. They are consigned to the *'Bicameral'* mind leaving the conscious one to concentrate on the way ahead. I follow this further when looking at waves to ask whether other long lost needs are suddenly recreated. All other animals have nothing but an unconscious mind. That is except possibly the primates and some members of the rodent family. Even a German Shepherd dog will leap endlessly for food just out of reach, but a chimpanzee will pile some boxes together to make it easier. As will a squirrel deduce how to get onto an impossible bird table. A cat will sit on top of the bird table and be surprised when no birds come to join it. Jaynes contends that the vast majority of mankind was like this until about 1,000BC. Mankind was a super intelligent being having learned to read, write and talk, defend himself and survive amongst far stronger animals but, in fact only so few had tapped into this conscious mind so to do.

With this, to a certain extent, I do agree. I think his date is wrong since there can be no time when universal use of all the brain occurred. Was it when they built the pyramids, whenever that was, and, if so, did all those people involved get a sudden enlightenment? Or was it just a few of the leaders? The obvious next question must be why? Why then? Why in Egypt and then in Central and South America? Why not China, Germany or Japan? Granted man must have summoned up every ounce of wit and ingenuity, based on knowledge at the time, for so many to survive during the immense period of time since Homo sapiens first emerged. He was still a relative weakling for hundreds of thousands of years before then, and so his relatively intelligent mind must have been at least in embryo state from the very beginning. Otherwise we would be as extinct as the dinosaurs. Even so, most of the world was just emerging from hundreds of thousands of years of Stone Age into this sudden Biblical Period of Enlightenment. Why?

During the ensuing three thousand years more and more people, first in the Far East and then in the West began using this conscious mind to enhance both civilization and their war making capabilities, leaving the Middle East far behind. The contribution of this part of the world being its natural supply of oil, and as the hot bed of the three great religions of Christianity, Islam and the Judaism. Simultaneously, all over the world except in the Antipodes and on the American Great Plains, mankind then progressed at more or less the same speed. They discovered copper, bronze and iron in that order; they built houses in mud, then with timber frames until eventually they could work stone and build bigger buildings that were much stronger. They discovered the arts at the same time. Useless metals like gold and silver, that were far too soft, became the precious metals to make jewellery and flatware, shiny stones like diamond, ruby, emerald and sapphire became the precious stones to go with the metals and so mankind could look now at other than the basic necessities of life.

The most significant result of this growing awareness was the transformation from an earth moving society to a building and constructive one. Previously all fortifications had been enormous earthworks like Maiden Castle and Salmesbury Rings in southern Britain, dug out of the earth by sweated labour over a long period of time. In the West the only large construction works were various stone circles of roughly extracted stone shards such as Stonehenge, built, presumably, for the worship of the sun. But for years until well after the birth of Christ most man made structures were of timber and/or earthworks.

Look on any map and you will see marked 'tumuli'. Tumuli are man made fortifications and they are dotted all over Britain and Western Europe. Even the small and historically insignificant ones were enormous feats of civil engineering in their day, involving hundreds – if not thousands – of labourers, using whatever tooling they had devised by that time, moving tiny amounts of usually very wet earth each time. And this was even though manpower on the land was not that great or plentiful. But all this happened in very small parts of the world other than in the Middle East. It was there that something happened to release that dormant side of our brain to suddenly give us the powers and the knowledge to create some stunning things. And it all happened in the fertile lands of Egypt in the West, Mesopotamia and Persia in the East, and Assyria in the North. During all this time the rest of the world slumbered in a Stone Age stupor. But, having said that, Stone Age Northern Europe was building the enormous henges, mounds, stone circles and monoliths, most of which required much planning and considerable logistical expertise. I think here of Stonehenge, Avebury and others right up to the work at Stenness in Orkney. And all was done without any metals or the wheel. I give my thoughts on why later on in the book.

Going back to ancient times, either before, after or simultaneously with Jericho, we must begin with either the pyramids or the Sphinx, in whatever chronological order, which involved not earth moving as such but physical building construction work with all that that entails. Physical construction begins first with a level site, and this must be surveyed very accurately, since any dips at corners will result in mis-shaped buildings. Then the site must be laid out to accommodate the buildings. Again surveyors of advanced ability are needed but if you are going to complicate things by aligning two sides exactly, and I mean exactly, to within seconds of the true North Pole you will also need the help of a very highly skilled astronomer.

It is interesting to ask how indeed they were aware of a 'North Pole' anyway, since they were supposed to think that the earth was flat and that the sun made its way back by way of the underworld to rise again in the east. That was why they built, if we are to believe conventional wisdom, the solar boats so that Pharaoh could make the journey in the afterlife. If they knew that there was such a thing as the 'North Pole', surely they would be aware that the world was, in fact, a sphere just like the sun and the moon and that it span on that axis? But just what was so important that they had to line the first pyramid so carefully with this point of which they should have no knowledge? And again, surely knowing this [perhaps by observing the Pole Star and seeing that it failed to move whilst the others all did] why would they want to provide a solar boat for the dead Pharaoh? Unless the boat came from a totally different period of time many thousands of years later.

But the Great Pyramids were surveyed as such. That is an indisputable fact for all to see. Briefly this is what had to have happened by a people barely out of the Stone Age and with no obvious metal tools other than those made of bronze [if built in 2,200BC, copper if earlier].

Before building proper could begin suitable foundations must be dug into the bedrock, any below ground basement work must be dug, excavated and carried away and then underground building completed. Then the building proper could begin but only when sufficient materials were ready. The Quantity Surveyor at the time would need to order many thousand limestone blocks, all cut to an exact size and with perfect sides and corners. It would only need a few running off by no more than one degree – almost impossible to measure – for the entire building to end up lop sided. All these must then be delivered on site on demand. Plus a large quantity of Granite blocks of various shapes and sizes in the fifty to seventy ton each bracket. But these needed exact angles, so that they could be placed exactly together with no suspicion of a gap, to form a sloping passage through the middle. As the building continued, various narrow shafts must be installed so that they lined up exactly with an obscure star which has taken the fancy of the builder. And these shafts must be a continuous perfect rectangle cut diagonally in advance through the stones so that as each stone was laid it matched its neighbour exactly. What a pity that all they had to work with were a few stone flints or, at best bronze, since iron was yet to be discovered. Nor had they any numbers, proper words or means of measurement, drawing or writing. How amazing.

Logistically this was a difficult task involving tens of thousands of workers both cutting and delivering stones onto site. All of whom must be housed and fed with a plentiful supply of water. Then there was the little problem of raising these stones into exactly the right position. Would they use wooden gantries with pulleys and ropes? Not really since all they had were palm trees, the hard wood forests having succumbed to the desert many millennia before hand. There was plenty of sand about so they could build enormous ramps up which the blocks would role but how do they get seventy ton blocks of granite, not laid out horizontally, onto an inclined plain where they locked precisely together? Not easy.

I am far from convinced about the sand ramp theory, particularly when moving such a large number of enormous blocks. Sahara sand is very dry and, in consequence, very soft. Any effort made to simply push the blocks across the surface would have resulted in a 'bow wave' as on a ship which would have brought the first one to a halt within a few feet. Did they then use rollers? Again these would only be effective if [a] the roller was made of a comparatively hard wood and was of significant diameter and [b] if the surface of the inclined plane was up to at least the standard of our roads of the mid 20th century. A roller cannot work on soft ground; it would merely sink in the moment any weight was put on it. If you compare the huge slabs at Giza with the round 'slices' of rock at Luxor, the latter could have been rolled up a crushed stone ramp with relative ease since the ramp would only need to be relatively narrow. This just could not be done at Giza.

However, the building would proceed from the inside out taking special care that it remained true to its polar alignment, true to it's exact outside dimensions and true to the inclination of the outside walls so that the final stone marked the exact centre of a perfect pyramid. This was a prodigious feat of civil engineering if ever there was one.

Having done this, let's build another for the brother Chefren but that one, when it is finished, will be lined on the outside with smooth alabaster. Then just to keep it in the family, another for the son, Mykerinos, but this time cover the exterior with smooth granite slabs. And when all is finished, by shear coincidence the layout on the ground of all three just happens to mirror three stars in the heavens. By another incredible coincidence, the shafts line up on the same stars. Again, amazing. But, whilst we are at it, we'll ignore the spare one built by the father of Cheops, Snedfu. It is called the Red Pyramid and he built it ten miles away in the desert. Just why, we will never know.

Or so we are led to believe.

And then we move to the sphinx. Now he is more of an earth moving, rather than building, exercise having been excavated from the bedrock at some time in history. Had he been built simultaneously or indeed after the pyramids, surely he would have faced them in honour and tribute to such amazing buildings. But he doesn't, he sits rudely with his back to them facing east to get the first rays of the sun. But he doesn't get the first rays as they are now since where he faces looks due east is as it would have been many, many years ago. Thousands of years in fact. Back to the days when the Sahara was a rain forest at least 12,000 years ago. To the time of the dawning of the present astrological age of Aquarius. To know this and work it out, again within seconds of true east, needs a very accurate knowledge of a thing called 'Precession" which must be clearly understood.

As well the earth rotating at 1,000 miles per hour and its trajectory round the sun in a year, it also has a tiny wobble at the poles which takes about 26,000 years to complete. This wobble is 'Precession' and is virtually impossible to deduce from simple observation of the stars. Particularly if you do not have a telescope, understanding of mathematics or iron for a compass, since all these were thousands of years away from being discovered. And yet they must have understood precession plus an awful lot more to do with the stars.

There is the Sphinx himself. Throughout recorded history he has been dug out of his covering of sand. Leave him only a few years and the desert will fill the trench around him leaving him, or so you would imagine, in pristine condition with little or no weathering. But he is not. Far from it. His main body has been weathered, not by the sand storms of ages but torrential rain of at least two thousand years. Not possible say the 'experts'. This phenomenon has been well recorded by now by others working on the same theme and I more or less accept what they have to say.

What raises its head for me is that, in order to expose the main body from the bedrock, [the head always protruded and must have been either added – for which there is so far no evidence – or have been a convenient outcrop] a large quantity of stone had to be removed. Some of this has been identified as enormous perfectly formed pieces on nearby buildings. If this is so, it must have been extracted in several very large pieces, raised thirty or forty feet above the main body and then expertly worked for its final purpose. Now, if the original object had been merely to clear a space around the main body, the excavated bedrock would have been broken into small, manageable sizes. Today this would be done with controlled explosives after which the big excavators would move in but, of course, we are talking of a long time before explosives and the only excavators were slaves who would have an absolute limit on what they could carry, due to the simple matter of their physical size.

So, again if we believe the 'experts', a significant proportion of this excavation was cut out in huge pieces and then raised onto the plateau where they were used on totally insignificant buildings of little or no obvious use. And cut with incredible precision. Just why would they bother? And what did they use to extract such huge lumps of comparatively hard limestone in one piece? It would be difficult today with our latest equipment.

In the meantime, the newly exposed basic shape of the incredible Sphinx had to be skilfully shaped into the figure of a huge crouching lion. As before, before they had discovered iron. According to accepted archaeology and palaeontology the only tools that man had in that period were Stone Age flints, copper chisels or, at best ones made of bronze. That fact is very interesting indeed. A very large 'pounding stone' where all the carving and extraction was achieved by simply hitting one piece of rock with another is one more favourite and long standing theory.

I have recently been back to see the Giza site again and from it I make these observations. The Sphinx itself lies at probably the lowest point on the plateau. He is at least 40 metres below the level of the Great Pyramid and he faces a hill at the other side of a small valley. Now if it was the intention, as everyone else seems to accept, that he was built to see the first rays of the sun in the eastern sky, surely they would have carved him out of the abundant bedrock so much higher up? I feel that the whole theory is flawed for this reason alone but I can offer no other credible one myself. I have no idea why he was built but cannot accept that it was to catch the sun's first rays.

So now we have irrefutable evidence that there were actually built, not three, but four massive pyramids and actually excavated and carved from bedrock one enormous figure of a crouching lion. The fourth pyramid, a few miles away and called the 'Red Pyramid', is thought to have been built by Cheops or his father. Now why, having supposedly built one a few years earlier, would he feel the need for another? And with an unused spare available, why build another two? Accepted 'experts' can date these exactly but I have many doubts about when they were built and who actually built them. More to the point, why?????

What is beyond any contradiction is that whoever was involved in this work over many years and possibly more than one period of time must have had the following advantages and skills.

1. They were skilled astronomers up to, and possibly beyond, present day standards.
2. They were skilled mathematicians who knew all about such constants as *pi* before there was even such a thing as a number. They understood angles and how to calculate exact ratios between height and base to achieve these constants.
3. They were brilliant surveyors.
4. They were brilliant architects and quantity surveyors.
5. They were stone masons without equal before or since.
6. They were incredible builders.
7. Their quarrying skills have probably never been equalled.
8. Their logistical skills are the same.
9. Their civil engineering knowledge and ability would be awesome in this day.
10. They were able to not only cut enormous pieces of rock in one piece from the bedrock, but to then face it to a perfection only possible with highly sophisticated modern technology.
11. They were able to move those stones over considerable distances from quarry to building site, and then place exactly, single pieces of around seventy tons. This would hardly be possible today even using the very latest quarrying, lifting and transporting equipment.

Moving away from Egypt, but remaining in the Middle East, we have other massive building, rather than earth moving, projects which were collectively known as the 'Seven Wonders of the World'. The Colossus at Rhodes was a huge bronze statue that came during the age of Grecian expansion; The Hanging Gardens of Babylon were a mighty stone and mud edifice dating from around 1,500BC, whilst the Pharos, back in Egyptian Alexandria was a mighty lighthouse plus an ancient library going back to the dawn of time.

Not included in this list is the amazing pillar erected by the Roman Emperor Pompey in Alexandria. Carved, supposedly from a single piece of solid granite either at the quarry above Aswan or on site by the coast, it is a huge edifice made all the more remarkable by the fact that it had to be floated down the Nile and then transported over land to its site. There it was raised to the vertical and placed exactly and truly onto a pre-carved base and set in place. The base itself is massive. There seem to be no marks on the base to indicate that it was placed there other than by carefully lowering from above. This must rank as one of the most amazing feats of engineering of all time. But all of these came at least two to three thousand years after the pyramids.

This takes us back to the bulge. Or, more to the point, two bulges. If we take on board what has been said above about Egypt and the Egyptians, an almost identical thing was happening in South and Central America and always attributed to the Inca and the Maya, other unremarkable and indolent peoples who again have contributed zero to the advancement of mankind. The Maya were thought to be around from about 1,000BC to 1,000AD. There is some doubt about the Inca. They may or may not have been about during that period. They were there in opulent and decadent glory when the Conquistadors arrived. However, as in Egypt, there is no evidence whatsoever that the incredible buildings in the Yucatan Peninsular, north of Mexico City, south to Peru in Cuzco or at Machu Pichu were actually built by any of them, or during that period. An infinite period into antiquity is suddenly halted by peoples who had acquired, from somewhere unknown, skills of prodigious variety and complexity not matched until the second millennium after Christ and to this day, never surpassed. One proceeded to construct five of the greatest works of civil engineering ever in Egypt, whilst another society across a mighty ocean built equally enormous pyramids, cut huge stones with incredible accuracy and vast cities as well, that were laid out with awesome precision, and who should not have possibly been aware of each other's existence. Or could they?

Effectively they were building these massive structures for over one hundred years and then they just stopped. In Egypt there were a few other minor pyramids of poor design and quality, but mostly their kings and queens were buried underground using traditional earth moving techniques needing little or no technology. Other big temples such as Luxor and Karnack appeared but their construction is simpler and more accountable. There then began the steady decline continuing to this day where the entire areas, on both sides of the Atlantic, continue to contribute not one single jot to the civilization of mankind.

And so we are led to believe that a simple society existing on the extremely narrow banks of just one river emerged from antiquity and obscurity around 3,022 years BC. They then messed around with pagan beliefs based on the river and the sun for from three to six hundred years during which time they constructed little more than a mud hut. The accepted interpretation of the hieroglyphics and drawings of the time prove this, and then, out of nowhere, comes a couple of generations of brilliant builders, astronomers, mathematicians, organizers and engineers, who build five of the greatest buildings the world will ever see, before disappearing again into obscurity. Whilst the same was being repeated in Mexico and South America many thousands of miles and one massive ocean away. At the same time or later? We will see. Over the following years the temples at Luxor and Abu Symbal were built and there is no denying that these are prodigious feats of engineering. But these are all feasible projects. Any engineer can see just how these were built and it is equally easy to see how the various monoliths were hewn from the solid rock. What always fills me with awe and wonderment are how these were extracted and then moved prodigious distances before being hauled into the correct vertical position where they have remained for several millennia. But mostly these were one offs, the pyramids required a constant supply, in the tens and hundreds of thousands, of huge, perfect stones scattered over a vast building site since, in order to complete all in the hundred or so years, most must have been a concurrent ongoing project.

But now the waters are muddied again. The very recent emergence of Google Earth allows us to see from the air the entire planet. This has revealed some astonishing things, especially in South America. Anthropologists studying the Amazon have found hundreds of massive earthworks, many away from the river and all of a similar construction. Between them are signs of long straight roads.

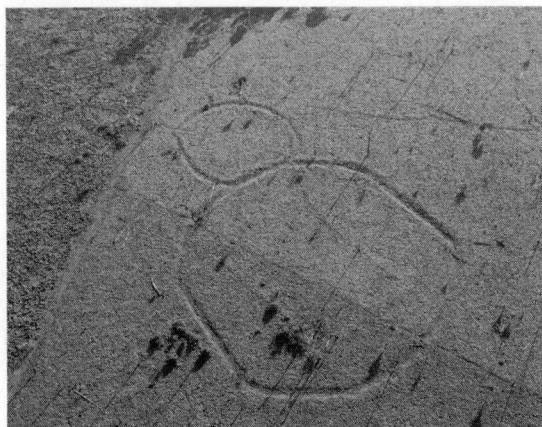

Aerial shots of early civilizations along the banks of the Amazon. Some of these show perfect rectangles and evidence of roads. It is a mystery of what happened to these people from the time of the first Spanish discovery until the arrival of the Portuguese.

The Amazon was first explored, by Europeans, in 1541 by the Spanish Conquistador, Francesco de Orellana, accompanied by Gaspar de Carvajel who chronicled it all. He had a suitable boat built at Quito in Peru which at the time was accessed only overland across the Andes. He set off down river in search of gold but could not return against the current. Consequently he eventually fetched up in the Atlantic some 2000 miles away. But on the way the trip was recorded and it was reported that they discovered many large towns that were heavily populated. This was subsequently treated with more than suspicion as subsequent expeditions, right up to the present day, could find no corroborating evidence. All that was found were small riverside groups of Stone Age peoples.

But the advent of satellite imagery allows us to see things from above and these earthworks have emerged. Some are carefully lined up on the exact north/south meridian and are huge with exact right angles at the corners. Others are perfect circles. They have up to ten metre walls and ditches and must have been built by a very advanced people, as described by Orellana. Towards the mouth of the river on some islands has been found some amazing pottery of enormous size. Much of it was for burial purposes but it is the decoration that is of interest. The carving is exceptional and much is even glazed using polychrome pigments. Shards of domestic pottery have been excavated at the sites all along the river and these show a civilization to match that of Egypt, but was it of the same period? First thoughts put it at around 1000BC but nothing is certain.

So now we have not one, but two bulges on our graph but the most amazing thing is that these two graphs, put one on top of the other, have just the one variable – when in history their bulges actually happened. Otherwise they are very similar. Is this a coincidence? Maybe, but somehow I have my doubts.

9

WAVES

Waves come in two categories. There are tangible ones and intangible ones. Tangible ones are the ones we can see such as the waves of the sea, whether they be thunderous breakers on a rocky shore or the mild ripple when a stone is thrown into a still pond. But waves they all are and they arrive at a steady frequency [the distance between two wave crests], whilst their power or intensity is measured by the height from the trough to the crest of the wave. So long as there is some force out there disturbing the liquid, the waves will continue ad infinitum.

Then we come to the intangible waves – those we cannot see but that are there nevertheless. The first ones of these are light waves which we see as a continuous effect, but which are actually made up of hundreds of different waves with each colour having a separate wave length. Our eyes act as a computer and automatically separate the waves on a continuous basis leaving us free to enjoy the whole spectrum before us. Some animals cannot do this and so only see in black and white. The phenomenon known as being 'colour blind' means that that person has a slight glitch in the brain that fails to separate some colours, and so goes through life unaware of at least two beautiful colours. The rest of us can see the colours that make up our spectrum beginning with Ultra Violet and ending with Infra Red. Outside that spectrum the wave lengths are either too short or too long for us to be able to pick them up. But they are there nevertheless, measurable with machines.

Other waves that the brain can pick up are those of sound and here we again can identify just a small band before the frequency gets beyond us. It is here that the animal world has the advantage. Animals have developed facilities to hear far more than we can. Have you noticed how your dog or cat will sometimes jump when you change TV channels? They have heard something that we cannot. Predators like lions, snakes and birds of prey have either finely tuned hearing, sight or smell so that they can detect the smallest movement in the undergrowth whilst their prey, like small mammals and birds, have similar advanced facilities to level up the playing field.

We all can see the waves in the sea which is a comparatively dense medium compared to the air above. We see them as ripples on the surface but beneath those waves are others that we cannot see. Divers may feel different currents but the ones of which I speak are those made by fish. A single fish or a shoal will send out waves

Here you are looking at a trillion waves, only one of which is visible to the naked eye. Whether on those distant Alps or on the Mediterranean beach, any single one of those other waves can be picked up if you have the correct receiver.

through the water that a predator such as a shark, otter or seal can pick up from a distance. A shark will smell the waves sent out by blood and home in on it. We cannot see those waves, whether anyone has tried to measure them I do not know, but waves they are and they are out there, all day and everywhere. The predator cannot see its prey but the waves tell it that the food is there.

All this shows conclusively that mankind and the animal world collectively have developed highly sophisticated mechanisms to see, hear and identify certain types of waves travelling through the ether.

But these waves with which we can relate are a miniscule proportion of the number of waves out there travelling at incredible speeds through the ether. Here we are not talking about millions nor billions, but trillions of different waves bombarding us 24 hours of every day. There is no escape. Whether on the top of Everest, on a deserted South Seas beach or a Tokyo subway, trillions of unseen waves are bombarding us all the time.

Yet this is a relatively modern phenomenon brought on by the advent of radio. Go back to pre-Marconi days and the earth was bombarded by a very large number of natural waves such as nuclear radiation [which occurs globally in tiny proportions] and other Ultra Violet waves that find their way through our stratosphere. This is why we get sunburned when too long exposed to the sun. Then there were shock waves from any natural disaster such as a volcano or earthquake but, apart from these, there was nothing man made to upset the balance. Natural selection over the millennia meant that we all built up immunity to these waves.

After these we come to man made waves and there are a lot of them. Marconi and the Curie family set it all off but in a small way. At the end of the nineteenth and beginning of the twentieth century the waves created by man were very weak and tended to peter out in a short distance. If you wanted a radio in the twenties you built yourself a crystal set and messed about with it until you picked up a weak signal. Long distance communication was done by way of a cable where you would send your telegraph by either Morse code or simply by voice. All telephone conversations were sent by way of a cable as indeed are a lot today. Of course it is a wave of some sort that sends the message down the line. And so it carried on until World War 2 when radio transmitters got more powerful and with the introduction of radar. We then had our airways becoming contaminated with Radar signals, albeit weak ones, emanating from the ground, ships and aircraft plus a mixture of radio signals from a plethora of sources.

Add in here that Television was becoming a commercial reality in the United States and even more unseen waves were filling our airways. Every single one of these waves must have had a man made method of generation and, per se, a man made method of retrieval.

Then it all changed when the first Sputnik orbited the earth. Soon we were able to not only launch and retrieve satellites but to leave them there as well, beaming down waves into the ether for the mobile phone with which you cannot do without, hundreds of TV channels in every language on earth and satellite navigation systems, beaming down a carpet of waves, so that you know within a foot or so exactly where you are on earth. The Internet has changed the world of information plus giving us some highly sophisticated surveillance systems that, if you are reading this in the garden, someone in Washington, Moscow or London can see you clearly. Anyone now can do this by tapping into Google Earth. We are not talking about weak 2LO waves of the crystal set days but mighty powerful ones to achieve this. Even more disturbing are the new stationery drones hovering above areas habited by 'celebrities' and, no doubt, criminals. Soon that will include most of us.

Then there are the Nuclear Power Stations emitting radio active radiation – not in life threatening proportions or anything like it – but enough to add to the above cocktail. Every hospital has an X Ray facility generating lethal X Rays but only in the tiniest doses as to make them safe but, nevertheless, adding again to the mix. It is too soon to say just what effect all this has on our long term health since we have had no time to build any sort of resistance or immune system to it all, but it is quite frightening to think that, as you sit in the peace of your garden, or on a quiet hillside miles from anywhere, every TV channel in the world, every radio broadcast in the world, every email, yes, all 2.5 billion of them, every twitter, every Facebook entry, every text message and every mobile phone message is being beamed at your head. Literally trillions of new waves, infinitesimal in size, all aimed at every corner of the earth. All you need is the right receiver to listen to what they have to say.

But, and this is the purpose of this section, what about the waves of which we know nothing? The principal of Feng Shui is that about your home and yourself there is a constant flow of charged particles which, if you can arrange things in the correct order, will bring great benefit to yourself. All this is seriously believed in the Far East and I am certainly not going to dismiss it as rubbish. Vast commercial buildings are constructed with the Feng Shui element being the priority rather than an afterthought. We can't see these waves or channel flows any more than we cannot see the TV and mobile phone signals, nor can we as yet detect them with any type of man made receiver, but does that necessarily mean that they are not there? No. No one can say that for certain.

Taking the argument further we enter the world of science fiction. What about Mediums communicating with the dead? Do ghosts exist and, if so, are they benign or harmful?

Personally, taken from my own experience, I have a problem dismissing ghosts or spirits that haunt our spaces. I give some examples.

Years ago, when I was a child, my grandmother moved into a small, isolated cottage in the Yorkshire Dales. Soon afterwards my brother and I spent the night there, sleeping on inflatable mattresses in sleeping bags in an otherwise totally unfurnished room. The floor boards were bare. About three in the morning I heard the distinct sound of someone walking about the room. I sat up to see my brother still hard asleep but the noise continued until it just faded away. I said nothing to my uncle and aunt until about twenty five years later when grandmother lay dying in her bed upstairs. My uncle was in the other bedroom and my aunt in the kitchen downstairs. Both simultaneously heard what they thought was the sound of granny coming downstairs. But there was no one there – she had just died. It emerged later that a clergyman had died in a fire at the house about a hundred years earlier.

I spent the last twenty five years of my working life amongst the stately homes of Great Britain. During that time I chanced across some ghosts but, I have to say, none actually first hand.

In York there is a medieval building called St Williams College and here our security guard had a 'spiritual experience', if that was what you would call it. When all had gone on the first night he heard distinctive footsteps on the bare boards upstairs. There was nothing there. During the night he sat at a desk opposite a stand where, to his horror, a large, heavy brass charger slowly rose off a hanger before crashing onto the stone floor. He was still sat there, white with shock when I arrived at 8.30.

A different security guard was on duty at Hoghton Tower in Lancashire when, in the middle of the night, a one inch diameter flagstaff sheared off and crashed onto some glass. There was no sign of other than a clean cut by a heavy sharp instrument. Two days later in the same room, a lady was holding a glass when it rose out of her hand about a foot in the air before hurling itself forward a foot and smashing as though it had hit a solid wall.

Yes, I do believe that there are such things as ghosts but what they are I have no idea.

What about mediums being able to contact the dead? We've all had a go at a séance or been to see an old woman who claims to be in contact with your loved ones. Many a music hall act was successful in doing this but invariably these tended to be a scam of some form or other. But, before we either embrace this fully or dismiss it as rubbish giving false hopes to the ignorant and vulnerable, let us first look at things logically.

The first observation that I make is that there are an awful lot of dead people in the graveyards of the world plus many more who opted to have their mortal remains cremated. Also there are the dead animals, birds, fish, insects, plants etc., etc. Where do all these fit into the great scheme of things? What about those who chose to be cremated? If there is an after life, is it split between heaven and hell? Whose decision is this? Is entrance to this dependant on being of the right religion – at the time and in that place - so that, for arguments sake, the Jews got it wrong and only those who followed Christ had the choice? Then what? Is it going to be just the good Catholics who went to Mass regularly and saved up their indulgences that are eligible for the big decision? What about those 'Good Catholics' from the Pope downwards who committed such appalling crimes during the various Inquisitions? Where are they now? Equally the same can be said for the 'Good Protestants' who went about burning Catholics and pretty girls as witches with such vigour. Does that mean that the rest of mankind must be tossed away into the abyss? And all those Muslims who have murdered innocent civilians in the hope of entering heaven where they then have exclusive access to those seventy virgins? Don't the 'virgins' get a say in it all? What about those who lived before Christ, before David, before Moses and before Abraham? Those of our ancestors, for that is whom they all are, who go back not a hundred, nor a thousand years but hundreds of thousands of years, back to the arrival of Homo sapiens on this earth? There cannot be a cut off point, where we can say that people who existed before our chosen 'God' manifested himself, were automatically denied access to a heaven.

'Ah,' say the religious leaders, 'where you go wrong is in imagining that all creatures have souls.' Souls apparently are denied to animals and vegetation therefore they don't count. That is except, of course, your pet cat, hamster or gold fish buried at the bottom of the garden. Equally early man had no soul because he didn't have this or that God to worship. It is all highly simplistic and a most convenient 'Mighty Bound'. But what is a soul, does it die with you or does it leave the body on death, float for a time before joining the rest in some idealistic after life? Do you then join up with your friends and family for all time? Supposing you had done granny in for her fortune, got away with it but that she knew? Again all highly convenient if true.

So what is your 'soul'? Can it be measured and does everyone have one? What happened to the souls of Hitler, Lenin, Stalin, Mao Tse Tung, Genghis Khan, Attila or the other mass murderers from history? Or are you all anonymous in the afterlife?

There is no medical evidence whatsoever of the existence of a soul. Medically, when we die that is it. No more. Our body is either cremated or buried where it decays as in the burial ceremony 'earth to earth, ashes to ashes, dust to dust'. And, since at the time of writing, only one person has ever claimed to have returned from the dead, the evidence is fairly conclusive. Everyone has one chance on this earth for how ever long it takes after which that is it. It is over, finished, history. Or so it would seem.

Some religions then think that there is a rebirth. As a punishment for our sins whilst on earth, we are sent back time after time to go through it all over again until we get it right. We are reincarnated where our soul departs the mortal remains and enters those of a new born child so improving each time until it achieves perfection or 'Nirvana'. This holds up providing the birth and death rate remain constant. Since mankind has always been increasing in numbers over the millennia, surely this leaves a vacuum where some people miss out on a dead soul and either go through life without, or start a new one afresh? Christendom and Islam both believe in an after life as, indeed, did the Ancient Egyptians before them, whilst the Jews believe that we enter the world with nothing and so should leave it the same. All that matters is what we do whilst we are here.

One theory to prove reincarnation is the evidence of deep hypnosis. Here the hypnotist takes the patient through a series of regressions, going back as far as possible, so that in one life a perfectly healthy man may have been a Jewish slave girl in the fourteenth century, a Roman Centurion or a great Lord. They describe the events and times very accurately. But could there be another explanation to this? We all know that we possess unique

123

genes that pass from one generation to another. Some of these genes contain malevolent features such as hereditary illnesses whilst others determine the colour of your skin and your racial origins. No one has so far identified them as such – which in no way proves that they do not exist – but it is my contention that we all possess a bank of memory genes. With these the memories and experiences of our ancestors are passed down through the generations. This could account for the experience of 'déjà vu' – that feeling that you have been there before, or seen something, when you know that you most certainly have not. When writing my novel, 'The Fairest Isle, The Foulest Deeds', some years ago, I imagined the small fishing port of Falmouth on the north coast of Jamaica and wrote it down. Some years later on a visit to the island I found Falmouth to be exactly how I had described it. My paternal grandfather was in the Royal Navy and travelled the world. Could I have got it from him?

Amongst all this one of them may have got it right but which one? If we only knew!! But, and now we enter the world of science fiction, just supposing that, as with television, mobile phones and radio, we could build a receiver that would pick up and translate those waves? What if it was possible to, through hypnosis or similar, to programme the mind to pick up those waves? Could the so called 'Mediums' be normal people with a slight aberration in their brains, where a portion inactive in the rest of us, works and so enables them to communicate with the dead?

If not then all those who claim the gift must be some sort of charlatan, giving false comfort to ignorant and vulnerable people. We just do not know for certain but, until proved conclusively and beyond all reasonable doubt, I am prepared to give the benefit of that doubt to the believers.

I most certainly believe in telepathy because it runs in my family. When I was a child in primary school in Leeds my brother was walking home alone and my mother's aunt was staying with us. When my brother was a good quarter of a mile from home my aunt turned to my mother to ask what the matter was because my brother was hurt and was crying. He had just walked into a lamp post and had a bleeding nose! Now I will send an e-mail to ask my son in Australia when it would be a good time to talk on Skype and more or less simultaneously the call will come through. It is the same with my other son and even my ex-wife. I will make to ring them, or vice versa, and they will at that moment be ringing me and invariably about exactly the same subject that is going through my head.

As I write this, only today do I read of a controlled scientific experiment between two scientists, one Italian and the other Spanish, and in sealed conditions in Italy and India, where both simultaneously came up with same simple thought in their own languages. I did a simple experiment myself by asking a close friend, my two sons and my former wife some questions. One lives nearby, one over 100 miles away, one in Australia and my ex-wife was in Thailand. At exactly 9.00am one morning I asked them to give three rivers, three cities of Europe and three names. I was thinking of my answers at the time. All came back with the Nile as one of the rivers and all knew one of my cities. As a 'red herring' I was thinking of a local river and my ex-wife also came up with a local river but not the same one. One of my sons came up with the River Rhone when I had put down the Rhine but had thought of the Rhone. No one got a name right. Does this prove anything? I don't know but I cannot dismiss it. Once again, no one knows but it is out there.

Taking this argument a stage further, throughout history, a small number of men – never women – went a stage further and became prophets following a face to face meeting with either God or the Angel Gabriel. As we have seen, there were a lot of prophets in the Old Testament all with the one purpose of warning mankind of its inevitable doom some time in the future. These petered out following the ascension of Christ, only ending with the appearance of Christ Himself to dictate to St John the Divine, some forty years after His death, His Revelations for the future of mankind.

Not content with that however, some six hundred years later that same Angel Gabriel appeared to an illiterate Arabian called Mohammed after which, for the next twenty three years,

Gabriel made frequent manifestations to Mohammed from which the Holy Koran was written. And what is written in the Koran? It is quite simply another version of the teachings of Christ.

So what made these men so special? They were all simple men. Christ was a carpenter, Mohammed illiterate, Moses an orphan brought up to subjugate his fellow Jews, Isaiah just an ordinary man as were the rest of them. Just what did they all have in common that, over a vast period of time that same Lord God and that same Angel Gabriel should choose them over all other mankind to give more or less the same message? And that message was effectively 'If you don't all behave yourselves and live in harmony together, you will lose the lot'. Could they all have had an aberration in the mind enabling them to open this channel of communication or was there something altogether different to consider? The 21st century must be ripe for another manifestation since now the whole thing is more than both a reality and possibility – it is a probability. For only now we have the means of a man made Armageddon.

There are other waves that must be considered to be intangible and these are the ones that distinguish that rarest of all phenomena and that is silence. Let me elaborate. Few of us are able to experience the wonder of total, still silence but it is, nevertheless a very real phenomenon. As I have mentioned earlier I lived overlooking the sea and in the middle distance was an International airport. To my left was a constant line of buildings making a typical Mediterranean waterfront. Behind me were a main line railway and busy road which I only heard if my rear door was open. By the early hours the airport was silent and there was little coming from the road or the railway. For much of the time it was total silence. There was nothing to break this silence when the sea was still yet all the time I got a sensation in my ears that can only be described as a feeling of pent up energy.

In contrast I have a friend who lives some thirty minutes away up in the Alps. The house is a good mile from the nearest road and here there is a magical stillness and silence, only disturbed by the breeze through the trees. Here I can sit and feel the sensation of peace and tranquillity in perfect silence that I never got on the coast.

So just what waves are going through the ether to cause this? Could they come from the sea or is it the residual power from street lamps and the railway? Something is left in the atmosphere there to cause this that is absent in the mountains but just what it is, I have no idea.

Some animals and fish have the extraordinary power of migration. Swallows spend the winter in Africa but then make the enormous journey back to northern Europe to breed. Always to the spot where they were first hatched. Throughout the world other birds like geese travel vast distances to and from their breeding ground but always return to the same spot. The most amazing of all are the fish.

Just what is there in their brains that can tell them after hatching to make their way out into the oceans and then, even more amazing is how they find their way back across an ocean and then into the correct river to breed? What messages do they get from the sea and river mouths that tell an eel, having swum all the way over from the Sargasso Sea, not to turn right up the Seine as its contemporaries are doing but to carry on and turn left when it gets to the Thames? Think of the salmon making a similar journey around the north of Scotland. Imagine that a huge shoal of them are coming as if on a railway journey. They get to the Moray Forth and some get off to go up the Spey. Another group know that they carry on until they get to the Dee, the next stop off at the Tay, the remainder ignore the Forth leaving some to turn up the Tweed, a few will go up the Aln and the handful left will home in on the Esk.

It is claimed that fish have no memory at all and this I neither accept nor reject because I just do not know. I just wonder what waves underwater, for that is all they can be, enable the right salmon to home in on its correct river ignoring all the rest in the process. Scientists claim that it is instinct but if that is so I must ask what instinct is. How does it help a lonely salmon pick out the far from obvious mouth of the River Aln in Northumberland rather than take the easy option of the Tweed a few miles up the coast?

As I say, there are waves about the ether and in the seas that we know nothing about but, because of that we must never deny their existence.

10

DO THE NUMBERS ADD UP?

Let us crunch some numbers.

Here I am going to look carefully at four construction projects over the years. One was from the 19th – early 20th century, one between the wars, one very recent using the latest technology, and the last being the four great pyramids around Giza. The others are the Panama Canal, the Hoover Dam and the Channel Tunnel. The only accurate comparison is in the amount of material physically moved. I then look at whether or not the material was used for building purposes or had to be disposed of, how the material was excavated and/or prepared for construction and then what was available in construction equipment at the time.

What type of terrain had to be overcome each time? How near to water and food supplies was the project? What about housing the work force and medical help when needed? These and dozens of other questions must be asked and answered of the first three projects before we can hypothesise on the fourth.

What is undeniable is that all were at the time massive and virtually impossible projects that were undertaken and completed as their physical presence today shows. Much faith plus a lot of sweat and tears, not to mention astronomic sums of money was needed in each case but, for this exercise, we are not interested in the money nor the politics involved, merely the engineering problems encountered and how they were overcome.

THE PANAMA CANAL

Before this was built or even mooted, the only ways from New York and the East Coast of North America to San Francisco and California were a dangerous wagon trail journey across hostile

Indian country, followed by an ascent of the massive Rocky Mountains. The alternative was an equally dangerous sea journey through the Straits of Magellan or around Cape Horn sailing against the prevailing Westerly winds. Each was a journey that would take many months. A simple canal through the middle of Central America used by the increasing numbers of steam powered ships would cut the time enormously. Most of all it would allow the passage of people to and from California to be carried out in relative comfort and safety. The implications for trade for the countries of the South American west coast, Mexico and all the American/Canadian seaboards were obvious, plus it now would make easier access for the East coast and Brazil to the Far East. It made a lot of sense. The presence of the Rockies and the granite formed High Sierras made a rail route impossible at the time.

Following his success in Egypt, Ferdinand de Lesseps was appointed as the first engineer to survey the area and he decided on a sea level canal, the same as at Suez. But this proved a disaster since a fast flowing river crossed the site several times, inundating it in the wet season. He had no real answer to the fact that the Pacific had a tidal range of 20ft against the almost nil one in the Caribbean. After several years struggle and losing large numbers of the workforce to malaria and other insect born diseases, the French ran out of money and had to abandon the project. By the time it was finished in 1914, 5,609 workers had succumbed, mostly through disease.

The Americans took over and decided to use a system of locks, taking it up to 85ft above sea level, where they could use the large natural Gaton Lake system for a significant part of the way. The biggest challenge here was cutting a wide channel, 8 miles long, through the Culebra Mountain. This mountain contained much mud whilst the bedrock was a mixture of sandstone and ironstone. Problems encountered included huge mud slides that must be cleared and dumped each time, whilst the exposed ironstone would oxidise when exposed to the wet air. This caused it to lose its strength and crumble, so precipitating the mud slides.

But they did have all the best equipment which they used to good effect. Surveying was an accepted science and so they could use the Theodolite to get the correct heights and levels all the time. Obviously they had paper, pens and pencils with which to do their calculations and drawings, any number of means to measure accurately distances, heights, liquids and solids plus the same numerical system and languages used today. They did not yet have a computer, adding machine, calculator or any electronic gadgets such as lasers or mobile phones. Initially they could use the telegraph and the Morse code for communication and, for personal transport, the simple horse was king.

A Marion steam shovel excavating for the Panama Canal in 1908.
These ran on tracks or rails and were essential in a project so big. Note the size
of the boulder in the bucket. It is about the same size as an average block used on
the Giza Pyramids.

Doing the actual work during the 34 years it took to construct were 39,000 people in all categories. These would include the actual labourers, who were mainly local indigenous Panamanians, plus a large number of West Indians from the now defunct sugar industry of the Caribbean. As well there were managers and a whole host of Civil Engineers from the USA together with a large team of ancillary workers who manned the hospitals, obtained, prepared and served the food; builders to construct the housing plus plumbers, joiners etc to maintain it; teachers for the children of the workers plus, of course, wives as well. All making a proper little town and community. Much work was done to try to eradicate the mosquitoes which had a devastating effect on the workforce, killing thousands in the end, but it was always a losing battle and they remain a problem even now.

One of the biggest problems with any construction project anywhere in the world and at any time in history is, and always has been, the removal of waste. The reader must be aware of this in the garden. Dig a hole for a post in stone, concrete or simple earth and you must stop every few minutes to drag out the spoil before continuing with the excavation. When you have finished you are left with a pile of rubbish which must be swept up into a bucket and dumped somewhere. If you work out the time involved, you probably take up more time on this than digging the actual hole. Inserting the post and securing with mixed concrete take up very little extra time after which the job is done and finished.

All construction jobs, no matter what size, use this self same discipline. Dig the hole, remove the waste, and build the structures. Job done. Of course, some require bigger holes, more waste, more building etc. In the case of the Panama Canal, 177 million cubic metres of waste was excavated against just 3.4 million cubic metres of construction work. Virtually all the construction work was done by pouring concrete. To build the Culebra Cut through the 8 miles of far from solid mountain, they used 100 massive Bucyrus steam shovels that could excavate 115 cubic metres per hour. These dumped the waste into 4000 wagons on rails that each carried 15 tons. 160 steam locomotives worked a twenty four hour shift as the job went on. To loosen the stone they used dynamite – 19 million pounds of it.

As work went on, the locks at either end were built so that sea going ships could follow the progress and be used to dump the waste far out to sea. By the time it was finished and opened in August 1914 it was, and remains, the biggest single construction feat ever. But, without the equipment – even though it was primitive by modern standards – and the ready availability of dynamite, it would have been a physical impossibility no matter how big the workforce. It would be fair to say that this was a muck shifting rather than construction exercise in the ratio of at least 9:1.

THE HOOVER DAM

The mighty Colorado River drains a vast area of North America. Rising high in the wilderness of Wyoming it collects tributaries on its way to the sea, in the process digging for itself enor

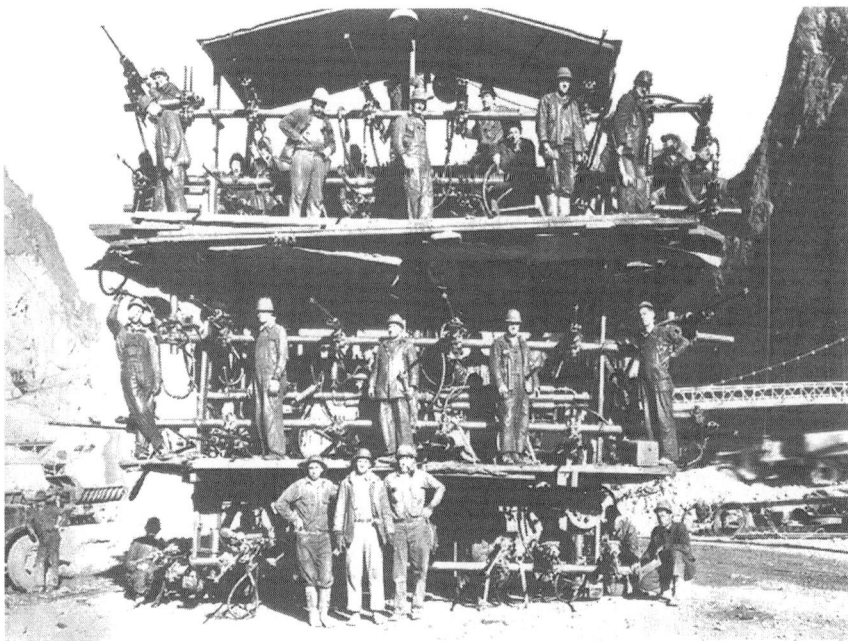

Workers on a huge portable rig used for drilling the tunnels to divert the Colorado River during the construction of the Hoover Dam. Note the big power chisels, or pneumatic drills, mounted on stands, needed to cut into the rocks. Attempting to do it just by hand would not have been considered and, by extension, had those tools not been available, the dam would never have been built.

mous canyons such as Nevada's Grand Canyon, one of the great natural wonders of the world. From here it gathers pace before plunging through Black Mountain Canyon, after which it meanders through Arizona and Mexico before discharging into the Gulf of California and then into the Pacific. Taking with it most of the water needed to irrigate large tracks of the Western Seaboard.

By the twenties California was a rapidly expanding part of the States and needed, in ever growing quantities, both fresh water and electricity. At the height of the Depression, a decision was made to dam the Black Mountain Canyon at Boulder and so construct a massive fresh water lake, while also generating a huge amount of Hydro Electricity to be distributed across Nevada, Arizona, California and Northern Mexico. President Herbert Hoover eagerly embraced the scheme which was known as the 'Boulder Dam'. President Jimmy Carter in 1977 decreed that the name should be changed for all time to be The 'Hoover Dam'.

As with the Panama Canal it was an obvious good idea at the time whilst subsequent events and years have done nothing to change that opinion.

Initial surveying and the usual preliminaries began in the twenties with actual work starting in 1930. Obviously there were problems, some the same as with Panama, others very different. This time the construction was in the desert which was very arid and temperatures in the canyon rose to an average 120 degrees during the day. The main need now was to have sufficient fresh water to keep the workforce from being dehydrated. 16,000 people worked on the project which involved building a new town – now Boulder City – to house the workforce and again all the same type of ancillary worker.

The first challenge was to build two huge tunnels through the adjoining bedrock so that the river could be safely diverted away from and around the construction site. The canyon walls which are both very steep and extremely high, had to be prepared to key in the concrete and this was done by workers in slings using jack hammers. This was a highly paid, but extremely dangerous exercise. Much excavation work was needed to prepare for the turbine houses and in all about 3 million cubic metres of waste was removed. Using massive dump trucks driving up winding roads this was removed from the canyon to be dumped away in the desert.

When construction proper began, the topography helped enormously. A huge bridge like gantry was built to span the canyon and, by using a mixture of ropes, wires and pulleys, buckets of ready mixed concrete would be mixed at the top and then lowered down to the workings. Each bucket held about 8 cubic yards – about the same as a normal Ready Mix lorry seen on the roads today – and this was tipped into a pre formed mould 50 ft wide by 60ft long by 5ft deep. This was so that the dam could be built up in a series of 5ft thick blocks of concrete. A fairly dry mix was used and so it did not take all that long to dry out. Had they simply tried to pour the lot quickly, it would have taken over a hundred years to dry out. Obviously the concrete was reinforced with steel rods and, as one level of blocks set solid, another was built on top of it in a series of layers until it was finished but, all the time, they were able, without the need for cranes, to keep pouring and mixing from above. While all this was going on the turbine houses were being built, turbines installed and the necessary wiring to carry the electricity immense distances erected. The excavation work was assisted by the use of 8.5 million tons of dynamite. In total they used 2.456 million cubic metres of concrete on the project.

Since the war technology had marched on somewhat. We now had both petrol and diesel power rendering the huge steam shovels obsolete. These were replaced by big earth movers, diggers and drag lines that could move about on tracks making it so much simpler to remove waste. Huge dump trucks would then get rid of it. Surveying equipment had improved, we now had typewriters plus the telephone making communication so much simpler while the supply on site of such things as steel and hardwoods was taken for granted. They were digging through sandstone which is consistently hard but the use of dynamite rendered its removal a very simple matter. They were still a good fifty years ahead of the micro chip era and so all calculations were still being done using a slide rule. As with the Panama project, they had full access to and knowledge of the calculus, trigonometry, algebra and geometry as well as up to date knowledge of the Theory of Machines, Fluid technology and the principals of heat engines. Huge drawing offices meant everything could be drawn out to the last detail and every calculation made, checked and double checked.

It was a massive operation that was finished in 1935 when new President F D Roosevelt formerly declared it open. This project is a more or less 50/50 split between being a muck shifting exercise and a construction one.

THE CHANNEL TUNNEL

Not since the melting of the ice about 10,000BC when the sea waters rose, has it been possible to cross the English Channel [or La Manche to the French] on foot. The straights of Dover are not deep but in all our recorded history, we have needed a boat to make the crossing. It is one of the world's busiest seaways both lengthways to and from the main ports of Europe, and across with a steady flow of ferries and hovercrafts carrying large numbers to and from Europe and the UK. It has been a dream of politicians from both sides for years to be able to cross, either by bridge or by tunnel, no matter what the weather was doing. Arguments against a series of bridges were mainly that they would be equally susceptible to the prevailing winds and so, after years of negotiation and planning, a tunnel was agreed and work began in 1987. The grand idea being that, as well as taking cars and freight, it would eventually be possible to get on a train in Glasgow, Edinburgh or Bristol and get off again in Madrid, Rome or Istanbul. The only obstacles to this are lack of high speed lines in the UK, and the infuriating necessity to have to change trains in London. To a certain extent one also has to change trains in Paris, Lille and Brussels.

It was, and still is, a brilliant concept made possible by Civil Engineering advances during the 20th century, even though the basic cutting method was actually pioneered in the early 19th century by Brunel when digging the Thames tunnel. For the Channel they could dig much deeper than could Brunel but they still had the same problem of a possible inundation should they hit a layer of thinner and porous chalk. Chalk rates at 3 on the *Mohs Scale,* one of the softest of all rocks. They built not one but three tunnels, one for each direction and a service plus escape tunnel in the middle should anything go wrong. The Service Tunnel came first using huge boring machines that advanced a total of 130 metres each week per tunnel. That is ten metres per day at each face. As the boring machine advanced, behind it ready made concrete rings were put in place and sealed so that only a fraction of the excavated rock was ever left exposed and at risk. Brunel had an army of bricklayers following his machine which achieved the same result. Huge Tungsten Carbide cutters chopped away at the Channel chalk but Brunel's men only had hand tools. Waste under the Channel was removed by rail through the Service tunnel simultaneously to either side with the French tipping it into the sea, the British building big sea walls and tipped behind them. Progress through the tunnel was measured by the latest Laser technology so that when the day came for the opposite excavations to meet under mid Channel, they were more or less exactly in the right place.

The Drawing office was now a highly sophisticated computer which could transfer geological reports into mathematical calculations meaning that for every metre travelled, they knew exactly what to expect and be able to allow for it. As well as the 11 boring machines used, they had access to the latest pneumatic drills, sophisticated drag lines, dump trucks and planing machines. The concrete rings were pre-cast in pieces, set in place then grouted to seal them. Other concrete for the two huge terminals in both countries was mixed on the spot to build the various platforms and ancillary buildings needed for a modern terminal. High speed rails of high quality steel were laid in each tunnel so that, by the time it opened in 1994 there was a total of 153 kilometres of tunnel and rail. 13,000 people were involved and they moved a total of 7.285 million cubic metres of chalk. Add to that another 3 million cubic metres of concrete poured and we have a project involving the moving of over 10 million cubic metres of material.

There were no problems about housing the workforce, hospitals, schools etc, since the whole project was carried out in an already highly developed environment on both sides of the Channel. Apart from diverting some railway lines and building some motorway access points, the entire infrastructure was more or less in place. The 13,000 involved were all to do with actual construction with few, if any, supernumeraries.

It was opened in 1994 by Her Majesty, The Queen and President Mitterand of France. It had taken seven years of actual construction and was a 60/40 muck shifting to construction split.

So here we have a comparison of how three massive modern day projects were carried out since the advent of mechanised earth moving. The only bridge between today and the works in ancient times was Brunel. His boring machine was lucky to do one foot in a day meaning that having six going continually he may do 2 metres a week. At this speed it would have taken 1,471 years just to dig it out and line it. Because of space he could not increase the man power which shows just how technology has progressed in 150 years. And this begins to put the construction of the Pyramids into some sort of context.

Using less sophisticated methods, the Hoover Dam was a 50/50 split moving 6.2m cubic metres of material and involving 16,000 people over 5 years. Of all the projects this was the easiest to do.

Not long after Brunel they began the Panama Canal which involved moving a massive 180 million cubic metres of material by 39,000 people over 37 years. This was a 95/5 split with just the Culebra Cut being the equivalent of the others.

The four Great Pyramids of Giza were built using 6.093 million cubic metres of a mixture of Limestone and Granite. When, why, by whom, how many involved and over what period of time? These are big questions. Does anyone have the answers?

The next chapter will look at this in detail.

11

THE GIZA PYRAMIDS – MISSION IMPOSSIBLE?

The smaller of the three pyramids of Giza. Note the sizes of the people in the foreground and the exterior coating of granite. We look carefully at just why this was considered necessary later on.

Before we look carefully at the Egyptian, rather than Mayan – or any other, pyramids I would just like to explain the various parameters within which I work. As I said in the Foreword, I am an engineer, not a graduate academic, and I look at everything through the eyes of an engineer. I wouldn't claim to be an unimpeachable 'expert' in either archaeology or civil engineering but neither am I an uninformed 'amateur' either. The one thing that I have learned more than anything else during my fifty year business career is that nothing in the way of ideas should be dismissed as impossible. Not one single thing, no matter how ludicrous or far-fetched in the orbits of technology, astronomy, time travel, electronics or ideas should be dismissed. I consider everything before coming to a conclusion and even then, if subsequent results prove me wrong – which has happened more than once – I simply look at it again and come to a different, but by no means definitive, one. When they built the first railways, the 'experts' said that no one could survive travelling above 30 mph, an iron ship must sink and it would never be possible for a 'heavier than air' device to fly. At the turn of the 19th/20th centuries, there was even an attempt in the British Parliament to abolish the Patent Office on the basis that there was nothing left to invent. In my last year in the sixth form at Leeds Grammar School in 1953, the senior Physics master told the class quite categorically that there would never be enough power available to send a rocket out of earth's gravity.

Years later in the late seventies my cousin died in Brazil. I was his executor and had to book telephone calls many days in advance to speak to people out there. They were what were known as 'person to person' calls where if you didn't get to speak to the correct person, you didn't pay the massive telephone bill. My calls were pre-booked in advance through an exchange in New York and that was cutting edge telephonic technology in 1977. How could anyone in those days have anticipated the enormous impact of the simple microchip and the mobile phone of today; the decimation in a quarter of a century of much of the manufacturing base of the West and the incredible advances in air travel shrinking the world so that now no one is more than about a day away from anyone else?

For my mother, who died at 99 in 2006, it was more of a mystery. She saw virtually the birth and maturing of the motor car, aeroplane, electricity, telephones, world travel and the electronic and the nuclear ages. Her mother, my grandmother, never saw a house with electricity. My paternal grandfather served in Queen Victoria's navy on ships that still had muzzle loading guns through gun ports on the ship. Add to that the eradication of smallpox, diphtheria, polio and tuberculosis to be replaced by AIDS, cancer, dementia and heart disease. Plus anaesthetics and artificial insemination as well, all of which were monumental strides in the progress of mankind. And it all happened in just one lifetime. What will the next century produce if we carry on at this pace? I rule nothing out. Not one single thing. No thought, no matter how absurd or how far in the realms of present day Science Fiction or 'pseudo-science', do I rule out. As this is being written, my daughters-in-law have both recently had babies. Just what will my grandchildren have to look back on if they attain anything near my mother's age? Had I been able to suggest to my own grandparents, the inventions and discoveries that have occurred in my lifetime, they would have thought me quite mad. I feel sure that some who may be reading this now, about my own ideas of what may happen in the lives of my own grandchildren, will think that of me. Those picking up dusty volumes fifty years hence will have a different idea.

You have read my chapter on waves. I see huge progress here with receivers being built to decipher those hidden intangible waves now so widely derided. I see space travel for mankind becoming freely available with methods of transportation now only seen in Space Fiction. I see us conquering that last great obstacle to science, the Fourth Dimension – namely Time itself. All pipe dreams as this is being written, but far from being impossible.

Having said that, there are other basic rules of physics that cannot be either broken or varied. Rub two soft items together and they will wear out as will two hard ones. A soft and hard together, lubricated, will go on forever. You cannot cut steel with butter but steel will cut butter. You can never cut a hard substance with other than a harder one. A softer one will not touch it. Heat will only travel from a hot body to a cold one, never the other way round. A moving body will carry on in a straight, or rotational line until an external force changes it. Liquids will always find their own level. In order to do any work on circles, you must understand and have a working knowledge of the constant *pi*. To construct perfect right angles in large projects the *3, 4, 5 triangle* must be understood. This is the Pythagoras theorem that, in a right angled triangle, the square on the hypotenuse is equal to the sum of the squares on the other two sides. Also knowledge of the principals of the *30, 60, 90*, the *equilateral* and the *equiangular* ones would help. All these constants you learn early on at school and were first promulgated over the years from the Greeks onwards. However, it must be said that Greeks always claimed that they, in turn, had learned a lot from Ancient Egyptian writings. To make maps and to do any type of surveying, the principals of trigonometry must be understood. You cannot make a map or lay out a building site without recourse to some type of trigonometry.

There are things of which I am suspicious, the first being coincidences. To a certain extent I will accept two coincidental happenings as just random occurrences. Three I will not. My golden rule here is when driving a car. Most times my journey is without incident but there are occasions when, within a short distance, there is a close call. This would always be the other driver's fault. Then there will be a second which makes me shake the head. Coincidence, not my fault again but if there is a third one then they were all my fault and I must concentrate before I have a serious accident.

The other thing that makes me suspicious is the round number. Again I give you an example. As we go through life a lot of money passes through our hands, usually equally in and out. We are called on to pay our bills on a daily basis. I buy a paper that costs 55 pence, I fill up with petrol and the credit card will show £54.97. A visit to the supermarket may cost £87.34, the electric bill may be £98.38, the mortgage £376.54 and so on. Hardly ever will you pay a bill [unless it is contrived to be so] of exactly £50, exactly £100, £1000, £5000 and so on. If I see a bank statement with lots of these round figures on it my first thought is that there is a fiddle somewhere. Someone is laundering a lot of money and, in the past, I have always been right.

It is the same with measurements. If a series of measurements or quantities, added, subtracted, multiplied or divided result in an exact round number, or even a mathematically significant one such as 'pi', I always go back to the round number and try to work out why that was the starting point, the others being convenient pointers.

For this exercise, and this subject, the one thing above all else that was just as relevant back in the year dot when man began to work, rather than just stack, stones, is the difficulty in so doing.

Beginning with the humble flint, through extracting the stones of Stonehenge, carving jade in China and working the massive granite pieces in Egypt, right through to tunnelling through the Rockies, the Alps and the English Channel, the problems were identical. There was and is no difference. To hew a narrow passage through limestone bedrock was the same then as it is now. They did it for all to see. No one is arguing about that. All I question are the three big ones of 'how', then 'when' and, most of all every time, 'why'?

And so it is with these reservations, but an otherwise totally open mind, that I look at the four Great Pyramids of Egypt. I do not ignore what was done in the rest of the world, nor what was done across the rest of Egypt, but in the main do exclude them from this volume. I look in some detail at all aspects of what happened in Britain and at Giza at the time in the hope that if any sense can be made there, it will apply equally across the globe. To cover South and Central America in similar detail would require extra volumes and result in much repetition.

As with the other three mighty projects I first ask myself the question 'Why?' There was an obvious need for a canal to shorten the journey to the American west; California needed electricity and water; a tunnel beneath the English Channel made sense but so far, like most of my readers, I have got through life without the need of a large pyramid. So has everyone else for the last four thousand odd years and, if we believe the Egyptologists, apart from a few hundred years or so, so had everyone else beforehand back to the ubiquitous amoeba from which we all presumably descend. So what, during that flick of an eyelid period of world history anything from 4 to 25,000 years ago, occurred to demand the construction of so many different pyramids all over the world?

Make no mistake about this, at the time there were a lot of pyramids being built. All over the world as the map shows and I think we should pause and glance at these before looking in some detail at those in Egypt. Some were crude earthworks of great height like the ones near Xian (home of the Terra Cotta army) in China. There are over a hundred of these from 20ft to 1,000ft high with sides up to 700ft long, some built as extensions to existing mountains but the interesting thing is that most point exactly north/south/east/west. Why? This makes 'The Great White Pyramid' easily the biggest man made structure, dwarfing that of Cheops – and it had a flat top. No one knows how old they all are but, according to Buddhist monks, documents at least 5,000 years old describe them as being very old even then. There is another big one in Bhutan Province called 'The Burma Tibet Pyramid' built in brilliant white limestone that is supposed to glow at night. It is flat topped and the same size as the Great Pyramid. Another has some superb stone work in the centre chamber and this is a step pyramid at Ziban on the Tibet border. The plethora of wonderful buildings in Central America and Mexico is well documented but there are others of a similar style in Guatemala, Belize and El Salvador, going into South America in Bolivia, Peru, and Columbia. All of which use precision cut stones of large, but relatively easily handled, size and without the need for mortar. A new site, previously unknown, has been discovered recently in the Amazon Rain Forest of Brazil. They spread upwards into the United States, particularly along the Mississippi Valley. One in Georgia at Cartersville is built very near to a large deposit of a very special ore – Limonite. What is so special about Limonite is that it is used extensively as radiation shielding for atomic bomb tests, nuclear reactors and in the space industry. It is what gives Mars its red colour. A coincidence or not?

But what about the identical ones, with a flat roof and perfect stonework, on Tenerife? These are obviously pre Columbian and were excavated by no less an authority than Thor Heyerdahl. Who built them, when and why? Back in North Africa, go down the Nile to between the 5th and 6th Cataracts into Nubia and we find about 180 pyramids with very steep sides of 68 degrees, 40 to 50 metres high and with bases about 51 – 52 metres. Here the coincidence is that they could have been built by the same chap as in Tenerife. They use perfectly cut coursed oblong stones – not very big - with corners of raised band masonry, but all the stones have been cut to the exact slope – in two directions. We need advanced geometry [or a good computer] to work that one out. Moving across the Mediterranean there are 16 small pyramids in Greece, little bigger than a room, thought to be observation towers and to pre- date Egypt.

Pravda reported in January 1999 that Russian scientists had discovered several ancient pyramids, 15 metres high with smooth sides, in Uzbekistan near to Samarkand. They said they were at least 2,700 years old. Pyramids exist in Germany where they are known as 'Cairns', the biggest being the Cairn of Barnenez, whilst a satellite picture has identified three in Italy, totally overgrown but, significantly, laid out to exactly mirror the belt of Orion. As, of course, do the three pyramids at Giza. Across the channel and into Ireland near to Drogheda is a large concentration of pre historic stones. These use the same design as the Egyptian ones and one has a horizontal passage at ground level, 18 metres long where, at dawn

Perfectly symmetrical pyramids in Nubia. Note the corners. If built of brick, as seems to be the case, these would have needed very big ovens in which to bake them.

on the winter solstice, the sun's rays shine precisely through a small window to illuminate the central chamber. There are no pyramids as such in the UK, the nearest being a perfectly conical mound at Silbury Hill in Wiltshire. In those days it was even harder to create a perfect circle as the base than a perfect square.

145

This one is 540 ft in diameter rising to a flat top at 128 ft and contains nearly 350,000 cubic metres of chalk and earth. Built as a step pyramid, it has eroded so that it now appears to have flat sides. There are numerous earthworks or 'tumuli' in Britain, most built over the years for defensive or religious purposes, but there are three near to York which again, incredibly, mirror the belt of Orion. And you know I don't believe in coincidences.

In Japan there is a superbly carved stone pyramid, 15ft square by 8ft high that looks like a miniature Great Pyramid and has perfect corners, is extremely smooth and that has been hewn out of one single block of grey granite. This is an incredible feat for Stone Age man. Nearby is a similar one with another some way away. All laid out in some pre-destined formation that so far no one has iden

The Pyramid of the Sun in Mexico. Again note the stone work on the corners and how they are so similar to those in Nubia.

tified. Under the sea, as yet unexcavated, between Japan and Taiwan are dozens of sites, including pyramids, submerged when the ice melted. By definition they had to be built pre-8,000BC. Moving down to Australia at Gympie near Brisbane are the remains of a 100ft tall step pyramid built, according to Aboriginal tradition, by brown skinned, blue eyed and blond haired beings who had come from Orion. Another structure, twice this size has been found in New South Wales, there are five identical ones in New Guinea whilst Magnetic Island, off the coast of Australia in the Pacific has one accompanied by a sphinx. Most interesting of all is one in Candi Sukuh in Java that is an exact replica of those in Mexico. Right down to having a twin head serpent God called Quetzalcoatl - as had the Mayans.

I have even come across a web site that has identified a series of perfect pyramids on Mars but, until we can actually go and see them, I think it better to discount them from this work. One remarkable theory is that these have yet to be built when the planet is colonized, their image being the result of a time aberration. A rather big hmmmmm... there I would think.

The ziggurat on Tahiti as drawn by one of Cook's artists in the 18th century. The natives whom he met there were still very much in the Stone Age, quite incapable of constructing anything like this. So who did, when and why once again? No European had ever been to Tahiti before.

And so over a period of time that I estimate to be of no more than 1000 years in duration, all over the world people needed pyramids, lots of them and very big as well. Most were cut and built with a precision that is envied to this day. Few were other

147

than solid. They were all in places where the previous biggest building was a mud hut and all subsequent buildings being little better.

The question remains. Why????

Conventional wisdom is unanimous on this. They were all built as graves for leaders. This may be so and I am quite happy to accept that the Giza pyramids were used as mausoleums for three Pharaohs. But I don't think that they actually built them. I think they were there, and had been for a very long time. Cheops and family merely used them at the time. What about the ones in Nubia? There were 180 of them. Were they all tombs and who were the masons who cut those stones with such accuracy? They could not do that without carefully calculated drawings showing a perfect rectangle to the front that, on some stones, sloped in two different planes. This was a truly amazing feat for a race barely out of the Stone Age. Were they all for the Kings, over a millennia, since not one is significantly bigger than the rest?

The ziggurat on Teneriffe is stepped like Mexico and Tahiti with corners similar to
Nubia and Mexico. All the buildings show perfect symmetry.

Why only the few on Tenerife? And how was it that they could be using the building techniques of Nubia to the designs of those in Mexico, and the one in Tahiti? Was this a one off grave for the leader at the time and, if so,from where did he get the idea? In China there are enormous earth mounds supposedly used as tombs for the Emperor about 500BC. But where did he get the idea from, use it for a time and then discard it, never to be used again? The Terracotta Army was built in an excavated pit, not entombed in a pyramid.

The pyramids near Samarkand in present day Uzbekistan that the Russians have discovered are a series of very smooth sided ones that are not very big. They offer no opinion as to their purpose, date or construction but present day evidence indicates that a smooth side may be significant. The ones in Greece are relatively small using random small stones that could easily be handled by one man and, whilst nowhere near as significant as the others, must have been built for some purpose.

And this is the ongoing problem. There are just so many of them, with too many similarities, but spread over such huge distances at a time when it would have been impossible for any simple land based race to have made it on foot or with pack horse. Until Marco Polo in the 13th century AD, no one is recorded as having walked from Europe to China and back. It would be possible to reach Samarkand and return to Egypt but Tenerife? It is just too much of a coincidence to believe that someone on the island, as with the rest of Western Europe, still on the edge of the Stone Age, should use the exact building techniques of someone two thousand miles up the Nile, but to the design of someone else, many more thousands of miles away, in Central America. After which they then build nothing else for thousands of years.

The other mystery is that there are so many of them dotted all over the world all of the same basic four side shape – never triangular – and so many have the same alignment of being exactly north/south/east/west. There are no other shapes. Only one built a cone, Silbury Hill, not necessarily to be buried in, but no convenient large cubes – always a four sided pyramid with or without a pointed top. And they got them so right. Virtually every one is a perfect pyramid with the capping stone over the dead centre and all, but for some well documented exceptions in Egypt, were so well built that they survive intact today.

Looking carefully at the Giza complex, the Great Pyramid in particular, there are some interesting anomalies. If we accept conventional wisdom that Cheops, during his lifetime, conceived and had this one built and that it was finished before his death, surely he would have assembled a veritable hoard of treasures to accompany him in the afterlife? And he would have needed a considerable volume of space in which to put it all. You only have to look at the incredible quantity of relics that came from Tutankhamen and the space he needed to store them. And he only reigned a few years before dying in his teens. The other plundered, excavated tombs of Upper Egypt all indicate vast storage areas, something that could easily have been accommodated in all three Giza pyramids when building from scratch. But they didn't.

Inside the Cheops pyramid is a descending passage 350ft long that ends in an unfinished chamber 90 ft underground. And this is exactly under dead centre of the pyramid, the top of which is 600ft above it. But this passage was a mere 3ft 4inches wide and only 3ft 9inches high making it impossible to transport anything large such as a sarcophagus or the huge furnishings from the later ones at Karnak. Yet the roof is superbly carved in an inverted 'U' shape when it would have been just as easy to cover with flat slabs. Experts think that Cheops changed his mind before this was finished but my feeling is that there could be a totally different reason.

Everything above ground level was put there during construction; all below had to be done by digging out and, without mechanisation of any sort. Just using copper, wood and heavier stone hand tools, only ONE man could work on the face at any one time. No 'ifs' or 'buts', just one man with one small copper hammer, chisel or what have you, had to crouch there and dig that shaft to end up exactly square through solid limestone for 350 ft. How and why???? And what, without the knowledge of even basic geometry or trigonometry, was the method of deduction to work out the angle to end up under dead centre? Look again at the rig for drilling the Hoover Dam tunnels, the huge steam shovels of Panama and the laser guided sophistication under the English Channel. One very small man, or child, one chisel, one bucket and one small shovel to remove the waste. Look at any metre square table in your church hall. That is the size of the tunnel at 26 degrees. Could you dig in that space? Just how could he both see and breathe in such confines?

There is a a 19th century drawing of children working in a shaft of the same dimensions as on the pyramid. The coal is being pushed in a wheeled cart, on rails, on the level and two children struggle to move it on the level ground. Only one child can stand in a position to work. If you now turn that into a 26 degree angle, remove the wheels and rails and you will see the problem.

Back to the Great Pyramid, off this downward shaft is the main upward one, the Grand Gallery, that ends, above ground, in the King's burial chamber. This is relatively small for such an edifice but, nevertheless, carries a large granite 'sarcophagus'. Off the sloping upward shaft there is a smaller horizontal one ending in more or less the mathematical centre of the pyramid, again exactly under the centre line. From this small chamber are diagonal small shafts that are blocked off just before they penetrate the outer casing. From the burial chamber are two shafts, almost parallel with the blocked off ones but these penetrate the casing at more or less the same height on the North and South faces. Now we have a fully ventilated burial chamber, something totally unique in funereal history. All walled and roofed in granite. So what did Cheops do with his treasure? He built a great big hole away from the pyramid into which he left his solar boat to take him, with the rest of his treasures, through the underworld of the night. It is this single fact, above all others, that makes me think and believe that he merely hijacked the pyramid rather than building one for himself.

The ratio of the total perimeter to the height is exactly the equivalent of 2 x *pi* or 6.248. And the angles of ascent throughout, 26 degrees, are exactly half the angle of the exterior which is almost 52 degrees. The main centre corridor is of such highly polished limestone that it is impossible to stand without some sort of ladder which, of course, they use today. Round numbers?????

Next we look at the second pyramid of Chefren which again is a massive structure into which, at the design stage, any types of chamber could have been built. But they were not. There are two entrances. The first gives a burial chamber at the end of a long passage that is below ground but the passage continues up again to another chamber at ground level in the exact centre of the pyramid. There is a second entrance to this. Above ground there appears to be nothing but solid masonry. The shaft, which penetrates the pyramid itself some 50 ft above ground level, runs for 200ft and is lined with both polished granite and limestone. The angle is steep at nearly 27 degrees – too steep to climb easily – and leads to what is assumed to be the burial chamber. In it is a small 'sarcophagus' 6ft in length with sides between 20 and 24 inches high and carved from red granite. There is no evidence of it ever being used which again is strange. For what I ask, if it was only to hold a mummified body? There is nowhere near enough space to store any treasure for the afterlife. And so far none has been found buried nearby. Curious if nothing else. It was then encased in smooth alabaster, since removed for building work in Cairo. The entire underground excavations must have been completed before they could begin the actual pyramid which suggests that what was left below was exactly what was intended to be left there. They would not have abandoned the underground workings and then gone to the trouble of building a massive and solid pyramid above, followed by repeating the exercise with a third pyramid.

The third pyramid of Mykerinus has its entrance in the north wall with a sloping shaft at nearly 27 degrees. Again it is exactly north/south, again extremely small and with walls and ceilings lined with rectangular well fitted limestone and granite blocks. After 70ft it levels off in the middle where there is an antechamber. We then come to a large 'burial' chamber, 30 x 15 x 15ft with a vertical shaft downwards into a second 'burial' chamber below. All this was excavated from the limestone bedrock – a feat in itself given the tools available at the time. The final chamber is

12 ft long, 8 ft wide and 12 ft high and it is lined in chocolate coloured granite throughout with the roof ones forming a dome shape. Amazing, and again little if any room to store the treasure, let alone a solar boat. Again no treasure has been found buried nearby. This chamber may be a natural underground cavern which its roof suggests it could be. It was intended that the entire exterior was to be encased in smooth blocks of granite, a few courses of which survive.

Now we cross the desert to the south for nearly ten miles to Darfur where we find the magnificent Red pyramid only just that bit smaller than the one of Cheops. It has an opening 94ft above ground with a shaft that slopes down at again 27 degrees for 206ft. This passage way measures just 3ft x 4ft for its entire length. This leads to the first chamber which is 40 feet high and is shaped as a triangle with 11 courses of perfectly cut granite, each overlapping the one underneath by the identical amount before meeting at the top. From here the passage continues to a second chamber, more or less dead centre in the pyramid but again with the identical granite ceiling. 25 feet above floor level in this chamber is the perfectly squared entrance to a third chamber 14 feet x 27 feet but with the same ceiling at a height of 50 feet. The access shaft to this chamber has perfect right angled corners throughout and is of constant width. And this edifice was apparently built about twenty years earlier for Snedfu who came before Cheops. These dates are open to question, but it is not in dispute that all four must have been going up simultaneously. Unlike the other three this has an exterior angle of 43 degrees, exactly the same as the Pyramid of the Sun in Mexico. The Giza pyramids mirror Orion's belt, add in the Red Pyramid and you find either Betelgeuse or Rigel in the same constellation. Interesting to say the least.

So here we have the four greatest buildings on earth at the time, not one of which was in any way suitable for its supposed purpose. This for the simple reason that it would have been impossible to contain all but a fraction of the paraphernalia that an Egyptian monarch would have demanded for his life in the hereafter. Not only that but you would have thought that having got it wrong on the first one, the mistake would have been rectified on the subsequent ones. But it wasn't. There was no effort made to vary the design except for the one thing. Three of the pyramids went down to the chambers, only the one went up and with some deliberation at that. For this single reason I suggest that the building order be changed so that the one supposed to be for Mykerinus came first, then the one ascribed to Chefren followed by the Red one with the mighty one of Cheops possibly the last of all from that era. I give my reasons later on.

Then many thousands of years later along comes Dozer who proceeds to build his stepped pyramid but he has neither the skills nor technology and it remains a very poor replica. The principal difference being that the stone working skills were no longer there. Another effort was made with what is known as the Bent pyramid since this suffered a collapse in one corner during construction leaving the edifice seen today.

Let us just ponder for a moment and consider just the one long and narrow shaft that is 350 ft in length and under 4ft square. Or one 206ft long which is 3ft wide by 4ft high. Both descend at an angle of 26 degrees, are perfectly straight and have perfect square corners throughout. They were excavated from solid limestone which is hard. Not as hard as granite, but hard nevertheless. Certainly harder than the only metals of copper and gold that were known at the time if, indeed they actually built them c2,900 – 2,600BC. Because of the size alone, only one child or very small man could work on these at a time plus others removing the waste from above. The mason must stop every few minutes to fill a bucket that would then be hauled to the surface. Of course people were smaller which helps but against that they would not have the same strength as a bigger person later on. Having said that, all the mummies seem to show people not that much different to a modern day Egyptian. Now my other hobbyhorse is modern day slavery of which there is a lot about. I know because I wrote the award winning book, 'World Slavery – The Bigger Picture', which tells the full story. It is not for the faint hearted.

There are numerous videos on the internet about this and I have just been watching some children extracting ore in the Congo.

They were using modern day lump hammers and large cold steel chisels, and were slowly picking away in a very ragged mine. They were taking out minerals that are sold to the electronics industry to make computers, mobile phones, etc, and all are working as slaves. Yes, vital elements of your must have new phone have come from children working in misery as slaves. If done only by hand, a long passage of 350ft could only have been done by similar children at the time. The big differences in this are that the walls of the mine are both rough and random, the angles and direction are the same and the children can stand up. The 350ft shaft is smooth, exactly even and with a constant angle of descent. Using the 'high tec' lump hammer and chisels of today it is obvious that progress is very slow, and if I am extremely generous in my estimation I would say that similar progress in ancient times would be no more than the equivalent of about 2 inches per day - if we are lucky. That is assuming that the chisel is hard enough to cut the rock. Copper is not. Bronze maybe if annealed. In order to achieve that, the child must extract about 320 lbs of stone per day. He is kneeling in what would be more or less total darkness and the supply of fresh air to breath would be short indeed. He must also rely on a constant supply of fresh, clean water, plus some salt, to keep him from dying from dehydration. 320 lbs of stone is the equivalent of 7.5 full suitcases that you would take on holiday. That is a lot of stone to be cut out and removed by one child at a time. Or a very small man. Even a series of them working in relays. I know the problems from my own experience of putting fencing poles into even a limestone bedrock. It is far from easy and my back still aches many years later.

But let us stick to this hypothetical scenario which may or may not be correct. Let us assume that the child did produce this quantity using the copper tools of the day and he progresses at 2 inches of perfectly cut tunnel each time. Just to cut this one tunnel alone would take 2,160 days or 5.75 years!!!!

This was nowhere near being the total amount of the excavations on the four pyramids. It was the tip of the iceberg in fact. In order to extract the necessary bedrock under the Red pyramid between 750 and 1,000 tons of limestone had to be extracted, all by using no more than simple copper chisels. Allowance must be made for natural underground chambers but surely they would only be come across by chance since we are many millennia away from being able to do a seismic survey? Again in the long tunnel only one man could work at a time and this alone would take at least six years to do. Extracting 1000 tons using no more than a simple steel chisel would take 200 man years alone. It could never have been done using a copper one. **Never, impossible**. Allow six years to dig the tunnel after which more men could be employed and you are still left with a prodigious period of time. And that is using steel that they did not have. Significantly they were thousands of years away from the discovery of dynamite or any type of explosive. Copper would hardly touch limestone, if at all. With granite there would be no chance. On the Mohs Scale copper registers in at 3 which is the same as chalk but softer than limestone, however, according to accepted wisdom, that is what they had and that is what they used. Iron registers at 4 – 5, steel is 4.5, hardened steel 7.5 – 8 with fine limestone around 3.5 and granite at 7. Copper at best comes in at only 3. Therefore it must be accepted that to conduct building and mining work on this prodigious scale, tools very much harder than any registering less than between 7 and 10 must have been used. And they would need to be metal since using rock on rock would cause both to shatter because both would be very brittle. And so, in order to even begin this enterprise, they had to have at their disposal a massive supply of something very hard, malleable and some method of turning it into tools.

THE MOHS SCALE OF HARDNESS. This has <u>never</u> altered over time.

Hardness	Substance
1	Talc
1.5	Tin, lead, graphite.
2	Gypsum. Chalk.
2.5–3	Gold, silver, copper, aluminium, *limestone.*
3	*Copper,* arsenic.

3.5	Platinum, *bronze.*
4	Iron, nickel.
4–4.5	*Steel.*
5	Tooth enamel.
5.5	Cobalt, glass.
6	Titanium.
6–7	Opal, quartz [fused].
7	Quartz, *granite.*
7.5–8	Emerald, *hardened steel,* tungsten
8	Topaz.
8.5	Chromium.
9	*Tungsten carbide. Diorite.*
9–9.5	Titanium carbide.
9.5–10	Boron.
10	Diamond.

Looking at pictures of the Mykerinus 'burial' chamber that is lined with granite, it is obvious that this is the roof of a natural chamber in the rock. If so, we must ask how they knew that it was there in the first place, how they were able to calculate its depth and so work out the exact angle of descent, and then ponder on the fact that the pyramid above was built using that as the dead centre point, with all the other pyramids set out to some exact and pre-determined mathematical positions and astronomical layout? And all done with no accurate means of measuring, and no adequate tools for the purpose. And only to bury three kings, now long dead and their treasure being quickly looted. Think about that as I return to my original parameters. I say that if the end result is some interesting mathematical constant or, in this case the alignment with Orion as well, just what was the prime object of designing, and then building, these enormous edifices? They must have begun with the knowledge that down there, in that exact spot, was a natural chamber that could be used to build a granite lined chamber just 12ft x 8ft in area. After which the enormous area must be surveyed to a bewildering accuracy with other downward shafts being excavated in, again, the exact and perfect spots.

One suggestion is that they did know that the hollow chamber was there, how we will never know, and dug their long tunnel only to end up above it. So they had to dig down vertically to the depth and then horizontally to come in from the side. Having done that it was prepared to accept massive pieces of granite with which to line it, and this all having to be done before adding the pyramid above.

And so we must return to the question 'Why'? Why go to all that trouble underground only to cover it in a solid amount of rock in the shape of a perfect pyramid? We simply do not know but almost certainly it had nothing to do with burial rights. I give my thoughts later in the book.

Now we ask the next profound questions of 'When and by whom?'

If what I say above is to make any sense at all, most of this work must have been done in a different time to the ones of which we are aware. And with the use of a totally different technology. Conventional thinking believes that mankind emerged from the Stone Age around 3,500BC in the Nile Valley but this is contradicted by the Bible that talks of events and places much older. What is indisputable is that the Temple of Solomon in Jerusalem, the remnants of which are now the Western or 'Wailing' Wall, was built around 516BC. In other words contemporary with the Greeks and well after the golden age of Egypt had fizzled out. But Jericho was built around 8,000BC, using skilled masons who could lay coursed stone work. I find no reason to doubt this when put into the context of the Old Testament but, if true, it means that there were skilled masons about in Palestine for a very long time who would have learned their trade from earlier craftsmen. Whilst in Egypt all was over, more or less forever, when they built Solomon's temple, it was still thousands of years after the time when someone had built Jericho. The Freemasons of today see Solomon's builders as their own forebears. What were these incredible builders and their descendents doing during those 7,500 years? What is more they were also able to work fairly large lumps of rock that would have been impossible to lift by hand for the simple reason that you could not get enough lifting hands around the blocks. So, to do the building, they must have been able to move the blocks both vertically and horizontally at the same time. Having said that, the supply of superior quality timber available in the Levant was much better than in Egypt.

Going back to the pyramids they also were built with huge stones, many times larger than the ones used in Solomon's Temple and again, that would not be possible to lift with human hands since it was not possible to get sufficient hands on them. It is a fact that the average man today, used to handling heavy weights, would struggle to keep on lifting much over 30 to 35lbs all day and every day. Baggage allowance on airlines these days is seldom more than 44lbs which is a big and heavy suitcase. Just how many of those could be carried all day in the desert heat of Egypt? Since each block weighed 2.5 tons it would need at least 160 strong men just to raise it off the ground. And again don't forget that people were smaller in those days.

From whom did those builders at the time of Solomon learn their trade? More to the point, where did the builders of Jericho learn their undoubted skills? Technology soon gets lost, especially when you have no means of simple written communication. As this is being written we are less than one generation away from losing the skills to deep mine coal in the UK. But we have these enormous gaps in time between the building – in that tiny area of the earth's surface – of many of the world's biggest buildings. That is like saying that today we will build from scratch the Panama Canal using the latest technology, that technology being last used when they built the temple of Solomon. And during that time our technological achievements have been limited to mounting a simple irrigation device to a water buffalo and the construction of a lot of mud huts.

Sorry, but I don't buy it. We must go back to the 'Bulge' which could have occurred anything between the bench mark 3,500 years BC and as much as 20,000 plus years earlier. It is my contention that ALL the pyramid type structures all over the world were built by, or by descendents of, the same people over a comparative narrow window of no more than 1000 years. Probably very much less. Yes, it is a sweeping statement that contradicts all contemporary 'expert' thinking and, IF correct, means a lot of text books being re-written. Obviously that will not happen because what follows is not in those text books and so cannot be right!

There are two things that lead me in this direction. The first are the pyramids on Tahiti and in Java which are the big anomalies. As I have made clear, I do not believe in coincidences as a rule but these edifices insist that you accept not one, but two. The design and construction are just too close to those at Meroe in Nubia to be the work of other than more or less the same team, whilst the overall design is too close to those in Mexico, again to be the work of other than that self same team. Our problem being that there are very big oceans separating them all and ships of the period were far from being robust. Certainly not strong enough to cross an unknown ocean to what should have been an equally unknown destination. And then having to take with them an army of stone masons with all their equipment as well. Unless, of course, there was a stepping stone in between which opens up another can of worms to be discussed later. But for what purpose must always be the question.

The second thing that bothers me with conventional thinking is in the writing and drawings of the Egyptian Dynastic periods. Pick up any illustrated book on Ancient Egypt and you will find drawings of everyday life. Virtually everything they did is drawn (or carved into the rock), from knocking seven bells out of an enemy to gathering the harvest and cooking the meal. We see pictures of them dragging a huge statue into place and every trivial thing that made up everyday life. Now building the pyramids must have taken well over 100 years, which is several generations, to build and few families would not have had male members so employed at some time or another. They would have dominated the lives of generations just as the pit dominated the lives of coal miners all over the world for generations. Why then is there little or no reference to these massive constructions in the communications of the day? Equally there is no reference to the mighty Sphinx which would need a big team with small chisels for a very long time. There are a few pictures of men making bricks; there is one showing them trimming a stone in exactly the correct positions that anyone would stand or crouch to trim a stone and it does show them using a chisel, and there is one showing them building out of brick a ramp, for what purpose is not obvious at all. But there is nothing that can be ascribed to a pyramid and all these are dated some 1,300 to 1,500 years after they had built the Giza pyramids. Assuming that they were built c.2900 – 2,600BC.

I think it is for the simple reason that they were there already and, to those alive at the time, always had been. Which takes us back to the questions 'When and by whom?'. I come back to this later but I think it fair to say that not after 3,500BC and possibly not before 25,000BC which is a very large window indeed. We must narrow it down a bit.

The third question is 'How?'

This is the biggest question of them all. Before you can even begin to assess the problem you must have some knowledge of the basic properties of stone and here I would invite my reader to put down the book, take out the car and drive to the nearest building site. Ask the foreman for an off cut which will be Limestone, Sandstone or Millstone Grit. Go to your DIY shop and get a flat cold chisel, a lump hammer and a hacksaw with High Speed Steel blade. Borrow an electric drill but buy a 6mm wood drill bit, the same for metal and the same for stone. And some goggles. With these tools, which are far more than was available in 3,022 BC, I want you to prepare all the sides to be exactly, and I do mean exactly, at right angles to each other, they must be perfectly flat and mirror smooth when finished. You need to finish with a mirror smooth perfect rectangular block. Any over-zealous dints and you go back to the beginning. And I'll allow you just one week to do it.

Good, back to the book and if any reader can honestly tell me that he [or she] actually achieved this then please let me know through my publishers. I would bet for the rest of you, when the back was hurting, bits of stone were flying everywhere and the wretched stuff was splitting in every direction but the one you wanted, you gave up. By then the wood and metal drills will have burned out, the hacksaw a smooth blunt offering and the lump of stone even worse than when you started. If you still need convincing of the problem, please take these self same tools and find a part of the garden where you can expose the bedrock. Into this bedrock I want you to insert a post 6" x 6" to the depth of 12".

The back will be now very much worse since most of your time will have been taken up getting rid of the waste, and all the time the sides of the hole will have run off to some degree. You will be on your knees which will be hurting a lot, you will need to scrape out the waste every few minutes and must keep getting up to stretch the limbs. If it is at all warm you will need a constant supply of drinking water as well. Now, in order to accommodate the post at 6" x 6" at the bottom, it will be at least 12" x 12" at the top. This fact is very significant indeed. And when you've finished you'll only have extracted a fraction of the material that child must have done every day to dig that tunnel. Obviously it should not have been the same child and, going back to my slavery book, there is no real evidence these were actually slaves either. Remember, we are still only considering the one tunnel 350ft x 3.3ft x 3.3ft at the angle of 26 degrees. When you have dug out the vertical hole, try doing it again but at an angle of exactly 26 degrees! No, better forget that one.

My next simple experiment for you to try at home involves wood. Any piece of square section timber, 3" x 3" upwards and another, the same size but round. Now mark on these, using a square, cutting lines on all four sides. They must be exactly square and meet. Using any type of cross cut saw carefully saw down through the two nearest faces. Do not alter the saw cut by turning it over and beginning again but carry on with the one cut until it is finished. In 9 out of ten cases this cut will have run off by the end whilst with the round one, virtually every single one will run off. To get a perfect square every time needs a very good craftsman who has been doing it a long time. Or a strong and powerful circular saw.

The third little experiment to do at home is related to the layout of the pyramids, done – or so we are led to believe – by peoples with no means of writing, measuring nor mathematical calculation. Here I invite the reader to take a sheet of blank A4 paper and using no more than a pencil, ruler and a simple 30/60/90 set square as used by children everywhere, construct first a perfect square and then a perfect hexagon (six sides). You may use a compass as well which means that you have far more technical equipment than was ever available to the pyramid builders. They worked to a virtual zero tolerance and so should you. Just see how many attempts you make before you come up with absolutely perfect results. I will not ask you to then put the finished work along with others into a pattern to match some stars, viewed only with the naked eye, and expect you to get the angles and proportions exactly right. Having done that use your ruler to draw a random four sided shape with two sides being parallel. Now copy it exactly on another sheet of paper with again no discrepancy at all. Not very easy, is it. Now do it in a massive lump of stone!! Then draw out two lines at first 52 degrees and then 26 degrees to each other without using a protractor. Again, far from easy.

Those who dug out the hole for the post will have extracted .5625 cu feet of rock. How long did it take you? 1 hour? 2 hours possibly, and so you worked at the rate of .28 cu feet per hour? That is .0023 tons of rock or 3.374 lbs per hour. If so employed, working all day for 12 hours, you would have extracted 40.5 lbs of rock. If this was the progress of the children digging that one shaft it would have taken all of 472 years!!!! Like us completing today a project begun to bury Henry V111. And they didn't have a steel chisel or a lump hammer made from something harder. Because of the physical constraints due to the section of the tunnel they could never have more than just the one tiny person working at the face at any one time. Because of the tooling that was supposedly used, those 472 years are a very generous estimate!!! And then they must begin the real excavation work which involved extracting and moving over a hundred times more material over not one but four pyramids at the same time. Now do you think that I may have a point? And we have yet to produce one single block for the construction work.

It is important to be aware of these practical problems when you look at the pyramids, wherever they are in the world. For they had these exact problems, but on a far greater physical scale and multiplied in the millions.

Staying in the present day, let us assume that Abdulla the Builder is called to the palace and is asked to tender for the construction of a something totally new. Something that has never been seen before and therefore totally unique. The King has decided that he needs a mausoleum building above ground and he has set his heart on a four sided pyramid and this is the specification:

Height	450 feet
Sides	750 feet

To be built with 2.3million stone blocks each weighing 2.5 tons.

Inside various passages going up and down, one needing excavations in the limestone down to ninety feet but only to be 4ft square. A steep upwards passage to be lined with single pieces of carved and polished granite and limestone between 70 and 80 tons each, and ending in a granite lined chamber in the middle of which is a carved granite sarcophagus. It must be laid out exactly on the North/south/east/west axis and built to a tolerance on the sides of plus or minus 2 centimetres. This is just under one inch, or the thickness of this book. The angle of the exterior must be slightly under 52 degrees and the interior angles to be exactly half this. There are to be zero tolerances everywhere.

Abdulla will look at this before going back to the King to query 'Why the granite?' and the reason that he asks this is because the nearest quarry is at Aswan, many hundred miles up river. Assuming, of course that he is aware of this and that he can easily identify granite as such when compared to other stone in the area. And it is all located well above the First Cataract, or waterfall, on the Nile. Getting dump trucks to carry that amount in one is no problem but he still needs a new infra structure to the quarry from the river with concrete roads and huge cranes at either end. He will need very big barges of at least 300 ton displacement to float the granite down river where, again he will need a purpose built dock and heavy lifting crane near the pyramid. A new metalled road will be needed with similar heavy lifting cranes at the other end. Unfortunately, no crane exists that will lift the final blocks up to the top chamber since this will need an 80 ton lift to a height of about 200 feet at a radius of 350 feet. The biggest available as this is being written will lift 120 tons to 243 feet high but only at a radius of 266 feet. So it must be done with two cranes, one outside and another set inside the construction work.

Also we have a problem in extracting the blocks in one piece. Dynamite may shatter them but only that or something more powerful could separate something so huge from the bedrock. In the 21st century AD there is little call or use for granite in such huge pieces. Modern practice is to blast massive blocks of several hundred tons and then cut them to size using pneumatic drills and pile drivers after which they must be cut to the exact angles and then highly polished to give the smooth straight sides. This COULD be done today using the latest laser guided equipment but it would be incredibly difficult and would take a very long time. Abdulla will go back to the King with his quotes pointing out the difficulties and will query again 'Why granite and why in such enormous lumps?' The same effect could be achieved by other, easier means using limestone available on site. But no. Granite it must be - to that spec. Reasons on a 'Need to know' basis.

Laying out is no problem using the latest laser, seismic and satellite guidance systems and the excavation of the underground will be done with a mixture of dynamite, drills and earth moving machinery. When it is finished a simple carved capping of limestone or granite will cover it up after which it is a simple back filling job up to ground level. A series of cranes on each side will lift the individual blocks into place but it is the creation of the blocks that is a problem. The use of dynamite is precluded by the need for so many that are so big and from limestone. Dynamite would blow it all into little pieces in which case they must be extracted one at a time using pneumatic drills and then be faced using giant tungsten carbide, or diamond, tipped saws. These will need setting in extremely rigid frames to stop them running off. Or they can be faced with computer guided chisels that will peck away until the desired finish can be achieved. Then a series of dump trucks will bring them onto site. If we can produce the stones at the rate of 1,000 a day it will take us just 6.3 years to complete. 300 a day will take 21 years for just the Great Pyramid, 64 years for all four. Just for the Great Pyramid will entail the use of 25,000 men on the blocks alone. For the others being built simultaneously, we need 7 million in total which means either lengthening the time span or increasing production to about 3050 per day. 3,050 limestone blocks being excavated and trimmed to such tolerances every day for twenty years is no more realistic today than it would have been at any time in history. 300 a day and it will take 64 years or more. That is just for the outer blocks, not the elaborate passages or any excavation work.

And this is using the latest equipment available at the start of the 21st century. We need now a very minimum of 25,000 workers on the stones alone plus those working on the granite, the infra structure and the design/management structure. It will be almost doubled when you add the back up teams building housing, hospitals and the essential supply of food and fresh water. In the heat each man will consume at least a gallon of fresh water a day doing manual work, less for the others, plus that used for a shower at the end of the day and for washing his clothes. We need a pumping station and filter beds for a minimum capacity of half a million gallons per day, erecting by the Nile, with an elaborate distribution system, and a team of plumbers erecting stand pipes and taps. This just for the quarry. We haven't begun with the construction yet. And do not forget that the whole area is infested with malaria spreading mosquitoes. There is also the not inconsiderable problem of any sewage entering and contaminating the river. Whilst all this is going on a workforce must be out there producing food and clothing, tools and ropes. Without suitable backup teams, nothing can happen. For the underground work adequate lighting is essential as are pumps to supply a continuous supply of clean air to breathe.

This should put the problem into some sort of context. Go back at least 4,500 years and it becomes an impossibility. To cut out the stones I use 4 men with pneumatic drills that keep lengthening the bit. Starting on the back face, this would be cut first as a long single cut for five or six blocks involving dozens of vertical and parallel holes. When driving along any road anywhere in the western world that has had to cut through a rocky hillside you will see the remains of those holes. Over time they will weather and it will be smooth but for many years the evidence is there for all to see. This is the ONLY way to extract, or leave behind, a pre-determined rock face. Then there would be two men cutting out the short lengths. Underneath there would be another four men (again per block) to under cut from the next one below. When all have finished a very small explosive charge will separate them from the bedrock. A suitable crane then lowers them to the quarry floor from above where they are trimmed using massive band saws of special tungsten carbide steel and so finished exactly square and exactly the right size. They are then transported by lorry to the site [one man per block] where a crane [one man] puts them into position [three men].

Just this exercise alone in 2,500 BC simply could not be done in any sort of reasonable time. On the Great Pyramid alone, to finish in 64 years they needed to quarry, face, transport and erect at least 100 a day. This would be years after the Pharaoh had died. As today, only so many people can work on a given sized block at once and so they must start with the cross cuts, cutting with what they had, which was either a copper, granite or diorite bit tied to the end of a strong piece of wood. They must cut diagonally to give a slope off which the waste could be scraped and this would need to be done after every two or three cuts. The back face would be done at the same time working diagonally from an open end. Then another team would cut away horizontally, which is a very hard and back breaking job, until the block was loose. I will come to Somers Clark later on but he suggests that having cut the side and rear faces from the bedrock, all they did to separate the bottom of the block from the bedrock was to dig out some holes into which wedges were hammered. The wedges were of timber or metal and if those were hammered with lumps of rock hard

167

enough, the block would simply separate along a natural fault line in a perfect straight line. With that I would have serious doubts. I would say that 99 out of a hundred would simply break into anything but a straight line. I have seen pictures of this being done and each time the block has separated unevenly away from the intended plane. Amazingly, in his book, Clark illustrates one such block after it had been extracted in this way and it is a very sorry looking mess indeed.

Using a series of pulleys [which they did not have since they had yet to invent the wheel!] it would then be lifted to the top of the quarry and somehow put down on the ground. From there, in a presumably finished state, another team of at least 80 strong men would drag it along the floor down to the Nile. They must lift it into a boat, cross or simply float it down the Nile, lift it out of the boat again and then drag it the final couple of miles onto site. Another enormous team is fully employed on a muck shifting project of building huge ramps, with solid surfaces of hard stones kept in place by huge walls built from mud bricks, up which the blocks are pulled, before finally being placed in their ultimate resting place. If we allow the 100 per day and are generous and allow just one day for the transport, even though most of the quarries were dotted along the Nile for hundreds of miles, and eight days for extraction, we need a massive 248 men per block per day which is 24,800 men per day on that alone. Plus, as before, the logistical staff, and, on top of all this, the veritable army of several thousands using a bucket and shovel continually building and demolishing the enormous ramps. All of whom need feeding and supplying with adequate amounts of water otherwise they would have died like flies in the heat.

64 years in those days is at least three generations and so accommodation and feeding would have to be arranged for at least 100,000 [including wives and children] people at any one time. Since, at the time, they were actually building not one but four pyramids more or less simultaneously – some distance apart – we are talking of a half million work force on the project which would have exceeded the entire adult male population at the time. Providing enough water in the right place would have been

impossible. The problems involved in trying to extract the enormous pieces of granite, with precise polished faces, when it was only marginally softer than the hardest known element at the time, Diorite [found only in a remote part of the desert between Aswan and the Red Sea] was an even bigger challenge. Whether they knew about diamond we do not know but if they did, there was no supply in Egypt.

They would also have to build enormous boats, bigger than anything known at the time, or else the hard won prize would sink to the river bottom. After all, the boats at the time were all made of Papyrus leaves and Palm Wood, the nearest decent timber available being the Spruce Firs on the slopes of Mt Herman in Syria. On a forum to which I subscribe this was dismissed because all they had to do was to tie it to some palm trees and off it would float. Maybe it would. Maybe that's what they did but they still needed an awful lot of palm trees to attach to those big lumps of granite. I return to this later on. And as yet no one can offer any idea of how they overcame the First Cataract without taking them out of the water and manhandling them overland and to the lower level. Do keep in mind that two laden long distance lorries, on a sledge, is the equivalent of one of these lumps of stone. Think in terms of two massive fully laden containers stacked one on the other and you have sixty tons. How are you going to move that lot over a waterfall and down to Cairo? The logistics of transporting a meaningful supply of harder wood i.e., pine or cedar over the hills of the Land of Milk and Honey at least a thousand years before the Exodus does not bear thinking about. Assuming always that the Egyptians knew where that was and that the trees were there. If in doubt about this simply study the Solar Boat in which Pharaoh would sail through the underworld each night. This, according to wall paintings and models in the museums of the world, was the leading edge of marine technology at the time. No one would have had a bigger or better boat yet I would submit that just one ordinary limestone block carefully placed in the centre would have been enough to sink it. In 2.900BC good timber in any quantity should have been of a far greater value than anything else, including gold.

In various museums around the world including the Metropolitan, the Louvre and in Cairo are models of contemporary boats dated around 2,000BC. That is 900 years after the pyramids are supposed to have been built. All show that the maximum length was enough to accommodate up to sixteen oars – eight on either side – giving a length of between forty and fifty feet. To transport the granite, ships of at least 300 ft would be needed, and there is no evidence of any of these around at the time. Assuming of course that they used boats.

As I say, it must have been a prodigious effort involving hundreds of thousands of people if, indeed, this was how it was done. And there is not a single drawing to commemorate it all either. But it is beyond dispute that all the Giza pyramids were built to the specification above, as indeed were the hundreds of others, all at more or less the same time, all over the world.

Which, more than ever, leaves the question of 'How?

To answer that we must go back to the beginning and ask 'Why?'

12

THE PYRAMIDS AGAIN

The fact that I dismiss the building techniques of the early Egyptians as being virtually impossible will, no doubt, bring tears to the eye of many an established Egyptologist. He will stamp his foot and scream heresy and ill informed 'amateurs' for disputing the old and established views, but I think that this is a point that deserves labouring.

As I say, and I know I am repeating myself in so doing, I look at it from the point of view of the poor chap who has to actually do the work, not someone who thinks that things may have been done that way. I am the one who scratches his head, says 'Good God' and gets an attack of the nerves when he reads the specification. And this is why Abdullah today would struggle. His forebear, Akehaten, would have it very much worse.

'The specification of the Great Pyramid gives four sides of 750ft each, exact corners and it to be aligned exactly on the north/south axis. Excuse me? North/south axis? What may that be? I thought the earth was flat and that the sun went down over the desert and came up again over the Nile, but now you say that I must line it up exactly to that little star just above the horizon that never moves? Why? Unless I stand a bit higher on the plateau, I can't even see it. Alright, a series of poles set in the right place will let me observe other neighbouring stars from which I can set my plan. It may take a year or so but, so what? Pity I don't have a simple telescope or the ability to write notes nor have access to simple arithmetic.

'Got that done and it is spot on but now you want it level. Dead level or your pyramid will not be true. My manager says to build a simple water channel around it all and then we can easily get the levels right but I ask you, with what? Concrete did you say? I've never heard of it. All I've got is a lot of soft sand and rocks.'

There is nothing that would hold water for very long. Wait a minute, I could make a lot of channels out of mud and bake them in some big ovens, the only problem being finding enough timber to burn in the furnace. But first we have to get the angles right. Exactly square you said. How do I do that? So far nobody has invented geometry or trigonometry and I know nothing about triangles. It may be a bit hit or miss this one. All I can do is measure the outside lengths and then use some sort of rope to get a diagonal. Then I merely juggle the corners until the two diagonals are equal – I think. Problem is my tolerance is only plus or minus a few centimetres.

'Or I can begin at the centre which will be where that enormous and narrow shaft will end up somewhere a long way underground. Why do you need that? Why must that be lined in your precious granite and how the devil do I find sufficient tiny people to dig it? Starting in the middle I know where the exact centre of the pyramid will be and so from there I simply must work slowly outwards keeping it straight and level all the time but, having said that, the entire site must be first laid out to some pre-determined mathematical and astronomical calculations that I can't do because I don't understand mathematics as yet. It hasn't been invented and nor will it be for several hundred years. It is just not possible without a more than working knowledge of trigonometry.

'Having done that another team is using a series of poles that can be lined up with the horizon so that I can begin with a level and square base.

'That out of the way and having marked the exact centre of the pyramid I must dig 90 feet down into the bedrock for a chamber to be built exactly under that centre line. There will be the long tunnel as well but why only just over 3 feet wide and, according to my spec., just over 3ft high as well? No one can stand up in it. Why can't they simply let me cover it with flat pieces of stone instead of an inverted 'U'? Don't they know that all I have to cut it all are pieces of copper and possibly flint on the end of a stick? And who is going to measure off and then mark the exact

172

spot that I must begin that tunnel, and just how do you think I'm going to be able to keep it straight with perfect corners and the precise angle with the gear I have about me? But dig it out I must and, in the fullness of time, I have the base of the pyramid ready with a long underground shaft leading to a chamber underground. Now suitably back filled, but with an access point left to lead to another long shaft from the outside, again into the centre of the pyramid axis plus the dead centre of the pyramid.

'Now it gets tricky. My teams across the river are churning out the blocks but each takes an awful long time. Two to three weeks each and I need 2.3 million of them. But how else can I cut them? I only have copper and flints to do the job and getting the underside smooth enough to slide is proving a massive problem. You say why don't I use rollers? Good idea. Where can you get me ten million hard wood rollers of about the same size and perfectly straight and round? The rain forest? Good. Err, what is a rain forest and where can I find one? Either Ethiopia or the Congo, fine sort it out. Delivery? By the Nile of course. No, I didn't realise that from Central Africa, where only nomadic wandering camel trains have been, there is an impenetrable swamp on the river through which the logs cannot pass, nor that from Ethiopia they would all be smashed going down the waterfalls or would be jammed up in the gorges. What about local trees? Palms would crush in minutes. Olive trees from the Levant, they are hard? Yes, but have you ever seen a straight olive tree? Acacia? the same as for olive.

'Sorry, they must be dragged. Whilst it may only take a few good men to pull a heavy rock on rollers across a smooth and solid road, it will take many more to pull it over the same road but as a rough track, where the friction, particularly at the beginning, of the rough base on the rough road will make it stick like glue. As progress is made the road will cut up and the suggested method of lubricating with water will only serve to wash out sand and mud leaving stones exposed. Also, if the ground is in any way soft, as across sand, the leading edge will soon gather a bow wave that must be levelled out.

'Having got it to the river bank, a wooden gantry has been erected onto which a series of pulleys will lift the block off the ground. Of course, I still need to invent the pulley and the wheel but we'll let that one pass. But then it must be moved in that state several feet in the horizontal out over the river before it can be lowered into a barge. My problem here is that I must use a cantilever since I can't put a support into the river. Or I can build a series of docks with cranes over them but, whatever I do, moving the suspended block a significant distance sideways is a massive problem. With some difficulty I devised a pulley system using diagonals that has achieved this and I have built another on the other side of the river to reverse the process. I will need dozens when in full production. This is not really a starter because the boats are neither strong enough, nor are there enough of them, there were no pulleys and there was no method of assembling any type of crane for the purpose. Also by using enough palm trees tied to them and simply floating across means that the supply of palms would be quickly exhausted unless they are re-used which means taking an equivalent weight of palm trees back up river again. [Again, I look at these numbers later on because the idea of using any sort of pulley is out of the question. They had hardly discovered the wheel which, over the known centuries, was hardly ever used anyway because of the lack of, in the first place something to make them from, and in the second the lack of tracks smooth enough to roll them on.] Whilst the river is in its annual period of flood all low lying trees will be submerged and it will not be possible to control any raft in the current. Trying to tow a pile of logs against the current is out of the question. Oh dear, it's not all that easy. Then the long slide up to the Giza plateau where the bottom outer layer is set out. This must be checked and double checked for levels and square corners because half a degree out here will mean a cockeyed pyramid. 52 degrees on all sides is essential but, by the way, what is a degree?

'I now take the long journey up river to Aswan to check on progress with the granite only to find that nothing has happened. The job has stopped because I can find nothing at all that will touch the granite. There is no material known to me, that is available to me in Aswan, that will cut granite.

'Nothing at all. Make no mistake about this, there is nothing in Aswan that I can use to extract granite in such huge quantities. There is nothing to extract it in small quantities either. There is nothing that can be used for trimming should it be extracted by using wedges from soaking wet wood.

'There are some small stones called Diamonds which will scratch it since they are marginally harder but I can't get them in anywhere near a quantity to make it possible to extract in one piece the enormous lumps specified. And now an order has come in for the Red pyramid wanting dozens of slabs about 4 feet thick that are absolutely square with precise parallel sides. And someone has decided to completely cover the entire outer four faces of the smaller pyramid in perfectly prepared granite slabs. They need thousands of them! Why do they insist on Granite all the time? Well I'm sorry, but until a method is found of easily cutting the hardest of all the stones, the job stops now.'

The above is a realistic assessment of the problems of the Contracts Manager on site. The more I look at it, the harder it becomes, especially when it comes to setting up the granite lined rising passage ways. Those slabs must be cut exactly since, once in place, there would be no means of taking them off again and re-cutting just because they ran off a few inches. They are made, both in limestone and granite as a parallelogram which must be very carefully worked out, marked out and then cut. And those of you who took part in my little experiment know how hard that is. However they did it for all to see but, as we see here, not with the tools and equipment available in 2,900, 2,600 or 2,200BC.

Let us return now to the 21st century and go through the same exercise using the latest machinery available. We look at just one block of limestone and an equal sized one of granite.

Each has six sides and for this exercise I will assume that each measures 6 x 4 x 3 cubits, a Royal Egyptian Cubit being about 21 inches. This is the average size of the blocks at Giza. Of the six sides being quarried, three must be free leaving the other three to be dug out. Having said that, some quarries used deep mining where the blocks were taken from very solid bedrock. At the top between the block and the bedrock at times the gap was very small indeed so that whoever cut them at the rear must have done so lying flat on his stomach. How he got the waste out I cannot think. But today, outside with the top face exposed, a series of holes will be drilled exactly horizontally and exactly vertically on each of the three sides [easy using computer and laser guided drills], effectively releasing [6 x 4] + [6 x 3] + [4 x 3] = 54 square cubits each time which will be cut at the rate of about 10 sq cubits an hour for limestone and about 1 per hour for granite. So the drilling on the limestone would take 5.5 hours and the granite 54 hours. Things are now complicated because, in each case, we need to free one of these drilled faces first [the small one] for, if we try to free the three together, the block will shatter leaving a large lump in the corner. This is especially the case with limestone which will fracture at any time.

The chances of getting blocks this size out of a limestone quarry in one piece are very small indeed. The nature of the stone is that it will so easily split along any one of far too many natural fissures. The reality is that we may need to start and discard ten before we get a good one. That is why we must at times go deep into heavily compacted quarries. What that does for the numbers does not bear thinking about. For final facing we use a wire, or saw, made of high tensile steel, .28mm in diameter which is electro plated with 40 microns diamond particles. With this state of the art technology we will saw through the small area taking about an hour with limestone (including setting up) and 2.5 hours for the granite. By drilling enough holes a simple small charge of dynamite will release the remaining faces after which all six sides are faced using tungsten carbide, diamond saws or the diamond wire to give the final finished size. This means that today, using the most advanced quarrying techniques available, each limestone block will take about 8 hours to produce and a matching granite one will take about 60 hours. Each would need 10 to 12 men.

176

Think about this. We need 2.3 million of them for just the one pyramid. There were four being built simultaneously, granted not all the same size, but, even so, needing about 7 million blocks in total. If it takes 8 hours to produce just one, then each quarry face, working a twelve hour day [i.e., during daylight] will produce 1.5 per day. To finish in 63 years we need 300 per day, so need 200 faces each employing 10 – 12 people. That is 2400 people simply extracting the blocks, using the very latest equipment for the limestone alone, the easy bit being the transportation on to site and then subsequent erection using a mixture of dump trucks, shovels and cranes.

Just how, all those years ago, using nothing but copper and flint tools, could they realistically have produced 300 perfect limestone blocks every day for 63 years? They certainly could not have done so by conventional quarrying. By using these very generous figures, they would take at least 30 times as long just to dig out the blocks. So 200 faces will now take 63 x 30 = 1,890 years before completion! Or have 6000 faces each employing about 100 people which is 600,000 men, as before, more than the adult male population of the entire country. Is this realistic???? Also it must be understood that at a maximum only three people could work on any one block at a time. That is two on the ten foot long rear and one on the side. When they had finished, and only when they had finished, could the two who would do the under cutting begin.

Houdin, in his book on the subject claims that the Great pyramid was easily built in 20 years. He says that now they think that much of the centre was simply filled with rubble so reducing the number of blocks needed. OK, let's cut the number down to 1.5 million needed. In 20 years we need 75,000 per year or 205 per day. Simple arithmetic says that this needs 137 faces working full time. For the full 2.3 million blocks there would need to be 210 faces employing around 12 people each at the minimum. This is 2520 people. To build all 4 during those same twenty years would need 640 faces employing nearly 8,000 people. And that is using the very latest mining and earthmoving technology today.

Let us now consider granite. Limestone is a relatively soft, porous rock formed from the minute skeletons of tiny marine creatures over many millennia. As one layer sets, another builds up above it and then that sets as well. But there is nothing to actually key them together which is why limestone splits so easily. In the quarry it is seldom found in one continuous lump of perfect limestone. You may get one good one and then the next three in any direction could just crumble away into rubble. So you need vast quarries and even more time to select your good blocks, some of which will shatter when worked. Of course it comes in various guises and as marble it does form into large solid blocks but that used on the pyramids of Egypt was most definitely not marble.

Granite, on the other hand, is an igneous rock formed by the rapid cooling of volcanic lava. It is very hard indeed. On the Mohs scale of hardness, to which we have already alluded, everything is graded from 1 to 10. The softest mineral is Talc with a value of 1 whilst the hardest is diamond at 10. Limestone comes in at 3 to 4 with granite rating at 7 just below Topaz, and Corundum. Rubies, Sapphires, Emeralds etc., all are in the 9 to 10 bracket. Gold is at 2.5, Copper slightly harder at 3 and Tungsten Carbide is another at 10.

From this, using the very basic laws of physics, it should be obvious that copper will not cut limestone and that to cut and face granite something like tungsten carbide or high speed steel are needed.

And so, with granite, we are dealing with something very hard indeed. But Somers Clark insists that the Aswan quarries show that they rejected as unsuitable large quantities in Aswan before finally finding pieces that were suitable. The addition of this to the equation adds years to the time estimate.

Look round any grave yard and you will see some old monuments in sandstone, but mainly they tended to be in white marble, which is a form of limestone, until comparatively recent times. Now granite has overtaken marble as the most popular material for headstones. They used marble because it is quite soft and easy to work – which was the same reason that the great sculptures used it. There would be no statue of David if Michelangelo had to use granite. I am indebted to Tingley Monuments of Novia Scotia for their detailed web site that describes just how they make their beautiful monuments. When you have read this, it will put into some context the problems of cutting, preparing and finishing an eighty ton block that then had to be carefully placed in position a long way up in the air.

First let me tell you what is available to work granite today. We have already seen the diamond coated wire in action, and then may have wondered how they cut the kitchen worktops now in fashion, to such fine tolerances. These are cut in thin slices from huge blocks imported from India, Brazil and Italy. These blocks are blasted from the quarry using nitro-glycerine. A multi blade saw uses a cast steel grit as the cutting material between the blades and the stone, the grit being made by the crushing of cast steel shot. The slices are then cut into manageable lengths to be finished later.

Lasers using comparatively little power will cut accurately into the stone without splitting it. Used in conjunction with a computer they will cut accurately to a depth of about 1/8 inch at a time making them ideal for carving inscriptions.

Water jets have tiny nozzles out of which comes water at 3000 feet/min and at 50,000 psi. To cut stone a nozzle of .003 inch is used and the water is mixed with a mixture of garnet and ruby as the cutting edges. Using about 8 gallons per minute they will cut up to 8 inch thick material to any contour to a tolerance of +/- .005 inch.

Sand blasters are used extensively for finishing work as are computer guided profile grinders and the polishing is carried out using huge hydraulic machines to give an even flat finish.

To make a simple granite headstone this is what you must do.
First drill a series of holes into the bedrock both vertically and horizontally. The drill bits must be of tungsten carbide and

must be both lubricated and cooled using water which, in turn removes the debris. Without this it would be impossible to extract the debris, the drill would overheat and the cutting edge lost. Fill the holes with high explosive and then detonate, at which point you are left with a large lump of misshaped granite. This is then blasted again until you are left with some manageable pieces each weighing about ten tons. These are then graded and up to 80% will be discarded as insufficient quality. The remaining 20% is transported to the factory.

These pieces are now cut to the required thickness using a diamond saw. Any joints needed are also cut with the diamond saw. These sawn large pieces are now polished using successively finer abrasives. There are four revolving bricks attached to the head which rotates whilst hydraulic pressure maintains an even and constant finish. During this process much heat is generated, closing the pores in the stone which gives it its unique gloss finish.

Now a stone cutter – he with hammer and chisel – assesses the grain of the granite and will cut out the approximate final shape. No state of the art technology yet can assess the grain quite like a good craftsman. The piece is then fitted to a template controlled contour grinder before the top and sides are finished using an automatic top polisher.

The inscription is drawn out onto a stencil which is then attached to the headstone. A jet of air and grit sand is sand blasted at the open parts of the stencil leaving the wording crisp and clear for all to see. It is now ready for the grave side.

It all sounds simple, which it is given the size of the finished product and the state of the art equipment available today. However, none of this equipment could have been used – had it been available – for the work in the pyramids since the individual pieces were so very big. So far I have not spoken to any modern day skilled stone mason who could even attempt the job and certainly not with only copper and flint to work with. Somers Clark [more of whom later] did some experiments back in the 1920s on cutting granite using the supposed ancient methods, with flint as one of the cutting agents along with emery, diorite and water. After every three cuts he had to clean the saw and he had to admit that he got nowhere because he could not apply enough weight to the saw. He tried drilling, but could not put enough weight on it or get it to spin fast enough. Again he got nowhere at all. He didn't see fit to question just where, in 2,900BC, the flint came from since there was none in Egypt. Surprisingly, for such a serious researcher, he just seems to shrug his shoulders and take the ubiquitous 'mighty bound' over the problem.

So now we return to the questions of 'Why' and 'How', not just for the pyramids themselves, but also the obviously essential use of granite as part of the deal. First we look to just where in the pyramid granite was so essential and each time we begin with the burial chamber. It couldn't have anything to do with preservation of the body since not one of the subsequent underground tombs felt it necessary, and it would have been very easy in comparison to line, say the burial chamber of Seti, than it ever was that of Cheops. However a lot of the sarcophagi are of granite but I come to them later in the book. No, that was not the purpose. The bodies were all preserved by embalming well after they had stopped building pyramids. There was no structural necessity for its use either. All the stones used throughout are under intense compression, something with which either sandstone or limestone could equally cope. In the Mykerinus 'burial chamber', the roof lining does not even touch the bedrock above. And the simple lining of a long passage, had that been deemed to be so necessary, could be done in anything that was easier to work. Even by simply smoothing the sides rather than lining them. Given the enormous problems of identifying the perfect pieces, quarrying, logistics, working and installing, few would have persevered unless it was **absolutely necessary** to use this material above all others. They did persevere which indicates that it was an extremely important element of the structure, if not the most important. WHY????

13

WHY GRANITE?

At this point I must digress and talk briefly about some ancient sites in Great Britain. But before doing so we must look again at the Earth and its formation.

Elsewhere in this book I look at the beginnings of our planet but here we consider the finished article.

At the centre of the Earth is a solid core of a mixture of iron and nickel. The outer core is a thick layer of molten iron and nickel and above this is the mantle which contains solid rock, or magma, to a depth of about 2,900 km. This magma then becomes molten to a depth of between 50 and 200 km. Outside of this is the crust which varies in thickness from around 7km under the oceans to an average of 35km under the continents and up to 80km under the 'new' mountain ranges. The 'new' mountain ranges being the Rockies, the Andes, the Alps and the Himalayas.

The crust is made up of a thick layer of coarse volcanic stone known as 'gabba' which is then topped with a thinner layer of fine grained igneous rock known as 'basalt'. The basalt is not of even thickness nor is it level, and on top of this we get the various layers of sedimentary rocks which are the subjects under discussion. The sedimentary rocks in which we are interested are Sandstone, Gritstone and Limestone and this is where they came from.

Sandstone. This is made up of tiny smooth particles of sand that have weathered by water or wind over a huge period of time. Over the millennia it gathers in layers, settles and then solidifies to become sandstone.

Grit stone or Millstone grit is a harder stone made up of rough, angular shards of earlier rocks that have weathered but not so as to become smooth sand. Effectively it is very coarse and hard sandstone whose origin may be one of the granites.

Limestone is calcium carbonate that comes from the minute skeletons of dead organisms that chemically fuse together to produce layers of rock. Oil and gas come from a similar decomposition of vegetable matter.

The **Granites** are all igneous rocks resulting from fractures in the crust allowing molten magma to erupt and then cool down. These result in a very hard rock, more so than the sedimentary ones. We see it as volcanic outcrops. I include here basalt as well.

Diorite is another igneous rock found in much less quantity than granite. It is harder but has most of the other properties of granite.

All may possibly have other minerals trapped inside them. These can be iron which, of course, is magnetic meaning that some otherwise inert stones can affect compasses and radio waves. Jades and other quartz rocks very often have an iron thread running through them and it is not uncommon for limestone to have the same. The problems at Panama were compounded by iron deposits oxidising on contact with the damp atmosphere and rusting away.

Looking at the myriad of Neolithic and earlier monoliths gives us few answers but does raise more questions. Putting aside many of the diverse and remarkable explanations for the answer to the question of 'Why?' promulgated by some 'experts', I went down many alternative and more logical paths to see what emerged. Unfortunately so far I have come up with nothing. Nothing, that is, that can be unconditionally proved scientifically. Many of these sites are simple rings made of stones obtained locally. Some use limestone and others sandstone. Grit stone is used as well. Invariably they used convenient shards of stone found locally that were left after the ice receded. But this does not mean that those shards are necessarily from local sites. The ice displaced stones and either dragged, or pushed, them for many miles. Many of these sites are situated on what are called 'Ley Lines'. These were only suggested in 1921 by an Alfred Watkins, who wrote a book – '*The Old Straight Track*' – on the subject, when he found that many towns and villages that had names ending in 'ley' fell on the same straight line. Leys are supposed lines of force that run through the earth in straight lines and, again only supposedly, to be used by ancient man to find his way across country. Many towns and village names end in 'ley' which means 'woodland' in old English. As in Bromley, Chorley, Burnley etc and a straight line from two that are far apart will invariably go straight through several others. To pass through one, maybe two, and we are looking at coincidence but when the line passes through six or seven we must ask whether or not there is anything in it. I don't know, and as always keep an open mind. Obviously, since most of Britain in ancient times was covered in forest, a large number of villages would have the suffix 'ley' in them. We must not read too much into this. What I do not dispute is that through the Earth pass many currents that we cannot see. We cannot see the magnetic field any more than we can see electricity, sound or light waves. The oceans of molten iron and nickel moving about above the iron core of Earth gives us the magnetic field but we cannot see that. The crust is made of basalt and, like granite, this contains an element of radioactivity, the sedimentary rocks do not, but grit stone can contain elements of granite. Limestone can also produce some radio and electrical anomalies. Also, as we have seen, all the sedimentary rocks can, and very often do, contain elements of iron ore which, as said, is magnetic as well.

Many of these leys pass through Glastonbury Tor which is a large granite outcrop in Wiltshire and home to the King Arthur legend. There is a stone circle nearby. Many of the leys pass through the old stone circles as well. The purpose of this little digression is to say that despite the circles using local stones, many include just one made of granite that was obtained many miles away. Stonehenge had perfectly good sandstone pillars quarried nearby at Marlborough which must have served the purpose for worshipping the sun. But beforehand they found it necessary to go to Pembrokeshire, miles away across the Severn estuary and across South Wales, to dig out the massive bluestone granite boulders we see today. And, whatever conventional wisdom thinks, they did not have any suitable boats that would float the stones by sea through the hostile waters of the Irish Sea, St George's Channel and the fierce tides of the Severn Estuary. They had to be taken overland to where they could safely cross the Severn, which was many miles off course for a straight line from Wales to Salisbury. And yes, I've seen the modern replicas of suitable boats, invariably built by skilled boat builders using 21st century technology, tools and expertise. 21st century AD that is, when there were plenty of good DIY stores selling the prepared timber. I did suggest trying it with just a bit of flint and some animal bones but that had no takers.

I bought some genuine flints and replica bones with which to chop down a tree, extract a large square lump of limestone even. No chance at all. But that is all they had to extract and then transport their incredibly precious cargo. Why would they need to do
that????

Why would they want to do that???? A favourite explanation is that on Salisbury Plain were deposited just the right number of Bluestone shards to the correct size during the Ice Age and the ancient Brits thought it may be a good idea to use them. Fine, except that the ice sheet came nowhere near to Wiltshire. But, having said that, the shards may have been left nearby on the correct side of the Severn estuary. Of course, this then begs the question of if the bluestone shards were conveniently lying about, why then extract the sandstone ones from Marlborough as well? Marlborough is hardly on the doorstep of the Salisbury Plain where Stonehenge was built. The other questions we must ask are how they knew that they must have granite in the first place, where there was a supply of granite and how they were able to identify it in the ground. It is not obvious to even a graduate geologist that one piece of stone is granite and the next grit stone. You cannot walk along a path and immediately identify a granite outcrop. So they must have known it was there and there must have been a very serious need for it. Another possible explanation is that the bluestones may have been put there by a different people in a different age and for a different purpose. One remarkable coincidence with Stonehenge is that it lies on the meridian of 51 degrees, ten minutes north and that the angle of the Giza pyramids is 51 degrees, 50 minutes, an error of just 40 minutes or 41 miles. Silbury Hill and Avebury are even nearer to the exact position. The

Rollright Stones are just 8 miles away from the 51 degrees, 50 minutes of latitude. Amazing, isn't it?

The Devil's Arrows at Boroughbridge in Yorkshire are another example of this seemingly astonishing waste of effort. They are three huge columns, out of an original five grit stone ones, that are set in a straight line with orientation NNW/SSE. The biggest is 8m tall and weighs many tons, but all are un-worked shards that come from Plumpton Rocks some nine miles away to the south of Harrogate. Why not erect them on site rather than go to the enormous trouble of transporting them to Boroughbridge? At the time it was heavily forested and there was the River Nidd to cross. There is the Whinney Hill stone circle in Northumberland which has three sandstone blocks and the fourth from red granite. There is no obvious outcrop of red granite anywhere near a site that then would have been surrounded by woodland. It is set on the moor above.

The remaining Devils Arrows Monoliths at Boroughbridge in North Yorkshire. These massive pieces of stone were dragged 9 miles through dense woodland and over a river valley. By whom, why and when?

The Cerrig Duon circle near Conwy on the North Wales coast is of sandstone but with just one stone of quartz. The

186

Maenhla standing stone near Brecon in Wales is 3.5 metres high and 3 metres wide. It is shaped like an axe and stands on its own with no obvious source anywhere nearby. It has been brought a considerable distance to stand on its own on an otherwise barren moor, but is now alongside a modern road that follows the route of an ancient Roman one.

The Rudstone Monolith [below]in the East Riding of Yorkshire near Bridlington. It is a grit stone monolith 8m high and weighing 40 tons. It came from a quarry at Cayton Bay near Scarborough some 9 miles away to the north. Again, why, why, why??? It appears to have been trimmed. The problems for Neolithic man c1500-2000BC of transporting over open countryside, or through a dense forest with its accompanying undergrowth, a lump of stone 40 tons in weight were more or less identical to those of an Egyptian doing the same 1,000 years earlier across the desert.

The Rollright Stones near Chipping Norton are a circle of huge limestone blocks. Apparently there are electro-magnetic anomalies nearby. And so it goes on. I could fill the book with lists of these but that is not the purpose. It is to try to decipher the message that they send out to us. What could it be?

Look at the properties of granite. As we have seen it is an extremely hard igneous rock formed when much of our planet was in a very fluid state. If not fluid, then volatile. It is very close, even grained, with little susceptibility to fissures and subsequent splitting, and does not easily wear out. It is inert except that it emits a small amount of the radioactive substance Radon 3. Apart from Uranium, it is the only radioactive rock. In the open air this is hardly measurable and perfectly safe but, in closed environments it can build up, contaminate the air, and be quite harmful to anyone spending much time in any chamber or room where it is used. Could this be our first clue? Let us look further at this aspect.

Radioactivity is measured in Becquerels (Bq) and 1 kg of granite contains 1,000bq. To put this into context, every adult human being emits 7,000bq all the time; 1kg of coffee emits 1,000bq and the average European house 30,000bq. 1kg of Uranium emits 25 million bq. So 1,000 is a small dose. But how many kgs will you find in one 70 ton block of granite? There are 2.204 lbs per kg and 2240 lbs per ton and so simple arithmetic shows that there will be 71.143 million bq in a 70 ton block. Or the equivalent of 3kgs of Uranium. The long passages to the burial chamber of the Great Pyramid plus the burial chamber itself add up to many times the one 70 ton block meaning that the total radiation in that almost perfectly sealed environment will be equal to a significant quantity of Uranium. All gathering in that top chamber before venting to the atmosphere. Also in the final chamber of the Mykerinus pyramid is a very substantial quantity of granite plus a significant volume in the long access shaft, all of which contain a measurable amount of radioactivity.

Granite contains traces of the very rare metal, Thorium, which was discovered in 1815. It has been used ever since for a variety of things including the manufacture of gas lamps. When the lamp is first lit, the light is a very dull blue but, as soon as the mantle warms up, it becomes a brilliant white. This is caused by the heating of a miniscule layer of Thorium. In this day and age Thorium has taken on a new lease of life as the prime fuel in a new generation of nuclear power stations and this is because it is radioactive.

One ton of Thorium can create the same energy as 200 tons of Uranium and 3.5 million tons of coal. It is expensive to extract but already power stations in India are using it as the prime source. It is the safest nuclear option and does not leave behind nuclear waste, which begs the question of why the west is not building these things right now, but that is for another work, not this one. I merely mention it in my fishing expedition in search for the answer to my ongoing question of 'Why Granite?'

Also, being so dense and free from faults, granite is a great insulator, providing the joints are sealed - which they are in all the pyramids. Then, looking at a section through the Great Pyramid, any number of different interpretations can be made of what we see.

Conventional wisdom says that we see an entrance way through which the Pharaoh's body was taken, then up the shaft to be laid to rest in his granite sarcophagus surrounded by all his toys and treasures. The lot then sealed off when finished. Others say that the chamber was an observation post to measure the stars but, to me, it looks like a sophisticated chemical lab with exact pre-determined lengths and sections of shafts to first accelerate a gas in the deliberately small section, then slow it down whilst passing the huge smooth sides of limestone, before some process was complete in the upper chamber, with excess gas being vented through the sides. Far fetched? Maybe it is. Who knows? All I look at are facts and I have already dismissed the burial ground theory, if only because that certainly had no need of granite. Nor was there any need for the extremely complicated mathematics needed for the layout. Subsequent tombs with enormous treasure troves did not use it at all. Something must take its place. So, for the moment let us hang on to this thread as a possible starter. Another interesting 'coincidence' is that the granite 'sarcophagus' is exactly the same size as that given in the Bible for the Ark of the Covenant.

So here we are, back in the UK with all these circles and standing stones, not to mention the myriad of circular henges and tumuli that were built during the Neolithic period. We know this for certain because before that the land was mostly covered with ice and so nothing can pre-date the Ice age unless it was in the south east of the country. Again why? Well let us look at what they all have in common.

The first and most obvious is that they all seem to be built on high ground. On exposed moors away from the tree line. Most low lying land will have been covered in trees or bush during the time when they were all hunter gatherers. The second is that they all seem to have needed to be built in that spot and that spot only. When it would have been just as easy to erect the Devils Arrow at Plompton Rocks where they were found, they dragged them across the tree lined countryside and over the River Nidd to the slightly higher ground of Boroughbridge. Is it significant that the Nidd is not navigable for very far but Boroughbridge is the furthest navigable place, for sea going vessels, on the Yorkshire Ouse? The other sites all seem to be on high ground which could suggest either the favourite explanation of a religious use or, I suggest as another possibility, that it could have been a security one where a lookout could see all around him. I did read that the extensive workings on Orkney may have been built as a contest between rival tribes. A sort of Neolithic Highland Games. I doubt it somehow. The favourite theory as this is being written is that they were all built for religious reasons to worship the sun and moon. I doubt that as well but I feel that the alignment of the sun with some stones may be significant as direction pointers. They may have been used as early timepieces to confirm the changes of the seasons.

Or they could be used as landmarks for the use of travellers and here I get into deep waters with my thoughts. I have absolutely no method of scientifically proving what I say below, but I'll give it a go. At least it's as good as 'The Highland Games' idea!

Please forgive me if I seem to wander with my thoughts but in the end I pull it all together.

I talk later in my book about my Australian friend Harry Gration who was blind. All he could distinguish was light and dark yet he was able to travel the world on his own and, as he said, see the sights. When he came to us he had just toured Scotland which he thought was wonderful. So how did he know that? It is also well recorded that Helen Keller, the remarkable American who was born both deaf and blind, was able to get degrees, write books and live a very full life. Again, how did she do it? I also have spoken before about the 'Bicameral Mind' which is the part of the mind that most of us seldom use because it is where the memories of normal everyday things are stored and are done automatically.

Here I'm talking about walking, sleeping, eating, sex etc., to begin with and progressing to things like riding a bicycle, swimming, driving a car or ballroom dancing. Things that you learn and then never forget because they are stored away in that part of the mind. The theory of the 'Bicameral Mind' is that also stored here are things that, because of our advanced civilization and way of life, we no longer need, and here it means fire, shelter, defence against an enemy and clothing to keep us warm. Also vision, hearing and taste, things we take for granted until we lose them. Modern man no longer needs to think of these any more. It was done for him in the past and over time his mind has ceased to consider them to be a need. In business we talk of this in terms of goals, where certain goals are set out and when they are achieved, they no longer remain as goals so can be struck off and the next one considered.

Now another thread regarding the piece about waves. Here I spoke about the birds that return each year across continents to their place of birth to lay their own eggs; of the salmon that choose the correct river to spawn and the eels that find their way from the Sargasso Sea to the correct river again. Add to that that a cat can usually find its way home even if it is lost a hundred miles away and pigeons that can find their way back home from any number of starting points. All have in common that they are members of the animal kingdom and, apart from some basic cunning, have zero reasoning power.

Neolithic man, whilst being of a considerable intelligence, had no previous history to work on. For him across the globe everything had to be discovered from first principals to include providing shelter, lighting a fire and hunting for food. The simple fact that he existed at all means that the very basic animal needs had been met and those are to eat, sleep and breed. That he had in common with all other animals. Unlike the animals he had to find clothing in the northern climes for warmth, fire for heat and shelter from the elements. But other animals, as shown above had the ability to find their way around, returning over many miles to familiar feeding grounds. Some say that it is instinct that gives them this ability, so just what is 'instinct'? The *Oxford English Dictionary* gives as a definition '*Innate propensity, especially in lower animals, to seemingly rational acts; innate impulse; behaviour; intuition.'*

Neolithic man also needed to find his way at times back to where he began and with a landscape heavily wooded it would have been very easy to get lost. Unfortunately for the Caucasian races we are too far into the modern era to make any meaningful comparisons but we do have the Native Americans and the Australian Aborigines who are not many generations away from being wandering peoples living in original conditions. It is well documented that these people could track for considerable distances and find their way across barren wildernesses. I have contacted the web sites of both these peoples and written to them, without result, to find out whether any of their peoples, following westernization, could still do that, now that it was no longer needed. If so, what in the brains of their ancestors was able to pick up something from the earth that their modern descendents no longer had the need for? And again, if so, just what in the earth could they pick up? And was what they could pick up exactly the same thing that the lower animals could, and still do, detect?

What, in the earth and the skies and the seas, could there be that all these peoples and creatures could pick up that was no longer needed as mankind progressed towards civilization?

And here we go back to our stone circles, monoliths and rows of standing stones. As I say, most are on exposed high ground, most are in seemingly isolated spots, many used stones transported many miles from their quarries and a significant few felt the necessity to include, at considerable inconvenience, a stone of a different material, that material invariably being granite. I have on my study wall a map of England where I have indicated all the appropriate ones of these. Onto this map I have drawn many of the so called 'Ley Lines' of Alfred Watkins and many of the leys, especially if drawn from Glastonbury Tor or Stonehenge, go through the sites that I indicate. Could this be some sort of proof that leys do in fact exist? That I cannot say.

Let us look at this hypothesis. The original Stone Age and even pre-Stone Age hunter gatherer who came across the land bridge into southern Britain will have been very little further on in life's progress than the animals around him. Quite simply his entire existence was to eat, sleep and breed using skins to keep warm and eating meat, most likely raw, from the animals that he caught. And that was that. He wandered the land as the ice receded over a considerable time frame until he found places to build semi permanent settlements where the first primitive farms were established. Those who settled no longer needed the ability to find their way about and so, over the generations may have lost the ability to do so, but the hunter gatherers still did. There the women and children would stay at home and the men go out over distances to catch and kill food. As time went on some form of trade will have evolved which would mean that they had to find their way from place to place. We know this because of flint remnants that have been found far from where flint is quarried. So how could they find their way?

Supposing that, like the animals, they were able to sense earth currents that told them where they were going? Supposing that they could find out by following a current that took them from one circle to the next, or to a monolith, and that monolith showed them in which direction they should follow? And could the granite stones, having only a tiny content of radon that may or may not interact with the earth currents, be put there for that exact purpose? So that the main stone edifices, being there as traffic islands on the ancient pathways leading, as many do on my map, to the protected circular henges that would then be used primarily as defensible and sheltered places to live.

While man was still in his primitive state this would be his goal. To build a network of stone markers across the land to help him find his way along the possible 'Ley Lines'. Once he had those standing stones which, with probably the only exceptions being Stonehenge and Rudstone, were never worked in any way, he no longer had the need for the ability to erect them. None are in any way decorative nor do any seem to have a structural necessity of any kind. And so few, if any, are dated later than the Neolithic which, to me, indicates that it was only when man still needed the 'instincts' of his animal past that he felt the need to build markers along the path. As he began to be civilized during his journey into the Bronze and Iron Ages this need receded until it was lost for all time, but peoples still living a primitive existence, even today, still have it and use it in the jungles of the world.

Is this feasible? Realistic? I don't know but having studied all the alternatives including the 'Highland Games' theory I think it may have some mileage in it. I have a problem accepting that ancient man would build so many circles in such inhospitable places for religious purposes. For this purpose it would be so much easier to use timber of which there was so much about. And then build their temples in a sheltered clearing rather than on a bleak and exposed moor. And would they have any means of knowing how long a hardwood structure would last compared to a stone one? I doubt it and equally doubt that it would be an issue anyway. If the circles, built on those exposed moors were for religious purposes, what about the single monoliths like the Rudstone or the three [possibly five originally] Devil's Arrows at Boroughbridge?

The one mantra throughout the book is that I rule nothing either in or out. That at the time of writing no one has been able to actually identify or measure a 'Ley Line' or a Feng Sui line of force, by no means indicates that they are not there. I don't know whether they are there any more than does anyone else, and I certainly do not patronise those working on the theories by describing them as 'pseudo-science' as they were to me once when I posed a simple question to an academic. He said that he could not discuss 'pseudo-science'. I keep an open mind. The religious theories may be correct and, if so, I can live with it. Equally so may my ideas be. Only time may tell.

This idea is dismissed by some because Neolithic man had sufficient intelligence to be able to identify landmarks such as hills to guide him. I say that that is the precise reason for my idea. Much of the land is flat and finding one's way through the overgrown floor of a dense and virgin forest is far from easy. Sense of direction is easily lost if there is no sun shining and distant vistas are obscured by mist and low cloud, or simply are not there until a higher ground is found where he could emerge and look around him. How convenient to do so and find a landmark placed there for the purpose. Then he could follow it's directions to the next one. If I'm wrong, I'm open to a better idea.

Having said all that I came across a piece in the American 'Science' magazine that reported a researcher at the California Institute of Technology, a person by the name of Joe Kirschvink, doing experiments along this line. He erected a 'Faraday Cage' which is a sealed container and it was made of aluminium. He insulated it from the Earth's magnetic field and designed new ones himself. In total darkness he wired up some students to an EEG monitor and then subjected them to measurable but different magnetic fields. He was able to detect changes in the brainwaves that exactly matched the changes in the magnetic field.

This is thought to be caused by a field sensing molecule in the retina called 'Cryptochrome' and this is known to be present in birds. Other experiments suggest that traces of 'Magnetite' could cause the same effect because it is known to be present in the beaks of some birds. In humans it occurs in tissues. Magnetite is a commonly occurring mineral found in iron ore and was first identified in early times when man became aware that it reacted to the Earth's magnetic field. In that context it was known as a 'Lodestone'.

If I project this idea into my work, could early man have used this ability to locate the granite in the first place? Is it possible that some of them had a highly developed sense of these things and by travelling across the virgin ground be able to sense that the stone beneath their feet was different? In this case could a traveller with the sense be able to inform a people, say at Stonehenge, who had identified for some purpose an urgent need for granite, that they could find a ready source by following the circles and markers all the way over to Pembroke where Bluestone was readily available?

Obviously much work by someone much younger and better qualified than me must carry out this research but if I'm looking in the right direction, it would answer an awful lot of questions.

14

BACK TO THE PYRAMIDS AGAIN

However, let us give the 'experts' the benefit of the doubt here and grant that they have employed 600,000 men on 6,000 rock faces churning blocks out at 300 per day. I now call on my transport manager – sorry, Logistical Advisor – to sort out getting the blocks to the river, over it, and then up the long incline to the site. The Great Pyramid is only the odd kilometre away, the small one less than another kilometre further on but the wretched Red one is many kilometres further into the desert. So now it is my turn to crunch numbers again. I keep as my reference point my suitcase which always weighs around the baggage allowance when you fly in the 21st century and it is usually 20 kilograms or 44 lbs. Now we all know that a full suitcase of this weight takes some lifting today, even for a fit young 6ft tall adult. Yes, I can lift one out of the boot of the car and then onto a trolley, but I certainly wouldn't like to have to hold it for very long. Now we have little wheels and smooth surfaces to help out, they did not.

A 5 ft tall Egyptian of the period would have had relatively the same strength, and so it would be reasonable to assume that his maximum continuous load could not have been more than about 20 - 30lbs in weight. Each block on average weighs 2.3 tons or 5152 lbs needing 160 - 257 men to physically lift it. You could not get 257 men around it so that is impossible. To drag this weight along a smooth road with no rollers is going to be difficult since the frictional force will be enormous with no possibility of building up any momentum. Given the strength of the men, we are going to need around 300 per block which will move it around a kilometre a day if we are very lucky. So we are going to need 300 men x 300 blocks for each kilometre. Let us assume that it is two kilometres from quarry to river and then a minimum of 3 kilometres to the first pyramid giving a total distance of 5 kilometres. Therefore we need 300 x 300 x 5 = 450,000 men just for the Great Pyramid. This must be on top of the 600,000 digging them out. All to be fed, clothed, housed etc, with their families, which will double the number. So now we must make provision for 2 million people before we even begin the construction work.

But let us still give them the benefit of the doubt and consider the river crossing. I was fortunate in that my flat in France looked out over a marina with a boat yard in the corner. Now the boat yard spends a lot of time pulling yachts in and out of the sea and they use a simple lifting mechanism. It is a gantry on wheels made of cast steel with a capacity of about 50 tons. You simply sail your boat into the purpose built dock, the crane comes along and straddles it, two slings are fed underneath, and a hydraulic crane lifts the boat into the air from where it is taken to a vacant lot in the boat yard. Simple. You will find one of these in every boat yard in the world, many small harbours as well.

In the centre is a fifty ton lift needed to lift those yachts out of the water. Even the smaller ones like the one in the foreground. That will weigh about 7 tons. The sailing yacht to the left will weigh about three tons or the same as a pyramid block.

Now this is the only way it can be done now and could be done in antiquity. Only with the greatest of difficulty could they be slid up a concrete slipway. With an uneven bottom, dragging up a wet river bank, would be physically impossible. They would have needed about 20 of these docks and cranes at either side of the river, with one massive one to cope with the granite. It would not be difficult, even in those days, to devise a pulley system, had it been available, with enough mechanical advantage to lift the blocks vertically, but just what timber they used is a mystery. They had no hard wood of any sort. Also they had yet to invent the wheel and there is ample evidence that they didn't use pulleys. We are still looking at the 4th Dynasty, but if you leap forward 1500 years to the trading ships used by the kings of that time, cartouches and paintings show sails being raised by ropes passing over and through holes in timber masts only. There is no evidence anywhere of any type of pulley system being used for any purpose at the time. There are no cartouches depicting pulleys and so it is assumed that they did not have them. Without the mechanical advantage obtained by pulleys I would say that it would not have been possible to lift using a crane or hoist. If it was difficult to slide the solid block on its own, it would have been very much harder trying to slide the crane with a 2.3 ton block swinging in it. All the blocks would have had to be very carefully lowered exactly into the centre of the boat otherwise it would have tipped over.

Sliding them in would have had the same effect unless a very long and shallow ramp was provided, both in and out of the boat. Any suggestion of a drop, even half an inch, and it would have gone through the bottom of the boat. The mere act of transferring the weight from the slings to the bottom of the boat without even a millimetre of drop would have sent the block straight through the bottom of other than a very substantial craft. This had to be done 7 million times without a single mistake. Surely there must have been the odd careless or even accidental mistake over more than a hundred years, in which case should we not expect the Nile to contain a considerable supply of submerged blocks? Has anyone ever looked for them? Conventional wisdom says that all the blocks were not transported in boats but by tying sufficient timber to them so that it would keep it afloat. Yes, that is possible as we will see but with the huge lumps of granite???? Again conventional wisdom says that it was tied to huge logs and then they simply waited for the flood to float it down stream. I do allude elsewhere of the problems of navigating a huge river in spate with a modern powered craft. With a raft and a few men with poles? Well, really, I don't think so. And, as with the idea that the Stonehenge bluestones were deposited by the ice, surely there would be several huge lumps of granite, or indeed limestone, scattered over the desert when they drifted off course? Many of those should still be with us. Are they? I'm not aware of any.

Well after I had written this I saw a news item about a boat, not a very big one, that had been damaged in the English Lake District. It had to be slipped out of the water and to do it they used a huge Caterpillar bulldozer, on tracks, pulling up a very gentle slope that was full of wet mud. Slipping it back again was more difficult because they had to use the same bulldozer pushing, the result being exactly as I describe in Appendix 3. By easing it in very slowly they succeeded. Using just humans would have been much harder but not impossible.

Let us consider the alternative. Again the blocks must be quarried and somehow got to the river bank. There they are attached to enough timber – palm or olive or what else?? – to keep them afloat. They must be coaxed into the river down a ramp of the type I used to launch my small boat each time. That was made of concrete and my boat was on a trailer. One made of mud and rocks would have not worked at all. As soon as anything gets wet it becomes unstable as anyone who has got stuck in a car in a field will tell you. They may use gravel but the river would soon wash that away. A muddy launching pad at each side would have been impossible to use more than once after which it would need to be reset. That would require even more men to add to the workforce. But, let us assume that this is how they actually did it. The timber was in short supply upstream and so presumably by some means or other, it was taken back upstream for re-use. Just how did they do that against a current that in places was fast moving?

The granite blocks in the 70 to 100 ton each region would have needed simply enormous boats just to prevent them sinking under the load. They would have needed a big crew of oarsmen to row them down river, and then to take the boat back up river again, since Aswan is over 500 miles from Cairo. Again, putting it into context, that is like floating them from London to Rome and then rowing back against the current!!! Also, bear in mind that 1,000 years later the cutting edge of boat design had no more than eight oarsmen at any time because the boats were made of papyrus in the main. And then we are back to the loading and unloading at either end. They could have built big air tight pontoons of timber, strapped the blocks to them and simply floated them down when the river when in flood, but they still needed the same unloading at the other end. And the same return journey for either or both pontoons and men. Or have a constant supply of materials to build the necessary boats plus a constant supply of skilled seamen to guide them down river.

However, even if we accept that this is how they did it, the whole theory has one massive flaw. Have you spotted it yet? Yes, the Nile flooded every year. The river would rise or fall at least twenty five feet in which case all the docks and cranes would be flooded. This has enormous implications for the logistics at the time. Let us look at the Nile flood before the Aswan Dam was built in 1970.

The river begins to rise in June each year due to the melting snows and rains in the Central African Highlands plus the annual rainfalls in Ethiopia. Together both the Nile and the Congo drain most of Equatorial Africa so we are talking about a lot of water going down a narrow valley. By July the river flow was much increased and this carried on through August and September to its peak in October. That peak was around 45ft at Aswan, 36ft at Luxor and 25ft at Cairo. Then it went down again so that for only six to seven months of the year all the benefit of the alluvial deposits were utilised to grow crops. The downside in 2,900BC was that for five months the river would be unusable for the transport down and across it of huge blocks of stone and that any docking or floating off areas must constantly be rearranged.

So a second set of arrangements on each bank must be built on ground 25 feet higher – obviously some distance away if progress was to be made during the flood. This would have had the effect of shortening the dragging distance on each side. Moreover it would not be unreasonable to hope that somewhere in the desert around high water mark would be the remains/ruins of those docks. They would have needed to be very strong to last for over a hundred years of constant heavy use. So far, to my knowledge, no one has found any. Conventional wisdom insists that canals were dug from the river to the side of the construction work and, presumably similar canals near the quarries. Where is the evidence of these, especially for the one out to the Red Pyramid? Even so they still needed exactly the same docking and loading facilities of which there is no evidence whatsoever. The fact that the Giza complex is some 60 metres or 180ft above normal river level means that they could never have been floated to the site. And they must allow for the rise and fall of the river. How??? Did they have the capability to build locks? I think not.

The current hot theory in Cairo when I was last there in 2010 is that the blocks were prepared on dry land at Aswan, attached to timber pontoons at the quarry and then when the river rose, they simply floated downstream. Again, how did they find enough timber to construct the pontoons? How did they load, and subsequently unload the blocks, and how could anyone control a huge craft like this as it first went over the 1st Cataract and then made its way north in a torrent? Watching any newsreel footage of big rivers in spate should convince any doubter of this problem. When I see my local river, the Wharfe, at times of flood going over a weir I realise that being on a huge raft would not be a good idea. It is a torrent at that place going over a simple fall of a few feet, far less of a drop than the first cataract of the Nile and with far less water.

The problem overlooked with this theory is that the Nile will not have been navigable in papyrus boats for several months each year. You only have to look at any big river today when in flood and you will see that the current will have swept everything away, making even a simple crossing a hazardous undertaking. Even with powerful engines few vessels sail against the flood on rivers like the Mississippi or Yangtze. Oarsmen heading towards Aswan would have little chance whilst those coming the other way with a seventy ton lump of granite would have no means of control. This has an enormous effect on the time scales for the construction. For months of each year it would have been impossible to transport any blocks at all.

Now we look at the properties of the pyramids themselves. I say to you quite categorically that, had there just been the few in Egypt and possibly a couple in Mexico, then I would, like everyone else, have stood back in awe and let it pass. But there are those others, hundreds of them dotted all over the world, and some of which are even bigger than that of Cheops. It was obviously unknown in the Classical world, or The Great White Pyramid in China would have been mentioned as being the eighth Wonder of the World. But it was not and only discovered recently and, as yet, has not been touched by archaeologists. What an opportunity lies there. Here I agree with conventional wisdom in that I think they were all built in a tiny window of about 1000 years which coincides with my bulge on the graph. My new graph [Appendix 1] now shows the same long lead in time interrupted by bulges of various sizes before returning to its varying pattern for the last two thousand years.

It is irrefutable that something dramatic happened to mankind during that bulge period that necessitated the construction of so many pyramids in such diverse parts of the world. And it cannot have been a sudden rush of blood simultaneously making local kings and chiefs demand a pyramid to be buried in. And then have it set exactly north/south, in formations matching Orion's belt, using the same design and stone-work. Two similar happenings make a coincidence. Over one hundred do not, yet all these structures are spread all over the world where their builders were totally unable to communicate with each other. Or were they?

Let us return to the properties of pyramids. There is a big industry out there making domestic pyramids [with no sides], so that they can be erected at home, and where you can sit and ponder in peace. It has been proven that placing a blunt blade in a pyramid in the right spot will result in it being sharp again next day. Also that food can be kept fresh within the confines and [I think significantly] they will recharge a battery. Let us say that that is our next clue. Obviously for this to happen the pyramid must be hollow. A solid one is of no use whatsoever.

What about the actual layout of the site at Giza? That greatest of all Egyptologists, Flinders Petrie, did a triangulated survey of the site back in 1880 – 1882 and fixed all the positions in relation to each other. And why did you not know this before? Why is it not recorded, as much of Petrie's work is, in the myriad of works on the subject? Could it be because it posed some extremely difficult questions? That could be the reason why. From this he proved beyond any doubt that all three were planned at the same time. His work, carried on subsequently by mathematician John A R Legon, also showed that whoever laid them out as they did, did so with an incredible mathematical precision that they fully understood. We are not talking simple arithmetic here but maths up to at least Masters Degree standard, something that the locals of the period could not have just stumbled upon and then forgotten afterwards, but the type that has taken us 2,500 years to fully understand. It also helps to have a powerful computer with the right type of programme.

I will not attempt to patronise you, the reader, by pretending to understand all of Legon's work since I do not, but I have sufficient knowledge of the subject to get the gist of what he has to say. And one thing that comes out loud and clear is that when added together many of the numbers ended up with known mathematical constants. Such as that a proportion of the height to total base each time comes out as 44/7 which is the exact number for *2 x pi*. Such as that if you draw a rectangle beginning with the outer east and south faces of the Great pyramid, projecting lines out at right angles to meet similar lines coming from the north and west faces of the third pyramid, you end up with the dimensions [in cubits] of 1732 and 1417.5. [Appendix 3] These are significant numbers to a mathematician since they represent the square root of the first two primary numbers multiplied by 1000. This is no coincidence or accident.

Legon then draws a part circle joining the outer points of the three pyramids from where, assisted by a CAD programme, he can deduce the exact centre, from which he can work out the diameter, which comes to exactly 35,000 cubits, a round number if ever I saw one. From this Legon calculates many other things and those interested in further research into this should go to his web site at www.legon.demon.co.uk. It is fascinating and well worth reading but I introduce these tiny abstracts to try to show that there was nothing accidental in the layout of the pyramids. They were laid out with an incredible precision to the designs of gifted mathematicians and highly skilled surveyors. Once again we must ask those three awkward questions of 'Why', 'When' and 'How'. In this volume I also pass over the significance of the mathematical' Golden Ratio' which appears over and over in the measurements of the Great Pyramid.

Introducing astronomers into the equation muddies the waters a great deal more as we shall see. Again I do not pretend to be an expert in their 'language' nor do I understand fully what they exactly mean but, like the rest of you, I certainly get the gist of their arguments which are quite breathtaking in their implications.

The first thing you should understand about this is what is meant by 'The Great Circle'. As we all know the earth is more or less a sphere whilst most of our maps show it flat – the Mercator Projection. On the Mercator maps the shortest distance between any two points is a straight line but, if you then transfer that line onto a true round globe, the further you go, the greater the added mileage. So you follow a curve taking you far from that line to get the shortest distances. That curve is the Great Circle. Typical examples being London to Los Angeles across the North Pole, and the old tea clippers that would go way down into the Roaring Forties, to the edge of the pack ice, on their way from China across the Pacific to Cape Horn.

There is an interesting site called 'Mapmakers from the Ice Age' written by a Belgian astronomer Jean Pierre Lacroix, with the aid of Cape Canaveral, back in 1998. He refers back to some maps studied by Charles H Hapgood in 'Maps of the Ancient Sea Kings', evidence of advanced civilizations in the ice age.' One of those maps that belonged to Turkish Admiral Pirie Re'is shows the entire world including the Americas and the Antarctic. From this he deduces that in that period after the ice had melted, a series of beacons were erected around the world as some sort of astronomical observatories to guide sailors on their journey.

Most of this is written in very technical language but the conclusions are easy to see. If you take Easter Island in the Pacific, the Nazca lines in Peru, Tenerife in the Atlantic, Giza as the centre, Mohenjo-Daro in Pakistan and Angkor Wat in Cambodia, returning to Easter Island, and draw a line between them all, it describes an almost exact Great Circle circumnavigation of the world near but not on the Equator, passing in the process many other historical sites.. It lies at around 30 degrees to the angle of the Equator. Further, if you take the Meridian of Alexandria as your base and Giza as the centre and then describe a series of circles you will find that Mohenjo-Daro, Stonehenge and the ancient French workings at Carnac all on one circle. Anghor Wat and the Chinese observatory at Gaocheng are on another circle

The Thornborough Henges in North Yorkshire, UK. They are huge. The length of the parallel straight embankments known as 'curcus' is 1.1km. The circumference of the centre henge is 722metres, exactly double the diameter of Stonehenge which is the same 360m and 366m that they are apart. They lie on 54 degrees north which measures one tenth of the Earth's circumference at the Equator. The zig zag line to the left is the public road from which none of this is apparent. From the air, covered in white gypsum they must have been spectacular.

whilst Nazca, Machu Pichu, Uxmal in Mexico and Chaco Canyon in the United States lie on another. On my map you will see that I have shown the sites of the principal pyramids throughout the world together with other non-pyramid shaped pre historic sites.

Taking the ones that mirror the belt of Orion it shows an exact straight line from Giza through Italy to Thornborough in North Yorkshire and its three tumuli. Take another straight line from the one on Samoa through Tahiti and you arrive exactly on Easter Island. These are as perfect lead in markers onto a beacon as you will find plus, of course, they are antipodal meaning that an approach over either ocean will guide the traveller onto the correct Great Circle course.

Of all our sites, the Yorkshire one is significant since it is the most northerly and the only one to have been engulfed in the ice. Now the ice would have easily destroyed simple earthworks of this size, and so it is safe to assume that these were built after it had receded in about 12 – 10,000 BC. After the ice had gone the waters rose and much of the Plain of York was left as a swamp. Right up to the 17th and 18th Centuries the Kings of England on their journeys north had to wait on Tadcaster Bridge for an escort across the swamp land to visit York. So the Ancient Britons would have had to wait until the earth was dry enough to build their tumuli, which I would say would not be much before 6,000 BC, but probably around that time. I would also think it safe to assume that Giza, being at the centre of the world at the time, would come first with the rest following over a period of time. This would put Giza in at no later than 6 – 6,500 BC with the rest following, possibly over a whole millennium. Or it may have been earlier as we will see.

I would further question the uses of all this information. The first and, to me most obvious observation, is that it cannot have been there exclusively for sea farers. If you think about it, assuming that our ship was sufficiently sea worthy and capable of sailing against the prevailing wind and the powerful South Equatorial Current, they would have needed very accurate guidance systems to find their way from Easter Island across the Pacific to the coast of Peru. Then what? They couldn't see the Nazca lines, or Machu Pichu, high up in the Andes. All they found was a very dry and inhospitable Peruvian coast. To continue their journey they had to climb the Andes and then make their way across Brazil to the Atlantic or go down to Cape Horn, return up the Atlantic and then pick up the trail across to West Africa before setting off across the desert to Giza. Going the other way would be just as difficult. Sorry but I don't buy that one either.

The only observation possible is that all this was meant to be seen from the sky using whatever navigation instruments were available at the time. Impossible? Ludicrous? Obviously, but what else can be suggested?

A further thought on the subject of very ancient stones. Look at the work on the Giza pyramids; then on Tenerife and then on Easter Island and what have we in common? All use carefully worked stone to a very high degree of sophistication. All use stones that have been quarried and then worked to give the finished result. Now check out the various monoliths and stone circles of northern Europe. They too use massive pieces of stone but effectively none are worked.

Each piece has been quarried, no doubt by using the simple method of finding a suitable weathered outcrop and then by identifying a natural fault line. Into this fault are inserted pieces of wood as wedges hammered in with large 'hammer stones'. The wood is soaked which causes it to expand. If it is very cold this water will freeze causing it to expand even more until the force causes a large shard to break away from the outcrop. And that is it. The piece is then transported to the site where it is erected as either one of a line or of a circle. I query why some stones were moved large distances. Could it be that there was no convenient outcrop nearby and that the shards had separated naturally, probably during the ice age, and that it was easier to transport them than to dig them out in the first place?

As we will see later in the book, all of humanity emerged from the eternal 'Stone Age' with the same basic intelligence and ability, give or take the odd thousand years. So what happened to give the inhabitants of Egypt, the Canary Islands, Easter Island, Machu Pichu et al, the incredible ability to do what they did that was denied to those living in colder climes? Something did, what was it?

15

AWKWARD QUESTIONS

I do not intend to rehash closely what so many gifted researchers have already covered and, should you wish to study what follows in greater detail then may I suggest that you read, amongst others, the works of Eric von Daniken and Graham Hancock plus the massive work by Michael Cremo and Richard Thompson – *'Forbidden Archaeology'*. Not to mention the myriad of Internet Sites, many un-attributed, that give in depth information on everything below. I merely mention things here for which there is no logical explanation today but, nevertheless, are accomplished facts that will not go away.

Typical Nazca lines. What can they possibly mean?

Being a simple soul I tend to believe what I actually see and look for the simplest, most obvious of explanations. Take for example the Nazca lines in the wild wilderness that marks the desert of the High Andes in Peru. These were marked out by a forgotten people using unknown methods during an ancient period long ago. They can only be seen from the air from where you can see various obvious designs of immense size that mean nothing at ground level. Since, in theory, flight was not possible before the

Wright brothers, armies of scientists have debated what their land based meanings are. I do not have that problem. I believe that they were designed to be seen from the air, when and by whom I do not know, but they were certainly messages of some kind. The irrefutable facts are that they are there and were marked out for a purpose.

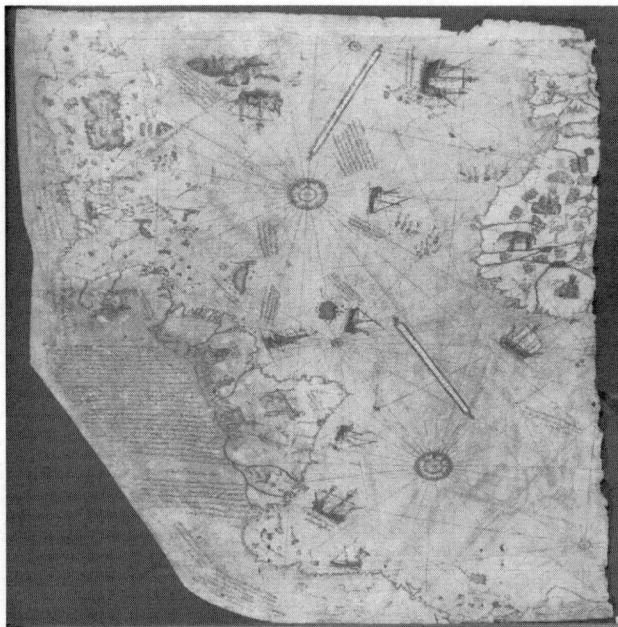

The Piri Re'is Map. Note the relative outlines of Africa to South America which show an error of no more than around 20 miles. At the bottom is Queen Maud Land in Antarctica which again shows more or less correct longitudes, as do the Bay of Biscay and the mouth of the Mediterranean. Drawn in 1513 it was copied from a far older map and this is the torn off Atlantic page. The rest is now long lost.

The next difficult one is the Pirie Re'is map. Again the story of this is covered by others and I too look a lot closer later on, but briefly for this chapter this is what it is all about. This was a map drawn by the Byzantine Admiral Pirie Re'is in the early part of the 16th century and discovered in an Istanbul library comparatively recently. In 1923 in fact. Its origins certainly pre-date Columbus and what makes it interesting is that it shows South America, and parts of the Antarctic continent free of ice. It shows mountains and rivers, now covered by 2 miles thickness of ice, in great detail and can only have been drawn by cartographers on the ground or from the air. Seismic surveys today confirm that it is very accurate indeed. The problem is that in the 16th century no one as yet had discovered Antarctica or the Americas and that it has been covered in ice for an awfully long time. But some intelligent being saw it and mapped it.

Pirie Re'is said that he had taken it from an ancient scroll, long since lost, but we must ask ourselves, just how ancient? Once again the facts are irrefutable. The map exists, someone drew it without guesswork and someone, one day, must come up with an acceptable explanation. One theory is that the continent sits on a plate and, that towards the end of the last Ice Age, that plate was situated somewhere in the Atlantic where it was the home of the advanced civilization of Atlantis. Could that have been a stopping off point between Tenerife and Mexico? Many people have thought so but any student of geology and ancient geography will point out that the continents of Africa and South America, which also sit on separate plates, were once very close indeed. The Amazon basin fits very easily into the Bight of Benin leaving little or no room for another wandering continent in between. Also the map shows it located in its correct position over the South Pole. And that it accurately shows the shape of South America must indicate that there were humans about with map making skills a long time ago. Also on this map the site of 'Atlantis', if it actually existed, is shown just where the Bahamas sit today. And no, I don't buy that one either. I return to this subject in Chapter 21.

Then we come to the Rock Crystal skull which emerged in the late 19th century at, of all places, Tiffanys who sold it to the British Museum as being Aztec. Now Rock Crystal is a quartz material and is up there with granite as being exceptionally hard and far from easy to work, yet someone, in ancient times, was able to carve an anatomically perfect representation of the human skull. Complete with detachable jaw bones. Or so we are led to believe. Another skull [coincidence?] appeared in the forties when it was sold to a Mitchell Hughes by Sotheby's and since then they have kept popping up all over the place. It has been calculated [not by me] that using the only method possible in ancient times of slowly grinding away with a mixture of diamond and water, the man hours required to complete just one added up to over 300 years working full time.

My feeling is that ONE of these MAY be genuine but not necessarily so. For the purpose of this exercise I feel that they merely side track the main issue and, genuine or not, have little relevance to this work. One interesting by line to this is that if it is indeed Aztec in origin, despite all their building achievements and skills at carving jades, there is not one scrap of evidence that they actually had any metals of any type to work with.

In 1903 the German industrialist and 'amateur' archaeologist, Prof. Albert von LeCoq, on behalf of the Berlin University excavated sites near Turfan on the Silk Road as it entered the Gobi Desert. Here he excavated some wall paintings which were then transported back to the Ethnological Museum in Berlin for safety, only to be destroyed by an allied bomb in 1944. He brought back over 300 cases of artefacts that seemed to prove the existence of an Aryan race in the area. The interesting thing about the paintings is that they depict local Asiatic faces with appropriate features together with red haired, blue eyed western peoples described by LeCoq as being 'Greek Gods'. Augustus John describes them as 'Apollo' like blue eyed blonds with decorations identical to those found on modern [1905] playing cards. At the latest these paintings were done around 200BC but that is not certain. They may have been much earlier but it is not up to me to challenge the dates. But who were these 'Greek Gods' living on the Silk Road? Where did they come from, when and why were they there? Is it coincidence that they are near the region of China's great pyramids?

What about the Sphinx, that massive stone carving sitting with his back to the pyramids facing for eternity to the exact point of sunrise on the summer solstice when he was first supposed to be laid out. This is another subject described by others in incredible detail elsewhere and so, again, I will merely lay out the salient facts.

The first and most obvious one is that he does not now face the rising sun at the exact moment that it appears since, due to the process known as 'Precession', discussed earlier in the book, the earth has tilted on its axis and he looks to the exact spot where it would have appeared no later than 12,500 years ago, at the dawning of our present Age of Aquarius, as we left the Age of Leo that had lasted some 26,000 years. A mystery to me that so far no one else seems to have picked up is just how, in all these structures from Stonehenge and the Irish earth works down to the Sphinx, they knew the exact moment of sunrise. And that it was the actual solstice, not the day before or after since they had no method of recording time.

This takes some working out even today with all our telescopes and computers yet they were able to do it then.

You may think this a doubtful observation. Surely it is the moment when the first rays of the sun are visible on the horizon but this is not so. My first observation is that the Sphinx does not look out to sea but over a rocky landscape and low hillside and so, when he first sees the sun, it will have been up for some time. Also, at dawn and sunset the sun is at a virtual tangent to the curvature of the earth, but immediately before the one and after the other, its rays must first pass through the atmosphere before striking land. This causes what is known in physics as a refraction of light, the same as if you put a straight stick into water at an angle. The stick appears to bend. It is the same with the sun's rays. As they enter the atmosphere they are deflected, so that a mere reflection of the sun is first up in the morning and last away at night. As the earth rotates, the sun's rays eventually describe an exact tangent with the curvature of the earth, and that is the exact moment of sunrise or sunset. Until then you see a dull red circle rising slowly on the horizon, of which it is clear, before that first bright spark right at the top indicating the true sunrise. Also, in Northern climes, the chances of any solstice, even the summer one, or equinox being free of cloud cover would be extremely remote.

Had the intention actually been to have him see the first rays of the sun, surely they would have dug him out higher up onto the plateau at the same level as the Great Pyramid? This is some 60 metres higher. Then he would have looked over the hillside rather than at it. To me this doesn't make sense since whether he was dug out before, at the same time or after the pyramids, there was all the room in the world to pick a better spot.

I am not even going to start on how they dug him out of the bedrock, suffice to say that they did for all to see. However the interesting enigma is the weathering. Pictures of Napoleon at the site show it submerged in sand with only the head visible. There are numerous pictures in the late nineteenth century showing the same and it doesn't take much working out that all that sand will be quickly blown about in a desert storm, soon filling the void. Once there it will stay forever until man comes along and clears it. And once covered it is forever protected from erosion. I would even go so far as to suggest that from the first covering following the encroachment of the desert it remained as such until it was uncovered in the 19th century. Yet the body shows that it has eroded badly over the years, not from sand but from several thousand years of torrential rain. The area last saw significant rain not later than 8,000BC when the area was grass land, and that period was some time after it had been rain forest. That means it must have been built well before that. 10,500BC perhaps? Or even earlier? The pyramids have not eroded due to water and so they cannot be considered as being contemporary. The exposed head is almost unrecognizable due to sand and wind erosion.

There are a staggering 39.5 million individual websites on the Internet relating to the UFO phenomenon. I do not pretend to have viewed them all, only a tiny fraction, and my conclusion is that either there are an awful lot of 'nutters' out there or that there could be something in it. However, unlike the ghosts, I have never actually witnessed one myself. Having said that, I may nearly have done so on the very morning that I wrote this piece. I lived with a clear view of Nice airport but a friend has a flat on one of the highest points in Nice from which she can see the entire city, port and airport. As we were talking on the telephone she told me to look out over the airport since some very fast jets of some description were approaching me, more or less overhead, and travelling in formation at a very high speed. I was on my balcony but saw nothing as she said they were disappearing into the clouds. Four fast jets make a lot of noise but I heard and saw nothing. My friend did. I just wonder what they were. In France, military planes are not allowed to fly low over built up areas near airports. I often saw military jets, but only well out to sea. It certainly makes you think.

Whilst doing the latest update of this book, I saw posted on the internet not one, but dozens, of pictures of UFO activity over London. Members of the public used their mobile phones to record several tiny white spots in the sky, attended by what could only be described as a 'mother ship', darting about until they disappeared behind some much lower clouds. There were too many people who were obviously strangers to each other taking these pictures for them to be a computer generated hoax, but of what they were photographing remains to be seen. Always remember that UFO means 'Unidentified Flying Object' which, of course, all these were.

Soon after this update was reviewed again in 2014 it was a fine late afternoon and I enjoyed a coffee in the garden of my now UK flat. To my right I could see in the distance some low fine weather cumulous clouds and above them, flying in the NE/SW air corridor were the vapour trails of commercial aircraft flying at around 35 – 40,000 ft. They flew over the cumulous but under a scattered covering of cirrus clouds – more commonly known as 'Mare's Tails' – and these are the highest clouds that have a ceiling of around 40,000ft. You see this clearly when flying on holiday. Once above the clouds, that is what you are, above the clouds. At 35 – 40,000ft there is nothing but bright blue sky with just a suggestion of very thin clouds at the same height. Above that there is nothing since the air is very thin and there are no clouds. Then I looked above my head to see another obvious vapour trail that had just been made since it had not begun to dissipate and that was well clear of the commercial air corridor and was in an almost exact east/west configuration. Then I looked again to see the cirrus clouds drifting underneath this trail and, by the obvious difference in the speed, they were a very long way under that vapour trail.

Now there have been planes that have flown at well over 100,000ft but they were specially built leaving the record for the highest altitude for a 'normal' plane at around 85,000ft by a Lockheed SR1. The highest commercial flights were Concorde at 50,000ft with the only planes currently flying at these extreme altitudes being the U2 spy planes which operate at around 70,000ft. Was my vapour trail a U2 or could it have been something else? If a U2, what was it doing over the North of England in 2014? Makes you think again, doesn't it?

Again, just before typing out the above, I read in the paper that a massive hole had appeared in the ground in a deserted spot in Outer Siberia. The Russians say that they have no idea what it is or how it happened. It is not a 'sink hole'. But it is there for all to see on Google Earth.

The one thing I absolutely refuse to believe is that we, on earth, are unique and isolated, being the single planet in the entire cosmos to support intelligent life. Or, for that matter, any life at all. That we are alone out of all those billions of stars, galaxies and planets takes a lot of believing yet, out of all those millions of sightings over the years, so far not one has set down and attempted to make themselves known to us. Or have they? Without us being necessarily aware of it. Now there is a thought to carry forward.

One thing is for certain, and that is that they will be technologically more advanced than us, for the simple reason that they are here and we are not hovering over their own planet. In what form will they manifest to us? Would they be as replicas of ourselves, or something else right down to a primordial sticky mass? My feeling is that they will be a lot like us, standing upright on two legs and with dexterous hands and arms. Why? Simply that no matter how advanced they may be, someone or thing has to do the simple bits like actually putting the space craft together with nuts and bolts. No matter how I try, I cannot envisage any method of being able to draw such a complex piece of technology in a computer, press a button, and a finished space ship appears in the next room. That I fear is stretching credulity to its limits. Someone or thing has to have built the computer and all its myriad of small components and all needing dexterous hands. Since writing this piece for the first edition in 2007, some nine years later the advent of the 3D printer has become a fact and you can, in fact, design something on the computer and it can be printed out as the finished article. Ten years hence where will this technology take us? As I said earlier, I rule nothing out at all. Had I suggested a 3D printer back in 2007 who would have taken me seriously?

Then there is communication when they do land. How did they get here since their host planet must be light years away and, according to Einstein, it will never be possible to exceed the speed of light? One light year is the distance a wave length of light will travel in one year at 176,000 miles per second.

That should put the lid on the whole argument unless some of those 40 odd million 'nutters' are right. Which means that either Einstein is wrong [which I believe], or that there are other ways of travel. Now we must enter the world of Science Fiction [or do we?] by considering Teleporting.

'Beam me up Scotty' is a phrase that will forever be Startrek as Captain Kirk is whisked back onto the Enterprise from some distant planet but, today, just how far fetched actually is it? We know that the US Air Force, from its top secret Los Alamos facility in New Mexico, has had a team working on it for years. Just how far they have got, they are not saying but I do know that as far as the technology is concerned, they understand what is needed but are still a long way off teleporting more than a single particle at a time. Teleporting a living being is an incredibly complex operation and it is doubtful whether it will occur in the immediate – or medium term – future. They will get there, probably not in my lifetime, but possibly in that of our recently born child. Or much earlier, as did the 3D printer.

But, if you think about it, we already use teleporting of a sort every day if we have access to the Internet. Every time we send an email, either the picture, text or moving image is instantly scrambled electronically, before being sent either to some far distant satellite from where it is beamed, in digital form, to the far corners of the earth. Or it will go along a fibre optic cable across continents and oceans in fractions of seconds to appear on your computer. One person only has the right receiver which picks it up, unscrambles it and then places it in the 'Inbox'. And all is done more or less instantaneously. The receiver can now be a mobile phone. When I needed to contact Brazil less than thirty years ago, this technology was most definitely the stuff of science fiction, but not now. With the present daily advances do not dismiss this as a possibility for the not too distant future. I include it in my things to put on the back burner for the moment. Every week I speak to my son in Australia on Skype. I have watched his lips carefully and the speech is more or less instantaneous. Thirty years ago, after he was born, this would have been most definitely the stuff of the comic papers.

Taking this argument further given the technology of 2016, now 3D printers can do amazing things. I could design something in London and send electronically that information to a 3D printer in Sydney or Los Angeles and the finished article will appear there. This can be anything in metal, carbon fibre, plastic or even pasta! To me, that is approaching teleporting. Just where this technology will take us in the next twenty five years I do not know but if they can eventually replicate a human heart in this way and send it across the globe, which I forecast will happen, it may begin to answer a lot of these questions.

The next awkward question that will not go away comes from the chapter on The Creation. One theme throughout, and from whence all the Gods come, is the story of the tall white man or woman [in Australia he was brown and blond] who performed miracles before disappearing to heaven either by floating away or by means of a ladder. Once again my problem with coincidences raises its ugly head. I could accept one of these, maybe two as the subject of vivid imaginations but when they leap up everywhere I prick up my ears. Again there was little chance of collusion because the distances over the big seas were involved, and so one must accept that there must be an element of truth in it all. So just who were these supposed giants who lived for prodigious years, where did they come from and, more to the point, where did they go? Again there are just too many similarities for these to be coincidental. They are fully discussed in the chapter on the myths of creation.

Then there are the Dogon people from Mali in West Africa. They migrated some 500 years ago from the Sudan to escape slavery and the imposition of Islam, settling eventually on a rocky escarpment near Timbuktu on the edge of the Southern Sahara. They believe that they were visited some 5,000 years ago by a race of extra terrestrial amphibians called the 'Nommo', and that these people or creatures came from a planet near Sirius. Yes, once again mention of Sirius from the Orion complex. But it was not actually from Sirius but a smaller star, since identified as a white dwarf, called Sirius 'B'. They called it 'Po Tolo' or just simply 'Po'.

What is remarkable here is that Sirius B is a tiny star, the size of the earth but with the mass of the sun, and is very faint and impossible to see with the naked eye. Yet they knew it was there, that it was made of a very heavy metal and that in an elliptical arc it orbited Sirius itself every fifty years. Every fifty to sixty years they have a ceremony to celebrate this. That in itself is remarkable since they would have had little to measure the passage of so many years and few, if any of them would have lived long enough to witness it more than once. The Dogon are also aware of Jupiter's moons, Venus and the rings of Saturn which again can only be seen with a powerful telescope. They understood that these were planets which orbited our own sun. They believe that the people will return as human beings [have they already been?] some day before reverting to being amphibians and ruling from the seas.

Sceptics say that missionaries gave them the information but artefacts positively dated to over 400 years ago show the relevant stars. There is no evidence at all that the missionaries also gave them powerful telescopes to provide the fake evidence.

I have great difficulty in dismissing all this as merely tribal myth. To me it is another small piece in the enormous jigsaw puzzle that we are unearthing. There are too many apparently unconnected things all over the world pointing in the same direction that, when put into the bigger picture, rather than being treated in isolation, make for interesting deductions to be considered. One just cannot take a 'Mighty Bound' over them all and move on to more convenient happenings.

Genesis 6.4 states quite categorically *'There were giants on earth in those days; and also after that, when the sons of God came in unto the daughters of men, and they bare children to them, the same became mighty men which were of old, men of renown'.*

Iceland had a giant in human form – Ymir – with a palace at the far side of the rainbow.

India had a Primordial Giant, a cosmic man – Purwha.

The Aztecs had the female Coatlicue with son Huizilopocth.

The Mayas had two gods in a story to mirror Genesis.

In Honduras a white woman came down from heaven to where she returned by ascension in old age.

Nicaragua had a heaven and fiery hell.

The Egyptians had Osiris ascending to heaven to the Elysian Fields and then the female Hathor held the ladder for the deserving to climb to heaven. Thoth taught them wonderful things.

There were the blue eyed blonds living on the Silk Road in China.

Etcetera, etcetera.

Not forgetting, of course, that Christ and Mohammed also ascended to heaven, as did Elijah and Enoch. Moses had a manifestation of God himself and that the Angel Gabriel flitted back and forth for thousands of years.

To me, the only conclusion has to be that there must be some truth in them all, or that they are all figments of vivid imaginations. You cannot accept without question Christ's ascension and then dismiss the rest as rubbish. It is all or none. I prefer to think the former. In this book, I go down that path.

There are the numerous finds throughout the world totally out of context with existing thought. An iron cup, not unlike a Scottish Quake, which is a cup for drinking whisky, was found embedded in a lump of coal in Oklahoma that formed 300 million years ago. Obviously man made.

In 1844 an iron nail, complete with head, was unearthed in northern Britain. It was embedded in a piece of sandstone aged around the 350 million years period. In the same year at a quarry by the River Tweed in Britain a gold thread was discovered in rock at a depth of eight feet. In 1871 a coin was discovered at a depth of 114ft in Illinois. In Illinois again, in 1891 a gold chain was found embedded in a lump of coal. It was obviously man made and decorative and made some 320 million years ago. In another Oklahoma

The iron cup from Oklahoma. Found in coal.

coal mine in the nineteen twenties miners discovered a long wall made of perfect square concrete type blocks so highly polished that they shone. It was over 100 feet long and the blocks were cubes about one foot square. Obviously it had to have been built before the vegetation decomposed into coal at least three hundred million years ago. The miners who found it in an old shaft mine said that the roof caved in on them when they found the first few feet. They took out some blocks which were literally mirror smooth on all sides. They then put staves in to secure the roof but the fall had exposed well over 100 extra feet of the wall. The mine owner was furious and forbid them to talk about it lest it stopped production. So who built it???

221

In 1938 in China there were found a pile of dusty stone disks, perfectly formed and with a hole in the exact centre. They have been dated at around 10,000BC. They are beautifully carved and have lots of tiny hieroglyphics that have been translated [by whom?] to say that they belonged to a people called the 'Dropa' and that they were survivors of a crash by their craft into the nearby mountains. When put on a turntable they emit a distinctive 'hum'. They seem to have vanished during the war. Are they for real or just one of the many 'hoaxes' that were supposed to have been perpetrated at the time? It was a lot of effort if that was the case. Just the one should have done the trick.

One of the beautifully carved 'Dropa' stones.

An iron axe with wooden shaft similarly embedded into rock not less than the same age was discovered in North America. And then there are the numerous examples of dexterity in the working of gold and the polishing and piercing of precious stones for adornment at times when man should have had time only for basic survival. In 1944, in Mexico, a hoard of ceramic models of dinosaurs was found. Carbon dating puts them at between 3 and 6,000 years old. How could Mexican Indians at that period have been able to make accurate depictions of a type of creature that became extinct millions of years earlier?

In his book, *'Human Devolution'*, Michael Cremo lists numerous examples of fossilised human bones dating back hundreds of millions of years. Some simply crumbled to dust as they were exposed leaving a perfect mould in the surrounding rock. These things cannot be faked and so at those times a form of Homo

The Mexican 'dinosaurs'.

sapiens must have inhabited the earth. The big questions must be whether or not they simply became extinct and then re-evolved in a later period or whether they survived over the ages.

In Abydos, near Luxor in Egypt are many small carved cartouches showing humdrum everyday life except for just one that identifies depictions of planes, helicopters and submarines. It has been tested by many to see whether or not it is a hoax, but apparently not. Amazing it would seem, but maybe not so as we will see.

Are these actually planes on the Abydos cartouche? It is carved amongst many others on a huge granite lintel. Until recent discoveries, it would have been impossible to carve this using modern hand tools.

In 1936 a young couple in London found a piece of sandstone out of which there appeared to be some wood protruding. They took it home, cut it open with a chisel and inside was revealed an iron hammer. Subsequent research places the stone at around 400 million years old and the iron to be 96% perfect. The wood was beginning to turn into coal.

These things exist, they will not go away and cannot just be swept away as an anomaly. For every single one of these you will find the usual detractors all screaming *'conspiracy theory, ha, ha, ha,'* and they may be right. On the other hand they may not. The iron cup and the hammer mean that a form of dextrous, intelligent being must have been well developed before the time when the dinosaurs ruled the earth. And well before the present continental set up was formed. They had discovered iron and knew how to cast it. They must have been the only warm blooded creatures at the time, but is it credible to expect us to believe that they then wandered the earth while continents were diverging, mountain ranges being formed, dinosaurs evolving and then becoming extinct? At a time

The iron hammer embedded in stone. My first thought was that it was somewhat crude.

when most forms of life on the planet were very basic indeed. And during this period of time all the other species of animals, birds and fish slowly evolved, most subsequently going into extinction? And again during all that time we, assuming that they were like us, the ultimate survivors with the ultimate intelligence, after millions of generations actually reverted back to the Stone Age and the ability to build only a mud hut before the 'bulge' on my graph occurred? With all this I have a problem especially since there is little fossilised evidence of very ancient, very advanced people. Only the remains in those rocks that once surrounded human bones. I certainly don't go for it, yet those artefacts, and those moulds, got stuck in the coal and the rock all those years ago.

Someone left them there before the arrival of the dinosaurs. Who were they? Are they our ancestors or what????

What about the Ark of the Covenant? And the Holy Grail? And why, of all metals, should the softest of them all, gold, be the prized one all over the world? And the hardest to work of all the stones, granite, be equally sought after and extensively used for mostly non-structural purposes? None of it makes any sense at all.

Time is the last great barrier to science and this, to a large extent, being governed by Einstein's edict that the speed of light is the ultimate speed, will take some overcoming. I feel that the answers to many of the questions posed so far will be answered fully if we say that Einstein may be wrong. Once we accept that then a whole host of possible answers emerge.

So that life on Earth, or anywhere else for that matter, can be maintained several important criteria must be met. The first is that we must have oxygen to breathe and then water to drink and to help produce food. We also need a very narrow temperature band in order to even exist. The present panic over global warming [or is it cooling? Scientists and other experts seem to disagree on this one] is talking about a rise in global temperature of one or two degrees only. This is an incredible narrow balance if it means the difference between survival or not. The Earth maintains its balance because of several things. The first is that it is just the right distance away from the sun to give us our temperature. It spins on its axis at a thousand miles an hour at the Equator to give us our days and nights and it rotates around the Sun once a year. Because it is tilted that rotation gives us our seasons. Without this happening one half would be permanent ice and the other unbearably hot. I ask you to consider a simple question. Why? Yes, why does it continue to spin like this, year in, year out since time began? A stupid question maybe, but I think not.

Think about it. I feel that few would not agree that the Earth, like every other spherical object in the heavens, was formed originally from a large number of spinning rocks and gases that joined, cooled etc., until we were left with a solid large round object happily spinning away on its own. Science agrees that, give or take the odd billion years, this happened with all our planets at about the same time and logic would suggest that the physical composition of each would be similar. Not identical, but similar. Alongside it is a moon, also from the same source that was originally spinning otherwise it would not be a sphere. The moon apparently no longer spins. The obvious answer to this is that being smaller it does not have the mass to keep it spinning. Fair enough. But every other round object in the sky began in exactly the same way, including our sun, but they all rotate at different speeds. Taking the 'solid' as opposed to the 'fluid' planets, Mars, at 13,300 miles of circumference rotates in 24.62 hours. It is half our size and so rotates with a tangential speed of 540 miles per hour. Venus has a circumference of 23,765 miles but takes 243 Earth days to rotate which gives a tangential speed of 4 miles per hour. Our moon has a circumference of 6790 miles and actually rotates at 9.59 miles per hour. By a unique scientific aberration known as Libration, which I am not going to even begin to try to explain to you, due to its rotation of the Earth and our trajectory round the Sun, the same side always appears to face the Earth. For exactly the same reasons we have to send a probe to look at the far side of both the Moon and Venus. So what keeps the Earth rotating at exactly the same speed over billions of years, not speeding up but slowing down at an incredibly slow rate, when the others plainly have slowed down dramatically?

Newton's Law of Motion states that any body will keep moving in a certain direction until an outside force changes it. So what outside force slowed the rotation of the moon, as well as Venus and Mars, but had no effect on our planet? Logic would suggest that after a period of time the rotation would gradually slow down as the first accelerating forces reduce and this seems to be the case with the others. But not that much with the Earth. If the Earth had no water as with Mars, there would be little outside force to slow it down. But the seas are there and moving all the time with the tides. These move in all directions and the seas themselves are subject to the effects of high winds which whip up considerable motion on the surface. Also the core of the earth is a molten mass, presumably stable since it is trapped and cannot escape.

Liquids on the move can do enormous damage as the victims of storms and tsunamis will testify and I would have thought that over the millennia the movement of the seas should be sufficient to have a slight effect on the rotation of the earth. If the water came from those 660 comets hitting us, that alone would have had some outside effect on the natural earthly rhythms but it doesn't seem to have done so. The sudden arrival of millions of cubic miles of water and rock should have caused an imbalance. But it didn't. I wonder why. Also, over time the poles have iced over and then been free of any ice covering as their positions shifted. Not necessarily at the same time either and this should have a huge imbalance. If one ice cap melts and the other does not it should all be thrown out but it doesn't seem to do so. Not even a tiny bit and that I feel is strange.

Recently I visited a 'Queens of Egypt' exhibition in Monaco which showed some remarkable artefacts used by different Pharhonic Queens. One exhibit made me look again. It was of a small non-descript group of wood carvings dating from about 1800BC. What was interesting was that they were supposedly carved from sycamore. Now sycamore is a deciduous tree that needs a lot of moisture and not much heat and is indigenous to Northern Europe and North America. It certainly is never seen in the Mediterranean region, but those areas of northern Europe were still very much in the Stone Age at the time. So where did the carvers get the sycamore, or could it be an erroneous attribution of either wood or date? Similarly, in the Egyptian Museum in Cairo there are various tools used in very ancient times, some of which have sycamore handles. This suggests that when those tools were being used during the time frame of the pyramid builders, there was no suitable hard wood in the country. The only indigenous timber in Egypt during the First Kingdom was palm, acacia, olive and fig. Not sycamore nor could it be found anywhere near. It would need a very substantial vessel to transport logs of sycamore across the Mediterranean but they could have got to the coast down the Rhone. Everywhere you look in the world's museums are tools with sycamore handles and no one seems to query where it came from.

In his opus, *'The Ship Under Sail'*, published in 1926, around the time when the tomb of Tutankhamen was discovered, and the study of Ancient Egypt was yet to become an 'ology', the distinguished nautical historian and writer E Keble Chatterton describes the very first ships on the Nile. He describes a picture of a ship on a vase in the British Museum dated at around 6000 BC. It is of a simple vessel with a mast and square sail. Then he goes on to talk about a people who invaded Egypt around 5000BC from the Red Sea. They brought with them artistic ability and united the land. They also brought with them the ability to build ships. Presumably they will have come from Sumeria in Iraq. They developed the square sail rig to take advantage of the fact that the prevailing wind in the Nile valley is north to south so enabling them to sail against the flow of the river. He compares these boats to the ones built in Burma to sail the Irrawaddy River and the ones in China for the Yangtse and Yellow Rivers. These are all places that could have had no knowledge of each other.

He cites contemporary illustrations from around 3400BC showing ships being built of clinker construction, which is where the successive planks overlap the one below, and of workers hacking away at the timbers to carve them into shape. This is interesting because it is 2000 years before cedar and fir was being imported from the Lebanon and Syria and nearly 3000 years before iron was first worked in Egypt.

Let us look briefly at this. First, clinker built boats, such as the fishing cobles of the UK coast, require very smooth planks of quite thick wood that are steamed into shape. We can make the comparison because a big coble of today is about the size of a big ship of that ancient period. If they are other than smooth a very large amount of caulking would need to be done to keep the water out. The planks would need to be long and more than one must be carved from each log of wood. Just where did sufficient long and straight trees come from of sufficient hardness for this purpose? They could not use the soft and porous palm. Having got the trees, how were they cut into planks of even thickness when all they had were small tools made from copper or bronze at best? What did they use as fastenings to hold it all together? Nothing adds up. That the ships were built is beyond doubt. That they could not have been built with the tools available must be up for question. So what did they use and where did it come from? The tools on display in the Egyptian Museum could not have built those ships.

On a recent visit to the Egyptian Museum I looked very carefully at some granite sarcophagi and some granite carvings of large proportions, all from various dynastic periods. One such sarcophagus interested me a great deal because on its mirror smooth outer surface were some very intricate carvings. As we discuss with the building of the pyramids, granite is a very hard substance, harder in fact than anything else around in Egypt at the time.

Granite is also quite brittle so that if you are able to find a chisel hard enough to penetrate the surface, a considerable force is needed to make an impact. The immediate area will shatter into little pieces. Yet into this smooth outer surface are carved in perfect detail small birds and other animals with extreme accuracy and in great numbers, all very close to each other with not one sign of the outer edge chipping off. This is remarkable because any such attempt today using the very latest tooling, even power tools, on a modern granite kitchen worktop would result in the holes running into each other. These carvings are of such precision that they resemble ones that would be carved out of hardening plaster using a very sharp knife. So how did they do it? Today we would use a laser, water jet or careful sandblasting, operations not readily available several thousand years before Christ was born.

It is interesting that I describe later in the book some Sumerian texts of around 3-4,000BC that were written on softening clay tablets. These tablets were baked in an oven after which they became as hard as stone and this was standard practice throughout the area. Could that sarcophagus have been carved and prepared in the same way? If so it would answer a lot of my questions as well as asking a whole lot more.

Jump forward in time now to just after the birth of Christ and the Roman occupation of Egypt. In particular to Alexandria and 'Pompey's Pillar'. Now this is a remarkable piece of civil engineering for several reasons. For some inexplicable reason, all other students of the period and places seem to ignore this. Everyone talks about Baalbeck but never Alexandria. The first is that it is thought to be one solid piece of granite, perfectly carved to be exactly round and tapering from 2.7 metres diameter at the base to 2.4metres at the top. It is 30 meters high in total, the shaft being 27 metres of one piece of granite. This alone weighs around 396 tons. It is architecturally and visually perfect in proportion.

Think about that. Here we have one piece of granite hewn from a quarry in Aswan over a thousand miles upstream, carved with incredible precision, using tools softer than the granite itself, either at the quarry or on site in Alexandria. If carved on site the weight would have been significantly greater. It has to be removed in that same one piece and transported to the river where it must be lifted with care into a suitable craft of at least 500 to 750 tons to be capable of supporting the weight without sinking. This vessel must somehow negotiate the first cataract since the quarry would be some distance above it. This could only be done during the annual Nile flood when this massive vessel would have to effectively 'shoot the rapids' and then continue downstream with the river in spate. All the time it must be controlled or it would simply spin out of control and end up beached inland when the level dropped. This in itself would be a hazardous undertaking today with powered craft. No book on the ancient quarries mentions the obvious quarry from where this was extracted.

Having arrived in the Delta, and taken the correct channel to the left on the way, it must then be taken from the boat and placed on land. No contemporary crane arrangement was capable of this yet it must have happened. The site is at the top of a significant rocky hill and this huge edifice had to be taken with extreme care on some sort of sledge or wheeled device the very considerable distance involved. Already in place was a massive granite base stone set exactly level onto which must be lowered the pillar. The base alone is huge as my picture shows.

I looked very carefully all around the base and the foot of the pillar and there is no evidence whatsoever to show that the foot of the column was first placed on the base and the pillar levered from the horizontal into position. Using this method would have been impossible because a point would be reached where the foot of the column would simply slide away and off the base. Considerable damage would be done to both and this would remain to this day.

The author standing in front of Pompey's Pillar in Alexandria. Note the precision with which it was placed on the base. Also the polished surface that is falling off.

Not so and all seems to be perfect with no evidence of repairs. It is very easy to prove this at home. Just get any length of wood or metal about 18 inches long. Stack some books so that you have a three inch high platform and then try to put the stick vertically on them. You must just use one finger of one hand. It cannot be done. I've just tried it again and every time the stick simply slid off as the angle approached 45 degrees.

The pillar is exactly vertical and exactly square on its base. It can only have been placed there by lifting from the horizontal, moving possibly a short distance of perhaps 5 metres and then raising it the approximate 4 metres in height, carrying it to the correct position above the base, before lowering and placing in position with extreme accuracy. Once in place it could not be adjusted, it had to be placed with incredible accuracy first time. You can see on the picture that this is so.

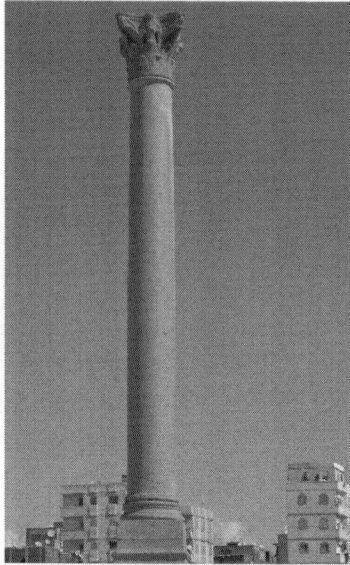

The pillar with its perfect symmetry and capping. To lift this vertically it must be gripped at no more than one third of the way up. There are no visible signs of this happening.

The pillar has a polished surface which around its base is falling off. Could this be significant? With a polished, tapering surface, how did the lifting gear get sufficient grip, without leaving

any marks, to raise 396 tons in weight? Having raised the pillar from the horizontal to the vertical, how did it then move the short dis-
tance so that it ended up in the exact correct position? Bear in mind that there is no single crane available anywhere in the world today, as this is being written, that could do this.

But it's there for all to see. How did they do it? We will see. There is one other remarkable thing about this column. Everyone knows that not very far away was one of the world's seven wonders, the Pharos. This was a giant lighthouse built of very solid limestone blocks and it stood until the fourteenth century when an enormous earthquake caused it to fall. But the nearby pillar remained standing. The Pharos was a very substantial building but the pillar was, and is, freestanding, yet the latter did not move at all. Interesting.

The amazing Antikythera Mechanism that could deduce complex astronomical problems well before 100BC.

A final and interesting anomaly is the Antikythera Mechanism that was discovered in Greek waters in 1901 in the wreck of a ship that went down between 150 and 100BC. From this it must be argued that it cannot be dated later than 100BC. What is interesting about this mechanism is its mechanical complexity and its extremely accurate function. It is the first known Orrery which is a device used for complex astronomical calculations.

It could predict with complete accuracy the Metronic cycle of 235 months and the Callipic cycle, which is four Metronic cycles or 76 years. It could do all this and allow for leap years well before these were discovered and incorporated into the Julian calendar. It also proposes a heliocentric universe, first discovered by Copernicus in 1.543AD. A heliocentric universe is one with the sun at the centre with the planets rotating around it rather than everything rotating around the earth. It involves lunar observations spread over many years which required extremely accurate timing. What are these two cycles? Don't even ask. They are used in work on the tides and involve some very advanced mathematics to fully understand them. I certainly have no intention of even beginning an explanation but the Greeks knew enough to incorporate it all to perfection in their machine. Even though the Med is non-tidal. The Greeks would have had to go to the Atlantic through the Pillars of Hercules to study tides. Did they and if they did, why? No other Greek writings mention this.

The device itself is 13 inches high, 6.7 inches wide and 3.5 inches thick. It is made of bronze and was originally mounted on a wooden frame. Into this are 70 separate gears including a differential set to calculate the relative movement of the sun and the moon. On it are inscribed, in a mixture of Greek and unknown other languages, the instructions for its use containing 3000 characters in all.

Obviously someone, possibly the peoples who spoke and understood the unknown other languages, at some time in the distant past decided that there was the urgent need for this device. They sat down to work out each function and were able to calculate the exact gearing needed each time to achieve it. Significantly they knew all about the planets and that they all, including the Earth, orbited the Sun, thousands of years before Copernicus.

234

They then had to design it so that each mechanism was accurately geared to the next which, in turn, must be equally accurately geared to the next until all 70 odd gears were working together. All must be housed in the above small container and all calculations must be done without the knowledge of 'zero' in the mathematics. Then all must be drawn out precisely with measurements calculated to at least the accuracy of a good clock and then, last of all, someone had to make it. This is what interests me.

Earlier in the book I invited the reader to do some simple experiments to show how difficult it is to make things entirely by hand and it is this fact that gives me a problem. I just cannot see how they can have made this type of mechanism without some sort of tooling. We are talking of incredibly tight tolerances here of plus or minus a thousandth of an inch otherwise it wouldn't work. For this a micrometer or Vernier calliper is needed but who made that with its fine thread? Tiny slices of perfectly round bar must be cut at an exact right angle, the gear slots which are triangular, could be cut by grinding or filing but then the spindles must be made of extremely thin rod and inserted in the precise centre of the gear, again to the same tolerances and exactly at right angles so that each gear ran true and meshed perfectly with the next. The tolerances of the wafer thin sheets on which the spindles were set were the same. And all this was done at least fifteen hundred years before the first crude machine tools and the first accurate measuring devices.

Various researchers have made models of the device but all have access to the latest precision watch maker's lathes and milling machines without which they would say it was an impossible task. I would agree but someone did it. Who, when, where and why? No one will ever know for certain.

16

THE ARK OF THE COVENANT AND THE HOLY GRAIL

I link these two together because they are both mysterious objects which may or may not have existed. I believe the Ark did but, if the Grail did, there is much doubt as to both its form and purpose.

Take the Grail first. This is supposed to be the cup out of which Jesus drank at the last supper. It was used by Joseph of Arimathea to collect the blood of Christ whilst interring Him after the crucifixion. Joseph is then said to have brought the Grail to England where he founded a line to keep it safe. The Grail, like the Ark, is said to possess magical powers, especially of healing.

Our problem with the Grail is that it vanishes from all records until it reappears in the 12th and 13th centuries as part of the Arthurian legend. And this is a legend that you can either believe, or dismiss as just a good story in fiction. This is all down to heroics between the various Knights of the Round Table centred on Percival, Lancelot and Galahad. The legend is well documented elsewhere and so I do not intend to take up time or space to rehash it all except to say that it has a lot to do with seeking the Grail.

There are many thoughts as to its size and shape. The most obvious must be that, if it was used to drink wine at the Last Supper then one would have expected it to be the size of a normal wine glass. Not as has been described as a large bowl or platter. Chretien de Troyes in 1180, as part of his poem *'Perceval, le Conte du Graal'*, describes *'Whilst dining in the Magical abode of the Fisher King'*, Percival sees a procession where youths carry magnificent objects before him during the meal. There is a youth with a bleeding lance, two boys with candelabras followed by a young girl bearing an elaborately decorated 'graal' or grail.' To me this is just a good part of the legend with nothing to do with the cup that Christ used. That would be something very simple – even made of wood, not something elaborately decorated. It would most likely have been a simple pottery bowl without a handle. At the 'Last Supper' those involved would have had their minds on other more important things than providing a valuable and lasting artefact to be handed down over the millennia. As for everyone else, it would have been a simple wine cup or bowl easily held in one hand.

So where might the Grail be today? Various suggestions have been put forward including several locations in the UK and some in the USA – taken there in pre-Columbian times. The Knights Templar were the traditional guardians but they vanished many years ago. This remains a great mystery, the problem being that, should the real thing ever emerge, few would believe

The Holy Grail as portrayed by Dante Gabriel Rosseti.

it. If made of wood it would have disintegrated into dust many years ago. Only if kept in a sealed tomb would the timber survive as with just a few of the tool handles taken from digs in Egypt.

Then we come to the Ark of the Covenant, that mysterious box covered in gold that eventually held the tablets on which were inscribed the Ten Commandments. But it didn't always contain the tablets and there was no suggestion that it might when the Israelites began their epic journey that was the Exodus. So what was so important that tribes of fleeing refugees had to put it into a gold covered box, and then have senior priests carry it all over the desert for years, so that it could be conveniently on hand when Moses came down the mountain?

Not so says the Bible in the chapter of Exodus. It was made by Moses on site after he was given the tablets. Sure. In the desert they had a convenient supply of Acacia wood – my Bible calls it 'Shittin Wood' - to make a box 51 inches long by 31.5 inches wide and 31.5 inches high? The Acacia trees of the Negev Desert are more shrubs than trees and so it would have been difficult to find sufficient to produce the amount of wood needed. This is around 50 x 5 ft long planks, one inch thick and six inches wide that would otherwise have all had to be conveniently prepared in advance and then carried by a retreating people across the Red Sea. And then enough of the purest gold to beat out and encase it completely, and put a thick gold rim around the lid? On top was a solid gold throne with two gold cherubim, their faces turned to face each other, their outspread wings acting as the Throne of God, with the Ark itself acting as His foot stool. Obviously we needed means to cast these. It was then covered with a cloth and carried by four priests holding carrying poles. We are talking here about an army of people with oxen and carts carrying all this on the off chance that it may be needed. I don't think so any more than do you.

Once again we must do our sums. Just simple arithmetic will do. For basic rigidity the box itself must have used timber around one inch thick which is a convenient figure for this exercise. All sizes are in inches, feet, pounds and tons.

Finished sizes are: 51 x 31.5 x 4   = 6426
                         31.5 x 31.5 x2   = <u>1984</u>
                                               8410   cubic

inches

This equates to 4.867 cu ft. The timber weighs 40 lbs per cu.ft therefore the finished weight is 195lbs. Four and a half of our suitcases.

It was covered in gold at presumably around 1/16 inch thick therefore if we take those same 8410 cu inches and divide them by 16 we get 525 cu inches of gold. Gold weighs 1204 lbs per cu ft and so there is 366lbs of gold. This before adding the decoration.

And then we must look at the tablets. No one knows how big they were and so I am going to assume that they were 12 x 6 inches by 1 inch thick. This gives 72 cu inches per tablet multiplied by 12 to give us 864 cu inches or .5 cu ft. Sandstone weighs 145 lbs per cu ft, therefore they weigh 72.5 lbs. I would think that they will have been made of mud that was then baked as a brick but it will have weighed about the same.

So the finished carrying weight of the arc before the decoration, cloth and poles is:
72 + 195 + 366 = 633 lbs in weight.

As always we use a fully loaded suitcase for the airline weighing 42lbs as our comparison and so this is 14 suitcases. The very most that any person, then or now, could carry for any period of time is around 25 to 30 lbs. And so it would need between five and six people holding each corner just to lift it off the ground.

If the raw materials were brought from Egypt they would be bigger and heavier to allow for wastage.

But on top was placed a solid gold throne that measured 2.5 cu bits x 1.5 cubits which would have to be about 2 inches thick for rigidity. Doing the same maths this gives a weight 2529 pounds or 1.129 tons. Hmmm! It would have been impossible to provide strong enough carrying poles, or strong enough fastenings, to make it possible for the now *extra* 25 men on each one to simply lift it off the ground.

However it did not stop there. They were instructed to build huge tables, a tabernacle and an altar, plus provide solid gold tableware and cutlery plus many feet in length of fine dyed linen, all described in detail in Exodus 25 to 27. The weights of the timber as finished would be around 4.5 tons. It is impossible to estimate the exact weight of additional gold, silver and brass that would be needed to complete these but it would be considerable. At the very least it would be another ton in weight, probably much more.

Joshua and Moses bowing before the Ark as envisaged by James Tissot in 1900. Two simple questions. 1. Could those thin poles have supported such a weight and 2. Where, in the arid desert would you find such long, thin pieces of timber?

And so we are led to believe that on tap in the Sinai desert, around 1400BC, there was readily available at least 5 tons of useable timber and several tons of gold, silver and brass. Add on fastenings and the acres of linen specified and you get a vast hoard. All of which must be carried by hand or on the backs of mules and donkeys. Wheels would be of little use in the desert, iron was yet to be discovered and we have already shown that sledges made of wood were not possible. And all of which must have been assembled together in Egypt and transported by a desperate, fleeing population which, one would have thought, may have other things on its mind.

Of course they needed extensive workshop premises, foundries, pattern shops etc. etc, which makes one question the whole idea. But, be that as it may, let us continue.

The Ark then preceded the Hebrews during the rest of their travels to the Promised Land. It was said that sparks flew between the wings of the cherubs and these killed serpents and scorpions, the River Jordan ran dry as the priests approached, running full again when the last of the people had crossed. It was taken into battle against the Philistines, who won and stole the Ark, but sent it back seven months later. They took it again in a subsequent war only to be overcome by mishaps and disasters. Wherever the Ark went people were smitten by boils so again, they gave it back. Over the centuries it had many resting places including the Temple of Solomon in Jerusalem. Eventually the Babylonians sacked Jerusalem and the Ark vanishes from history. Following the line begun by the union of King Solomon and the Queen of Sheba it is believed to have found its way to Ethiopia where it is supposed to lie to this day in the Chapel of the Tablet, at the Church of Our Lady Mary of Zion, in Axum. It is now kept under constant guard and only the head priest is allowed to see it. Or so we are told. Getting the Ark with all its gold from Jerusalem to the Ethiopian Highlands at the time would be another logistical challenge.

Originally the Ark was supposed to hold 'Aaron's rod that budded' plus 'a pot of manna'. This latter could be significant for it was manna 'from heaven' that kept the tribes alive for forty years. This surely means that they will have needed rather more than a single pot, whilst it would not have been possible to carry the lot from the beginning? How could they possibly know to carry enough to last forty years? The only possible answer must be that they had the facility to make it as it was needed.

So just what is 'manna'? For this we must go to the Jewish book, the *Kabbalah*, which contains much traditional knowledge including, in one of its books, the *Zohar*, details of the Ancient of Days. Here I refer to the works of the Fiebag brothers, translated from the German, who with two English engineers, George Sassoon and Rodney Dale have done much work on this subject.

241

Their article is *'The Holy Grail – Chalice or Manna Machine'* and should be read on line to get the full story. Look it up on the Internet. However, briefly Sassoon and Dale in 1978 came to the conclusion that the *Zohar* described a machine for the production of manna. This machine was contained in the Ark or even could have been the Ark itself and, by several simple processes was able to turn dew and an algae culture that required the radiation from a nuclear powered light source. [When researching this book, by this time I had already come to the conclusion that the granite in the pyramids was there as a source of radiation, well before I came across this piece of information. There is no question of finding the facts to suit the theory. I was just as surprised as, no doubt, are you]. They quickly deduced that it must be extra terrestrial. On that, I leave it to my readers to make up their own minds.

At the top was apparatus for distilling dew and this was a curved cool surface. Over this the air flowed to condense the water. At the centre was the light source and algae which circulated through pipes, separating oxygen and carbon dioxide and providing cooling. This chlorella sludge was then taken to another vessel where the starch content was dried to malt like substances [it tasted of honey and wafer] from whence the dried matter was then collected and stored ready to eat.

The Israelites took this with them, in the Ark, at the beginning of their wanderings and from it they were able to survive. The Ark would contain the nuclear device and it is easy to see why it should be considered Divine. After all, from nowhere it provided a steady stream of food for forty years. The presence of a nuclear device would account for the sparks that killed the scorpions and serpents whilst exposure to radiation would account for the Philistines being covered in boils.

So far, this is the best explanation yet of the powers of the Ark of the Covenant. From here the Freiburg brothers deduce that it is the Manna machine rather than the Holy Grail that was taken to Europe and it is from this that the Arthurian legend begins. But that is no concern of this book.

17

WHY GOLD ?

Warren Buffet, one of the world's richest men, put it succinctly in an interview with the British newspaper 'The Guardian'. "It gets dug out of the ground in Africa, or someplace. Then we melt it down, dig another hole, bury it again and pay people to stand around guarding it. It has no utility. Anyone from Mars would be scratching their head." As do I today. It was quite useless yet from virtually Day One of us becoming 'civilized' it has been the most sort after commodity on Earth. Only now through the rapid advancements in medical and electronic researches has the true value of gold become apparent.

Throughout all my research for this book, only the one metal keeps coming up time after time. It quickly appears in the Bible. So just what is gold and what properties does it have that make it so special? The first is that it is one of only two that are called 'naked' metals in that they can be mined as the raw metal rather than having to be extracted from an ore bearing rock. The other is copper. Gold is the only metal that never oxidises so will carry its shine forever. Gold is malleable and can be beaten into incredibly thin sheets as in gold leaf for decorating porcelain. It is soft and so useless for any type of tool but, because of this, is ideal for making jewellery and the mounting of stones. Not one of which attribute is very much good to a people eking out an existence in tents or mud huts while they either wander through the desert or attend their mealy patch.

There are industrial uses. One is as a catalyst in various chemical processes as well as, now, having a series of medical uses. The advance of micro-technology in recent years has opened up a huge new market for gold.

It is as the catalyst that is of interest and could be the reason why it was sought after in ancient times with the ornamental use being a by product. And there is one use that it most certainly could have been part of, and that is in the manufacture of a fuel cell which will generate electricity. Any advanced civilization would need a supply of electric easily generated at source, and the simple fuel cell is by far the easiest.

Very simply this is how it works. There are lots of sites on the internet describing this in great detail but this is the simple gist of the idea.

Take a supply of rotting vegetables [plenty about] and mix with water [plenty about]. This produces methane gas. The methane is passed over a gold catalyst which turns it into Hydrogen and Oxygen. The hydrogen then passes through an electrolyte with more gold, mixes with oxygen from some air passing through a similar electrolyte, also with added gold, the end result being water – used to continue the process - plus a charge of electricity.

So, very simply, we have electric that we could not have obtained without the gold.

Gold is a very good conductor of electricity and is being used more and more in high tech electronics. Very often now you will see gold plated connections on tiny components of your computer, mobile phone or ipod. Also it is used extensively in the world of nano-technology. But again, not of much use to a tribesman in ancient times, wandering the desert or attending to his mealy patch in the Delta.

In those days, gold supply compared to total world population, was relatively high and it had little value to the ordinary people, being of decorative use to the rulers only. And yet someone, when penning the Bible, felt it necessary to mention it 300 times, in the process foretelling that one day in the distant future it would have an enormous value.

The oldest recorded history of Britain, going back to the Bronze and Iron Ages describes lost treasure of gold, again totally useless to the people of the time.

For thousands of years all trade was done by barter. Ships captains carried only enough bullion to pay for essential supplies, bartering the cargo for goods produced locally. Any cash would be in the main silver coinage or, even in the 18th century, simple cowry shells. Very little was in gold which again was still more or less universally a decorative material. It was only in the late 18th century, when world trade needed something rare and tangible, when banking had become an established method of doing business, that it was agreed that the currency of each country would be set against the value of the British pound weighed in gold. This was the Gold Standard and all paper money was merely a promissory note guaranteeing to exchange them for gold by the central banks.

Gold achieved its destiny as the most sought after commodity on earth on its discovery in California in 1849. By then the world's banks were hoarding it in large quantities and the producing nations became exceedingly rich. And all foretold with such incredible accuracy so many years ago. Just how could that be possible?

But all my arguments above come to nought when it is pointed out that there was indeed a 'control' part of the experiment when Columbus discovered Jamaica in the West Indies. The inhabitants were the Caribs and Arawaks who were a pure and unsullied Stone Age people. They had never had contact with the Europeans or with any of the religions. Their only tools were primitive, sharpened stone, cutting devices and they had no knowledge of any metals except the one – gold. This they used for decorative purposes and they traded with it with other islands. They put little value on it and happily handed it over to the Spaniards, but the fact remained that they knew about gold. As did the Incas in Peru and the Aztecs in Mexico, all well before any European could possibly have pointed out its apparent value. The whole history of Latin America is based on the fabulous wealth of the Inca gold. This I find quite amazing. The quantities of gold used by the Incas was astonishing. They used it in huge quantities yet modern researchers and explorers have never found where it came from. Apart from decoration, to them it had no monetary value.

All my other research into some essential need for gold has hit a blank wall. So far no one has offered any alternative suggestions other than the one suggested by Zecharia Sitchin which I discuss later.

18

TIME

In the forties a Professor J W Dunne published two unreadable books, 'Serial Universe' and 'An Experiment with Time'. In these he tried to explain that Time itself could be reduced to simple mathematics. Had he access to modern computers with their sophisticated programmes, he may have succeeded but all he did was to confuse his audience. There was, however, one little experiment that anyone can do to show how it is possible to see the future for someone else.

You are stood on the side of a valley, on the opposite side of which is a winding road and on that road is a car travelling fast. As you follow him you see that around one corner there has been a landslide taking the road away. The driver cannot see this, but you are able to see very clearly that he is rapidly approaching sudden death, and you can do nothing about it. He arrives at the scene, the car leaves the road and he is killed, and you saw it all, before, at the time and afterwards from your one vantage point. In those few moments you saw that person's past, present and future, something he could not.

Dunne reasoned that if this could be reduced to a mathematical formula, then it would be possible to see the future. But he never succeeded. Other ways of seeing someone else's future are hiring them for a job. You know precisely what they will be doing on Monday morning, they do not. But it is only when we can accurately forecast our own futures [that is if we really wanted to] that we can say that we are making progress. And that will involve time travel, something that is still very much in the realms of Science Fiction.

The problems of travelling at beyond the speed of light are well understood. If you leave the earth at twice the speed and are away for a year, you should have advanced a year in age, but is the light back on earth then two years behind you so that, in fact, you arrive back a year before you set off? In fact the answer is somewhat different in that for every year that you travel at this speed, time on earth advances by a substantial multiple of it, so that you can be away for a few years and return over a hundred years into the future. Could this explain the extreme ages of the Jewish elders in the Old Testament?

Time travel for us is still somewhere in the future but, as I said earlier, when you consider the changes in the lifetime of my mother, how can you possibly dismiss it during the lifetime of the child born today? I am not alone in believing that this not only may, but will happen eventually. The distinguished Professor Ronald Mallett of Connecticut University, where he held the chair since 1975, wrote a book on the subject of how he was attempting to construct a time machine. This is not the work of a crank but someone able – and willing – to look at the problem laterally and to decide that everything is possible. At the age of 62 he still believed that it would happen in his lifetime. Certainly it may in that of today's child.

With this I think we have enough evidence to come to some conclusions, most of which Academia will not like at all. However, all are the result of simple practical logic, not because of accepted thought. Please bear with me and read the lot, in the order that it is written, before coming to your own conclusions. As I said in my foreword, I began with some pre-conceived ideas based on the knowledge generally available in the book shops. Had I been given the sometimes incredible, sometimes preposterous, answers that follow, before I began, I too would have dismissed it all as a massive flight of fancy. All my conclusions are based on simple arithmetic, simple basic physics and chemistry and the never ending logic that says that if a thing is physically impossible to do, then it is physically impossible to do it that way. It is only when we start to question things and then seek a practical alternative that we eventually find the truth. However impossible that may be to accept. If we consider carefully and logically what then turns out to be impossible, it surely follows that we must seek the answers elsewhere, wherever the journey takes us.

Part 2 attempts to do just that.

PART 2

19

THE PLOT SO FAR

Before we look any further I must declare that since the first edition many new works on the subject have come my way. Many were out of print in 2008 but the advent of 'Print on Demand' has enabled many such works to become readily available. I am wrong to say 'new' works because some were written before I was born and before, as I said earlier, the subject of ancient Egypt had become an 'ology'. Amongst them I refer to a book, already alluded to, and suggested for me by none other than the British Museum. It is by Somers Clark and R. Engelbach and was published in 1930 when the Tutenkamun artefacts were still being extracted and catalogued. It is called *Ancient Egyptian Masonry and the Building Craft*. At the time Somers Clark was an archaeologist working in Egypt for the museum in Cairo. He had access to much material that is not available to someone like me, and was able without much difficulty to visit the quarries from where the stone used in all the construction work across the land came. This has caused me to revisit some of my own theories which I change accordingly. Anyone looking at this subject must be prepared to consider other points of view and that I do. Other works that I consider relevant are mentioned as we go along but I must say that it has come as a relief to find that other, far more eminent, researchers than me have been looking down similar lines and that my ideas have turned out to be not a million miles from theirs. Until categorical and irrefutable **facts** come my way, I will always remain open to other theories on this subject.

I have also reinforced my theories by agreeing that these questions cannot be answered by coming at the subject from one angle only. The cold, factual archaeologist has certainly done his bit as have those who interpreted the religious aspects. I look at the very much bigger picture by considering the ideas of <u>**all**</u>, no matter how apparently 'off message' they may appear to be. You cannot accept without question the opinions and timelines set down by Herodotus so long ago, and then ignore the works of someone like

Charles Hapgood. It is from people like him that the really good ideas come.

I think that before any conclusions can be made by anyone, the ghosts of the extra terrestrial element must be laid once and for all. If we believe that there was no visitation on earth by any other being ever, then little can make sense. We are back to the pure Darwin of Natural Selection and the Survival of the Fittest. We believe that the Egyptians had a rush of blood to the head and suddenly acquired out of thin air a prodigious technical knowledge and building skill that they then promptly lost. As did the Mayans, Aztecs and the Incas at more or less the same time. As did the inhabitants of Java, the Canary Islands, Australia, China, North America and parts of Europe. All got it at the same time, built enormous edifices – some even on the same exact Great Circle line to circum-navigate the earth – and then just packed it in. That there are mathematical facts relating to the astronomical layouts of many buildings is simply a matter of coincidence. That as a building project at any time, there would not have been enough man power to build them as has been previously thought, but they did it anyway. A convenient 'Mighty Bound'. That the Piri Re'is map is another inconvenience. Another 'Mighty Bound', or a gigantic fraud even. Better still, simply get out the airbrush and send it into oblivion. All the inexplicable artefacts embedded in ancient rocks do not fit into accepted theory so must be ignored at best, or preferably airbrushed for convenience. Let's have another 'Mighty Bound' and move on. Better to just bury the evidence in the deepest museum vaults as 'pseudo-science' and forget them.

We must then dismiss Genesis 6.4 which claims that the sons of God mated with the daughters of man, and then what else of the Bible? We must also dismiss the Virgin birth, Resurrection and Ascension of Jesus, the ascension of Mohammed, the Holy Ghost and much else since these all have extra terrestrial connotations. The Revelations, the story of Moses, Elijah and of Isaiah never happened. There was no Angel Gabriel and therefore all Islam is a fake. No matter how many people on this Earth believe any of it, and that is the vast majority, they are all wrong and the few academic atheists are right. Is that it?

3

So where do we stop? All the prophets must be wrong as well leaving us with a cold, empty philosophy where everything must be as it appears, leaving no room for doubters of any sort, and every awkward question answered with the all enveloping 'Mighty Bound' theory.

Well I am sorry but I do not agree, and I hope that what I have said so far will have given you enough information to form your own opinion. At least it should have opened minds to alternatives.

To me, as a sceptical engineer who deals in practicality and logic to solve puzzles, the evidence is overwhelming. *'But,'* I hear you say, *'where are your extra terrestrials today? Why did they stop coming if they have these powers? Where were they during the Great Wars when we needed them most?'* And, do you know, I cannot give you an answer except to say that we just do not know whether or not they have ever returned. My guess is that they have done so periodically, but now it is so easy to meld into the background that they could exist unnoticed. Just look at the way the jihadist terrorists wander in freedom throughout Europe with all the best efforts of our intelligence services coming to nought, even though the names and faces of the 'most wanted' are so well known. Who would believe them anyway? If someone strange turned up in the pub and asked for a room, explaining that he was just in from Sirius, having been dropped off by a space ship, with the object of sorting out the Middle East, you may be inclined to ring the police and get him sent to the funny farm. In what form could Christ possibly return for his Second Coming? You can see the headlines *'Man claims to be Christ'* followed by the derisory interviews on television by some of our [to them] cleverer interviewers. It would, and will if it is destined to happen, be very difficult to achieve.

It is my contention that in the past, going back millions of years, we have had visits from space. Most will have just come and gone having found that the earth was not very hospitable to colonize. The visitors may have stayed for a time and it is an interesting thought that most of the extremely ancient finds embedded in the rock either pre-date, or are around the beginning

4

of the dinosaur periods. All are dated c300 million years ago. Not 500 million or 200 million but all over the world at around 300 million. Could a form of humanity exist amongst such creatures? Any evidence of humanity would have been eradicated by the dinosaurs, one would have thought, but what about the wall in America? Someone built it and it was left behind amongst the rotting vegetation. Could they have just upped and moved on to somewhere else, which may explain the almost total lack of fossilised evidence that Darwin hoped someone would eventually find? Could that help explain why mankind over the subsequent millennia, if indeed he was around then, never progressed out of the Stone Age? But, around the 12 – 10,000BC mark, possibly earlier and possibly not pre Ice Age, a group came – how we will never know – and settled all over the earth.

Why then? A good question but, if there is a spark of truth in the above it will be obvious that these people, having come such enormous distances, must embrace a form of 'Time Travel'. Otherwise it would take millions of years to get here. If they were seeking another planet to colonize it would not have made sense to do so when we were overrun with massive dinosaurs. Equally it would be stupid to make the attempt in the twentieth and twenty first centuries when the earth was more than adequately armed and seriously over populated. Instead they may have chosen a period when the indigenous population was small, stable, benign, ignorant and unarmed, so that they could create a new world in their own image like the one they left behind. Is that not what God is supposed to have done according to Genesis? To communicate they drew maps and, using convenient local labour, built the massive edifices that remain to this day. The centre of their world was Giza on the Alexandria meridian and all measurements emanated from there. Over the years they bred with the indigenous fair skinned women who bore them a new race of powerful and intellectual children. Some of those children may have gone on to become the Pharaohs of Egypt and others to become the elders of the Hebrews – those who lived so long. Given hindsight, of which we are all expert, if any of us were given the chance to start it all over again, where and at what period of history would we choose today. Think about that. Exactly when would it have not been too late?

A new book by Timothy Good entitled *'Need to Know: UFOs, The Military and Intelligence'*, highlights the plethora of UFOs in our skies. He points out that the sightings during the two world wars showed a marked increase in activity, observed in the main by high ranking military personnel including Earl Mountbatten of Burma, and this goes somewhere along the road of my theory that the extra terrestrials would have checked out this period in time. Against this is the Roswell 'hoax' or otherwise where a UFO is supposed to have crashed, conveniently in New Mexico, revealing a 4 ft tall humanoid person. Unfortunately this remains shrouded in mystery being still 'Classified' information. The American government would do us all a favour by coming out and giving us all full access to the files. Of course, all these supposed sightings could be just another giant hoax, but I tend to agree with Bill Gunston OBE, one of the world's leading aviation historians and a Fellow of the Royal Aeronautical Society, when he asks whether it is credible to query the observations of so many eminent military men with so much to lose by lying.

Add to those distinguished personnel myself, with my 'near miss' and my high flying vapour trails, making it difficult for me to dismiss it all as a flight of fancy.

We are talking of long periods of time here. If they built the pyramids before 6,000BC, as I think they did, it was not until 2,500 years later that the first Pharaoh appeared to begin the First Dynasty. That is for us looking back to the time of Solomon and the Queen of Sheba. Before the Exodus even. During these prodigious periods there was plenty of time to assimilate into the local culture and for new tribes to appear. We are talking of nearly one hundred generations of each family. During this period their skills did not seem to improve and, if anything, they became as indolent as their hosts. For whatever reason – lack of resources is always the favourite – but here I am talking raw materials more than anything, they failed to capitalize on the enormous progress made soon after they arrived. Perhaps there was trouble in their host planet forcing a group to seek a home elsewhere? Had they had their own Armageddon and knew what to expect, which caused them to labour the point here? As we have seen, someone knew something that they should not possibly have been aware of at the time.

6

According to the Old Testament of the *Holy Bible,* these people were called *'The Nephilim'* which is Hebrew for 'fallen' and refers to them as Human/Alien/Angel half breeds. The angels being the 'Fallen Angels' of the *Book of Enoch* which was omitted by Guttenberg, as well as from the King James, versions of the *Holy Bible,* for the simple reason that it was thought not to exist. This important book of the Old Testament was first proscribed by, amongst others, Augustine since it was way off message to the doctrines of Christianity at the time. It was considered to be 'apocryphal' rather than 'factual'. The only people now to take it seriously are the Latter Day Saints who include texts in *The Book of Mormon.* One of the Nephilim leaders was called Anak who lived in Canaan which was to become the Promised Land of the Hebrews. The Anakites were a powerful race, bigger than everyone else, who built cities – presumably Jericho and Hebron – and eventually they had their wars with the neighbours. All this is well covered in the *Bible.* I refer here to *Joshua 11:21, Joshua 11:22, Deuteronomy 2:11, Deuteronomy 2:21, Deuteronomy 9:2, Genesis 6:4, Numbers 13:22, Numbers 13:28, Numbers 13:33* and so on. They are mentioned in The Dead Sea Scrolls and numerous other ancient Hebrew manuscripts. One would have thought that they must have existed from all that. Enoch thought so.

But the *Book of Enoch* did in fact exist intact and was discovered in 1773 by the explorer James Bruce in Ethiopia. He brought back with him four copies, now in the Oxford Bodleian Library, that were eventually translated, first by the Rev Richard Laurence in 1821, and then by R H Charles later in the century. Charles brought out the definitive version in 1912. For the purpose of this book I quote from the 1883 version of Charles with some later confirmation from the same source.

Once more we must put this work into the context of the times. Enoch was seven generations down the direct line from Adam and, along with Christ and Elijah, was one of the only three people to ascend into heaven whilst still alive. He was sixty five at the time and the great-grandfather of Noah. He did not return. The work that makes up the Book of Enoch was actually penned around 200BC quoting exactly what Enoch had said. This is further confirmed by the discovery amongst the Dead Sea Scrolls, in Cave

4, of 7 fragments in the Aramatic text of traces of the Ethiopic work. It is a big book but I have selected various verses which make for interesting reading.

7.2 'And when the angels, the sons of heaven beheld them [the women on earth] they became enamoured of them saying to each other, Come let us select for ourselves from the progeny of men and let us beget children.'

According to Charles in his 1893 version they then landed on Mt Herman which divides Israel and Lebanon from Syria. There were about 200 of them.

7.10 'Then they took wives, each choosing for himself whom they began to approach and with whom they cohabited, teaching them sorcery, incantations and the dividing of the roots of trees.'

7.11 And the women conceiving brought forth giants [this is a loose translation from the Greek which differs considerably to the Ethiopic version] and they [the women] bore them [the angels] three races. First the giants, the giants brought forth the Nephilim who in turn brought forward the Elioud. And they existed, increasing in power according to their greatness

8.1 'Moreover Azazyel [one of the Nephilim] taught men to make swords, knives, shields, breast plates and the fabrication of mirrors, and the workmanship of bracelets and ornaments, the use of paint, the beautifying of eyebrows, the use of stones of every select kind and all sorts of dyes so that the world became altered.

8.3 Amazarak taught all the sorceries and dividing of roots.

8.5 'Barkayal taught the observers of stars.'

8.6 'Akibeal taught signs.'

8.7 'Tamiel taught astronomy.'

8.8'And Asarudel taught the motion of the moon.

Now we are getting somewhere. Read again about gold – were they responsible for its popularity? The dividing of roots is about agriculture whilst the astronomical references speak for themselves. Significant is that the world became altered. The object of this book has always been that some outside force did the altering.

9.18 'Destroy all the souls addicted to lust and the offspring of angels for they have tyrannised over mankind.'

9.19 'Let every oppressor perish from the face of the earth.'

9.20 'Let every evil work be destroyed.'

12.5 'Then the Lord said unto Enoch to tell the angels of heaven who have deserted the lofty sky and who have been polluted with women.'

12.7 'That on Earth they shall never obtain peace and remission of sin. For they shall not rejoice in their offspring, they shall behold the slaughter of their beloved, shall lament for the destruction of their sons and shall petition forever but shall not obtain mercy or peace.'

There are many more chapters in the book, much of which is taken up with Enoch's vision of a journey to heaven and hell but I feel that the last two verses to be highly significant. Realising that introducing these angels onto the world that was still enjoying its long drawn out Darwinian march through the eternal Stone Age, they had irrevocably changed things for all time. And it was not necessarily all for the good. Here he is prophesying the coming wars that would consume mankind right up to this day and that the perpetrators would, in those wars, lose their own offspring as well, whilst all their prayers to their 'Gods' for salvation and justification would never be answered. Recorded subsequent history proves this to be an incredibly accurate assessment.

I fail to see how academia can simply dismiss all this since acceptance as being even possible turns the whole subject completely on its head. How all the reams of paper, all the hundreds of books on Ancient Egypt and the Biblical lands can simply treat all this as yet another 'Mighty Bound' is beyond my comprehension. It is only by accepting as a strong _possibility_ that the Nephilim did arrive from an unknown source somewhere out in the solar system. The _possibility_ that they proceeded to colonize all over the world and that they bred with the indigenous local people, so giving mankind that much needed boost of extra intelligence that changed us from hundreds of thousands of years as wandering Stone Age tribes into Modern Man. And all was done in the relatively short duration of 6 to 8,000 years.

I accept, with some reservations, that the Nephilim did colonize the earth around 6,000 BC, maybe earlier, but I doubt that they were quite the giants that the Bible suggests. Enoch certainly does not labour the point. What you must remember is that people in those days were very much smaller than we are today. Someone 5 ft tall would be a big man whilst the women would all be 4ft to 4ft 6 inches tall. A race of people in the 6ft to 6ft 6 inches region would appear to be extremely tall to these people. They would, in fact, appear to be giants. I do not see them being 18ft tall as has been suggested. If they were, then all parts of the anatomy would be bigger in the same proportion. They would need enormous legs to support the added body weight which would increase by at least 8 times while, without descending into vulgarities, mating with a 4ft woman would have been extremely difficult for him and painful for her.

But now go back to the chapter on the Myths of Creation, in particular the Gods of Ancient Egypt. The first Egyptians as such are supposed to have emerged from across the desert by the Red Sea around 5000BC. They had the vizier, or magician, Thoth who deduced the 365 day year. He was endowed with all the wisdom and knowledge. He invented arithmetic, surveying, geometry, astronomy, medicine, surgery, writing and music before ascending into heaven. He remained one of the principal figures in Egyptian religion, but does not his story mirror much of what Enoch was saying? All the wisdom attributed to Thoth is also said to come from a few of these Biblical people.

So what happened to them all? Did they just vanish from the face of the earth? The answer is 'no'. They did not just vanish for their distant descendents are with us today. I have no means of proving this genetically by doing DNA tests and I would be interested to hear from any young Geneticist doing his or her PhD who would like to use this as a thesis.

This is what I think happened – over a very long period of time. First it must have been about 20,000BC, then again circa 15 to 12,000BC until around 8 to 6,000BC when these people arrived and stayed. From where they came we will probably never know but my guess is that it could have been a planet somewhere near Sirius or around the region of Orion's belt. How they got here over that vast distance, we will never know. I say Orion's belt because this turns up more than anything else. I would qualify it by stating that it is only from a planet in our immediate solar system that these people, for want of a better name, came and Orion's belt occurs so often in our monuments. We see the arrangement of those stars in that way. A being coming from that area would see a totally different alignment of the sky. Only by looking upwards from Earth does it appear that way. Other explanations, which I discuss later, are that they came from one of our own planets called 'Nibiru' and that it had/has an interesting orbit of our sun. Of course another explanation is that they were in fact of 'divine' origination, given the references Enoch attributes to them. On the pages to follow I explore all options, no matter how bizarre they may first appear to be.

Why they left their own homeland, again we will never know. But they turned up here armed with technology beyond the wildest dreams of the average peasant with whom they mixed. This may have included a form of nuclear capability, they probably needed to keep a supply of electricity. But, although they had the mathematical ability to calculate the length of the year to within a few minutes, they do not seem to have had any method of keeping time, like a clock. If we believe accepted archaeological evidence of today they set their monuments to coincide with sunrises at various solstices and equinoxes around the world, so knowing exactly what day of the year it was. They would be aware of the use of Artificial Insemination and could quite easily have brought enough sperm to create the docile domestic pigs, cows, horses etc. that we know today. They could have brought seeds of edible plants [*Enoch 7:1*

'They taught them [the indigenous women] charms and enchantments, the cutting of roots and made them acquainted with plants'.] Do not forget that it is generally agreed that agrarian farming and settlements began around 7,500BC. We just do not know. The written work of this period was destroyed first by the Romans when they burned the Alexandrian Library and then in the west by Cortez when he sacked Mexico City, burning all the old records as heresy. What did we lose? It does not bear thinking about.

It is my contention that as they bred with the indigenous population of Egypt they gradually made their way into neighbouring countries. They became the first Pharaohs, which line eventually collapsed because of intense incestuous inter breeding. Do not forget that the average reign for a Pharaoh was less than ten years. Another branch fell out with the Pharaoh and was led by Moses to found a basis of the Jewish race. The Patriarchs of the Jews going back to Abraham may indeed have been all Nephilim or their descendents. Both the Jewish and Arabic peoples are considered to be of the same Semitic race. Many Egyptologists have always thought that Moses was a kinsman in some way of the Royal House. Moses may have taken with him some of the last vestiges of their dying technological knowledge in the Ark of the Covenant as it made its journey through the Exodus, to end up in the Promised Land of Milk and Honey. Others made their way across the sea to Crete where they again bred locally to become the Minoans. They took with them their building skills and mathematical knowledge to create the Temple of Knossus and the Labyrinth. The history of the Minoans is well documented. This was another brilliant civilization appearing from nowhere before just running out of steam. And then vanishing just as fast.

Others ended on mainland Greece to create the Golden Age of Greek architecture and learning. Another group made their way to Italy, forming eventually the Roman Royal houses, and built the incredible Roman buildings. Could they have had the technology still that enabled the Romans to build the monument in Alexandria and the wonders of Baalbek? Some may have been in Italy already, having built the three pyramids near Milan. As part of the Roman Army they settled in France, ending up in England, in Scotland and

Wales, all the time breeding with the indigenous populations. The Angles and Saxons then drove many of them out of England. Every population that contained their blood grew and flourished over the next two thousand years giving us modern civilization as we know it today. Where they had little or no influence like sub Saharan Africa, most of North America and all of Central Europe and Asia, the people remained stuck in the steady progress of the Darwinian theory. Even the most diehard and intransigent of anthropologists and Egyptologists must accept this as a self evident fact. It is not

A pre-Columbian Inca bust from Aramocacha, in diorite, showing the distinctive 'Roman nose'. Also note the apparent ease with which they were able to cut diorite, amongst the hardest of all stones.

racist to observe that, on the earth today, are large pockets of peoples living in abject conditions from which they are unable to extricate themselves without outside help. But, when those people are assimilated into a civilized society a reasonable, rather than significant, proportion are able to rise to the top. They have the basic intelligence but lack the will to use it. Of course, the objection to this idea is the building of so much in Central and South America which happened, and then stopped, most falling into ruin. That should not be the case for it confirms the theory. Others may have landed in those parts of the American continent and, for whatever reason, used the local labour force to build the incredible places that remain. Again, as in Egypt, they had a skill in cutting stone that is virtually impossible to replicate. The stones at Cuzco in the Andes are incredible, even more so than in Egypt. Did they begin in Peru before making their way north to end up in Mexico where, again, they simply ran out of steam?

So how do I know this as a fact? It is simple. It is the nose. The Roman nose. This feature on the anatomy of many people is a nose that comes more or less straight down from the forehead with little or no bridge. In many cases the top of the nose is, for want of a better term, 'hooked'. The nose is not straight but has a distinct bend in it. Pictures of Rameses 11 show that he had one, as had Nefertiti and Cleopatra. All the wall paintings in Egypt show the same. Frescoes in Crete show figures with the nose. Statues of the Ancient Greeks and Romans mostly show the same straight nose and today you will see it on many French and Welsh people. Seldom on a Scot or Irish person for, of course, the Romans stopped short of those borders. Napoleon is a typical example. So indeed is Wellington. How ironic if they turn out to be kinsmen. A great number of Jewish people all over the world have this feature. Barbra Striesand is typical. It is my contention that every person on earth who has a 'Roman' nose will have somewhere a common gene that takes them back as direct, if very distant, descendents of the Nephilim who arrived so long ago. I think that it could be significant that the Incas also sported that same 'Roman nose'. Drawings done by the Conquistadors of the indigenous populations show some people with this feature and some without – exactly as it should be. Those people are true descendents of 'The Gods'. Now all we have to prove, one way or another, is whether or not they were actually 'Gods' or mere mortals like the rest of us.

What is the state of play with the other problems?

Amongst the 'Definite Certainties' we must include the 'Bulge', although now altered to show similar bulges in other parts of the world. We cannot isolate the four Giza pyramids from all the other ancient monuments of the world. Easter Island and

14

Stonehenge with their primitive stone work were just as important a part of the 'Big Picture' as was Giza, Machu Pichu, the Nazca lines and Angkor Wat. We must dismiss once and for all that these were built solely as tombs for Pharaohs. They were not. They had an important part to play in the far bigger picture of the new civilization introduced from afar.

We now may know 'When' they built them. We think that it would be around 5 – 6,000BC – the time scale is advancing a little but narrowing down. But who built Jericho? Must we adjust our dates back by another 2000 years? As for the 'How' they built them, at least we now know how they could not have built them. We know that the numbers just do not add up when you compare them with the three other massive modern civil engineering projects. There was but the one way to build them in a reasonable time and that will be discussed later in the book.

I think we have come to the conclusion that, whilst it eludes us for the moment, Time Travel and teleporting are possible and were used all those years ago. It will happen for us, possibly being one of the accepted things that our child of today will look back on as an everyday happening. If you had mentioned Skype to my father, who died in 1980, he would not have believed that by simply looking at a TV screen on my desk I could see and talk to my son in Australia. Will my grandchildren be able to do the same in person when contacting their cousins overseas? I feel that the 'teleporting' of a person, a spacecraft even, may indeed be a possibility in the not too distant future but as for doing the same for an entire planet, well, I doubt it. It has been suggested.

We have identified that we are being bombarded by an unacceptable number of, hopefully benign, waves of known origin such as mobile phones, the internet, GPS and television, plus a lot of which we know nothing as yet. These are the spiritual waves of other worlds and lives, and that just a few living mediums are in possession of the right 'receivers' to be able to pick them up and transmit them. We will look more closely at these later in the book.

Amongst the 'Definite Maybe's' we have identified just why granite <u>may</u> have been so important in the construction process. It certainly was not necessary structurally nor was there any need for it visually. We have seen that they may have had a basic nuclear capability which may have been used to produce, in the first place, a form of electric power, and then generate the energy to produce the 'Manna' that kept the Israelites fed during the forty years in the desert. Without this electric power, once the imported radioactive materials began to fail, their entire civilization, plus the means of returning to the host planet would be lost for all time. Which is why, in the absence of Uranium, the vast quantity of granite was so important. I see no other logical explanation. This possibly explains the powers of the Ark of the Covenant. The boils suffered by the Philistines were probably radiation burns. This is why it was carried by priests who kept the lid firmly shut most of the time. The gold, like lead, would act as a radiation shield rather than for pure decorative purposes. Another thought is this. Could the supposed 'Curse of the Pharaoh' actually be radiation sickness following prolonged exposure to the granite?' Yes, I do know that there was no granite used in quantity in The Valley of the Kings. The objection to this whole idea is that if they had the ability and resources to find and extract granite, surely they could have saved a great deal of effort by going out and finding some uranium? Could it be that the nearest supplies were in Niger and Namibia in Africa and Kazakhstan in Europe? But if they could with ease find diorite in Egypt and mica in Brazil and work it with such accuracy, one would have thought that finding uranium would have been easier. After all, it does give out radio activity which mica certainly does not.

Could the obviously essential need for granite in stone circles, and especially at Stonehenge, be that its radiation properties enabled it to contact with the mysterious lines of force in the earth so derided as 'pseudo-science' by the 'experts'? They had to have a very good reason to go to all that trouble when there was plenty of perfectly good sandstone about. And there had to be considerable geological knowledge to be able to identify it.

I ask the reader, who is blessed with 21st century education and knowledge, whether he or she could confidently identify millstone grit, sandstone or granite in any virgin terrain? Think again about Stonehenge. The first edifice was of timber but that was

16

obviously not thought to be fit for purpose. Just why, if the object was only to worship the sun at the solstice, I cannot think. There were no roads about at the time, and they could only have used the sun for direction finding, but they had to go the very considerable distance to Marlborough to extract the second stones. There is no evidence that at the time they had invented the wheel which means that the massive Sarson stones had to be physically dragged the 20 miles that would have been wooded for part of the way. That in itself was a prodigious feat of civil engineering. So who would do that and why, having decided that still the building was not fit for purpose after going to the extreme lengths previously of identifying, and sourcing, of the granite beyond the Brecon Beacons across the, to them, treacherous waters of the Bristol Channel? And they would have exactly the same problems as the Egyptians in transporting them onto the site. It had to be very, very important to go down that path.

The 'Not Proven' includes what happened to the Holy Grail - that is if it existed at all. There is no answer at the moment to the question 'Why Gold?' There is no logical reason for its value in those distant days. Except that the Nephilim needed it to set their precious stones.

What about Armageddon? Only someone, either able to travel into the distant future, or who has witnessed its actual effect on their own distant planet, could possibly bang on so much, and with such emphasis, about this. It is no good making dire predictions about possible natural disasters for, no matter how good, nor how bad, are we all, there is now and never will be, any means for man to control the natural geological movements of the earth. If Vesuvius wants to go off again, it will do so in its own time and there is nothing that we can do to stop it. Only someone with detailed knowledge of Atomic explosions and their aftermath, or who knew about man created viruses with no known antidote, could make these predictions. Armed with sword and spear it would be impossible. It does, however, still leave some very big questions.

Pirie Re'is just will not go away. He has thrown up one of life's great anomalies to which the 'only' answer is quite

17

preposterous. That answer is that it was drawn by someone, either on the ground with accurate surveying equipment, or from the air, possibly very high up using a form of photography. That it shows an accurate layout of South America in pre-Columbian times is remarkable but nothing like as astonishing as the fact that it shows part of Antarctica accurately as a habitable green continent with flowing rivers rather than being covered by two miles of solid ice. It could only have been drawn before the ice cap began which is some time before the period under discussion.

As with the iron cup embedded with coal, it must have been done whilst our visitors from elsewhere were sizing up just which period of time they would make their appearance. Do not forget that we have already suggested that there must have been an extra terrestrial visitation before or around 6,000BC, with the beings who landed staying on to become the Nephilim. And that, owing to the vast distances involved, they must have used some form of Time Travel during which they could manifest themselves literally at any time in our history. To me the only logical answer, for answer there must be, is that they arrived in the Carboniferous period, left behind rubbish [as travellers do] and in this rubbish was an iron cup and an axe shaft. They did a certain amount of mapping which was left behind on earth when they finally decided on the 5 – 6,000 BC colonizing dates. Over the years since the ice cap formed, any form of writing or drawing would disintegrate into dust therefore, and here we are getting in deep, it would be drawn at the time, but then carried forward artificially in time, in the craft that landed at our chosen time. So it remained intact in the Alexandria library. This is what I think happened. So far I have yet to hear of a better explanation but my mind is open to one. Against that is the physical evidence of the hammer which is very crude, whereas anyone able to make it from iron so pure should have been far more sophisticated.

Now we will look in more detail at the big questions that have raised their heads so far, particularly in the context of the original quest which was 'Is it possible to believe in God, Christ, Islam and other religions whilst at the same time accepting that Darwin was more or less correct with his evolution and 'Survival of the Fittest' theory?' Slowly we are getting there and return first to one of our rhetorical subjects of 'How' they built the Pyramids.

SHIPS, PULLEYS, TOOLS AND LIFTING GEAR

Since the first edition I have spent a great deal of time studying and thinking about the tools used in Pharonic times, the materials available at the time and the sheer physical problems that the engineers and builders on site had to overcome before producing the buildings that are there for us to see today. It is worth going over it all again very carefully because it is fundamental to everything that follows. Ship building technique was just one enormous limitation on what could, or could not, be achieved.

My first observation is that I do not necessarily agree that the four great Giza pyramids were built during the accepted period which was the 4th Dynasty from 2,900 to 2,650BC. There is confusion here. According to Egyptologist Jurgen von Bekerath Cheops is dated as 2,604 – 2,581BC but Somers Clark, whose book was edited by Petrie himself, says he reigned from 2,900BC. Be that as it may, I use 2,600 as my base when the only metals known were copper and gold. I still maintain that the pyramids came from a very much earlier period; I think that they were all designed at the same time; I think that the site was surveyed to accommodate them all, the sizes, angles of the sides and mathematical implications were understood and carefully calculated and all before the first cubic foot of rock was removed. There was a carefully thought out reason why those buildings, in that shape, in that place and at that time were so **absolutely necessary**. And, most of all, there was no point whatsoever in digging out that first cubic foot of rock unless they knew with **absolute certainty** that it was physically possible to end up with not three, but four, perfect four sided pyramids, each with a capstone exactly central above a chamber far beneath it in the rock below. The extension of this is that they knew that they must extract 7 million huge limestone blocks, plus hundreds of granite ones of varying shape and size, and that they knew **exactly** how it was to be done. And they knew that those designing them may be long dead before they were all finished. So there must have been a long term need for them all. A 'one off' need, nevertheless, because once they were completed, for whatever purpose was necessary at the time, they built nothing else on such a scale. And they then had no further need for granite at all.

Let us look at the state of play in 2,600BC. What was available to our engineers, our architects and our builders if they were actually built between 2,600 and 2,450BC, or even a bit later. That is over a 150 year period which means that those people who decided they were so essential would be long dead before the last was completed. As would be their sons and grandsons as well. From this it follows that the necessity that was so pressing at the beginning was still there 150 years later. And having built those four pyramids, they would suffice, there being no need in the future to build any more. Could that absolute necessity be merely to bury four kings, after which their descendants merely went up river and dug holes in the ground? If those kings were considered to be 'gods', surely the ones following on would have thought that they too needed something similar for people to worship because they also must be 'gods' as well? Those descendants did build some remarkable palaces and erected some amazing obelisks, but not pyramids. Most of those are over a thousand years after the accepted pyramid era. So what, over just 150 years, possibly shorter or equally possibly longer, was that need that had not been there earlier and ceased so soon afterwards? Whatever theory is promulgated it remains a fact that the need for these buildings was very much a 'one off' occasion that did not recur.

First let us look at the raw materials available, what they were, how accessible were they and how easy would it have been to use them?

1. **Timber**. Timber was the first raw material used anywhere in past times because it was relatively easy to work and, most of all, it regenerated itself time after time after time. In Egypt in 2,600BC the only timber available that grew on the banks of the Nile was the **Palm** which gave a material of little lasting use because it was soft and without much strength. It provides coconuts for food and refreshment and oil for cooking as well. Then there is the **Acacia** tree, or

more likely bush, which is much harder but not available in big enough pieces to be of use for other than short items such as handles for tools. It was never suitable for cutting into planks of any size. The **Fig** tree produces figs for eating and dietary needs and that is about all but the **Olive** is both a hard wood and the producer of both foods and oils. From neither can planks of timber of any great length be produced. I would presume that they may have had the vine as well. They seemed to have used sycamore which is an anomaly because that tree is only indigenous in much colder climes.

2. **Stone.** For this project, enormous quantities of stone were needed. Quantities that would not be equalled until some 5,000 years later when building the three other huge civil engineering projects described earlier. But they all used concrete. Three types of stone are involved and they are **Limestone, Sandstone** and **Granite** with **Diorite** being a much harder fourth one. The Giza plateau, and all of Lower Egypt for hundreds of miles upstream, is limestone and so that was available, on site or nearby in unlimited quantities. All they had to do was dig it out. Sandstone was not a significant contributor to the process but granite was. Granite was only found some 1,000 miles upstream above the first cataract at Aswan. A cataract being a waterfall not unlike a very big weir used to dam rivers in the UK today. At Aswan there was enough granite for the purpose, the two problems being extracting it from the bedrock and then getting it from the quarry onto site so many miles away. Diorite is even harder than granite but is only available in small quantities many miles away scattered in the desert between the river and the Red Sea. The obvious question of why the limestone was not quarried from nearby deposits, but from a considerable distance away, must be considered and answered.

3. **Water.** The obvious need for water was in floating the rocks to somewhere near to the site, but it had the other vital use of being there in quantity to keep the population hydrated and the livestock and the plants watered. This came in a never ending stream in the form of the river, but

that was it. Once the area turned to desert from being a savannah somewhere around 8,000BC, only the river sustained life down a very narrow valley for thousands of miles. There was little in the way of regular rainfall. Also it must be admitted that water from the Nile, then and now, is far from being pure. It always carries silt washed down from afar whilst in those days it would also have been Egypt's sewer as well. Some sort of purification was needed to make it drinkable.

4. **Metals.** So what metals were available in 2,500BC? **Copper** was first to be discovered as a metal with any utility at all. On the Mohs scale of hardness it appears at No 2 being little harder than calcium or gypsum. It is malleable and is widely used in the electrical industry, especially in wiring. When 'annealed' it develops a harder surface which makes it usable to a very small degree for tooling purposes. It could, for instance, in its annealed state be used to scratch a drawing onto some wood or limestone. Annealing is a process of hardening where the metal is heated to a high temperature and then suddenly cooled in cold water. It is also called 'case hardening' when applied to iron or steel. There was plenty of **Gold** in Egypt from the dawn of time and there still is. From very early times it was used for decorative purposes and is, of course, one of the first things to be mentioned in the Bible. Significantly there were no **Tin** mines in Egypt, tin being needed to form bronze. The nearest tin mines in Africa were all sub-Saharan in Zimbabwe. The nearest to Egypt were in the Balkans with most coming from mines on the Germany/Czech Republic border. From there it found its way to the Baltic and the Mediterranean by way of the Amber Road. The Amber Road was an old trading route from the Baltic to the Mediterranean that took Amber beads to Italy, some of which found their way to Egypt where they were used as decoration on the breast ornament of Tutankhamen. There were tin mines in Cornwall and we do know that much of that went overseas but only in sea going craft at a much later date. And so the only metals indigenous to Egypt, that were available to Stone Age man who had the temerity to

want to build a pyramid c.2,900-2,500BC, were copper and gold, neither of which were any use at all. A long copper chisel as displayed in the Cairo museum would simply buckle if any force were to be applied to it.

5. **Workforce.** As any employer will tell you, a good, willing and skilled workforce is essential for the success of any business operation. One requiring much digging through solid rock, and then the logistical nightmare of transporting seven million stone blocks of varying sizes over distances of up to one thousand miles, obviously needed one such body of men. An equal number was needed for the actual placing of the boulders in the right place, plus a positive army of highly skilled stone masons able to cut all the materials with a precision only obtained today by machines. On top of this significant numbers of architects, engineers, surveyors, managers and mathematicians were essential for a successful outcome. Since the operation would take several generations to complete, a backup staff producing and preparing food was essential. They needed people to grow the crops and look after livestock. They needed some sort of medical facilities and, most of all, they needed the wives and family of the workers living nearby. Obviously all would need somewhere to live, sleep and to breed. What are the numbers involved here? Who knows? My early estimates remain in the millions, all of whom must be housed, fed, clothed and watered with the water being the most important. Otherwise, in the desert heat doing such back-breaking manual work, they would have perished from dehydration. They also needed skilled ship-builders to construct the ships/barges or whatever to get the stones down river to Giza and to go overseas to buy timber and tin. They needed people to cut the timber and make the miles of rope that was going to be used, and they needed another workforce building dwellings for the wives, workers and ancillary staff to live in. All of this added to the numbers until we get to far more than the entire population of the country at the time.

That then is a realistic assessment of what was available to that first engineer when the whole project was commissioned. However you try you cannot ignore, or take any bounds, no matter how mighty, over the above facts. It was no use whatsoever beginning those first underground tunnels unless the engineers knew exactly how they were going to extract, prepare, transport and erect on site those massive granite blocks.

I keep going on about ships because they were fundamental to the whole process. The only highways across the world in Stone Age times were waterways. Carrying any commodity overland was always difficult as those first colonising Australia and America found. Yes, across the open prairie or the deserts a horse drawn wagon could be used, but not over the Rockies or through the Australian Bush. The rivers or open sea were always preferred and it was no different in Stone Age times. From the dawn of time mankind needed ships, so what type of ship was available in Egypt in 2,600BC?

Contemporary wall paintings of cargo ships from an early dynasty.

Queen Hatshepsut, had erected in the Valley of the Queens at Luxor two huge columns that came from Aswan. They were made of granite and were floated downstream in an enormous barge that was about 300ft long but that was some 1,200 years after the planning of the Giza complex. Somers Clark states that in the Cairo museum is evidence of a cedar wood boat built for Snedfu, the father of Cheops for whom the 'Red' pyramid at Darfur, some distance from Giza, was built. And that is it for boats of the 4th Dynasty. Evidence of boat building for the time is sketchy at best. There are models in the museums of the world but none showing other than simple vessels of eight to ten oars with one or two paddles for steering and very often with a single either square or lateen sail. This to take advantage of the prevailing north to south prevailing wind that helped progress against the current. Pictures of Minoan ships of a contemporary period show more or less identical designs using no more than ten oars each time.

According to Herodotus the boats of the 4th Dynasty were constructed by joining lots of small pieces of wood together, invariably by *'mortice and tenon'* joints, and then covering them with layers of papyrus. There was no keel as such and lateral rigidity was obtained by a series of thwarts across the beam of the boat. The one used in 1,400BC had the cargo itself as the method of keeping it in shape. The 'Solar Boat' that was dug up as part of the treasure of Cheops had a keel and could have survived a light breeze at sea but I wouldn't have wanted to be on board in a gale.

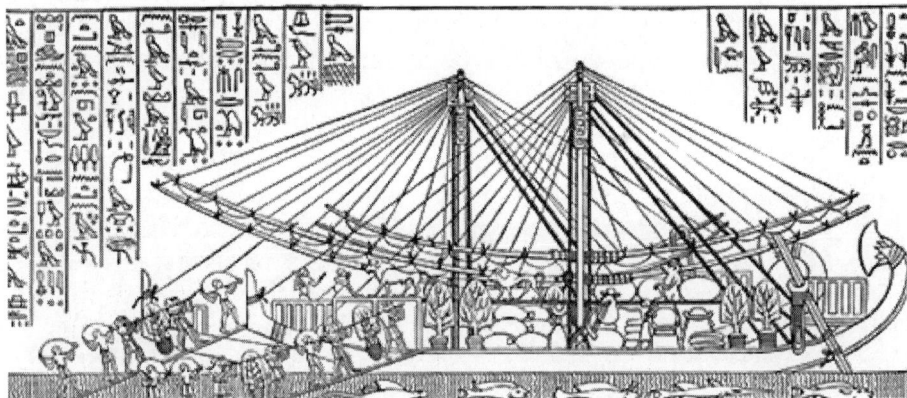

An interesting drawing in the tomb complex of Queen Hatshepsut, c 1,500BC, some 1,000 years after the supposed date of the pyramid builders, shows a sea going ship being loaded with goods for export. This is interesting because it shows just how big one of these ships was plus the method of loading. One person is holding a bag that will weigh no more than around 30 lbs, exactly as it would have been during the early dynasties. The cargo seems to be a mixture of grain and plants. There are no oars, only sails.

Apart from the one reported for Snedfu, none of these boats would have survived very long in any sort of a sea. A boat for ten oars would not have been much longer than around the 30ft or ten metre range. Any breeze much over force 4 on the Beaufort Scale would have built up a sea that would overcome it. I know this because I have a lifetime experience of sailing in all type of sea conditions in small boats. The one built of red cedar is significant because the nearest cedar is in Syria and the Lebanon which would indicate trade across the open Mediterranean, possibly with the Minoans. Either the Syrians brought the timber to Egypt or vice versa. We must ask how and it what quantity? But this does show that in ancient times overseas trade was being undertaken, but at the same time raises the question of how the Syrians got the logs onto their ships, or did they prepare them as planks first? We will never know.

What is immediately obvious is that boats of this construction could not have carried large lumps of stone. Yes, maybe one special one for one special purpose, but not for everyday use over a period of at least 150 years. The picture of the seagoing ship that I use as my illustration emphasises this point. Clearly it is being loaded piecemeal with labourers carrying the cargo by hand and this was how it was done until the advent of cast iron and steel during the Industrial Revolution in the 18th century, AD. Until then they could not construct a strong enough crane to lift large items. Only by the middle of the 19th century AD did cargo cease to be carried by hand onto ships in favour of lifting by crane. Until then putting massive single heavy items onto a ship was very difficult indeed. This picture shows that to carry the potted trees, two people were needed. To lift a block weighing between two and three tons many more would be needed and it must be obvious to all that it would have been impossible to load a 70 ton granite block onto a ship like this. But that was all they had.

It was not until well into the 19th century AD, that ships were big enough and strong enough for this type of work. The 'Blackwall Frigates' of the 18th and 19th century as used by the like of Cook and Bligh and then as emigrant ships a hundred years later were the work horse of the seas. They carried people, goods and raw materials across the globe but little came aboard using heavy lifting gear. Only the advent of the iron ship, and the ready supply of good steel to make cranes, allowed this. Remember, the entire world industrial revolution only began in 1781 with the opening of the Iron Bridge in Shropshire. Without good cast iron and steel, heavy lifting was a very difficult process.

So what else could they, did they use, for the purpose and here we must go back to our simple arithmetic? Consider first our 70 ton block of either limestone or granite. Both have more or less the same specific gravity of around 2,690kgs/cu.metre.

Palm trees are a soft wood with a specific gravity of 300kgs/cu.metre so how many kilograms of palm is needed to support every kilo of stone? The average size of an Egyptian palm tree that would have been used I estimate to be about 6 metres high of which four metres would be suitable for the purpose. It would have a diameter of around .5 metre average and those are the dimensions used for this simple exercise. How many of these trees would be needed to support one 70 ton block and one 3 ton one?

The area of the section of each tree is *pi* x the radius squared and so that comes to 3.142, x .25 x .25 = .1963 sq.mtrs.

A 4 mtr tree therefore consists of 4 x .1963 = .7855 cu.mtrs.

An exact replica of one of the ships that took the first settlers to the James River in the USA in the 17ᵗʰ century AD. This was about as big as it got for commercial craft by that time. This vessel could neither load nor transport a 70 ton block of granite.

I prefer to restrict my maths to simple experiments and so I obtained a small block of limestone that weighed 2.6 kgs. Using a simple bucket full of water I made a raft of pine since there was no suitable palm available. It took 2.95 kgs of pine to float it. Since the specific gravity of pine is 450 and palm 300 it follows that it should need .666 x 2.95 = 1.947kgs of palm tree. From this a 3000 kgs block would need 3000/2.6 x 1.947 = 2246 kgs of palm. 2246/300 = 7.488 cu mts or 10 trees just to keep a balance. Palm soon becomes saturated and therefore heavier in which case they would probably have used around 40 to 50 logs [if trees cut into 4], all of which must be evenly held together and then strapped with rope to the block. Some method would be needed to control it and then we must consider the not very easy task of getting one lump of stone and fifty heavy logs, all tied together, into the water at one end and out again at the other. The combined weight would amount to 5.5 to 6 tons.

By simple extension, if fifty logs were needed for a 3 ton block, then to travel around a 1000 miles with a 70 ton one we would need 233 palm trees! That just does not add up at all.

That is it. There is no room for doubt here. Each 70 ton block would need about 233 trees and each small one would have needed at least ten since the distances, and so the time in the water, would be much less. Either they used boats of sufficient strength that could make use of natural buoyancy or they used timber in those quantities. One or the other and that is it. Obviously the boat wins but there is no evidence to support it.

And so our next question must be just where did all this timber come from? Taking just the smaller blocks we need 70 million trees, albeit over a long period of time. Let's break it down a bit. The Great Pyramid needed around 2.3million blocks to be built over a period of, say 75 years. A palm would grow to the required dimensions at the rate of between 2 and 3 ft per year which means one growing to 6 metres, or about 20ft in height, would take between 8 and 10 years to grow. Therefore, over the period, there would be between nine and ten growths. If, as others have suggested, they only took twenty years to build them all, then there must have been huge and dense forests across the entire river bank since there would be insufficient time for new growth to mature.

2.3m x 10 = 23m trees. If each growth is 8 years we must divide the 23m by 8 which gives 2,875,000 trees, cut down, at a time just for the blocks. In the UK sustainable forests plant 1,000 trees per acre and so by using this we see that we need 2,875 acres of palm tree under growth all the time. There are 640 acres in a square mile meaning that all the time for 75 years there had to be 4.49 square miles of palms growing near the quarries in what was then, as it is now, arid desert. Anyone taking a Nile cruise today will tell you that from Cairo to Luxor the river bank is fairly well forested in palm but from Luxor to Aswan it is not. It is more or less desert all the way. So they must cut the trees downstream and then somehow or other float them against the slow moving current several hundred miles up to Aswan, get them over the rapidly running torrent of the cataracts and safely to where the hundreds of massive granite blocks were waiting. As I say, to an engineer it just does not add up. Let us not get started on how they cut down the trees if they only had copper to work with. Bronze even.

I leave it to the reader to decide how credible this is. Against this is that to get a boat, big enough to hold the huge granite blocks over the First Cataract twice, takes some explaining. In the early days of America as the pioneers made their way west, the main thoroughfares were the Missouri and Mississippi rivers. The wealthy took the steamer but the average pioneer had to use a raft. There was unlimited timber available, they had modern saws to cut it and so they used rafts to travel south with the current. They used a primitive oar at the rear to control it and this was called a 'riff'. The combination of the two became 'Riff raff' to denote the lower classes. Be that as it may, the significant thing is that they could only go the one way on a raft, not back against the current.

How did they move the stones? Well I illustrate the well known and well used picture used by every other book on the subject that I have read. It is used as absolute proof of the way that large lumps of stone were moved. I cannot argue with that because it does show an 80 ton statue being dragged by apparently 170 men on a sledge. I say that it proves conclusively that this could not be how it was done in 2,500BC. For a start this picture depicts a statue being moved during the XV111 dynasty or 1,200 years later. It does show a sledge but it also clearly shows a man on the front pouring either oil or water onto a track to reduce friction. Underneath are three men carrying extra pieces of track as either spares or to lay out later on. There is a foreman of sorts directing things. The statue is very carefully tied to a huge purpose built sledge with what looks like 'U' bolts on the side, something unheard of in the Vth dynasty. A copper one would not have had the strength.

This is a very important, much used, image showing the movement of a large statue. The period does not matter because the method is the same. This is how to move large items if you have no metalled roads, rollers or wheels. Here the statue is being dragged correctly from the front. The sledge has the correct upturned bow to ride over obstacles and it is being dragged along rails. Engineers are shown carrying spare rails and above is someone pouring a lubricant onto those rails. The overseer is standing on top to guide the operation. An obvious large body of men are employed but there is no sign of coercion as if they were slaves. It is correctly strapped to the sledge and even the tourniquet used is shown which means that it is an accurate description of a unique event. There are no comparable scenes anywhere of people doing the same thing to build a pyramid. One anomaly that no one else has picked up is the cleat securing the strapping to the sledge. That looks very much like the ones I used on my boat. It had to be at the very least of bronze or iron for strength. Not available earlier in 2,600BC.

This is obviously a very special 'one off' worthy of the painting. Show me a similar one of a large stone of around 2.5 tons and another of 80 tons, but not of a statue, and then I'll believe it. How else did they do it? I do not know.

We must also ask what they used for ropes. No one seems to have considered this one. Today we use special hawsers made from many layers of metal twisted to give high tensile strengths but even so, it would need something very special indeed to pull two, yes two, fully loaded containers on any sledge across sand or a rocky surface. I would say that today it would be difficult, in 2,500BC impossible. Yet they did it over and over again. How?

What about **Tools?** The shortest chapter in Somers Clark's book is the one about tools for the simple reason that few remain. In the British Museum there is a splendid adze of bronze mounted on a wooden haft that came from a tomb containing carpenters tools. I find it amazing that no effort has been made to identify the timber used since this is fundamental to the whole process. If it is sycamore, where did it come from? I have studied pictures of this and make the following observations.

I think that it is possibly either olive or even acacia. It is not palm. It is conveniently shaped so that the bronze tool or cutting edge can be carefully tied on to it. The museum says that it has been prepared by another adze but I do not think so. The tool marks for an adze are small where the material has been hacked out a bit at a time but the marks of this tool are long and continuous as when a plane has been used. So far no one has come across a plane in ancient Egypt. The haft is about 18 cm long. This is obviously way after our time since the cutting edge is bronze and we only had copper. This is perceived to be a carpenter's tool but significantly no similar one from any period has yet come to light that would, or could, have been used to cut stone. That is stone being excavated to provide a long and steep passage through limestone or to extract and trim massive blocks of granite. The ones used would be of a similar shape and size but for stone they must use at least bronze or iron and for the granite, well??? And no, they could not dig tunnels and shafts using a shaped lump of diorite or granite which is one of the favourite theories as this is being written. You only have to ask yourself how big a stone you could hold and then hit something with today? The result would be torn tendons in both hands and arms before an inch was extracted. That is assuming that the worker had not been blinded by the flying debris. Stone hitting stone with force is not a good idea since it shatters easily.

32

The Cairo museum seems to have the most tools but even those are few and far between given the time scales involved. There is a long copper chisel that has obviously never been used; copper mason's chisels; moulds for making bricks; various mallets where

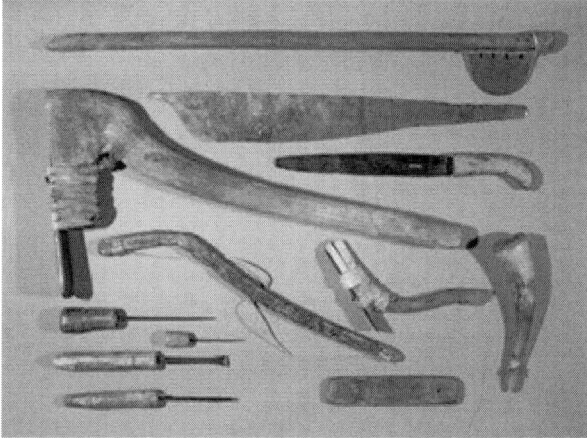

A selection of carpenter's tools made from bronze. The timber for the handles is not known but would need to be strong. It could be acacia. According to the British Museum, the bronze tool was strapped on when the leather thong was wet and it would tighten as it dried. Since they are all of bronze from a tomb dating from the New Kingdom, some 12-1500 years after the pyramids, we must assume that the earlier ones were no better. Is it reasonable to believe that these, but of copper, were the only tools available for the work? From my experience, unless the tool is attached mechanically to the haft, no matter how tight the bonding of the leather, it would soon work loose under constant hammering. In 1,500 years this was as far as they had advanced in tool design.

the weight is usually of granite or diorite; a copper plasterer's tool of unknown date; a square, level and plumb tool; various stone pounding balls made from diorite; diorite and black granite polishing tools; a mason's length of cord for measuring and some crushed wedges of an unknown wood. And that seems to be it.

The Flinders Petrie Museum in London has an equal amount of very small tools, none of which are remotely suitable for digging the smallest hole in limestone.

Again we must be practical and look at the hand tools available in the twenty first century AD. A pick axe with a steel blade has a handle no more than a metre in length. It can only be used with two hands where the operative stands over the work being dug out with legs spread out. Or sideways where he can get enough swing that would be needed to make an impression. Anything any bigger is out of the question. Heavy hammers are about twelve inches or a third of a metre long. Sledge hammers needing two strong arms are longer but not for continuous use in the stifling heat of the desert.

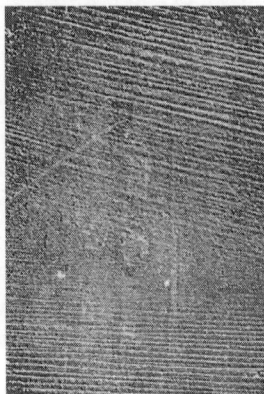

The saw, and other, marks left on the rear of a small seated statue of Mykerinus in the Cairo Museum. It is of basalt. Note the parallel saw cuts and the symmetry of the other marks. Only by holding a strong saw in an equally strong frame, on which an even, but very heavy, pressure be maintained could this effect be obtained. The other explanation is that it could equally be the marks left by the shuttering used if the statue was actually moulded instead. Either explanation opens some unexplainable 'cans of worms'. I think that it is from shuttering and that the marks are from both sawing and textiles.

Lifting and using any one of these for very long soon leaves the arms very tired. If the arms are above the horizontal the heart must work so much harder to pump the blood into them. An adze is either very big like a pick axe or much smaller and lighter like a hammer. The continuous use of any of these plays havoc with muscles and tendons in the arms. It does for modern man in exactly the same way as it did for the Ancient Egyptian. To use both pick axe and sledge hammer, the operative needs a lot of space around him. They need to be swung at arm's length for maximum effect. To work in a tunnel no more than 3.3ft square only a small tool pecking away could be used. What my father would have said was 'bringing a toffee hammer to the job'

With those tools and, presumably others like them, they apparently built not only the pyramids but all the other great and small buildings and edifices that we see today. No one anywhere has ever found any remains of long drills that were supposed to have been used, according to Petrie, to hollow out the sarcophagus in the Great Pyramid. There is some evidence of this type of tool being used to make boats – small ones – and cut timber, on the pictographs painted on the walls but, again, they come from a later period. We must never forget that in 2,500BC all they had in the way of metals were gold and copper, the two softest of them all. That sarcophagus shows marks made by a saw. It would have been impossible to build a saw that would slice through granite, out of copper. It just could not be done. Even if the actual saw had been made from copper, it would have buckled and collapsed under the huge weight needed to saw into the material. Yes, ground granite and diorite could be used as the cutting edge but in order to make progress enormous pressure must be used, a fact that Somers Clark quickly identified. Again, could just that type of tool have been sufficient to construct all those buildings? I leave it for the reader to decide but if not, then just what did they use?

Petrie himself said that it would need a saw 8ft long made of bronze using a diamond face to cut the Cheops sarcophagus from the solid granite block. It needed the same bronze but as hollow cylinders, again using crushed diamond, to drill out the centre of the same piece but only if a constant pressure was exerted. That pressure, according to Clark, had to be at least one ton in weight. I would add that much water would be needed to keep it all cool. He also came to the same conclusion, as did I on my sarcophagus in the Cairo museum, that it would be a physical impossibility, then or now [20th century for him] to cut the fine hieroglyphics in diorite bowls that were found at Giza. These show parallel lines 1/30th inch apart and 1/150th inch wide. No physical cutting tool has ever been found that would do this. Only something like a very carefully set up laser may suffice. Or a knife cutting into a soft compound.

The **Stone.** Let us look again at that through the eyes of an engineer, an architect or mason of the 4th Dynasty. Just what had he got? Very simply, he had limestone in abundance on site, he had granite about 1000 miles and one waterfall away up river and then scattered over thousands of square miles of desert he may find outcrops of diorite. Obviously he needed to know that it was that little bit harder than granite, and how to identify it when it was found. That is it. Nothing else. He had no diamonds at all or other precious stones assuming, of course, that he was able to identify them when he discovered a convenient mine. Diamonds, fresh out of the ground, look somewhat different to the cut and polished gem on the left hand of your wife.

Metals again are easy. He had found the 'naked' element metal of copper out of which he could make cooking utensils with stone as a tool to hammer it into sheets and shapes. He also knew about the other equally useless metal of gold which too could be used to fashion decorative items. Neither had any utility at all in 2,500BC for use in the construction industry. And that is it.

And so, armed with all that, he set to and built some of the greatest buildings the world has ever seen! It does not matter whether you are building a garden shed or the Channel Tunnel, every single aspect right down to the last tiny detail, must be considered before construction can begin. In this case not one, other than the ready supply of stone a long way away, aspect of the contract could even have been considered as being remotely possible. Not during the 4th Dynasty of Egypt, that is.

21

MAPS OF THE ANCIENT WORLD.

Gerhard Kramer was the most famous of all the 16th Century cartographers. He changed his name to Gerhard Mercator which is how we know him. It is his projection of the world that is most familiar today. It shows the entire world laid out flat. The Earth, however, is not flat but spherical, which means that the relative sizes of all the lands are incorrect. The Mercator Projection, as it is known, is therefore merely a means of establishing the relative positions of all the countries, rivers and seas to each other. To draw this, all that is needed is simple geometry.

To get an accurate drawing of the relative positions and sizes of the countries, and then put them down on a flat piece of paper, requires rather more. It requires a working knowledge of spherical trigonometry and how to calculate it. For that you need a very good mathematician and Charles Hapgood regularly used friends at the nearby Massachusetts Institute of Technology – the MIT – to help him out. Hapgood studied the ancient maps using both the Mercator projection and the actual thing over many years. He gave this study to his students as their degree subjects so getting access to some brilliant young minds that were untainted by existing thought. All could look at the subject with open minds and clear objectives. Most of all, in his brilliant book, '*Maps of the Ancient Sea Kings*', he names them and gives them full credit for their work. That is another reason why I soon came to like Charles Hapgood.

So what did these 'brilliant young minds' discover. The first thing was that they did not just study the Piri Re'is map in isolation. They looked at others including Mercator's atlas of the world published in 1538. They looked at the '*Dulcat Portolano*' and the works of Ptolomey and the various map makers of the Renaissance. I will quote the *Dulcat Portolano* below and so must explain that 'portolano' is taken from the Spanish 'porto' meaning 'port' and a 'portolano' was a method of finding the way from one port to another. Another thing to understand, that is essential to this section, is that, until John Harrison invented his chronometer in the 18th Century AD, it was impossible to estimate longitude. Latitude was understood from measuring the angles of the sun at mid-day but it was impossible to know longitude. Mercator, Piri Re'is et al had no method of doing that.

Until it was possible to build suitable ships, ocean travel was not easy but from the 13th century onwards ship building became more sophisticated, and adventurers were looking further afield. Maps were needed and across the classical world map makers were doing their thing.

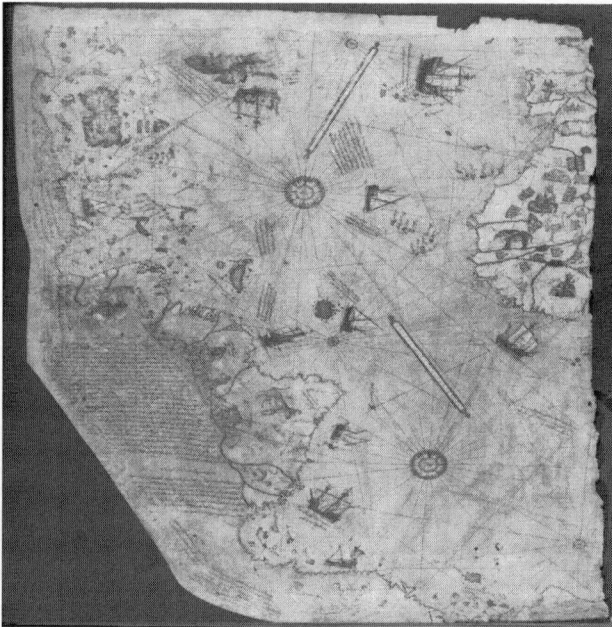

I show again the Piri Re'is map because it is so important in our quest. Since it is now proven to be genuine we have to ask over and over again who drew it and just what were his reference points? Did he use a triangulated survey or is it taken from the air?

But from where could they get their information? Only from seafarers themselves, but all maps drawn from the observations of those people are very poor and inaccurate. But other maps were being drawn that were extremely accurate indeed, one of which was the Piri Re'is map.

Piri Re'is was an admiral in the Turkish navy at the time of Suleiman The Magnificent in the 16th century. At the time the Ottomans were in control of Egypt and from the extensive library at Alexandria, from much earlier times, various documents had found their way back to their own capital of Constantinople, our Istanbul. At the Sultan's palace of Topkapi these documents were kept and they included maps. What was on the maps was remarkable to say the least. All contemporary maps at the time included the Mediterranean, the Black Sea, some of the land beyond the Red Sea, the west coast of Europe up to around Denmark, some suggestion of the Baltic and the southern portion of England only. Ireland was merely a blob. All were extremely crude indeed. That was the known world at the time, Columbus had yet to 'discover' America and the Atlantic was the great unknown. Obviously no one knew of the existence of an even bigger ocean to the west.

Piri Re'is found an ancient map which he copied and it was of the entire world, not as a flat Mercator projection, but as a true spherical version based on the layout seen from around 250 miles high with Cairo as its centre. Please bear in mind that all Hapgood's work, and those of his students, was involved with maps and not about Ancient Egypt. He was only interested in the maps and their interpretation. His only agenda was to find the truth and, with open minds, that is what they sought.

On the Piri Re'is map, discovered at the Topkapi in 1926, was an extremely accurate depiction of the Mediterranean and Black Seas plus the entire Atlantic showing both North and South America including the west coast of South America and, most significantly, the Atlantic coast of Antarctica free of ice on its northern shores. When Piri Re'is drew his map Columbus had only just discovered the Antilles and a tiny part of mainland America, both Central and South. Yet there was a map that showed the lot. So who drew it? The part of the map concerned was only a fragment, the rest of it being lost for all time.

As I have indicated, knowledge of spherical geometry is needed to do this and that is done by the use of what were known as 'winds'. A wind is an arbitrarily placed reference point in the form of a circle that is then bisected, usually 16 times. These lines are then projected across the map where they cross the lines from similar winds [which we today would call a 'Compass Rose'] so that exact points can be established. Obviously the more winds, the more accurate the map. The Piri Re'is map shows five such winds, one on the latitude of the Gironde in France with a longitude to the west of the Azores; the next is just to the west but on the latitude of southern Morocco. Just to the east of that is one on the Equator; then one in mid Atlantic on the latitude of Rio with the last being due south of Nigeria at the latitude of Patagonia. From these the intersecting lines are drawn on the map with amazing results.

The relative latitude and longitude of the African, European and American continents are more or less accurate, some to as near as around twenty miles. Hapgood gives all this information in great detail but for this exercise I am only looking at the bigger picture. The layout of the Mediterranean is so accurate that it could have been drawn today using the latest satellite technology, as is the Bight of Benin in Africa which would have taken years to survey, again using only the latest technology. But the one big inclusion is the Antarctic which depicts Queen Maud Land free of ice. Now it is under a mile of ice. Seismic maps have shown that the coastline, rivers and mountains on the 1513 map to be more or less the correct outlines. The latitudes are correct and so are the longitudes. A comparison made of the longitude of a point on the Guinea Coast of Africa with a known point on Queen Maud Land show the longitude to be exactly right. It is important to realise that a degree of longitude on the Guinea Coast is around 65 miles, it being just north of the Equator but at 70 degrees south, i.e, Queen Maud Land, it is only about 2 miles. This leaves the opportunity for error to be great but it simply isn't. The map also shows rivers and lakes where today we only see the Sahara Desert.

Let us look at more maps, all drawn from ancient originals. Unfortunately they have not a high enough definition to be worth reproducing here but all are there to see in the Hapgood book. The ones drawn by Ptolemy and his associates during the

Romano/Greek period of around 400BC are crude in the extreme and were taken from information given by seafarers of the time. But others drawn in the 13th to 16th centuries from the ancient originals are remarkable. Mercator, for his atlas of 1538, drew a map of the world showing it to be round and to have the two poles. He shows Queen Maud Land with accuracy, Patagonia and the Straights of Magellan leading to an accurate outline of the Pacific Coast of South America. Antarctica is quite accurate in shape and the relative position of it to South Africa more or less correct. He shows the North Pole as being sea and not land, the correct layout of North America, West Africa, the West Indies and the Baltic but not Western Europe or the British Isles.

The *Hadji Ahmed World Map* of 1559 shows again a round world but of the northern hemisphere. It is elongated to include the South Atlantic where Africa, South America, Madagascar, India, the West Indies and the West Coast of the USA and Canada, right up to Alaska are correctly drawn. Significantly the northern ice cap is land free and the Bering Straight is correctly positioned with the gap between the Americas and Asia. He shows India and South East Asia with Antarctica as well.

Another map by Oronteus Finaeus in 1531 is centred over the South Pole and shows the whole of Antarctica free of ice, the outline amazingly accurate and the relative latitude and longitude of the Straights of Magellan to be true as well.

Let us now put that into accepted present day historical facts.

11th century. Leif Ericson from Norway discovered North America.

1470. The Portuguese explore west coast of Africa.

1483. Bartholomeu Dias reaches the African Cape of Good Hope.

1492. Columbus discovers the Bahamas.

1493. Columbus discovers Cuba and Hispaniola.

1498. Columbus discovers South America near Trinidad and then explores the Orinoco.

1498. Vasco da Gama reaches India.

1502. Columbus discovers Central America and Mexico.

1519-1522. Magellan fleet completes first circumnavigation.

1577-1580. Francis Drake circumnavigation.

Between 1522 and 1580 there was just one other circumnavigation and so they were not very frequent, presumably because so few ships were available that could cope with ocean weather. All the expeditions lost craft due to storms.

From this chronology it must be obvious that the voyages of discovery were, in the first place, just that. They were done for commercial reasons seeking, in the first place, spices from the Orient and in the second gold. Lots and lots of gold. They were not interested in any cultural discoveries or any lengthy cartographical work. They merely marked on a map approximately where somewhere was and its approximate shape and this is confirmed by the crude attempts made in map making at the time. In 1513, whilst by now most people accepted that the world was round, it was still some 30 years before Copernicus came out with his ideas about it being something other than being around which the universe spun. His revelations had an enormous affect of celestial navigation.

In 1513 Central and South America had been discovered but not explored and the rest of the continents were virgin territory. Mainland North America had yet to be re-discovered as had the rest of South America. In 1538 the Magellan expedition had returned some 16 years earlier and so Mercator may have got his information from there but, in general, those early maps, copied from much earlier ones, could not have received much, if any, information from the navigators of the time. They were prepared for the navigators, not by them.

Looking at their impressions of northern Europe it is interesting to see that they all draw the Bay of Biscay with some accuracy as do they the French coast and the Netherlands up to Denmark. The entrances to the Baltic are fairly accurate as is the outline of England up to the Humber in the east and Lancashire in the west. None show the coast of Scotland or Ireland nor do they indicate the presence of Orkney or Shetland but some show Iceland. Ireland is always a simple blob on the map. Curious to say the least

What must we deduce from this?

Hapgood is unequivocal. He insists that they were drawn by some previous civilization, or possibly extra-terrestrial beings, in antiquity, before the ice caps were formed. Being a simple soul who tends to accept what appears to be the obvious, I must agree with him. So when, that is the question, as is why?

Queen Maude Land was last free of ice at around 3,000BP. The entire continent was last free over a million years ago. This has been scientifically proved by the taking of sediment samples in the Ross Sea in 1949. This was the 'Byrd Expedition' that included Dr Jack Hough, of the University of Illinois, who took and analysed the samples. By analysing the radioactive content of the samples and identifying their content some remarkable geological anomalies were discovered.

It is a proven fact that silt from a flowing river will deposit fine grains of sand but the sediment from a glacier falling into the sea is quite different, being much coarser. The samples showed that Antarctica had been a temperate land, free from ice three times during the last million years. It was last so in part in 4,000BC after a considerable period of relative warmth when rivers ran through the land. The Orantes Finaeus map shows rivers flowing from mountain ranges by the coast but none flowing from the interior, suggesting that it may have been ice covered at the time. The Ross Sea would, according to Hapgood, have iced over before Queen Maud Land which means that it could have been ice free as recently as 1,000BC. Could anyone, from the air, accurately draw maps of the land, mountains and rivers through over a mile of ice? I doubt it in which case some person, or being, drew these maps any time before 1,000BC. Had they the map making knowledge necessary to conduct an accurate sea level survey of such a huge area, which must now include South America as well? The other question is 'why?'. The *Dulcat portolan* shows an incredibly accurate Mediterranean and Black Sea, as does Piri Re'is, but as soon as Piri Re'is tries to draw, an island like Crete from contemporary information, provided by seafarers, he gets it hopelessly wrong.

The Ptolemaic map of around 40AD as redrawn by the monks of Constantinople in 1300.

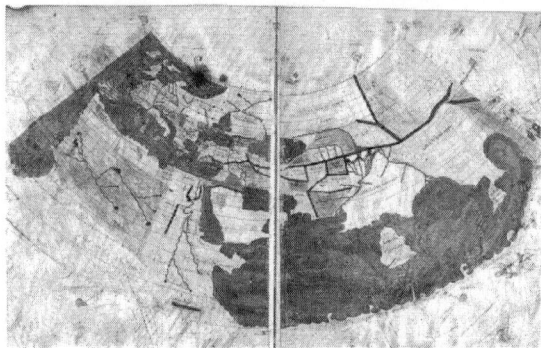

The world as known to Ptolemy, redrawn in Constantinople in 1300. This shows a good impression of the Mediterranean, the Black Sea and up into the Baltic but also it shows only the southern part of England in the British Isles.

The reason that much of the British Isles on all the maps is lacking anything north or west of The Wash could just be that when the maps were drawn, that area was covered in ice. Ice to that extent was there at around 20,000BC so we must ask whether the Antarctic ice was absent when the northern ice sheet was not. If not during the last Ice Age, could it have been so during an even earlier one? In any case it does place living and highly intelligent peoples on Earth at around 20,000BC. Against that idea is that sea levels were high enough to flood the North This is another piece in our jigsaw showing that our planet's timeline may not be exactly as the Darwin, and only Darwin, experts think it to be. It shows that there was intelligent exploration and recording being done during many millennia before and around the writing of the Holy Bible and the construction of so many important ancient buildings.

Compare the Pirie Re'is map with these two maps. They show the known world according to the Greeks and Romans and then what was known just before Columbus. The Pirie Re'is one must obviously have been done during a different civilization at a totally different time.

The Frau Mauro World Map of 1459.

The Frau Mauro World Map of 1459. The known world pre-Columbus. Note here the contours of West Africa in particular and contrast those to the ones shown on the Piri Re'is map. Obviously it would not have been possible to make a full triangulated survey of such an area during the brief time scales involved.

45

22

HOW THEY <u>COULD</u> HAVE BUILT THE PYRAMIDS

Bear in mind all the time that my theories depend entirely on the extra terrestrial element, without which none of this would be either necessary or possible. By simple definition, these were people of an advanced technical civilization, who were able to transcend immense distances and periods of time with apparent ease. If you accept this as the possibility then it is not unreasonable to expect that they would have had other tools in the box, having anticipated the possible need. Amongst those tools would be a compass with the knowledge of how to use it. The previous chapters must have shown even the most diehard of the detractors that there are huge unanswered anomalies in present thought.

The specification then called for, first, exact right angles at each corner for the finished base, and these must be built to tolerances of plus or minus one or two centimetres [they used the cubit which was about 21 inches]. The area to be surveyed was immense. Somers Clark shows a drawing where the base of the Great pyramid alone covered an area equal to that of St Peter's in Rome and St Paul's in London combined with much room to spare. The only way to do this is by understanding the principals of triangulation, something supposed to have been discovered thousands of years later by their distant descendent, Pythagoras. [Even though Thoth was supposed to have invented geometry.] And they must be small triangles pre-determined on the drawings. A project of this size must have had some drawings with which to work. It could not have been on the hoof guess work that resulted in the ratio of *pi* being so accurately arrived at. So they would be marked out in the sand, probably with lengths of rope of the exact length joining them together. The lengths would have to be fairly short to overcome the catenary effect. A Catenary is the mathematical term for the sag in the middle of a long rope. No matter how tight you pull it, every long rope has a catenary which would have totally thrown out all previous calculations. Simply laying it out on the ground would mean variations due to the uneven surface and, with these tolerances over such an area, it would have been unacceptable. From this it would be obvious that they had some means of measuring. Very carefully, using hundreds of tiny interlocking triangles they would arrive at the perfect square. But, before any building could begin, the other two pyramids must also be laid out to the predetermined sizes, in the precise predetermined layout, to end up with the mathematically exact figures identified by Flinders Petrie and John Legon. It took Petrie, using modern surveying techniques, over two years to do his survey; it would have taken these people much longer unless they had a satellite navigation system of which there is no evidence at all. So they were not in a desperate hurry, always assuming that this actually how it was done. The finished result ended with the centre of the smallest pyramid being exactly above a natural opening in the rock. This cannot have been a lucky accident. Somehow or other they knew that it was there and everything was designed and built around it. How they did this and why, we will never know. But it was an incredible feat of surveying unless very advanced 21st century AD equipment was used. It is my contention that they must have had that type of advanced knowledge and equipment. That equipment to include some method of doing a seismic survey of the ground beneath them.

I agree with accepted wisdom in that they began in the middle and worked slowly out, but the entire site must have been laid out first to get the correct layout and proportions. Only by so doing could they arrive at the precise mathematical results. And the exact dead centres to work to. This, in itself was a prodigious feat for anyone, even today, without accurate means of measuring, calculating and recording. If in doubt, just try to work out where to start digging, and at what angle, to arrive at the exact dead centre of the pyramid. To draw out the 26 degree angle and deduce just where they must begin their digging to end up in exactly the right place was an amazing feat in itself. That there are different ante chambers on route may indicate that they got it wrong on the first two but right when setting out the big one.

Several years later they would address the problem of the levels, which is far from easy given the vast acreage involved - plus lack of a Theodolite, but level they must be – exactly – or we would end up with a misshaped pyramid. Today, on site at Giza, you can see how much rock was excavated just to get things level. It is my contention that they built the small one first to an exact design and that was more or less finished when they began the middle one. The reason for this is that they only had the one descending passage to the naturally formed central chamber. If I am correct in the assumption that, apart from direction beacons, the primary use was either to generate power or to recharge what they had brought with them, it would appear that the small one either did not work or did not do the job well enough. But if they were, as they must have been, all laid out simultaneously that cannot be the case. That they built the second one to a similar design but much bigger, indicates that the small one may have worked, as designed, before being encased and sealed with Granite plaques. They would not have done so had they not been perfectly happy with it. But the second one they would seal by enclosing it in an outer layer of limestone or alabaster. Both were solid blocks of stone when finished which rather obviates the tomb idea. Obviously this worked but they then changed the design, first on the Red Pyramid some miles away with elaborate inner chambers, still below ground, before changing things again to give the Great Pyramid its unique layout. The big difference with the last two was the apparent need for substantial extra quantities of granite, to be found – inconveniently – over a thousand miles to the south near Aswan and above the First Cataract of the Nile. There had to be a very special reason for this. All four pyramids used vast quantities that were of neither structural nor cosmetic necessity. One also has to question the construction of three totally solid ones if the sole object was to bury someone below ground.

Levelling was in fact the easy bit even though the site is sloping and much excavation would be needed to arrive at the level site. Had they built a little higher up much of this levelling would have been avoided. So why, as with the Sphinx, did they not choose a more obvious site? Beginning in the middle, either by sighting the horizon or by using small troughs of water, it would have been very easy to keep everything level as the base expanded. The tricky bit was getting the angles exactly right so that the capstone was exactly over the centre of the pyramid. Half a degree out on any face and the thing would be well out of shape. To work this one out and then execute it so accurately had to mean the use of instruments and a detailed knowledge of geometry. If not as I have suggested, just where did that come from? And you must also add that the individual stones, all 7m of them, must each be cut with an incredible degree of accuracy. The placing of the final exterior blocks on each level and each face had to be very carefully measured so as to end up with the correct angle at all times. It would only have needed to be out by the length of just one block on one face and the capstone would not have ended up over the exact centre each time. Again, a prodigious display of surveying technique, even today.

The next task would be to identify the exact centre of each, and then to excavate through the limestone bedrock the underground passages and chambers which, one would have thought, was the principal object of the exercise. Here I have a problem if all they had was bits of flint or copper with which to dig. Those who took part in my little experiment earlier in the book will know how difficult it is to just dig out a 6 inch square hole to a depth of 12 inches in either sand or limestone using steel chisels. Just chipping away with a bit of flint is really not a starter and nor is it using copper chisels and lumps of stone as the hammer. As always one must be practical and realise that if you are holding a chisel with one hand, only something that can be comfortably gripped can be used in the other. However, it cannot be denied that they did it, ending up with perfectly square walls and floors, the ceilings being added if it was done by simple excavation. It could be done today using the 'Open Cast' method of extracting what they needed and then simply putting all the waste back into the hole. Since the ground above these excavations is covered in pyramids, it is impossible to say which method they used.

So how do we overcome this one? As I say, they could not have done it if all they had to work with was a flint chipping. Nor could they have used copper or bronze because they were softer than the bedrock. That would have been impossible, no matter how many people were working on it. As with digging out big blocks, only a limited number of people can be cutting at any one time or

49

they would simply get in each other's way. And this holds good using today's pneumatic drills. Especially in steep tunnels only just over three feet wide and high. Even more so if those tunnels had then to be lined with smooth blocks of granite. As I have said, there were no known means in 2,500BC of extracting and working the granite. There were none at all. Let us be clear about that. **Using tools and materials known to be available in 2,900 – 2,200BC, not one aspect of building the Giza pyramids could have been attempted.**

I took this picture of the Great Pyramid in 2010 to show the size of the project. Those are fully grown adults at ground level. From those it is possible to get a proper perspective of the sizes of the blocks used. Looking at this it takes no imagination to believe that 2.3 million of them at least were used on this pyramid alone.

So far no one has found any tools that could realistically have been used for any of this. Small pieces of bronze with sycamore handles as displayed in the Cairo museum are not a starter. None of the ones that I have seen anywhere could have been used to dig out the tunnels and holes under the pyramids of Egypt. It would be impossible now, as it was then, so they **HAD** to have used something else. Furthermore, no tools have come to light that could have carved the numerous granite statues and sarcophagi in every museum of the world. Being a 'hands on' engineer and researcher I made for myself a chisel from copper, and an adze, as near as possible to the ones on display in Cairo.

They were useless. They would not touch limestone no matter how hard I tried.

Now you must agree that whoever built these works, it is inconceivable that they would begin the laborious tasks of setting out and levelling, without having a very good idea of how the job as a whole would be done, so that a finish time of a realistic period would be achieved. You can't believe that after setting out they would have a crisis meeting because no one told the architect that they couldn't dig the hole or produce the blocks. No, they set out to build knowing exactly how it was going to be done.

There is an ancient site of great antiquity at Abydos, some distance up river from Giza, called the Osireion, which has a massive entrance gate. The lintel on this gate is a solid piece of granite and, with the sun in the right direction some faint parallel curved lines can be seen quite clearly. They cover the entire face and are evenly spaced. Now I have spent enough time at a work bench smoothing over exactly this type of line in wood, aluminium and steel to know exactly how they happen. On an unrelated project I recently bought some thick MDF which the DIY store cut to size for me using a big circular saw. Those sawn faces show the exact same result as the one at Abydos. All were made by the same thing – a circular saw. As soon as I saw a picture of the gate it screamed out at me that it was not only a circular saw of immense size, but also, because of the constant spacing, it had gone through it like a knife through butter. I know of nothing today that would produce the same result. All Egyptologists accept that this pre dates Dozer

Let us be absolutely clear here. Those cuts could only have come from a circular saw of immense size, strength and power. There would be no need or purpose to have an army of little men with copper chisels trying to reproduce marks that meant nothing to anybody. In the process defacing an otherwise perfectly flat surface that someone else has taken an eternity preparing. There can be no mistake about this; a circular saw was used to build this structure. This could not be a simple straight saw worked by a man at either end since the cuts would vary in depth and position. The only way then, as now, to finish up with parallel, curved, cutting lines like this is a power saw. Simply projecting those arcs into a full circle indicates that either the stone was cut high up on stands or that the blade went into a deep pit with the stone at ground level. The cuts show that it was set up in the exact position to give maximum strength for an anti-clockwise rotation.

The Osirieon itself illustrates this point. The vertical exposed walls are beautifully cut and absolutely straight. The horizontal lines are both parallel and at the exact right angle to the outer walls, being precision cut as well, to leave an almost ground finish between the stones with not so much as a millimetre of a gap anywhere. But the ends, not to be left on view, are simple rough cut rock. I return to this point later when discussing the building stones.

Now the possession of a saw like this, driven no doubt by somehow utilising the power generated by possibly the electrical, or even, nuclear capability, would indicate that they would have other toys in the cupboard with which to excavate rock. As they gradually made their descent to the final chambers they kept the sides and floor at the constant angle of descent and of constant straight width, leaving the walls perfectly vertical. This is only possible using machinery. Otherwise it would be nigh on impossible to keep it from running off anywhere.

Another example of this is a basalt [extremely hard] small statue in the Cairo Museum dating to the time of Mykerinus. I illustrate it earlier. It shows perfectly straight, even and parallel saw cuts. Going back to our experiment on the 3 inch square piece of wood, no one, using a hand saw could finish with hundreds of equally spaced and parallel saw cuts. By hand the saw varies in position all the time. The only way this can be done leaving those marks is with a mechanically operated saw of exactly even weight on each cut and set in a very rigid frame. Again, no 'ifs' or 'buts', that was not cut by hand.

You only have to walk down your own High Street and look at the inevitable big hole that is being dug. If it is being dug entirely by hand, with a pick axe, shovel and pneumatic drill, the edges will be uneven and the walls anything but perfectly vertical and true. But, if they first use a stone cutting saw before digging out with a small excavator using its back hoe, then a perfect clean cut will be found – as found on your nearest pyramid. As we found when digging our little hole in the garden, the biggest problem now would be excavating and removing the waste, and that would probably have to be done by hand – a long and laborious task given, as discussed earlier, that because of the physical size of the builders, it must be done a few pounds at a time in a bucket. In fact a chain of people passing buckets to each other would have been used. Or, as of now, they had mechanical means of accomplishing the task. Another thing to remember is that the tunnels are so very small and so very long, which would render excavation on this scale using only simple flint, copper or bronze tools impossible.

There is ample physical evidence of this today. In the UK there are thousands of disused mines for coal, tin and iron and the access tunnel walls are anything but straight and true. This is because they had no need to be otherwise. The narrow ones, where only the small children worked, are about the same size as the ones on the pyramids. No one would bother to go to the trouble of building them with exact corners and constant dimensions, and then to line them with granite, unless it was **absolutely necessary**. This was obviously the case in Egypt and we must ask the question of 'Why?' In the UK coal mines only the floor was relatively smooth to allow the children to drag the coal in wheeled trolleys, usually on iron rails, to the surface. Two children were needed at least for each small container of coal. The one and only reason for any shaft to be perfectly smooth and even is to allow a constant stream of some fluid or liquid to flow. As a mechanical engineer I studied the flow of air through pipes in the automotive industry.

We are still building just the smallest, the one of Mykerinus, of the three principal pyramids and eventually we arrive at our first chamber, located 70 ft down a 26 degree descending passage in an exact north to south direction, at right angles to our eventual pyramid entry somewhere higher up on the north face. The specification calls for the entire passageway above ground level, and continuing for a significant distance below, to be lined in granite. Then we must continue south with an even smaller shaft that even the Egyptian of the day would have had difficulty standing in, that must be dug out of the bedrock, before we arrive some forty feet further on in a second chamber, to be dug out of the bedrock as a double cube based on 15ft. That is 15ft x 15ft x 30ft which equates to 6,750 cu.ft of bedrock to be excavated, and removed up those same small shafts, to give again perfect walls and ceiling.

Near the centre of this is another opening leading to a steep ramp in a westerly direction. This to lead into a small chamber, off which is another ramp leading into the final chamber, which must be 12ft long by 8ft wide, exactly on the north/south meridian, but this must be lined entirely, floor to ceiling with granite. The ceiling to be formed with 18 slabs of nine each side, facing each other as a typical ridge, but then the underside must be carved out to form a perfect cylinder. This was a structural impossibility for the Egyptians of 2,500BC without some external assistance and intelligence. Here we are talking, not about far from simple muck shifting out of bedrock of limestone, but very intricate and dangerous deep mining. I am not aware of this being replicated at any time anywhere else on the globe. Again simply impossible without a considerable mechanical help, and immensely complicated by this tiresome introduction of granite located so very far away. Also it would have been impossible under any circumstances to ascertain in the first place that the chambers were directly under the proposed dead centre line of the yet to be built pyramid, and exactly on the north/south meridian, without some method of extremely accurate measurement and recording. This type of accuracy is only possible using very advanced civil engineering practice of the type used when building the Channel Tunnel. There could never have been any question of guesswork involved.

Let us be perfectly clear about this. Using only the tools on display in the Egyptian Museum in Cairo, this would have been impossible. Forget time scale and manpower, this could never have been achieved using the equipment available in 2,500BC. No matter what theory is put about, those shafts and that granite were not excavated and installed using those tools.

Somers Clark thought that it was all surveyed with a mixture of long ropes and rods of a fixed length put end to end. Yes, that could be done but we must always go back to the fact that before that first chisel mark was made the entire site had been surveyed and laid out. The distance between the outer sides of the first and third pyramids is 1714 cubits. That is 967 metres. How anyone using mere ropes and rods could lay out this area to those tolerances and to be a mirror of Orion's belt is beyond me. As a 21st century engineer I would say that it could not be done. Not now and not then using those tools. The finished sizes of the pyramids were all decided by these dimensions alone. Just why we will never know.

To me it is now becoming obvious that the sole purpose of this exercise is to provide a single, granite lined, chamber with perfectly fitting masonry in the exact centre of the pyramid and on the exact north/south line, with granite lined passageways to the surface. But, as contracts manager that, at this stage, has nothing to do with me. All I have to do is build the thing.

Starting with the walls of the far room, we need eight blocks 12ft long by 2ft wide by 1ft thick, plus five more of about the same size at one end and five more nine foot long at the other. Our slabs in the roof, of which we need 18, are 5 to 6 ft long, 1ft 6 inches wide and again about one foot thick. With the knowledge that the specific gravity of granite is around 150 lbs per cubic foot we can easily work out that the long wall blocks will weigh 1.607 tons each and the roof ones .6026 tons each. In one lift each man can lift about 35 lbs; therefore we need 38 men just to raise the roof ones off the floor and 103 men to lift the wall ones.

Just to move around, not to work, just to move around, each man needs about six square feet of space. To actually work he needs about 20 square feet as an absolute minimum. The room is 12 ft x 8ft, or 96 square feet, therefore its maximum capacity, just to move around, not to work, is 16 people. To work in, only about four people at a time could be employed. It is so now and it was then. Four, and only four people at any one time could work in that chamber, whatever they were doing. Plus, of course, there would be a massive problem of lack of oxygen unless some form of airflow was devised. There was the other not insignificant problem of providing a continuous amount of adequate lighting once the work was out of the rays of the sun. But then any type of naked flame would only serve to exacerbate the problem of lack of oxygen. Again, if you are in any doubt at all, just see how many painters and decorators can work at any one time in your own lounge, dining room or bedroom. It is easy to find out the square footage and you will find that this holds true every time.

In anybody's language, these sums simply do not add up at all, plus we have the added problem of negotiating extremely narrow and low passages with huge and heavy blocks of granite. So just how did they do it then, and how would we do it today?

Again I digress back to our little experiment where I asked you to find a lump of either sandstone or the softer limestone and, using virtually any tools you could lay your hands on except a stone cutting circular saw, I gave you a week to produce two adjacent sides perfectly flat and true and at exact right angles to each other. I didn't ask you to try granite because I knew you would have had difficulty in getting started. And I doubted whether, other than a highly skilled mason, any of you could succeed.

It is interesting to look at the problems comparatively recently of extracting large quantities of granite. There is an fascinating section in 'The Age of Gold' by H W Brands where he describes the problems Leland Stanford had when driving his Central Pacific Railway across the High Sierras. The High Sierras at that point were solid granite through which he must dig some big tunnels.

Attacking them with simple steel picks and shovels was a waste of time and so they used dynamite inserted into deep holes, drilled using tungsten carbide tips, to loosen the rock ready for clearing. But even large charges of dynamite had little effect and so he began using the highly unstable new product – nitro glycerine. With this it was reported that they were able to proceed by 2ft per face per day. And this they considered to be excellent progress. Also they had no need to end up with large lumps of rock to make into blocks. The smaller the waste, the easier it is to move. Bear in mind also that they could drill the necessary holes using pneumatic drills, something that the ancient Egyptian did not have.

Another practical example of this is the Stanedge Tunnel on the Huddersfield Canal in West Yorkshire, England. It is the longest canal tunnel in the country at 5,698 yards or 5,260 metres long. It was built in the late 18th century AD and the bedrock is mainly limestone but there is an outcrop of grit stone half way through. Above at ground level they sank bore holes at 200 metre intervals to provide a flow of air, extract the waste using buckets on ropes that would be hauled to the surface using pulleys and horses and by lowering a measured length of rope they could be sure that all was at the correct level.

The method of extraction of the rock was for one man to hold a long iron bar on his shoulder which would be hit by another man from behind using a heavy sledge hammer. Each time the bar was turned as in a drill and when the hole was deep enough a charge of explosive was inserted. The waste was then loaded into the buckets and disposed of up the bore hole. The tunnel is roughly finished inside and has two natural caverns. It is approximately 3 metres by 2.5 metres meaning that 55,650 cu.mtrs had to be extracted. It took 17 years to construct in total and that equates to a progress of around one metre per day.

Contrast this with the supposed progress in building the Red Pyramid at Dashur. Now Dashur is some ten miles south of Giza and about three miles from the Nile. It contains 2 million blocks of stone, not quite as well trimmed as at Giza and the entire outer surface was lined, only some of which remains. I have described the extensive need for granite earlier. Forget the underground excavation for a minute but just concentrate on the main solid structure. 2 million blocks of approximately, say 2.5 mtrs x 1.5 mtrs x 1.5 mtrs comes to 11.25 million cubic mtrs of stone to be extracted, trimmed, transported and erected. That is over two hundred times that of the Stanedge Tunnel. In actual fact the true figure is nearly 300 times that of the Stanedge tunnel. We know that it took seventeen years for that but, according to expert opinion, that is the time it took to build the Red Pyramid! Do those figures add up?

When researching this to find out how things may possibly have been done I made for myself a scaled down pyramid block 12 inches long, 8 inches wide and 6 inches deep. It is made of granite, weighs 50lbs and it took me just 2 hours to produce. Subsequent ones take about 30 minutes. It is perfectly square, smooth sided and they will sit either side by side or on top of each other with a perfect fit. And I didn't use a saw.

"Alright smart ass," I hear you all saying, *"just how did you do that?"*

And my answer is simple. I cast it in a standard shuttering and it was that that took the time to make. A simple 5:1:1 mixture of granite chips, granite or hard sharp sand and a mortar mixed with water and poured into a mould, when set makes a perfect granite block. When it has settled it has all the properties of granite including its radon content.

Returning to our pyramid, if this is how it was done, the builders will have had to cast these pieces of granite on site one at a time – an easy task for four to six men, after which the shuttering is removed and then I have no problem about raising these into place using simple leverage and fulcrums. Somers Clark says that they used a series of rocking sleds to progressively raise all the stones and that is certainly a possibility. The roof ones will have been cast with the curve there rather than, as thought elsewhere, hewn out Sistine Chapel style from underneath.

And that is how they must have built them all. I would go further and say that it was the only way to do it. We have already seen that producing 300 blocks a day quarrying, when each would take at least 2.5 weeks, would require a ludicrous 6,000 quarry faces working simultaneously, innumerable docks and cranes at different levels to load in and out of barges to cross the river, plus an immense army pulling them across the desert. The Red Pyramid is over 3 miles from the river. That needs over two million blocks to be pulled that enormous distance at a few yards an hour. That means at least a week for each block. No, sorry, not a starter. It would be impossible now as it was then to find enough timber in Aswan to build big enough pontoons to float them all down river for that is the only way to do it without using a crane. After the Napoleonic Wars in the early 19th century AD, both Britain and France looted Egypt and took away with them two edifices called 'Cleopatra's Needles'. They stand today on the banks of the Thames and in the Place de la Concorde. It was not possible to load either onto a ship and so they were towed along whilst tied to pontoons. One sank and had to be retrieved. Going back 5,000 years, they only had that technology and so it was the only way to transport huge lumps of stone. Smaller pieces, on the other hand, could go into boats. Using nothing but solid lumps of stone could not have been attempted using the equipment available at the time.

But mine is very much a starter. I do not pretend to be the first to come to this conclusion as others have been there before me. Notably a scientist from Israel named Joseph Davidovits who published on the subject some time ago. He also came to this conclusion which, by the use of simple arithmetic, can so easily be proved to be the only correct solution to the problem. It is the only solution that does not rely on an enormous supply of very sophisticated machinery or labour. Obviously he is dismissed as being a fool by all conventional Egyptologists, but not by me.

He thought that by using an esoteric mixture of materials it would be possible to create a concrete like substance that looked like stone and, to a certain extent, I do agree with him. That would account for the absence of weathering, particularly at the corners after, on the smaller pyramid, at least five thousand years of desert storms.

It is rapidly becoming obvious that these people did have machinery, especially a capacity to cut stone to an incredible accuracy, plus either a sophisticated understanding of the mechanics of pulley systems and some knowledge of the law of the lever. They most certainly were able to trim the stones to perfection and then assemble in very confined spaces, some very large lumps at not insignificant heights. I do not buy the theory of a series of monks with large trumpets levitating them into the air with the vibration of their sound. This theory comes crashing down, if you'll excuse the pun, when you ask how, having placed block [a] onto its pillars and you begin to lift block [b] to put next to it, do you stop block [a] from waltzing off into the ether before crashing down when the monks ran out of puff? No, they must have used a leverage system, the only part of which gives me a problem being just what did they use to make the levers? We already know that there was little, if any, hardwood about and palm would simply crack, splinter and break when used in this context. And here I must be guilty of the 'Mighty Bound' theory, for levers they must have used, made of what, we do not know. Cedar from the Levant being the only possible answer. Casting each piece on site overcomes all of this which is why I say that it is the only way to do it without machinery. No simple lever from any type of wood or metal could raise the corner of a seventy ton block of stone.

The only other answer is one that everyone, including me, will think to be preposterous and that is that they had some means of transcending gravity. As with the monks and their trumpets, is it at all feasible to lift enormous weights and transport them over considerable distances other than by using something like a Chinook helicopter? I do not know but it is something that must be **considered**, especially when we look at what the Incas did.

So now we have our underground works complete on the smaller pyramid, it is all back filled to the ground level and our mining team, complete with equipment, can move onto the next one. We no longer need the mining equipment for the rest can be done, given time, by hand. Sufficient limestone must be quarried, broken up and then processed to extract the lime which will be used as the base for the mortar in our blocks. The knowledge that furnaces must be built and used to extract the lime must have been there. A form of cement must be used in making concrete and this must be readily available. Portland Cement has the finished look of limestone and is manufactured by heating to a very high temperature crushed limestone and silica which comes from sand. To this is added iron ore and other minerals but just the mixture of the lime and silicon, both of which were readily available, suitably heated would suffice. When mixed with water this makes a perfectly adequate cement. The residue, which will form the basis of our blocks, and limestone, is so much easier and softer to work than sandstone. Davidovits describes a different mix and he may well be correct, I merely suggest the principal here.

It will be broken up in the quarry, loaded onto sledges drawn by oxen, asses or donkeys to be taken down to the river bank where it will be loaded into dumb barges. Or be simply carried as seen on the ship being loaded earlier. A drawing in the Cairo museum shows a team of oxen pulling a loaded sledge. At the other end the process is repeated and the sledges will bring the stone and lime onto site. Although I say 'sledges', that is one aspect where my theory falters. Somers Clark says that wheels were only used ceremonially in later dynasties on account of the appalling surfaces at the time. However the problems of wood supply and damage caused by rough terrain are still there as previously shown. If the terrain was unsuitable for wheels, then it most certainly will have been even more so for dragging heavy blocks, on sledges or not. How they got the material to site remains a mystery. For this idea to work it will be premixed with desert sand and mortar, of which there was a lot, in the correct proportions before being put into buckets and handed to a human chain, at the end of which is a shuttered box into which it is poured. There, water will be added, using a series of what are known as 'Archimedes Screws'. This is a long tube in which is a continuous spiral with tight tolerances to the side of the tube. One end is put into water at low level and, when the spiral is turned – easily by hand – the water goes up the tube to the next level. A series of these could take the water right to the top with relative ease. Water is added as it is going on until the box is full, after which it will be left to set. This operation will be repeated many times around the pyramid so that the whole structure rises at the same level until it is finally finished. Now only a fraction of the work force is needed. The actual pyramid itself would begin at the centre and slowly edge outwards at the exact level and towards the same exact pre-ordained corners necessary to give the correct ratio to find *pi*. Very slowly it would spread up and across until the final building was complete.

Another problem with this theory is with the Red Pyramid which is slightly further from the river. Just how could they have got enough water to make the building blocks, and to keep the work force hydrated, over such a distance? Equally we must ask that if, indeed I am wrong, how did they drag the solid blocks of limestone and the enormous ones of granite over the same distance. However they did it, they still needed enormous quantities of water to keep the workforce alive. My only thought here is that there must have been a branch of the river nearby on which the barges could float. The water needed to keep the work force hydrated by using the quarried block theory would far exceed that needed to cast the stones on site. It was done, one way or the other, and so there must have been enough water about. That is the only real flaw to the theory. How did they get enough water onto site for the building and to keep the workforce hydrated? This applies to all the pyramids, even the later ones. Using conventional theory it is worse because the provision of adequate, clean, drinking water that would have been needed to keep this enormous army of people hydrated to do the work, would be impossible.

Being entirely of limestone, the bedrock all around will contain an element of clean and pure water and so, whatever method was used, simple bore holes into the water table could have provided all the water needed, even out at Darfur. This theory allows for advanced technology that would mean that pumps of sorts must be used as would a quantity of pipe work which is a possibility, but the idea of thousands of men dragging boulders across a harsh desert is not. Then, as now, without adequate food and water the workforce would simply perish. One other thought is that had they had some form of pump, they must have sunk bore holes into the various shafts done to get air into the underground passages. Like a lack of water, lack of fresh air to breathe is fundamental to the entire process. They had to have had some method of ventilation and some method of getting water before the project could begin. On balance I think that must have been the case. Is there any evidence at all of ancient bore holes into the water table? Or into the underground workings? If so, we must ask what type of rig was used so to do?

Back to our pyramids which are slowly taking shape. Where needed, the granite is brought down the river from Aswan, having been crushed into small pieces by bigger and heavier lumps, and this is delivered onto site in just the same way. When we get to the last pyramid with its enormous central granite works we must be very careful. First the floor must be cast and it is obvious from the start that all the finished blocks will be far too heavy to be either lifted or moved when finished. Because of the steep angle they cannot be cast in situ for the simple reason that, when mixed, the mixture is liquid which will obey the simple self levelling laws of liquids. Therefore these blocks are cast level, but above, where they are destined to fit. When they are set, the shuttering is removed, then like the launching of an ocean liner, they can be slowly lowered into place. Simple gravity will assist them to slide the last few inches to join the next block. If the shuttering is correct, they will fit to perfection – which, of course, they do. And so it slowly takes place over many years. Whatever system for generating or conserving power is used, will now have been happily chugging away in the depths below the smaller pyramid, augmented by more power from the Red Pyramid ten miles away, even more from the second pyramid, before the mighty Great Pyramid comes on stream.

And, as I freely admit, the only real unknowns being what they used as material for the extremely long and immensely strong levers that must have been used throughout, and in just what form the power [electricity?] was actually generated and then used. I also concede that so far there are no obvious remains of furnaces to produce the cement nor is there any evidence of the type of fuel they must have used. A massive and continuous supply of timber would be needed, but from where would it come? There is no physical evidence of furnaces big enough to 'bake' the blocks to make then so hard as to withstand many millennia of wind and sand erosion. There is no evidence of pipe work from the river to be near any of the pyramids nor of any pumping or excavating equipment. There is no evidence of bore holes or drilling rigs and there is no sign of the necessary pumps and pipes that would be needed. Any more than there is the similar lack of evidence of dock side facilities for loading and unloading the huge blocks. Or any sign of a source of hard timber to make the sledges. Or blocks at the bottom of the river following an accident. The alternative again, for we must consider all alternatives, is that they had access to the technology to use solar power. There was a continuous supply of sunshine throughout the year which, properly harnessed, could easily be used for this purpose. We could do so now which means that they could have done so then.

There should be evidence of the enormous amount of material removed, after the completion of all the pyramids, of the huge ramps that would have had to be built if conventional wisdom is to be believed. I cannot imagine that, having finished the project, they would excavate the millions of tons of debris and scatter it far away in the desert. There is certainly no sign of it today. Look as carefully as you can but you will find no evidence at all of the debris that had to be used to build ramps up to the pyramid sides. It would have had to be excavated of which there is no evidence at all.

I also take a 'Mighty Bound' when saying that the material was brought in carts which, in turn must have had wheels, and this is a long time before the wheel was supposed to be invented. But I can see no other way to do it. No container would survive the journey dragged over rough ground unless it was made of steel but of this there is absolutely no evidence at all. And, of course, it would have needed furnaces to smelt the iron etc, etc.

This, I submit, is how they **could** have built the pyramids everywhere in the world. Some were simply stone shells filled with earth, and just the central chambers and their passageways stone lined, but all were built simultaneously by the same people for the same common purpose. Alright there are different designs but so what? You can just see the Mayan king [no, his ancient predecessor] looking at the plain ones on Giza and saying *"We can do better than that."* And then his compatriots in Java and the Canaries copying, for copies they are. More or less exact copies of style, with the stone work being copied either by, or from, the people of Nubia above the 6th cataract of the Nile.

The one thing that we do know for certain, because there are pictures of people so doing, is that they knew how to cast bricks at the time. I would say that the Nubian pyramids are all built from pre-cast bricks that were baked to make them solid. It is a very simple progression to move on to casting bigger lumps of masonry. This is the only clue in Egyptian wall art to any aspect of pyramid building.

Any other way is defeated by simple arithmetic and logic as I have shown. Again I digress. I spent the last thirty years of my working life in the exhibitions industry where the massaging of attendance figures was an art form. One staggering example was a small agricultural show high up in the Yorkshire Dales which had a couple of marquees, a small ring and a beer tent. Claimed attendance in the one day was 25,000 people. This is the same number as you see starting a big marathon. It did not take much working out that to park all the cars they would have needed a field several hundred yards wide and five miles long! The actual figures were nearer 250 locals.

I illustrate this to show beyond doubt, if I need to by now, that no matter how many mighty bounds you may take, you cannot argue with the figures. If a single stone weighs 1.6 tons and it is being used in a tight spot, where no more than about four people can work, and it is at the end of passage ways where only one can crawl at a time, then it cannot under any circumstances be carried there nor put into position without help. Also you could not commit far more of the country's entire workforce than existed to one project for several generations at a time. Someone had to produce the food, build the houses and look after infrastructure [if any] as well. No, the figures do not lie and they should be the first consideration, not the last, when offering a theory. The last thing, that should be the most obvious, is that this type of civil engineering project needs a huge amount of planning with lots of people in different disciplines. When first mooted there had to be an overriding need for it; the expertise to carry it out and the certainty that it could be achieved in a reasonable time frame. That it was feasible must have been easily recognised with all the above objections considered and overcome.

So now we think we may know 'Why?' They were most likely to have been built as in the first place navigational aids from the sky and then for others sources of a type of power. Or vice versa.

We think we know 'When?' They were all built around 5,000 – 6,000BC.

And now we think we may know 'How?' They used a method of casting all the materials, in a manner not unlike that used so much later when building the Hoover Dam. Even given the advanced quarrying equipment available plus an unlimited amount of suitable stone it was never even mooted that the dam face would be built mainly with excavated stone.

Before we move on from this point I return to my comments about the granite sarcophagi in the Egyptian Museum in Cairo. Here I mentioned the facts that the top was both round and very smooth and that on it were tiny incisions, very close together. As I commented, if using a simple hammer and chisel, as one small dart was finished, the material adjacent would be de-stabilised. As the next one was begun, the edge would chip. Granite is not as smooth as a material like basalt and there is no way to prevent this happening using a hammer and chisel. If you don't believe me, try it for yourself. It will happen for you as well. Try it on an off cut from a kitchen top company. Any attempt to use a chisel, no matter how fine, will never result in a clean cut. Another effort a fraction of an inch away will result in both joining together.

But, as always, those darts and bird carvings are there for all to see and were installed when the sarcophagus was new. How could they have done it? Today we would use a laser, water jet or sand blasting, all methods requiring lots of power. If I am correct they may just have had that power. If I am not correct they must have used something else.

And so we are still left with how they were able to cut and trim the granite so easily. Without doubt some of the pieces of stone are indisputably solid granite that has been worked by someone. I am thinking here of the 'sarcophagus' in the main pyramid. That, as we have seen was sawed on the outside using a massive saw but the inside was hollowed out fairly smoothly using huge hollow drills. They left a core that could be simply broken off. We know they had no diamonds at the time so could they have used something like diorite as the cutting edge with a slow turning drill under immense pressure cutting into the rock? The questions must be of what was the cylindrical drill bit made, what was the power source and mechanism and what was used to generate the necessary pressure?

66

Moving to the middle of the three pyramids, that of Chefren, we again look at the 'sarcophagus' and the way in. The supposed sarcophagus is cut from solid granite and an American engineer by the name of Chris Dunn checked it out carefully. Like me, he was far more interested in the 'hows', 'whys' and 'where froms' than normal mainstream Egyptology. He took with him two items of interest. One was a ground flat straight edge accurate to .002" and the other was a flashlight. Putting the straight edge alongside the walls of the sarcophagus and the light behind it he found that almost no light showed through. It was as accurately ground flat as was his straight edge. He looked further to some coffers, again of granite, in the chamber on the way in. Moving the lid of one he found the same thing. Both the bottom of the lid and the top of the coffer were ground to the same tolerance so that when put together they formed an hermetically sealed unit. One must ask why?

Like Zacharia Sitchin, the works of Christopher Dunn came my way as this revision was nearly finished. Since he is an apprentice trained engineer, as am I, I give his thoughts more than a passing glance. He spent more time than I did examining the workings of the stones and also he brought with him some accurate measuring devices. With these he identified equally flat surfaces at the temple, supposedly for bulls, in sarcophagi in the Serapeum which is at Saqqara. He was equally interested in the perfect ground corners where the vertical and horizontal planes met. The finish in those areas was as near perfect as you could get and could only have been done by a cutting tool of just 5/32 inch diameter. And this was supposedly only to bury a bull! Now the complex is closed as being dangerous but I remember it well from my first visit back in 1963. Dunn is quite certain that the interior of the huge granite boxes with perfectly ground lids could only have been done by using a sophisticated machine tool. I agree with him.

Another engineer, Donald Rahn of Rahn Granite Surface Plate Co, Dayton, Ohio, in 1983 measured the symmetrical helical grooves in that sarcophagus and found that they advanced at a rate of .100 inch/revolution. The diamond drills that his company used rotating at 900rpm penetrated granite at one inch in 5 minutes which is .0002 inches/revolution. That means that the drills cutting into that sarcophagus advanced 500 times faster than cutting edge technology in 1983AD.

Back to Petrie who examined a bowl from the Vth Dynasty made of granite. On this were incised hieroglyphics with lines just 1/150th inch wide. More lines were found incised, not scratched, that were just 1/30th inch apart. These were parallel and relatively deep and carved into one of the hardest stones on Earth.

So how today could we achieve this? With the advent of space exploration, NASA found the need to be able to extract rocks of all types using minimum pressure and power. They needed this technology for the various rovers that they intended to place on Mars and to that end invented the ultra-sonic drill. This uses the same technology as the Ultrasound devices used in medicine. It is now used as an alternative drill in dentistry. Granite is composed in the main from three substances, Mica, Feldspar and Quartz with the quartz being the harder. They found that by causing the waves in the Ultrasonic drills to vibrate at the same frequency as those in the quartz, the quartz would simply crumble away in its path. They found that a drill weighing 1.5lbs could drill holes of .5 inch diameter in granite using just 10w whereas a normal drill would need 750w. Although no one has tried to do so, it is theoretically possible to make a tool the width of a needle that could harness ultrasonic technology to reproduce the same effect on a piece of diorite, but first they would have to use a special lathe to turn out the bowl in the first place. As did those people in 2,500BC.

From this it must be obvious to all but those who will not see, that whoever did that work had 'MACHINE TOOLS' and 'ADVANCED TECHNOLOGY' that we in the 21st century AD cannot even begin to contemplate.

Look at all the other sarcophagi and sculptures made of granite. There are thousands of them in every museum in the world. Some are quite small, others very big but all have the one thing in common and that is that they have flat backs, bases and parts of the sides. As though they have been taken from slices of a rectangular granite column. The other way to end up like this is to cast them in moulds. My sarcophagi base was obviously rough cast.

The top had a rough cast inside with the smooth exterior. It would have been simplicity itself to remove the shuttering before the main mixture had finally set and cover it with a very much finer one that could be smoothed over whilst still wet. The incisions must have been carefully made before it set which is why they are so precise and have no chipped edges. Again I say that there was no other way to do this. My earlier mention of the straight saw cuts on the one in Cairo illustrate this. They may not have been cuts in the stone, they could just as easily have been cuts in a much softer shuttering material that would replicate on the finished article. Sitchin says that the Sumerian writings were all carefully etched into soft brick panels before being baked rock hard in an oven. From there it is a simple and plausible extension to using a granite based base.

Looking again at the pillar in Alexandria, its production as a single piece, I insist, was beyond even the Romans. The only way it could have been made and erected would have been by casting it in pieces, in situ, and then covering the outer surface in a thin layer of very much smoother granite screed. In places this is now chipping off in an even layer around the base revealing the rough cast core for all to see. There was no other way for this to be made for many reasons, the principal one being that then, and now, it could not have been lifted vertically onto the plinth.

But back to our pyramids which are now fully built and in use for whatever reason was first deemed necessary.

There then followed a huge gap in time before the founding of the First Dynasty in 3022BC. At least 2,000 years during which time possibly the host planet so far away had its Armageddon or similar and ceased to exist leaving the now distant descendents of the Nephilim abandoned on Earth with their technology and power sources becoming a distant memory. They had certainly lost the ability to communicate with each other and each assimilated into its own environment. Some, as in Java, the Canaries, Nubia and China did not last long since it would seem that they failed to breed with the indigenous populations. In Egypt, the Middle East and the Americas those early settlers now became 'Gods' in their own right as is shown in Egypt in particular.

69

But one thing is for certain and that is that many of the stone working skills were not passed on. Over a period of three thousand years, even in the now desert climate the tools, if of iron or steel, used would slowly oxidise away leaving subsequent generations to find their own. Anything made with an iron base is soon lost to oxidisation. As new materials like bronze and iron became available they were able to make better tools again including saws, for much of the stonework in later years is obviously sawn. Around 2,600BC Dozer built a pyramid which was a very rough copy of Giza but his supposed temple nearby was superbly cut with saws. Not necessarily at the same time nor for the purpose of which we are thinking. Another effort was made but this collapsed in one corner to become the 'Bent Pyramid' of today, after which they obviously decided to call it a day and revert to simple burial in vast underground caves, mainly at Luxor in the Valleys of the Kings and the Queens. Please compare the rough workings of the walls and ceilings of these compared to the superb stone work at Giza.

From this period onwards I have little argument with accepted history. Like so many others I am in awe of the achievements of those people. The workmanship in gold and hard stone is breathtaking, as are the massive statues and monuments, all of which it is possible to see just how they did it. The one massive anomaly has always lain on the Giza plateau and I feel that the few big mistakes made have been by taking Giza in isolation, ignoring the existence of the other pyramids and a steadfast refusal to consider a realistic reason for the existence of things like the Nazca lines. Most of all and to this day, they totally ignore the mathematical evidence of the likes of Flinders Petrie. To me that is criminal negligence. This man actually surveyed Giza minutely and came up with some very difficult figures as we have seen. I have just looked again through the magnificent work by Konemann, first published in German, called *'Egypt – land of the Pharaohs'*, profusely illustrated and of more than 500 pages, not one of which mentions this aspect of Petrie's work. Had it done so and then expanded on it as I, and many others have proceeded to do, then the whole work must be re-written. Surely this is an attempt to bury awkward evidence as conclusively as those ancients hoped they had done with their Pharaohs. The trouble is that, like the Pharaoh and his treasure, this will keep popping up until it can no longer be ignored.

Before we leave this part of the story, there is one thing that those with opposite views will throw at me every time and that is the physical evidence of a vast quarry out of which it is patently obvious they cut large stones. Yes, I see it very clearly in the Konemann book, there for all to see. So does this throw my theory out of the window right now? No, it does not, for two simple reasons. The first is that this quarry dates from around 1,300BC, possibly 4,000 or more years after the pyramids were built, and the second proves my point entirely. This is just one quarry of one rock face. Where are the other 5,999 like it that we would have needed to produce our steady supply of 300 blocks a day for nearly 65 years? So far no one has produced any evidence anywhere of quarrying of that magnitude in the vicinity of the buildings.

As you know, I don't like coincidences and certainly will never accept three in a row, dotted all over the world. We have seen that here at Giza much use has been made of granite, the sole function of which seems to be in some way related to electronics/nuclear uses, just what we do not, as yet, know. We have seen that the pyramid in Georgia, USA, has a Limonite mine nearby. Limonite is an iron oxide being an insulator in the nuclear industry. Now it appears that the huge pyramids in Mexico at Teotihuacan contain significant quantities of Mica, a difficult, fragile material with the nearest supply some 2,000 miles away in Brazil. It has no structural utility whatsoever, its only use being as an insulator in the electronics/nuclear industries. These cannot be simple coincidences. There has to be a common link.

Back to the quarry. As I explained in earlier chapters there becomes one point in time when the large stone must separate from the bedrock. Once again I rely on you, the reader –especially the male ones – to prove my point. At some time in our lives we have sawn through a plank of wood and just as we get to the final cut the wood breaks leaving a splinter at one side and a gap on the other. It is the same with stone. No matter how carefully you cut it out every time there will be a final cut where the blocks separate and invariably this will leave either an indentation in the block or one in the bedrock. In glassmaking it is called 'The Pontil Mark'. This would not be a reason to reject the block and therefore it would be reasonable to suggest that out of the seven million or so blocks used, a fair, if not significant, proportion would have that indentation visible. If the traditionalists can show this to be the case then I am wrong and they are right. I have never seen one but, so what? As always, I am open to correction.

I took this picture of a corner of the Mykerinus pyramid to show that after at the very least 5,000 years of wind and sand exposure, those limestone blocks are totally free from erosion. Look carefully and you will see no evidence on any of them of a 'pontil' mark where they separated from the bedrock. The simple law of averages says that half should do so but they do not.

I have studied the corners of all the three main pyramids, in particular at the stones. As has been described, limestone is a very soft rock made up of many layers and this is self evident if you see it as exposed outcrops on hill and mountain sides. And in buildings. York Minster has a huge permanent team restoring the eroded limestone carvings and stonework. As it becomes exposed it first hardens before corroding away. A softer layer will corrode faster than a harder one leaving an uneven finish after only a few years. Rain accelerates this, as does wind, especially when blowing sand about. I ask you to look carefully for evidence of the layers and their subsequent erosion. This is very important indeed. Those rocks have sat on exposed corners for at least five thousand years if we accept modern chronology and so should show considerable erosion. Look at the Sphinx. His body was eroded by rain. After the desert came that was covered in sand but the head was not. That eroded so as to be almost unrecognisable as the lion or whatever that it is supposed to be. There is none on the blocks because they were cast and not hewn from the rock. There are no saw marks either.

You may ask why, having devoted so much time to the pyramids, the Sphinx has been almost forgotten. Surely he is just as big a part of the mystery as everything else? Yes, he is very much so. The problem is that he comes from a different period of time during the Precessional era of Leo some 20,000 years earlier. We know this because he is facing dawn when the constellation of Leo would appear on the horizon at dawn first and that last happened 12,500 years ago. We are now in the Age of Aquarius and will be for some time. The other thing, as has been mentioned, is that he is badly weathered by several thousand years of torrential rain and it is thousands of years since the desert took over in North Africa.

The Sphinx is proof beyond doubt that we had visitations for a long time of other Nephilim who may have come, stayed a while and then gone, or simply died out for one reason or another – possibly disease. We will never know, but that someone came, carved out the enormous beast for whatever reasons they thought fit, and then simply vanished leaving Egypt and the rest of the world to continue its slow and inevitable Darwinian progress, cannot be now in doubt.

23

THE EXTRA TERRESTRIALS.

I have to admit that when I wrote the first edition that came out in 2008 I had never read or even heard of Zecharia Sitchin. I only came across his work by chance as this second edition was nearly complete. I'm glad I did because before I had felt somewhat isolated in some of my thoughts. These included the continuous references to the biblical Nephilim, the 'Book of Enoch', my ideas that Cheops may have simply used the big pyramid at Giza but that it was actually built very much earlier, and that there must be some link between all the great monoliths and ziggurats across the globe. I had thought through and written my piece on the impossibility of the human time line years before I read that he, too, had come to the same conclusion. Yes he, after far more and detailed research than I could ever have done, came to these same conclusions. And he had no doubt whatsoever of some sort of nuclear capability back in very ancient times. As always, I am looking at life many years before it is all supposed to have begun in 3,000BC

So who is, or was, he? Sitchin was a Jewish journalist based in Israel for most of his life where he studied the Sumerian clay tablets and other ancient texts, identifying in the process the possible extra planet in our solar system of 'Nibiru'. He came at the problem from a totally different angle to me. I look through the eyes of a practical engineer; he saw it all through the ancient texts. Others look at it through the eyes of the archaeologist whilst others are fixed on the views of anthropology. Mainstream archaeology sees it only through a very narrow interpretation of what has been discovered earlier and its own interpretation of anything new. It studies the remains and the texts with the main thrust being what they were used for rather than how it was actually done. Anything that is remotely out of context is dismissed and carefully airbrushed from history which is why I, and Sitchin agree that the museums of the world hold a great deal of stuff that 'should not be there'! Unfortunately, if one only sees it through one's own eyes, rather than trying to identify a much bigger picture, a great many 'mighty bounds' must be taken to prove the point. It is easy to get carried away with the religious significance of a building if you can safely ignore the fact that the people at the time only had a few small copper tools to work with and so could not have built it. In this volume I have tried to see the bigger picture by reading the works of others from every angle and every discipline possible and have used them to help my case. I know that I am not one hundred percent correct but, then, are any of the others?

That the pyramids were built cannot be denied. That there are hundreds of them all over the world cannot be denied. That they were all built over a relatively short period of time – about one millennium – as part of one massive master plan is difficult to deny. That the three Giza pyramids, plus the associated Red Pyramid, were built as one off tombs for the Pharaoh of the day cannot now be believed. The mathematical and astronomical evidence, quoted here from impeccable sources, plus the new evidence in this book, should prove to even the most sceptical of academics that previous theories are basically flawed and further research should be done along the path I illustrate here. I also must add that many other researchers, both 'amateur' and professional, have come to similar conclusions. I have merely put my own slant on things.

We have arrived at a possible date of around 5 – 6,000BC which gives time for the Nephilim to have become established in the post Ice Age, and consequently post diluvium period [that is if there actually was a universal flood, which I doubt], when the Earth was settling down to become the world we know today. A few [relatively] years earlier and they could have ended up with some mighty buildings at the bottom of the sea. As, of course, we do when considering the remains under the seas of Japan. Unless they were submerged following an earthquake, of which there is no evidence, they had to be built pre-8,000BC. Our date of 5 – 6,000BC gives around 2 - 2,500 years before the emergence of the First Egyptian Dynasty, by which time around 100 generations of a mixture of Nephilim and fair skinned Semitic and Arab blood, with the new higher intelligence and building knowledge, was able to spread over the known world of the Middle East including Mesopotamia, Arabia and Persia, and across the sea at Crete. According to existing thought the human population of the

Americas was now between 300 and 350 generations old and had spread across the continents to become the various races we know today. Not all came into contact with the Nephilim but those that did were settling, or not, in Central America and, as Incas, Aztecs or Mayans they, in turn, gradually spread down into the Andes and up into the fertile Mississippi valley, travelling up river as far as Ohio to the edge of the former ice sheet. The same was happening in other parts of the world. During this period, with the superior new intelligence, mankind as a whole was able to change from a nomadic way of life in tiny tribes of wandering 'animals' into both the agrarian and city dwelling communities that exist today. Few can argue that cities and farming began around this time. Again, simultaneously all over the world. Also there has to be some explanation for the different racial groups that could not have simply 'evolved' in such a short period of time, especially in the Americas.

Having decided earlier that some early Nephilim bred with Hebrew women and so founded the Twelve Tribes of Israel, this time scale coincides with the time frame of the Holy Bible. By accepting that the Hebrew elders may have been some of the original colonizers who must have understood and used Time Travel extensively, the prodigious ages of the likes of Noah and his family can be accepted as fact and that is a major step forward. So yes, I think that my time frame will not be far out, but probably it will be nearer the 5,000 than the 6,000 BC when it all happened.

Let us now consider what could have happened for them all, some considerable time after they first arrived, to decide simultaneously that Pyramid building was a necessity. As I said at the beginning of the book, I have got through life so far without the need for a personal pyramid, as my reader, I am sure have you. They needed navigation points all over the world and these needed to have first been able to be seen from the air, and secondly must be set out with a mathematical precision difficult to emulate today. Just why, we will never know. They must send a message so that the right people, or beings, could understand them. Giza may have been chosen because it was, in the first place hospitable, and was more or less the dead centre of all the land mass on earth. It lies on the 31st meridian north of latitude and, a coincidence I can live with, since the Greenwich meridian is purely arbitrary, it also lies on 31st meridian east of longitude. And since everything revolved round Giza it would be logical to make that world headquarters for all. At the time it was also a green and pleasant land before being engulfed by the desert. Only from above, and a long way above,

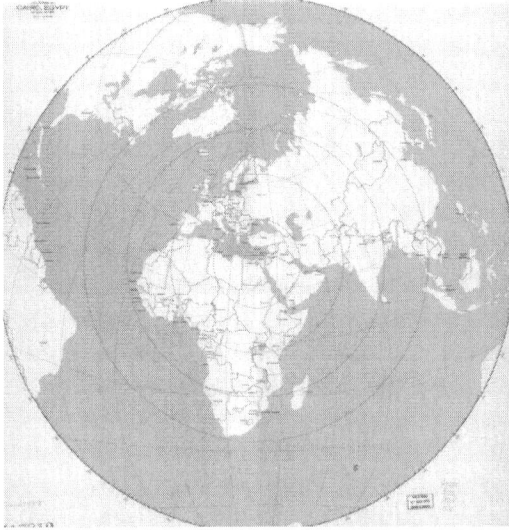

A world map drawn during WW2 centred on Cairo. Note the similarity with the Piri Re'is map, especially South America. To obtain this effect Spherical Trigonometry is essential.

could Giza be seen as the approximate centre of the land masses. The Ancient Egyptians should have had no knowledge of any of the other lands and continents. There may have been a totally different reason which I will come to later. The Piri Re'is map is a projection of the actual earth from a point about 250 miles above the dead centre of Giza. Now that cannot be a coincidence.

And so all roads must point towards Giza and, to a large extent, they do. As we have seen before, the Easter Island, Nazca, etc Great Circle line shows the shortest way around the world going by way of Egypt and the South Pacific. If you picked up the North Yorkshire tumuli you then had a straight line through Northern Italy to Giza. Wherever you went it was possible to find a suitably sited group of pyramids, or even a single one, or equivalent massive monument, all with clues going back to the single Giza site. Most of the other pyramids around the world were stone faced and earth filled or simple earth mounds, and it is not our purpose here to describe how each of them was built. If we could establish the methods of Giza then the lessons should hold good for the rest.

Obviously Giza was chosen and the first thing that any engineer or architect would do would be to survey the site and lay it out exactly as was intended. But why build anything at all? Why not do as they did at Nasca and simply mark the information on the land as Thornborough type earthworks if the sole object was to be seen from the air? There had to be a secondary reason. The north/south layout would have needed to be ascertained and this, having been done, would allow them to put the first markers into position. It would have been impossible to find the Magnetic Pole since we are many thousand years before the discovery of iron on this Earth, and magnetism as such was not identified until around the 4th century BC. Even then it was not understood as being a force running through the earth. But there was no other way to determine the exact line to the Magnetic Pole other than with a compass of some sort that responded to magnetism. So did they understand magnetism as such? I would think that they must have done but, like so much else, it was lost as time went on. Having said that, if they could survey and draw the maps so accurately, they must have had equipment for smaller layouts. As I said earlier, using just a length of rope and some measuring sticks was not a starter with areas almost a kilometre apart and covering an area of nearly a square kilometre..

You can work out that the Pole Star could be over the North Pole and the Southern Cross [out of sight in Egypt] over the South Pole but, first you have to know that there is a North Pole, and why there is one, and then you must know how to find it. Also, the certainty that the Earth is round and not flat, and that it circles the sun, rather than vice versa, must be clearly understood. With greatest respect to the experts, I feel that this scientific knowledge would be way out of the league of any ordinary Egyptian, following the natural descent according to Darwin, of the period. It would be out of his comprehension.

Cheops built his solar boat on the assumption of the contrary. Only someone with an accurate compass, who knew what he was doing, could do this. Also it must be observed that this was fairly common knowledge, for other pyramids, like the 'The Great White Pyramid' on the Tibetan border with China, are also set up in the exact same way. This cannot under any circumstances be considered to be a unique coincidence. This simple fact holds good, even if you stick to the flawed theory that the three Giza Pyramids were built around 2,900 – 2,600BC. There is no evidence in any paintings or carvings anywhere of people using a compass to navigate.

All of which takes us back once again to our first rhetorical question which was, can we believe both Darwin and the Bible?

We must go back to when the Bible was first written down and this was many years after the first people mentioned in it were about. I think that I have provided by now a good idea of from where those people, both before, and then after, Abraham, came. I think, and I would be surprised if anyone could prove me wrong, that beyond any doubt they were all early generations of the Nephilim. Whilst they obviously had incredible technological knowledge, there is nothing to say that, like their hosts, they would not be very superstitious. Or that they would have been, for want of a better word, 'good' people. They were certainly promiscuous if the Bible is to be believed. The first thing to enter their heads it would seem was to 'have it off' with the local women! If, as I suggest, that they had been on a Time Travelling exercise, leaving behind garbage in previous encounters, they may have been aware of the Ice Ages, the continents moving and the millions of years that the dinosaurs roamed the earth. They may have become aware of the seas beyond the Mediterranean and Red Seas and would know of the existence of whales [and that they are not fish], something that the inhabitants of Palestine, Egypt or Arabia could never have known. The chances are that this could just be history's first 'Mighty Bound'.

Some explanation had to be given for the 'Creation' so why not the six day theory? The mixing of the bloods with the Nephilim will have left those with still pure blood in awe of the blond giants who were the children of their women folk. Some will have seen the expedition leader and that these children were in his image. Over the years he became the God figures of the Mayans, the Aztecs, the Incas and the Egyptians, and the patriarch of the Jewish race. And of course the Biblical founder of the human race - Adam himself.

Going on through Genesis we find another 'Mighty Bound' when God creates woman out of Adam's Rib after which she eats from the Tree of Knowledge, discovers in the process good and evil, and is cast out of the Garden of Eden forever. Then there are some interesting pieces which go back to my earlier puzzles. Genesis 2:11 and 12. *'The name of the first is Psion: that is it which compasseth the whole land of Havilah where there is gold.'* 12: *'And the gold of that land is good: there is bdellium and the onyx stone.'*

Now just why, before He had even created Eve, before they were aware of the Tree of Knowledge, should they be thinking of gold of all things? And the way it is worded, to me it sounds extremely avaricious. Both gold and onyx were then, as they are now, purely ornamental and of limited practical use, especially in those times. Go along a bit further to 4:22 *'And Zillah, she also bare Tubalcain, an instructor of every artificer in brass and iron.'* Brass and iron????? We are supposed to be talking about several thousand years before these were discovered. Chapter 5 goes on to show the prodigious ages of the descendents of Adam which, as I have already pointed out, can only be explained by a long period during which Time Travel was possible. These people were fathering children when well over a hundred years old and that is only possible with Time Travel. What is interesting here is that only the men seemed to have lived these extreme ages. Only some of the wives and daughters are mentioned which makes me wonder whether all the Nephilim were male and that there was something in the make up of men only that allowed them to indulge in the Time Travelling. Or that the whole idea was to provide a whole new breed of humans, something that realistically only the men mating with local women could do. Would a small local man have necessarily been attracted to a huge female invader? Not sexist, just realistic.

I think that we must pause and consider those prodigious ages for a moment. I have given a possible explanation but there is another one which seems to be the favourite at the time of writing. We are looking here at the time that was well before the Gregorian calendar of the 365 day year. In those days years were measured arbitrarily, sometimes as Lunar years which came around every month and others based on a whole variety of astronomical observations. Considering the age of Noah at around 950 years, based on Lunar years it would have him at 80 modern years. Fair enough, that sounds about right, but the theory wavers and then sinks when we apply it to others. Genesis 11.11 *'And Shem lived after he begat Arphaxad five hundred years.'* That puts him at 48 modern years old. 11.12 *'And Arphaxad lived five and thirty years and begat Salah.'* This puts him at three years old. 11.13 *'And Arphaxad lived after he begat Salah four hundred and three years, and begat sons and daughters.'* And so he was 36 when he died.

Genesis 5 gives the generations of Adam and this shows Adam himself at 930 years [77.5 modern years], Enoch 365 [30] and Methusalah 969 [81], all of which agree with the theory. But what about Nahor 148 [12.33] who begat 'sons and daughters'? His son, Terah, begat three sons in his 70 [5.8] year life. And this is the problem because there is no 'catch all' answer to the paradox. Not all of the patriarchs lived to these prodigious ages and so the 'Lunar Year' theory must be suspect. Carrying it a stage further, if everything in the Old Testament is ruled by the Lunar Year theory, all time scales come tumbling down by a factor of twelve putting Adam and Eve at around 300BC and the Exodus at around 120BC. And this leaves an awful lot of Biblical history to be compacted into a very short period of time.

Genesis 17 contradicts the theory when the Lord God is talking to Abraham and then in verse 17, *'Shall a child be born unto him that is one hundred years old and shall Sarah, that is ninety years old, bear?'* Genesis 18.11 *'Now Abraham and Sarah were old and well stricken with age...'* But they did have Isaac and Ishmail so just how old could they have been? No 'normal' human being, no matter when in history, could bear children when they are *'ninety years old and well stricken by age'.* Only someone very different could possibly do that. Those writing Genesis were asking this same question even then and were commenting on the obvious age of Sarah. Only if she was from an alien stock could she, at ninety years old, have born children.

These old ages then carried on with Noah through the flood until the arrival of Abraham some time after 3022BC, since he appears in Egypt where the Pharaoh takes a shine to his fair wife, Sarah. On leaving Egypt in Chapter 13:2 we learn '*And Abraham was very rich in cattle, in silver and in gold.*' [The reverse italics are taken from the Bible.] He then goes on to father the child by Sarah when she is in her nineties, she eventually dying at 127 years old. After her, Abraham remarried and fathered more children before finally expiring at 175 years old. In Lunar years these mean that Sarah was 10.58 modern years old and Abraham 14.58. None of which makes any sense at all. After Abraham the ages gradually returned to normal spans which were eventually somewhat less than today. And that reflects the fact that mortal women with whom they mated were just like us. Only the alien men could produce children at great ages, their progeny when mating with the local women could not.

This latest fact is interesting because it raises yet another question of 'Why?'. After all this time of returning to their kinsmen in the host planet, should they now slow it down, and then cease altogether? My thoughts are that the other planet had either ceased to exist or that it may now be uninhabitable after its own example of Armageddon. The alternative is most likely, and that is that those left on Earth ran out of the ability to make the journey due to lack of fuel, or lack of whatever material the vessels were made of, thus leaving all future generations to be marooned here for all time. If there had indeed been problems at home, future Nephilim may also have lost the ability to make the journey. Gradually the technology would be lost and Darwin remains to continue his remorseless process, except now he has had one enormous leg up. And left a large blip on our Bulge graph. Over any period of time, mere mortals no matter how big the latent intelligence, soon lose technology. Equally they were slow to acquire it as well as was shown in northern Europe which took so long to emerge from its Stone Age past. But this spurt in intelligence effectively stopped evolution as such in its tracks. Only those peoples who had no contact at all could continue along that path.

The alternative to the Nephilim being extra terrestrial must be considered. Please excuse this brief excursion into a Science Fiction scenario. Just supposing that they were actually people from our own future who had mastered Time Travel? They also would be big and possibly blond as well. Suppose that 200 of the men decided, possibly after our almost inevitable man made Armageddon, to return to the past to change the course of history. As before they land on Mt Herman and begin the sequel of events already described. Is this at all possible? Maybe, but then surely they would have the benefit of the satellite navigation and tracking systems enjoyed today. They would have intimate knowledge of exactly where all stocks of Uranium and other radioactive materials are. If they were going to need a nuclear capacity surely they would have looked to the west first? This is where their settlements would have been, not in the rain forests of Egypt at the time. They would have no need to straddle the earth with pyramids and the complicated lead in lines. They would not have needed the Nasca Lines or the other major land marks since they would have the maps, some evidence of which [other, and better, than Pirie Reiss] should remain today. But it doesn't. To get the radiation needed they had to use the incredible quantities of granite that we have identified. Also out of 200 men it is hardly conceivable that every single one would be of pure white Aryan stock. Amongst them would be a fair proportion of coloured and other ethnic peoples to make up a balance.

I feel that, on balance, they must have come from elsewhere, probably escaping their own Armageddon on a planet unknown to us out there in space..

But what bothers me most about the Bible is that the chronology is actually very good indeed. Some may say too good. It was obviously written many years after the episodes illustrated but, if we now fit all the evidence unearthed so far in this book, it all slips very conveniently into place. Let me make this quite clear. I began with the chronology that resulted in the first 'Bulge' and this was based on what I knew at the time. Only the chronology published in such works as the Times Atlas of World History and Konemann's Egypt. This is information available to anyone as the accepted history of the Ancient World. Subsequent research means that a new version of the 'Bulge' must be drawn and it is this new information that I offer to the chronology of the period. The chronology fits the book, the book has not been written with this in mind, with facts and opinions adjusted accordingly. But now we have a variety of 'Bulges' for those far distant days.

Rather than Jericho standing out like a sore thumb 5,500 years before anything else, we now have Tiahuanacu in Bolivia to put in at a suggested date of about 15,000BC and Mohenjo Daro in Pakistan at anything between around 12,000 and 2,000BC. I put the Sphinx much earlier. Significantly this is around the time that primitive Homo sapiens were supposed to be entering the Americas. Findings in Brazil have discovered evidence of humans living at least 20,000BC and archaeologists there now think that man was present at around 100,000BC which means that they are now confirming my thoughts. As I say in the previous chapter, I have little argument with the chronology of Dynastic Egypt from which it is possible to follow events logically through time until the present day. That means that accurately measured time effectively began in 3022BC. And we can equate the happenings of the Bible perfectly, with the common dates universally accepted for the Exodus as being not before 1447BC and not after 1250BC, which is a very narrow window in this vast period of time. I would use the earlier date and, from this we can go back through the generations as described in the Bible, to give us a date around 3,730BC for Adam and Eve and then 1,870BC for Abraham. Abraham being the father of Isaac and grandfather of Jacob whose 12 sons were to found the Twelve Tribes of Israel. All that fits perfectly.

By this time the memory of the first of the Nephilim will have receded into the far and distant past, elevating them as the Divine ancestors of the Egyptians, hence the variety of different Gods whom they worshipped for so long. But, because of the anomaly of the prodigious ages of the current Jewish leaders, the remnants of the Nephilim must have still had thoughts about making their last journeys home. The time scale for it all being the same as from now, whenever you read this, back to before the first dynasty of Egypt. And, presumably, but not necessarily, all by word of mouth. The Hebrew, however, just stuck to the one God who, after the Exodus, had now delivered them out of bondage into the Promised Land of Canaan as has been reported many times elsewhere. The Egyptian worshipped his own version of the first settlers but under the names of Osiris, Ra, Thoth et al.

This still gives us gold being much sought after, and then iron and brass nearly 2,000 years before they were discovered in the Nile Delta. This must remain a mystery unless it was all written well after copper, brass, bronze and iron were common products, which the narrator would probably be unaware had not been around forever.

And so over the years the blood line of the Nephilim would gradually weaken as they spread throughout the world, leaving their only legacy today which is the Roman nose.

From all this it has become obvious that under no circumstances can the Nephilim be considered in any way, shape or form to have any claim to divinity. They were just as mortal as any of the elders of the Hebrews, those in Central America or China. Or even the Ancient Britons who were eking out an existence after the ice had gone. I think that they were given a divine status all over the world where they set up their colonies and built their pyramids or other vast temples. If your fair skinned and blond visitor had appeared to you in deepest Mexico and then guided you and your kin into building a huge 'temple', surely you would feel obliged to dedicate it to him and all his equally big sons and grandsons whom your women folk have borne. Yes, he would be divine alright, but only to them.

By now we have more or less achieved our objects for the book. Yes, there is absolutely nothing that has turned up to in any way totally refute Darwin. Except, that is, the final evolution of mankind and the question marks over the jumping between species. There has always been enough of the world's population who could never have been in any way in contact with the Nephilim and who have remained, as it were, the 'control' for this massive experiment. They remained, until well into the second millennium after Christ, on the same slow progress through eternity as they had for the hundreds of thousands of years since the emergence of Homo sapiens. Most were little further advanced than the Stone Age when the European colonists came to 'civilize' them, but those who bred with the Nephilim have gone on to produce modern civilization as we know it today. Alan Moorhead in his brilliant account of the area, *'The White Nile'*, tells of how Speke in 1862, having discovered Lake Victoria, travelled through Burundi and Buganda where he found the inhabitants still very much in the Stone Age. They had no perception of the wheel, lived in the most primitive conditions and were both indolent and incredibly cruel to each other. Slavery was rife with Africans capturing each other to sell on to the Arabs, whilst morality was non-existent.

And the Bible has shown an amazing consistency with regard to its chronology leaving little doubt that most will probably be true. But this is just the secular side of the book. We still do not know about those prophets who preached Armageddon and how they could possibly have known. We still have not touched on the appearance of Christ and the visions of Mohammed; why they were chosen and why they appeared just when they did, again during a relatively short period of time and in the same tiny area on earth.

I had got to the proof copy stage of this work when I watched with interest a programme on the British television network of BBC4. It was entitled 'The Extra Terrestrials' and fronted by the Astronomer Royal. Those interviewed for opinions included some of the foremost and highly respected astronomers in the world. I sat up and took notice. What did they know that I, a simple bumbling 'amateur', did not?

I was astonished with what I heard. I could not believe what I was hearing and seeing. One had come up with a formula for the number of life bearing planets in the universe. It contained six variables that must be multiplied together, but the variables were arbitrary, the last being anything from 100 to 1,000,000!!!!

Mighty bounds were taken as professors told of massive oceans that simply came and went on Mars, the explanation being that Mars does not have a core the same as the Earth yet it had been formed around the same time and in the same way. But it was in the form that the Extra Terrestrials would take that really amazed me.

They said that their intelligence would be so much higher than ours, the analogy being the same as trying to teach a monkey quantum physics. The final conclusion was that they would overcome the huge distances by coming, not as beings, but as robots that would be so powerful and so intelligent that they would destroy us all! That is a new view of Armageddon for me. One thing they failed to consider was that robots do not need food but they do need a lot of power. Where could they charge up their batteries? Could it be that they needed the pyramids to produce the necessary electricity? Now there is a thought to carry forward.

But the interesting thing for me was the presenter. If I am correct, and judging from this programme I may be far ahead of them all, the man himself may just be a descendent of an extra terrestrial himself! He had the distinctive nose. Yes, the same nose as the kings of Egypt and the 'Giants' of Genesis.

How ironic! I must say it made me feel much better and far more confident with my own views.

24

BACK TO THE QUESTION OF 'WHY'.

So is that it? Have we proved that we are all now descended from someone from outer space? Or still just from the apes? No, we have not but we are going to get to something very near. Please bear in mind that all I'm trying to prove is that the timeline of man may not be as is normally thought. It is not to explore in detail all there is to know about the various archaeological sites across the globe. I merely visit Mexico and South America as I do the UK. If what I have to say holds good there then it should everywhere.

I have little problem with Darwin up to, say, 200,000BP. It may be earlier or later but not later than 25,000BC. I have no problem with the timeline of Ancient Egypt even though the accepted, and never challenged, official one was thought up by the Greek historian Herodotus taken, apparently, from earlier scripts now lost from the Alexandria library. From there I have no problem with the Greek, Roman and European timeline up to the present day. Similarly I have no problem with the timeline of the Americas from 1492. But I do have with all pre-Columbian America. And I have a problem with pre-dynastic Egypt and Mesopotamia. I also feel that the Ancient Brits were not quite the backward Stone Age people as usually represented.

We are now back to the questions of 'why'??? Only if we can get some definitive answers to those questions can we look realistically to the 'how', after which we must ask about the 'when'? The two 'whys' that scream out at me still are the needs for both granite and gold. Taking granite first, it is a scientific fact that granite contains Radon which is a mild radioactive emission.

But limestone also has some interesting electrical properties as well. It is also a scientific fact that water flowing through or around limestone will provide an electrical charge. Another scientific fact is that limestone, or granite, if subject to heat and then cold will trigger an electric charge. If granite and/or limestone are compacted tightly together they also will trigger an electric charge. There are measurable quantities of electricity at Silbury Hill and with the 'Rollright Stones' nearby that are a circle of granite stones. The monoliths of Easter Island have also shown a propensity for an electric charge.

From this, if we were to want not just a little amount of electric but a large one, we would erect a very solid and very large lump of limestone. We would erect it near some water. We would also build it somewhere where it got very hot during the day and very cold at night. Just leaving it in the ground will not do. It must be huge and exposed to both heat and cold on a very regular period. The tropics are obviously unsuitable because it doesn't go cold at night; Europe is not suitable because it is not at a low enough latitude for the warmth all the year round. Also it rains a lot and even in summer there may not be all that much sunshine. But there is more than one place on this earth that effectively tick all the boxes and they are Mexico and Giza. Especially Giza.

Let us look again at Giza but from this angle. If a large **solid**, with the emphasis being on solid rather than hollow, pyramid is built with tightly fitting limestone blocks that is then sealed with either smooth alabaster [limestone] sides, as was the second pyramid of Chefren or, as in the smaller one of Mykerinus, with smooth blocks of granite, it may do the trick. There would be an edifice that during the hot day would heat up and then in the cold desert night it cooled, and there would for all time be a changing temperature that in turn was producing a charge of electricity. Underneath would be tunnels where any equipment would be installed to tap into this and the access to that area, if lined with granite, would generate a radioactive element as well. Put three of these in close proximity, may they interact to produce some very usable means of power? The tunnels would all extend through the solid mass to appear some way up one side, which of course they do.

And that is exactly what we have got on the Giza plateau. We have four such edifices that are totally useless as tombs but state of the art instruments for an electric/nuclear capability.

Alongside is a river that never dries up. It flows all the year round with much of the flow being through underground natural limestone passages. By doing this it creates a permanent charge of electricity that changes its magnetic field. That fact alone may explain why, with the enormous amount of limestone available on the spot, which would have been no harder to extract than anywhere else, it was felt necessary to leave it untouched. Instead they subjected themselves to the incredible logistic challenges of quarrying so far away. It can only be because they did not want to disturb the natural underground channels. It can hardly have been for aesthetic reasons of landscaping. It also goes to a certain extent to explain where all the clean, drinkable water came from.

The granite facing blocks on the Mykerinus pyramid. Note how tightly packed together they are and that they were finished smooth on site. A smooth finish would absorb more heat than an uneven one.

So does that help? Yes, it most certainly does. It answers the question of 'Why granite?' It answers the baffling question of why dig those thin granite lined passages underneath an otherwise totally solid lump of rock; it answers why they dug the blocks so far away as well. It does not answer the question of 'Why was the layout so mathematically perfect in all aspects. In particular, in relation to the 'Orion paradox' and the problem of arriving at the exact angles of the sides so as to leave a mathematically accurate end result.

Now we must consider my pet hate of the coincidence. We have seen already that not only does the Giza complex mirror Orion, but so do the three Milan pyramids and the massive henges at Thornborough in the North of England. We have also seen that Thornborough was covered in gypsum that made it glow white from the sky. What else is coincidental? For this we must cross the Atlantic to Mexico and just the one complex of the Pyramid of the Sun at Teotihuacan which is very near to present day Mexico City. That too is a four sided pyramid but not as big as those at Giza. It has an angle for the outside walls of 43 degrees. Now 43 degrees, like 52, is an odd number. If you take a circle and bisect it you get two segments at 180 degrees to each other; bisect it again and you get four at 90 degrees; bisect those and you get eight at 45 degrees and doing it again you end up with sixteen at 22.5 degrees. All relatively easy angles of ascent for any surveyor, at any time, who had the concept of a circle. But the numbers of 52 degrees, 43 degrees and the passage descent angles of all the tunnels of 26 degrees make no sense at all. Yes, the 52 degrees was necessary to arrive at the function constant of *pi* but that in itself would have been very difficult to measure with any accuracy. That it was done on all three pyramids is baffling and so, as always, there must have been an absolute necessity to do so. The 26 degrees is half the 52 but still would take some working out, even today, without access to even the basic schoolroom instruments. Digging tunnels at that exact angle would take a very competent surveyor and sophisticated instruments, especially when deciding on the exact place to begin digging. What about 43 degrees? That is the angle of the Red Pyramid at Darfur. Why should that be different and be so isolated as such? But it is not, because the Pyramid of the Sun also has a side of exactly 43 degrees. As a diversion, the latitude of Silbury Hill in England is 52 degrees and its angle is 31 – the latitude of Giza!!!

What else has the Mexico complex got that is interesting? Well the first thing to note is that it was built of bricks. The second is that the size of its base is to within a few feet of the large one at Giza. Then there is the labyrinth of excavated, incredibly long and narrow subterranean passages, that resemble huge drainage channels to guide water from the nearby San Juan river, through the complex and back out again. The exterior is in the shape of a ziggurat in that it is stepped but then enclosed in very accurately cut stone. Inside the pyramid proper are to be found large basalt carvings and a floor covered in two inches thick sheets of mica. That is the most amazing thing of all because mica is a very brittle mineral, of no structural integrity at all, and only of use in the electrical industry. There is no mica either in or anywhere near Mexico, the nearest supply being in Brazil which is thousands of miles away. Obviously there had to be an absolute necessity for its use and the knowledge of how to locate it from virgin land. Like diorite in Egypt, mica in Brazil is not the sort of thing that one just stumbles across and then decides that it would be a good idea to dig it up and transport it huge distances.

What else is coincidental and/or of mathematic significance? Let us go back to Thornborough in North Yorkshire. We have seen that it is the same as Giza in that it mirrors Orion; its circumference at 722 metres is exactly double that of the diameter of Stonehenge at 366 metres; the circles are respectively 360 and 366 metres apart; it lies on the latitude of 54 degrees north which is exactly 1/10 of the circumference of the earth at the equator. Like the edifices in America and Egypt it required a large, strong and primitive workforce to build it. It contains around 235,000 tons of earth that had to be excavated and carried in small buckets onto site. As did Silbury Hill but Stonehenge did not to that extent.

That I think may go towards answering the question of 'Why granite'? Yes, someone did need it in buildings of various sizes that were built according to the labour force available. A circle of timber posts at Stonehenge would not do; one of sandstone proved ineffective and so they had to go across the land to West Wales to find an adequate supply of granite. In stone circles across Britain and Europe there are odd pieces of granite that must have been put there for a reason. I still feel that it is because ancient man was able to utilise a part of the brain that has long become dormant in modern Homo sapiens. There was in ancient times, if we are to believe this hypothesis, a need to find directions across huge spaces and there was also a desperate need to generate power. The power need was not necessarily there across the globe hence the erection of the bigger monuments in just Egypt and Mexico.

'But,' I hear you say, 'you have been going on about hundreds of other pyramids across the globe. Were they all for generating electricity?' I do not know. Much more work must be done and it will take years, if ever, for them to be excavated. My feeling is that some of the remote ones such as Milan and the Pacific were, but most of the smaller ones in Mesopotamia, Nubia and Egypt were probably erected at a much later date for religious or burial purposes. In Sumeria, which is Mesopotamia, in 1910 an American named Samuel N Kramer from the University of Pennsylvania discovered the remains of seven ziggurats that were all built of mud bricks. The special thing about this being that the bricks were baked in a kiln rather than being simply left out to dry. Apparently they were then as hard as stones which is interesting because I also think that the big pyramids in Egypt, which is not that far away, were also built of a form of brick but we'll come back to that later. What he discovered confirmed exactly what was written in Genesis Chapter 11, verses 3 - 9.

'And they said one to another, go to, let us make brick and burn them thoroughly. And they had brick of stone and slime they had as mortar.

And they said one to another, let us build a city and a tower whose top may reach heaven, and let us make us a name, lest we be scattered abroad across the face of the earth. And the Lord came down to see the city and the tower which the children of men builded...........

Therefore is the name of it called 'Babel' because the Lord did there confound the language of all on earth, and from thence did the Lord scatter them upon the face of all the earth.'

Kramer, in his book published in 1956 'History begins at Sumer', identifies that the Sumerians had or had invented the knowledge of the following :

The wheel; the wagon; the kiln; metallurgy; medicine; textiles; music; maths; geometry; the ability to measure distance, weight and capacity; astronomy; the zodiac, irrigation systems; transport systems and the circle with the ability to divide it into 360 degree segments. They also had the lunar year of 12 months plus the knowledge of the need for a leap year. All was written on clay tablets that are carbon dated as being pre-3000BC. This is amazing because the Egyptian 'God' Thoth also had discovered most of these which were also brought to Earth, according to Enoch by a whole host of the beings that the Bible calls the *'Nephilim'*. Could they all have in fact been one and the same people?

So here we have proven written evidence before 3,000BC on clay tablets details of happenings that must have occurred much earlier, but how much is hard to say.

Sitchin, in *'There Were Giants Upon the Earth'*, identifies a people called the *Anunnanki* as being these first Nephilim. In the Ashmolean Museum in Oxford, England, are two Sumerian tablets catalogued WB-62 and WB-444 which show that the timeline of man on earth, civilized man at that, going back all of 456,000 years. He believes that they did not remain on earth but kept returning before finally settling for good around 13,000BC. To some extent that agrees with my own, independently thought out hypothesis. But 456,000 years in the Stone Age????

So is that it? Can we now say for certain that the pyramids of Giza and of Mexico were built not as tombs but for the generation of electricity? I would say the answer must be yes. Was the granite needed for its radon content? I think yes but Chris Dunn thinks not. He feels that it was necessary for its Quartz content. It is his opinion, and he may be correct, that the entire Giza complex was designed to vibrate in harmony with the Earth itself so creating microwaves that in turn could be used to create hydrogen that in turn generated power. Getting the power from the source to the machines is the tricky bit and for that question I have no answer. Dunn thinks that, bearing in mind that we are dealing with a very advanced civilization here, they may have had satellites and that the narrow shafts which I suggest are for ventilation, may have been aligned to those satellites and the waves were directed through them. Far fetched? Yes most certainly but far from being impossible.

Both our theories fail to address the problem of what the granite boxes in the Serapeum, that are so meticulously machined on the inside, were used for. They are wedged in tight passageways and are enormous. The one with the precision corners and ground flat inside and lid measures 13 ft long x 7.5 ft wide and 11 ft high. The basic block weighed in at around 90 tons and, according to quarrymen that Dunn consulted in America, would be extremely difficult to extract in one piece using today's equipment. To go to all that trouble there had to be a very important need for it. I presume it was for storage, as in some type of nuclear device [the Arc of the Covenant I have already suggested in a similar but mobile use].That would not necessarily be there for the scenario of Chris Dunn. But it would for mine. There most certainly would be a need for sealed storage capacity in very solid containers if there was a nuclear element involved. His use for the shafts and the possible use of satellites would apply equally to my ideas.

Another aspect that Dunn identifies that I had skipped over is that the supposed 'King's Chamber' in the Great Pyramid at sometime suffered a cataclysmic explosion. The walls are all pushed out by about an inch but the outer casing was unaffected. Egyptologists put this down to an earthquake. Afterwards it was felt necessary to seal the gaps left behind as best they could so that production could continue. In the Dunn scenario it was a build up of hydrogen that caused this; in mine it was a nuclear bomb! What I was not aware of is that the central 'sarcophagus' is apparently made of a chocolate coloured granite, the nearest supply of which is in North America! Just why would they go to the trouble of sourcing and then transporting over several thousands of miles of ocean just one piece of granite? Dunn offers an explanation with which I can live. It is his assertion that the block started out as the same red granite from Aswan but during the heat of the explosion it simply changed colour. A broken corner does suggest that it had at some time melted under excess heat.

So what else does Dunn say in his works, *'The Giza Power Plant'* and *'Lost Technologies of Ancient Egypt'* that is pertinent to this work? Plenty, that I can assure you, and I suggest these as essential reading for anyone who still harbours doubt. He looks at things objectively, and like me, begins it all from first principals with no pre-conceived agenda. He is incredibly detailed in his work and his conclusions are compelling. I quote some passages that made me smile. I have long thought that a series of documentary films on this subject would be a winner, but apparently it has been done. A long time ago though, in 1978, by the Nippon Corporation of Japan. They got approval to erect a pyramid on the Giza plateau using one ton blocks of limestone but everything else must be done to the ancient, accepted methods. The blocks were cut out ready for them but -'*Once cut into approximately one ton blocks, the stones could not be barged across the Nile. Floatation apparently was not the simple answer as had been suggested. The blocks had finally to be ferried by steamboat.*

The teams of one hundred workers each tried to move the stones over the sand and they could not move them even an inch!'

I had worked that out for myself. In the end they couldn't raise them off the floor and had to fall back on large cranes and helicopters to finish the job. Another experiment contradicted this. A group of Egyptologists said that they were able to easily move a one ton block of limestone over wet mud as though it was weightless. This proves my point exactly. No doubt the underside of the block was smooth with no protrusions as would be the case straight from the quarry. An ample supply of very wet mud would provide the ideal surface, especially along the flat but, as I said with regard to pushing your large SUV vehicle, once in motion it is no problem, it is the moment the suspicion of a gradient is encountered that it all changes.

Following his report on the Japanese experiment Dunn comments; '*It now remains for those who are absolutely convinced that the ancient Egyptians constructed the pyramids using primitive techniques to build a pyramid themselves, using the same techniques that they propose the Egyptians used. As part of such an attempt it would help if they cut just one seventy ton block of granite from the Aswan quarry which is some five hundred miles away, using their hardened copper chisels or dolerite balls and then transported the block to the Giza Plateau with their barges, ropes and manpower. If the proponents of traditional theories of constructing the pyramids are able to accomplish this feat, then we should give serious consideration to their proposals about pyramid construction.'*

Exactly! That is just what I have been saying. I could have written that myself.

Returning to the theme of whether the Dunn theory of microwaves being used to create hydrogen is correct, or my ideas about a nuclear method, plus a heating and cooling process involving underground water currents to generate power, let us look briefly at further details, especially those discovered by Flinders Petrie. He measured the long 350ft descending shaft that goes half through the masonry and half through the bedrock. This descends at that 26 degree angle and is straight to within just one quarter of an inch. Those are tolerances that would not be considered on any modern day building project and would be impossible to attain using ancient quarrying methods. It has always been my thought that the only need for this would be to allow a gas of some sort to pass over it with absolute zero interruption. [I used this technology in the '60s when developing ram pipes to increase the performance of cars – it worked!] And again using Petrie's research, let us look at the casing stones on the Great Pyramid that had to be fashioned one at a time to allow for inconsistency in the general construction. These most certainly were not cast on site but hewn from the bedrock in a distant quarry. When placed together the gaps between them were on average .20 inch wide. Almost a ground finish. This is the thickness of three or four sheets of paper.

How big were these blocks? They were all around five feet high, twelve feet long and eight feet deep, weighing in at between 16 and 20 tons each. And there were 100,000 of them. Few quarries today would even attempt the task. Again we must ask 'Why?'. Would there be a need for such an accuracy to seal the building if it was just for a tomb? Obviously the answer must be 'No'. For a device that merely resonated with Earth currents? Again, doubtful. To seal a nuclear device? Yes, most certainly.

All the time we must settle the 'Why' question before anything else can be considered. I return to the immense size of the project. Using present day cutting edge quarrying technique, how long would it take to extract all that stone? I could only guess until I came upon the answer in Chris Dunn's book. *He quotes that in the research for his book, '5/5/2000 Ice: The Ultimate Disaster', author Richard Noone asked Merle Booker, technical director of the Indiana Limestone Institute of America, to prepare a time study of what it would take to quarry, fabricate and ship enough limestone to duplicate the Great Pyramid. Using the most modern quarrying equipment available for cutting, lifting and transporting the stone Booker estimated that the present day Indiana limestone industry would need to triple its production which would involve all thirty three quarries in the State, and that it would take TWENTY SEVEN YEARS to produce the stone. And that was just for the Great Pyramid. Add in the other three and you see the scale of the task.*

As always we realise the size of the project which must have been absolutely essential for those living at the time.

Throughout his works Dunn never questions just where this sudden, if indeed it was sudden, burst of technology came from. All the time he merely refers to them as pre-dynastic Egyptians. So could any group suddenly attain such technology so quickly? Yes, they could. We did. The Iron Bridge was erected in 1781 which is approximately 10 to 12 generations ago. So in that time we went from being an agrarian society into one that could send a probe to both Mars and Jupiter in far less time than the 4th and 5th Dynasties of Egypt. But I still do not think that they did. I still feel that there was just too much technology spread across the entire globe for them all to do so, especially when the indigenous peoples have since proved quite incapable of anything similar.

For the Dunn theory to prevail, the uses of the second and third Giza pyramids, and the fourth one at Darfur, must be identified. All of these have workings underground only and the Earth current theory, plus the method of distributing the power depend on the pyramid, rather than the underground, being the most important. Obviously these three were built with an underground need only. So does that help my case?

I believe it does. Obviously I have no means of proving any of this scientifically and so it must be conjecture. A theory like all the others. I feel that the other three pyramids had only the underground workings to such accuracy so that some process could be undertaken to prepare the raw material that would eventually end up under or in the Great Pyramid. The need for such close tolerances remains a mystery but the equal need for such massive quantities of granite must indicate its use for its content and content only. That content can only be either quartz or radon. Nothing else, it was not structural at all. The containers in the Serapeum would have little use for the Earth current theory but huge necessity for sealed nuclear storage. I don't know for certain but that is my best guess – or theory if you like.

It remains my conviction that it all came from peoples like us from somewhere far away at some time between 12 and 6,000BC. A cataclysm which could be anything from a nuclear war to a famine, a disease or the shifting of the poles wiped them out leaving only the strongest of their buildings to remain. And just a few of the strongest of the leaders to leave their mark on society for the future.

25

THE NEPHILIM AND NIBIRU

Let us look at this possibility a little closer.

Sitchin says that on those tablets in the Ashmolean is written evidence of a human timeline back 456,000 years. As I remark independently to this and well before I read his works, I think that buried in the cellars of museums across the globe is the evidence to prove most of these ideas but, since it blows all existing academic theory out of the water, it is better to keep it hidden and airbrushed from history. He also goes on to say that the Anunnanki had a different life cycle to us. A year to us and a year to them were not the same. I make this point earlier when I look at the ages of the Hebrew elders such as Abraham, Sarah and Noah. In earthly terms they could not have survived to those ages, not now, not then if they were normal Homo sapiens. They certainly could not breed when well over 100 years old! There is no anthropological evidence of anyone previously living for these prodigious periods. Therefore the Holy Bible, on which the three great religions on earth are based, must have a fundamental flaw here and, as I say earlier, if it is wrong here, and with the first few verses, then just when is it correct? You cannot just 'cherry pick' the bits you like and take your 'mighty bound' over the rest. A 'mighty bound' is different to the 'airbrush' because it is something that is there for all to see, but is inconvenient, and so must be left to one side but the 'airbrush' is where you pretend that it isn't there at all. The 'airbrush' is the most used instrument of research for many historians.

Sitchin rarely uses either of these. He goes the other way and digs in the tiniest detail when seeking his evidence, much of which I have to confess, is remarkable to say the least. Where I differ is that he is of no doubt whatsoever about his findings. He is adamant that he is correct whilst I say, *'Wait a minute, let's look from another angle'*. So what is that angle after all?

As I say, it is his contention that they all have a different life cycle to us and if that is true then it answers completely that anomaly in, and identified by, the Bible. He thinks that they were not, as I suggested, on a time travelling exercise because their own planet was actually in our own solar system and not somewhere in a galaxy out there in outer space. That makes sense except that now we have the most sophisticated observation equipment ever and it has not turned up so far. To that I remark that only recently more than one planet has been discovered in the Constellation of Cygnus some 500 light years from us. One is Kepler-1861 which is the same size as earth and orbits its sun at the outer edge of a life supporting orbit. In other words it could support life but is too far away for any realistic interaction with us – at the time of writing. If we can find that then just where is Nibiru right now?

Sitchin believes that the Anunnanki came from a planet in our solar system, orbiting our own sun and it was called Nibiru. A lot of other people believe in the existence of Nibiru. Do I? I don't know but keep an open mind. The difference being that we have a circular orbit but Nibiru has an elliptical one so that for some of the time it is just the right distance from the sun for life but then it spends more time far out in space. Is this feasible? Yes, that's what comets do. They come near to us and then they hurtle out into space before returning centuries later. So yes, that could happen. But surely it is either too hot or too cold out there? Yes again, and it is Sitchin's contention, backed up by inscriptions written on clay tablets that now reside in the basements of museums, that they kept the atmosphere habitable through the use of either a powdered or flaked gold that shielded it from the sun and insulated it at night. We have our layers of atmosphere that filter the rays of the sun, he thinks that they used a form of gold for the same purpose. Again is that feasible? I don't know. I would have thought that the gold should have fallen to the ground since it is one of the heaviest of metals. As always I cannot help but look through the eyes of an engineer who obeys the basic laws of physics. It could be out there due to centrifugal force, but could Nibiru not have a core of a heavy molten metal giving it a strong gravitational pull and magnetic field? Possibly an inert substance and so have little in the way of gravity? Yes, that is a starter but a thin one at that. If they had little gravity they would not need huge rockets to get themselves airborne. But why should they do that? Sitchin believes that it is because they had run out of gold without which they would all perish that they came here in search of it. On Earth they sought gold everywhere which is why from virtually Day one of the Holy Bible it is mentioned. Look again at the wording of Genesis 2-11. *'And the name of the first is Psion, that is it which compasseth the whole land of Havialah where there is gold. [12] And the gold of that land is good: there is bdellium and the onyx stone.'*

So what is 'Bdellium'? It is a resin that seeps from an obscure bush that is indigenous to Ethiopia, Eritrea and much of sub-Saharan Africa. And 'Onyx'? That is a gemstone used in the jewellery trade and for decorative purposes. It is a quartz of crystalline construction with a Mohs Scale hardness of between 6.5 and 7. It only comes from such areas as Australia, Brazil, Madagascar and Latin America amongst other countries of the world. The nearest to the Middle East is the Czech Republic and parts of Germany. Interestingly it was used during the 2nd Dynasty of Egypt c.3000BC. Bdellium in ancient times may have been a word used to describe a crystalline rock. It puts the land of 'Havialah' somewhere south of the Sahara Desert where these three mainly useless materials could be found but that then throws everything else out.

Sitchin, as do most other researchers of whom I am aware, never worries about where rocks or timber came from. When I began a blog on a British website looking into the Neolithic remains, especially the circles and megaliths, the others were astounded to find someone actually looking into that aspect. No one had ever done so before. One said that it was *'a breath of fresh air'* to find someone coming from a whole different angle. I do that sometimes. Yes, as a logical engineer I must ask why the Bible should emphasise first gold so early in the work and now I query how they knew of onyx and bdellium which again only came from so far away? Just where did, in 3000BC, the Egyptians find it when it's nearest source was again so very far away? To get from Central and Northern Europe to Egypt in 3000BC would require a long and perilous overland trail – over or around the Alps – by donkey or ass followed by the voyage over the far from benign seas of the Mediterranean. Or they could have gone up the Rhone but unfortunately the prevailing wind is north to south – the Mistral –

which throws that one out. They could have found it near the coast of southern Africa and brought it by sea, if they had boats strong enough for the purpose. Which leads us obviously back to the original question of 'Why?' Surely there was no urgent need for either material?

All roads lead us inexorably back to the 'granite and crystal' conundrum and the need for some sort of electrical and possibly nuclear requirement. Do bear in mind that I came to this conclusion some ten years earlier when the first edition came out. Now I find that another writer whose work has received more than its fair share of acclaim has also come to that conclusion. He thinks that they did need lots of power and that the need to keep revisiting their original home meant that it was in some sort of trouble. Was this man made, one may ask? Was it their version of our 'global warming' crisis? Or had they had a nuclear 'Armageddon' of their own making? This line of research begins to answer some of my earlier questions so let us look closer.

First the gold. When the Spaniards arrived in Latin America they were greeted as 'gods' by the indigenous inhabitants who willingly handed over the gold. Now a native of Latin America has totally different racial characteristics to a Spaniard, the most obvious being their colour, their size, their faces and that they did not have facial hair or beards. The Spaniards were white, they were bigger, they had European features and they grew beards. Most of all they came seeking gold. The 'gods' of the Latinos were tall, white, had European features, they had beards and they sought gold. Ergo, the invaders were in fact the 'gods' returning!!!!! The gold, which had no value other than for decoration, was willingly handed over to the returning 'gods'. By that time all memories of the original reason for the need for gold would have been lost which is why they used it for decoration in such quantities. And that is what happened in fact. Sitchin believes that the use of mica at the Pyramid of the Sun God was as a purifier of water in the hope that from the waters would come a form of gold. Is he correct? Hmmmmm?

Then the bdellium and the onyx. Again only if it was absolutely **necessary** would they be accessed and used. It is the accessing bit that intrigues me. If the onyx came from Madagascar or Germany, how in the first place did they know what it was, and that it was there, second how was it first recognised and third how did they mine it? There is no evidence of human existence on Madagascar in pre-dynastic times and northern Europe was only inhabited by Stone Age hunter gatherer tribes. So now we have onyx, bdellium as either a resin or a crystal, mica and then granite, as with the bluestones of Stonehenge et al, as being minerals that were of no utility whatsoever to their apparent final use. But being identified as necessary and then being located, extracted and carried over enormous distances in the Middle East, Northern Europe and Latin America. And all by peoples who cannot possibly have had the faintest ideas of the existence of the others at a time when basic survival was the order of the day. In order to find one source of a material such as onyx one would be forgiven for thinking that incredible areas must first have to be explored before finally locating it in Germany. If not, how on earth could they have found it, which brings us back to one of our rhetorical questions of 'WHY'? Just why did they need both onyx and bdellium to go with their gold???

Let us return to the nuclear aspect of the equation. I have already said that to me the Ark of the Covenant, if it did exist at all, must have been in some form a small nuclear device. That it caused boils suggests radiation; that it is encased in gold suggests a radiation shield and that Israelites were fed with manna from heaven for all those years suggests that they must have been able to make lots of it. That means that they were carrying around a very precious nuclear device covered in a very precious metal. Going backwards in time it also suggests that they brought it with them from Egypt. No matter how many bounds you take, you cannot find enough of the right timber and the enormous weight of gold out there in the Sinai Desert. They could not have built furnaces to cast the gold either. In Egypt were the pyramid complexes of Giza, also set up to produce some sort of nuclear energy through the mixture of the granite and limestone. From that it suggests that maybe, just maybe, the information and detailed knowledge of what made the pyramids so successful, and then redundant again, in a very short time was in fact either held or stolen by the evicted Hebrews who had probably been in charge of it in the first place.

They who were fleeing were the last remnants of the 'Nephilim', now interbred for generations with the indigenous populations of the area. As they fled over the desert may they, in fact, have merely hid in the desert until all living memory of them had died out, rather than have taken the more obvious route along the coast on their journey to their promised land? It is a matter of historical fact that, following the Exodus, the creative genius of the remaining Egyptians quickly eroded to zero whilst that of the fleeing Jews did nothing but develop right up to the present day. It is widely accepted that the Incas had no written language at all and nor had any of the peoples of the Middle East until the Sumerians invented the cuneiform. How do we know that? Anything written on any type of paper is lost over time as the paper turns to dust. Just look at how fragile the Dead Sea Scrolls are and they are around 2 – 3,000 years old. Go back another three thousand years and there should be nothing left, which there isn't. We will never know what was stored in the library at Alexandria but, even so, most of that would have perished over the last 2,000 years.

Many people have queried why, if the Sumerians and Egyptians were so clever, did they produce such primitive writing? Good question. It is my thought that both cultures knew exactly what happened to paper and so felt it better to commit the information onto something more durable like stone. What better than to use a form of 'shorthand', for lack of a better word, and simply carve the message into soft clay as tablets that were then baked to become as hard and durable as stone? Or carve them as small pictures in stone so that it would remain very much longer? Were the Ten Commandments carved onto some convenient blank stone tablets with bronze hammer and chisel or etched in clay as before? I feel the latter to be the case.

Keeping with Sitchin because he has much to say about all this, he does believe that the Egyptians of old, and the Sumerians, did have advanced and sophisticated nuclear weapons as well. He looks at the biblical story of Sodom and Gomorrah. The tale of Lot and his wife as they fled Sodom. All this comes from the texts written in ancient scrolls and on tablets safely locked away in the vaults of the British Museum. Obviously it needs a skilled scholar of ancient texts to in the first place read these; in the second translate them into a modern tongue and third to interpret what they say. He says that all this is a post diluvial battle between the 'gods' that now lived on earth. He says that one had a 'spaceport' at a point in the Sinai Desert which the other had to destroy and that it did using five nuclear bombs. The texts say '*awesome weapons*'. If that be the case then surely just the one would have sufficed?

According to the Bible, Abraham pleaded with one of the angels who had visited him to spare the cities, on the grounds of what we now know as 'collateral damage', or civilian casualties. He argued that one in ten were righteous citizens. That evening two angels were dispatched to the city to verify this but were mobbed by those who wanted to sodomize them. They agreed to delay the action to allow Lot, who was the nephew of Abraham, and others to escape before dropping the bombs which did in fact obliterate the area. According to Genesis 19; 27 and 28,

'And Abraham got up early in the morning to the place where he stood before the Lord.

And he looked towards Gomorrah and toward all the land of the plain and beheld and lo, the smoke of the country went up as of the smoke of the furnace.'

And then a wind sprang up which spread a nuclear winter across much of Arabia and the Persian Gulf, engulfing Sumeria and Mesopotamia in the process. Sumeria never recovered. The ancient texts recorded, according to the Sitchin translations, as follows.

'A storm, an Evil Wind, went round the skies causing cities to become desolate, causing houses to become desolate, the sheepfolds to be emptied, causing Sumer's waters to become bitter, its cultivated fields grow weeds.

On the land of Sumer fell a calamity unknown to man, one that had never been seen before, one that could not be withstood. An unseen death roamed the streets, it let loose in the road, no one

can see it when it enters the house. There is no defence against this evil which assails like a ghost. No one can see it when it enters the house, through the highest and thickest wall it passes as with the flood, through the doors as a snake it glides like a wind [and] through the wind it blows in. Those who hid inside were felled behind doors, those who ran to the rooftops died on the rooftops. It was a terrible and gruesome death.'

We have seen exactly what is described above when reading about Hiroshima and its consequences. Of course, Sitchin knew that so did he make a suitable 'mighty bound' to help with a convenient theory? Possibly but, then again, possibly not because in the Sinai Desert to this day as now seen on Google Earth there is a large area of obviously charred rock that stands out against the otherwise featureless mountains. Equally it is a fact that the area is one of the driest on earth which would mean that rainfall would not wash it away. Hmmmmm again? Maybe not.

To finalise this let us look at another but totally different angle that was certainly not available until very recently, and that is the human genome. It is only very recently, writing in 2016, that it has been possible to use human DNA as a forensic testing tool.

As recently as 2001, only just before I had begun the research for the first edition, it was established that rather than our genome having in excess of 100,000 genes, it did in fact have just 30,000. Once more let us put that into context.

A fruit fly has 13,600 genes and a roundworm has just over 19,000. We share 99% of our genes with the chimpanzee and 70% with mice plus many with all the other plants, animals, fish and fungi of the world. But that leaves less than 300, 233 actually, that are totally unique to Homo sapiens. *Nature* magazine, issue 409, shows that these genes are unique from all other species and affect our physiological and human functions that are absent from the apes. Just these few genes, and this is not fanciful hypothesis, separate us from all other animals. They make us walk upright and shed our body covering hair. All other accoutrements that are necessary for the survival of animals are made obsolete because of these few genes. It is known that it is possible by way of what is known as 'horizontal transfer' for genes of, say a fly, to pass into a pig, and by extension into a human. We can absorb more genes from bacteria so could we, did we, get those extra 233 genes from another species from somewhere far away? After all, did not the Lord say that he would fashion Adam in his image? If not by the transfer of genes then what? Sitchin believes that was what happened. Do I agree? Maybe, maybe not because all humanity, whether descended from the Nephilim or not, must have these same genes. After all we do share all the same physical attributes, whatever race we are across the globe.

Where did these Nephilim come from? What is the evidence for Nibiru and where is that now? If they were extra terrestrial then they came from one of two places. The first is that they were divine and were in fact 'Gods' sent from afar to save the human race. Probably not. The second is that they were mortal and had come from a distant planet, but how distant, that is the question?

Forget what ancient texts may say, let us look only at facts. First the people. Since the offspring of those first settlers and their descendents ended up with one head, two arms, two legs and ten each fingers and toes it must be assumed that they were a lot like us. Technologically they would be far more advanced, not as far ahead as current academic thought would suggest, but physiologically they would not be much different to us. In which case the criteria for survival for them would be more or less the same as it is for us. They would eat the same type of food, drink water, maybe wine even, sleep at night and reproduce as we do. The extension of that is that their own planet of 'Nibiru', for argument's sake, must have also been very much like our own. It would need an oxygen bearing atmosphere, plenty of water and with more or less equal night and day. So as to be neither too hot nor too cold, it cannot have orbited its own sun at a very much different distance to our own. They may even have been orbiting our own sun. They need only have begun their own 'Industrial Revolution' a mere hundred or so years before we did to get to the necessary level of technical knowledge.

We've already considered that it may be a planet that has become detached from somewhere in the region of Orion but, because of the time taken, even at the speed of light, for it to get here through outer space I feel that that is not a feasible concept. Could it have been the mysterious 'Dark Star' written about by others? Could it have an elliptical orbit as suggested by Sitchin? Again I doubt it. The ellipse idea fails for the same reason as does the outer space one because life could not be maintained at such extreme temperatures for the times involved. No amount of powdered gold could keep any planet from freezing over. That is if it could remain in the atmosphere. No, that would not work at all.

The 'Dark Star' idea is that there is a nineth planet in our own solar system that is hidden away in the asteroid belt. Nibiru sits there undetected because it is thought to be a big asteroid. Again, I don't think so for the reason that the asteroid belt is too far from our sun to meet the life bearing criteria. Could it have been Mars when that had its supposed atmosphere and water? Yes, it could. The rotation is good, distance from the sun acceptable and it would make sense to seek a new home when things began to go wrong. The downside to that argument is that with no atmosphere, rains or wind the abandoned cities should be still visible now. Apart from someone claiming to have spotted some pyramids on the planet there has so far been no evidence unearthed to suggest any form of life at all. So again, I very much doubt it.

So with what are we left? The 'divine' one is still strong but first just think of this scenario. Suppose that in ancient times, as shown on some ancient carvings, there was an extra planet that met all the criteria, that was on more or less our orbit but not necessarily concentric with it. That planet is inhabited by mentally further advanced peoples who may just have had their own nuclear war, destroying most of life in the process. They need to relocate and do so by coming to the nearest host which is us. Is that not why we are looking at Mars? They may have known about us from previous visits over a great period of time but sometime around the 20 – 15,000BC period they needed to settle for good. But before finally doing so they must make frequent return visits home.

Just why they would need to do so, we do not know, but they found suitable places where there was an existing primitive society, living in a hospitable place, that had sufficient man power to do the heavy work in building the various edifices we see today. Again, just what they were able to use we cannot even guess at, but whatever it was it enabled them to work rocks and move earth with ease. It enabled them to dig narrow but perfect holes through rock to incredible tolerances and it then left tantalising clues about how clever they were. I show the stonework at Cuzco in Peru to illustrate this. It is a breathtaking display of absolutely useless utility. There are three concentric walls averaging six metres high and around 400 metres long that were built to be freestanding from stones so carefully worked that it is not possible to insert a piece of paper between them. The biggest stones are in the 120 to 200 ton range and the total volume of stone is over 6,000 tons.

There are hundreds of these massive stones making up three long walls. Note the carefully rounded edges and the jigsaw puzzle interlocking of each for absolutely no purpose whatsoever!

Just try to work out the angles and shapes in this piece of stonework on paper. Then think about how you would cut those stones from what appears to be grit stone, and place them in those exact spots so that they fit with a zero tolerance all round. And then replicate it on three freestanding walls 400 metres long. Each stone a different shape and size that fitted exactly in its place. I submit that no normal, and here I emphasise the word 'normal', people living in the High Andes all those years ago had the tools and expertise to do this, assuming of course that they felt the need so to do. To me this has all the signs of someone 'showboating' just to show how clever he was. Unlike all the other ancient sites, this one has no obvious utility whatsoever.

The people, or creatures, or whatever who built all these edifices all that time ago knew exactly what they were doing using some form of technology that is way beyond us even now. These stones in Peru, and there are more at Machu Pichu, show that my theory of how it would have been possible to build the pyramids by casting as blocks applies only to normal human beings. Anyone who could carve these stones with such ease and to such precision in Peru could also have done the same when cutting the massive ones at Giza. Anyone who could raise these massive blocks, some of which are in the 120 to 200 ton range, from the valley floor onto the site and then place them firmly in place could also have done the same at Giza. In Egypt, when this was finished, the people bred with the local women leaving their descendants still with us; in South America their descendants seem to have merely reverted to being very rich and decadent versions of the existing population.

So what about Nibiru? Did it, could it exist? The answer is yes, yes it could have done. Let us think about that. Supposing that out there in our solar system is that extra planet called 'Planet 'X' or Nibiru and it has an elliptical orbit of our Sun that takes 3,600 years according to Sitchin. OK, let's believe that. He says that it is far bigger than us and it was a crash between it and another planet that caused us here on Earth to break off resulting in the Earth and its moon. Is that feasible? No it is not. Not at all. As we've seen throughout this book, the simple application of basic physics precludes this argument because both the Earth and the Moon are more or less perfect spheres. You only get a natural sphere from a spinning hot substance, not from colliding planetary objects. Also we must ask the obvious question of what was happening to all the seas when it was going on. No, that idea is one that I am amazed is still out there as being 'fact'.

Could it be lying in the asteroid belt? Yes, but not if it contains life and, if it is out there, it cannot be anywhere near the size suggested to remain unobserved. So in what form could it be?

In order to support life similar to our own the same criteria must have been met. That means all that I've indicated before with the principal one being that it must be more or less the same distance from our sun as us and that it must orbit at the same speed. So why have we not found it as yet? One suggestion is that it is on our orbit but diametrically opposite to us so that it always sits hidden behind the sun. Possible? Yes that is possible. If so it is well within the range of our present day space programme and so a more advanced people should be able to find us with ease. The other thought is that it was there within our own orbit, and easily seen and accessible, but now it simply no longer exists. That would account for the many ancient inscriptions that show an extra planet. Could a man made, or even natural, catastrophe have overtaken it resulting in it simply exploding sometime in the past? Yes, that could have happened. It could have, in antiquity, have collided with another now long gone planet and, as Sitchin suggests, have left others behind, possibly now large jagged fragments in the Asteroid Belt. The inhabitants with their advanced technology could have seen that this was going to happen for some time in advance. They could have planned for it and sent away their best brains to create a new version of themselves on another planet. Obviously most would perish but their seeds would flourish on Earth which had a small and basically backward population. By mating with them they could replicate their own society.

Far fetched? Yes it is but we must look at the facts, nothing else, and consider only what <u>could</u> have happened. We know that something dramatic happened between 20,000BC and 5,000BC to change mankind forever. We know that the Bible agrees with that statement; we know that across the entire world are far too many structural anomalies that exist; we know that the indigenous peoples of those lands had nothing like the mathematical and technical ability to build those structures and we know that someone was mapping our planet in the very distant past before the ice engulfed the Antarctic continent. All these things happened for all to see and there has to be an explanation. Only the last of the ones above can I see as being remotely possible, but whether or not I am correct I leave for others to decide.

Another researcher looking into the DNA aspect of the riddle is the young American engineer, Perry Marshall. His angle is that only 'God' Himself could have designed the various genomes in living things to make them advance and that it could never have been because of random mutations. He gives several analogies.

The first is a simple sentence such as 'That is a good very idea'. You or I could easily change it to 'That is a very good idea' or 'That is a brilliant idea'. 'Very Good' and 'Brilliant' each have eight letters and because we change the design of the sequence through intelligence it is the work of seconds to make that change. So could we eliminate the 'intelligence' bit and replace it by random selection? How many permutations would be needed if we simply relied on random 'natural selection'? The answer is 'billions' and even then it would be a fluke if the correct answer came up.

He then describes how Microsoft employ 40,000 software engineers to produce each update of its Windows programme. If the software could simply and randomly update itself it would save a great deal of money, but it cannot because it needs a superior 'intelligence' to feed in the correct sequences. A list of notes of music on a sheet mean nothing as Eric Morecombe famously told Andre Previn on the 'Morecombe and Wise Show'. He said that he was playing all the right notes but not necessarily in the right order. It needed a skilled musician to put them in the right order. We get ill with a bug and are given an anti-biotic which makes us better again. We get ill again but the bug has some intelligence in its DNA that identifies the anti-biotic and so it uses a different method of operation. If the bug relied on random changes to combat the medicine it would be killed very quickly.

Marshall describes the entire atheist theory as being that throughout the timeline of life on the planet, there has always been a random mutation that has caused a new and better species to evolve. He uses these, and other, experiments to show that evolution could never have happened randomly but that there had to be some greater being out there doing the thinking or designing to make it all happen. I would have thought that the chances of a new and inferior species would be the same and so, using the laws of averages, we would in fact remain the same, never advancing nor retreating in our evolutionary progress.

Do I agree? Yes, to a certain extent because it is what I deduced way back in 2005/6. I realised most of this as I have indicated earlier. I still cannot accept that at any time in history a simple small fish randomly had a gene change that enabled it to

113

breathe air and walk on land any more than I can accept that randomly a lizard suddenly changed its genes to cease laying eggs and suckle its young. If that be the case, why has 'evolution' as such not at some stage gone into reverse? Could a lizard evolve from one of us, or a pig or a cow? If not, how could we have evolved from one of them? I am sure that there is much more to it than that but, since Marshall is very much younger than me, he and his fellow researchers may find the answer long after I am gone. Read his work in 2050 and see what he has to say.

Another random thought along these lines is with plants. Plant a seed and the stem will emerge into the light and the roots will grow in the opposite direction. It does not matter what position the seed is planted in, it will always find its own way, both up or down. It is enclosed in a dark environment but will always find its way to the light. How and why? Think of one of us placed in a dark round ball in a weightless environment. In one spot is a trap door to let us out. The odds on finding it begin at 1 in 360x360. Those are the odds of a simple plant finding its way to the surface if left to a random selection. But some intelligence in all plants enables them to get it right every time. From where does that intelligence come?

26

WAVES, GHOSTS and GHOULIES – THE SPIRIT WORLD

Many years ago, while on holiday in Portugal, I met an Australian named Harry Gration. Harry was on a world tour and, as he put it, 'was seeing the sights', except that he was totally blind and had been since he was five years old. All he could make out was whether or not it was light or dark. He came to stay with us in Yorkshire having been on a tour of the Scottish Highlands. He said he found them beautiful at which I asked him how he could possibly know that. But he did. Losing his sight resulted in some mechanism within his brain compensating, so that he was able to absorb the light waves without actually being able to see anything.

In the 19th century there was born a lady named Helen Keller who, at the age of 18 months became both blind and deaf. Yet she graduated from Radcliffe University, wrote twelve books and died in 1968 after an incredibly full and active life. Most communication was done through the palms of her hands but she could talk and converse. Again, losing two senses merely accentuated something in her brain that, like my friend Harry, enabled her to carry on. The point I am trying to make is that in our brains we all have some hidden and unused cells capable of picking up waves of which we are as yet totally unaware. They enable the blind to 'see' and the deaf to 'hear' but in forms of which none of us understand. This must be another good subject for a PhD thesis.

It is my contention that in northern Europe mankind had possibly only had a brief contact with whoever built the great buildings elsewhere. I think that they were all following the basic evolution of Darwin. They built whatever they built as servants, or slaves, or whatever of the others but otherwise they had no other advanced knowledge. They used what their brains allowed them to use. They were learning everything from *'First Principals'*.

For this reason we cannot dismiss out of hand the thought that some of us _may_ have the basic quirk, for lack of a better word, in our brains that enables us to contact the spirit world. As I said earlier, ancient man may have used earth currents to find his way about using parts of his brain now long unused today. Others may also have parts that are active uniquely to themselves.

Like the Extra Terrestrial ghosts that must be laid to rest, we must ask ourselves very seriously whether or not we believe that a Spirit World of some sort can exist, for the answers to other questions do rather depend on it. If we categorically dismiss it all as a load of rubbish, as many do, then either a lot of things are going to take a great deal of explaining, or there are a vast number of liars, charlatans and fraudsters out there, all trying to deceive us. You cannot believe in any of the great religions and discount this as rubbish.

And this gives me a problem since simple logic must say that they cannot exist but, if simple logic is correct, how do I explain my own personal encounters with ghosts? I assure you that my security guards at the time were in genuine terror at what they had witnessed, and the thoughts of my childhood encounter still raise the hairs on the back of my head. And since I have absolutely no other explanation, I must accept that there is something in it. Michael Cremo in his opus 'Human Devolution – A Vedic Alternative to Darwin' digs very deeply into the subject. Vedic, meaning the Sanskrit, is a look at the problem from the point of view of the Eastern religions which are heavily into this sort of thing. In the book he gives pages of examples of scientifically observed séances with people actually contacting the dead, furniture moving, etc, to the point where it is difficult to deny the facts. One thing that did interest me was who was actually doing the research. Who attended the séances on a regular basis? It is common knowledge that Newton was, first an alchemist seeking gold, with his mathematics a secondary consideration, but the number of other top scientists quoted in the book is remarkable. Presidents and Fellows of the Royal Society were all heavily into Spiritual Research for many years. Not merely trying to prove it was a hoax either.

As with the extra terrestrials, if the deniers are correct then much must come to a halt, and out of the window must go most of the Jewish, Christian and Muslim faiths. Plus, of course, anything from the East that has reincarnation at the centre of its philosophy. The ascensions did not happen; the Angel Gabriel must be a figment of the imagination together with the Virgin birth. We are straight back to Darwin being the one and only solution.

But I do not believe that they are correct. There is far too much evidence to the contrary. Again, in Cremo's book, he looks at *Marian Apparitions*, in particular the one at Fatima in Portugal. Far too many people were involved over a long period for that to have been a hoax perpetrated by some simple children. They saw angels first, before there was the appearance of the Virgin Mary, and the eldest of them was only nine years old. She was a shepherdess out on the hills, not the type who could cunningly think something like that up, and then make it stick. The evidence of too many near death experiences of rational people cannot be dismissed out of hand, whilst there are so many ghost and poltergeist stories from all over the world that some, if not all, of them must be true. The '*Book of Enoch*' is all about his spiritual visions. It is well worth reading.

If we are to believe unconditionally that some sort of a spirit world does exist, in what form does it take? Where are all these spirits right now as I write this and you read it? Are they swimming about in the ether above our heads, waiting for a signal so that they may manifest themselves in some form or other? Are only a chosen few of us, programmed with the right receiver to pick out of all those hidden waves we discussed earlier, our own only contacts in this other world? I must have some sort of receiver because I heard that ghost all those years ago, so why have I never come across another in the subsequent seventy odd years? I have certainly spent enough time over the last thirty years alone, at all times of the day and night, in some of Britain's spookiest buildings, but not once have I been contacted by the 'other side'. These are all baffling questions with, seemingly, no possible answers. And now I am guilty of doing what infuriates me with other writers – asking the eternal questions with little or no idea how to answer them. These are my thoughts which may or may not hit the target. As I say, I just do not know but I can offer an idea and, most of all, my mind remains open to other conflicting theories. In fact, none of us really knows at all.

So let us think about this carefully as logical human beings. It seems highly improbable that some sort of spirit world does <u>not</u> exist at all. In which case it must be a possibility that it does. It cannot be far away and, like your TV set or mobile phone, can be put into operation at any time of a medium's choice. All the medium must do is set up the séance, go into a trance and then call up his, or most likely, her contact on the other side, who will then talk to her in some form that they can mutually understand.

The astonishing thing is that having, in many cases, a random and anonymous group taking part in the session, a similar group, who know at least one of those present, has gathered on the other side. So that when the medium asks whether anyone present had an Uncle Fred and the answer is positive, she can then pass on the message that Aunty Joan and Cousin Audrey are all up there and wishing them well. I have never come across a story of a medium contacting the relatives of a very bad person, telling them that he is roasting away in the depths of Hell. It is always that the subject is either in or on the way to heaven. Also the medium never tunes into someone speaking a different language, or a long dead ancestor of the subject speaking a Dark Ages dialect. Always someone no more than one generation away and very close to the subject. I am not being facetious here, merely stating the facts.

So do Heaven, Hell and Purgatory actually exist and are they part of this spirit world? In fact has this spirit world anything whatsoever to do with Christianity, Judaism or Islam? Do the religious spirits, from whence came the Marian Apparitions, differ to the spirits that manifest themselves to the mediums, or as ghosts, or are they all on the one spiritual level existing in some sort of parallel universe? And that this is only accessible to us when our soul departs our earthly body on death. Do we then proceed into this spirit world automatically as of right, or is there some sort of pre-ordained selection procedure? A procedure where the undeserving and patently wicked amongst us are denied and sent, either to Hell, or some sort of eternal oblivion where their souls must, if we believe the eastern religions, suffer eternal reincarnation over and over again until they behave? These are all very difficult and profound questions indeed.

The Eastern religions believe a great deal in reincarnation so that on death your soul departs its earthly body and enters that of a new born child beginning again. As you live these many lives your soul should gradually improve on the long road to 'Nirvana' where only perfect souls exist. This is given as the reason why, under deep hypnosis, you can be made to regress into earlier lives which are accurately described. I have suggested the alternative 'Memory Gene' theory.

The Catholic version of Christianity believes that on death you first visit purgatory where you wait for as long as it takes before being finally selected to go to your ultimate destination. By the use of various incantations whilst on earth it is possible to obtain indulgences which are thought to speed your progress through purgatory. With this latter fact I am at the very least, sceptical. It could be just a ruse by the clergy to claim more control over its congregation but, on this, I am quite prepared to be proved wrong.

So let us put together what we now know and see if there is anything with which a simple logical mind like mine can live.

We have to accept that there must be a spirit world of some sort out there. That is fundamental. If you still think it is rubbish then what follows will be even greater rubbish. It would appear that in some way the divine spirits that contain Christ, God, the Virgin Mary, the Archangels and possibly Mohammed [although he never claimed Divinity], are part of the same world of the secular spirits like our Cousin Audrey and Aunty Joan. From this it seems that only the secular spirits can be contacted by us through our own 'receivers' who are the mediums tuned into the right wave lengths. The divine spirits make their own appearances as and when they want to. They remain eternal and intact, out of our reach, but with us remaining firmly within theirs. We cannot contact them no matter how much we pray. And they materialize on only very rare occasions. The secular spirits seem to vanish after about a generation, possibly to a different level out of reach of mortal man until he, too, joins them as he inevitably must one day. Those spirits who manifest themselves as ghosts are the problem. Usually they have died a violent death and it is just possible that, because of this, their soul may have remained trapped in the mortal world for eternity. They manifest themselves, always in the self same habitat and in the self same way to a variety of different people. They are able to choose to whom they appear and must be on a different wave length altogether to the normal secular spirits. Probably you do not need to be a programmed receiver to see a ghost since they do appear to almost anyone at all. As the secular spirits are selective, only speaking to people whom someone may know, the ghostly spirit is never so. He or she will appear to anyone at all, providing that that person is in the right place. Again I am open to correction, but so far I have never heard of a secular medium being able to contact at will either a Divine spirit or ghostly one. Various clergy over the years have conducted services and said prayers at the places where the poltergeists are present in an effort to exorcise them but few have succeeded. If they have so done then that effectively proves as correct all in this chapter.

The Divine Apparitions appear very seldom and usually to someone of total innocence. At Fatima the Virgin Mary appeared to three children aged 9, 7 and 5. At Lourds the recipient was the child Bernadette, the Angel Gabriel appeared to the young and illiterate Mohammed, Christ appeared to the monk and hermit St John the Divine. They do not make an appearance at a football match or the Democratic Party Convention. From this it would appear that the Divine spiritual world is possibly connected to the secular one but on a different level, all existing somewhere in the ether that surrounds us as a type of wave. Do not forget that, as you are reading this and probably thinking that I have flipped, also out there in that self same ether, or through tiny wires and fibre optic cables, are all your telephone calls, all your emails which include enormous documents and pictures – many of which are moving, all your TV channels, your radio waves, now billions of internet sites, your GPS signals and much more. And all the unseen magnetic forces flowing through the ground, none of which you can see, feel, smell or hear. But you know they are there because with that right receiver you can switch them on or off at will. We are not normally able to tune in to the spirit world except through the chosen few mediums.

Mediums are tuned in, by what means we know not, but tuned in they are, so that at will they can switch to the spirit frequency, but only the secular one. A very chosen few in the past have been able to switch on to the Divine frequency and contact God, or his chosen spokesperson, in person. They include Christ, Mohammed, Moses and various prophets of old. The Divine frequency can choose to whom it speaks from above whilst the secular one can be contacted only from below. A bit like having two different channels on your TV set, one of which only works when the weather is doing a certain thing.

This is how I see this other world. Like a long spiral staircase with various resting and sorting stages on the way. As we climb it over the years, for now we are entering eternity which has no end, we are gradually assessed on our earthly pursuits and either proceed further or stay forever at that level with only the few ever arriving at either Heaven or Nirvana. Those left at the different stages may be reincarnated if the Hindus and Buddhists are correct; if Christ is correct many will be diverted back to the fiery pit of Hades. Most will be left in limbo, unable to go back for they were not all that bad or able to proceed because they were not that much good either. Of one thing I am **absolutely certain** and that is that there will be no fast track to the top for someone who has just killed himself and hundreds of innocent civilians, of whatever faith or creed, with a homemade bomb. And then gone on to say that he, or she, has done it in the name of God, or one of his prophets.

This now leaves us with one final question. Is it possible for a mere mortal to cross the great divide that separates the secular from the divine? I would say that the answer must be an unqualified 'Yes'. After all, as a child Mary should have been one of us, only achieving divine status on giving birth to Jesus. Mohammed was certainly of this earth and of the Arab people. Did he cross the divide? As I say, we will all find out in the fullness of time.

The one thing that we will never know until it is too late, and which no theologian of any faith can tell us for certain, is just what a good person is. And what is a bad one? Just what is the criteria for this decision? Does writing this book make me an instant candidate for the fire or give me a fast track to the top? Who knows? No one does but, again, we will all find out in that same fullness of time.

27

WHAT HAS GOD GOT TO DO WITH IT?

It is never the purpose of a book like this to offer comment on current affairs since most, if not all, of what is taking place today is quickly forgotten a few days later. As British Premier Harold Wilson shrewdly observed *"A week is a long time in politics."* Also I must emphasise that what I say next contains no intended racist message nor is it intended to offend anyone. It is simply a statement of current and historical fact that under no circumstances can be either denied or overlooked.

Few would argue that just one part of the world has been, from the distant and ancient times of this book right up to the present day, the number one hotbed of eternal trouble. That is the Middle East and, for much of the time, bang in the centre have been the Jewish people. The Exodus was Egyptians against Hebrew right up to the Russian Pogroms that sent so many to America in the nineteenth century. Hitler used them as his excuse for the Second World War, killing six million in the process and then Stalin killed off at least another 20 million both before and after the war. And now, having finally settled in God's 'Promised Land', the strife is far worse, exacerbated by the more zealous of the Jewish Fundamentalists insisting on taking land belonging to nearby Arab Palestine. I have to say, theirs is just as rightful a claim since it is based on an equally long period of time, and is backed by equally Fundamentalist Muslims. After all the Canaanites were in The Land of Milk and Honey well before Moses arrived.

One side blowing themselves, and innocent civilians, up with personal bombs followed by the other sending in tanks or rockets to destroy a village, is certainly no answer to the long term solution. Nor is one faction of Islam being out to destroy another any way to a lasting peace if, in fact, that is what any of them actually want. As I write this in 2016 one group of Islamist fanatics have occupied a large slice of the Middle East causing a power shift and population upheaval that will reverberate around the world for generations to come. The only victims are fellow Muslims who must seek refuge in the 'enemy' strongholds of Western Christendom.

The other serious hotbed of trouble was based in Europe and centred on England. After the Ice Age, Britain was more or less at peace until the Romans came in 43AD. Then came the Angles, the Saxons, the Jutes and the Danes before the Normans settled after the 1066 victory. From then on England has been at war in more theatres than any other nation on earth. Many times have we fought the French, the Spanish, the Danes, the Dutch, the Turks and the Italians. We have fought the Arabs in the Middle East, the Indians in India and the Chinese in China, the Russians at Crimea, the Boers in South Africa, the Afghans in Afghanistan, the Argentines in the Falklands, innumerable native tribes in occupied countries across the world, even our own people in America, Wales, Scotland and Ireland and, of course Germany twice. And now we are finally extracting ourselves from the mess in Iraq and Afghanistan. The reasons for this would need another book and are of no consequence in this one. I merely mention it because it shows that, over many years at the centre of many disputes have been the Jews, the Arabs and the English. Hebrew, Islam and Christianity, the very people who, if we are to believe the scriptures, God is supposed to have put on the straight and narrow to lead mankind in peace, friendship and understanding. There is a fat chance of any of that happening at any time now or in the foreseeable future.

Now this is very interesting and please bear with me as I offer you some carefully considered thoughts, born many years ago, to filter through. Most came from fierce arguments with my dear friend, Derek Shaw, when he was preparing me to become a Confirmed member of the Church of England. He would offer something and I would say it was wrong. Then we would have an interesting hour of intellectual discussion on the subject. It was wonderful. How I miss him now.

Hebrew, Islam and Christianity [and in each case I generalise rather than discussing the various offshoots and sects] have the one common God. The God of Abraham who, if we are to believe the Old Testament, was in constant contact early on with

124

many of the elders of the Hebrews and they, according to my theme, were either the Nephilim or their descendents. Whether they were all secular and not divine is open to question. If all were secular how do we account for the Ascension whilst still alive of Elijah and Enoch? Now the Nephilim are first introduced to us in the Bible, and so may be equally considered to be Biblical figures as anyone else. If I am right and they had this ability to transcend time then, as well as leaving all their rubbish all over the world in impossibly ancient times, [*OK, someone put it there. If not them, then who?*] could they also have peeped forward in time before deciding when and where to settle? And when they got to the beginning of the twenty first century they would rightly be somewhat horrified. Not as bad as if they had arrived in 1942 or 1916 but, nevertheless, pretty horrifying.

Global warming, apparently so rampant that it could precipitate another Ice Age, tin pot dictators having nuclear weapons and desperate to use them, the Middle East in probably its worst turmoil ever, fundamental Islam desperate to take on the world, diseases like Cancer and Aids out of control and a worldwide lack of very much moral or spiritual guidance nor, for that matter, any desire for any either. Slavery, especially of children, rife all over the world and the most powerful nation seemingly determined to remain at war with 'Islamic State' and 'Al Quieda' – James Bond's 'Spectre'. The all enveloping evil organisation which, to have as an enemy, is Manna from Heaven for Presidents and Prime Ministers who have been proven to be otherwise totally inept at every other thing that they have attempted.

And this is the nearest we have got so far to the Biblically prophesied mankind generated Armageddon of which we were warned. Again the mixture is as before. As it was in the very beginning and as, it would seem, destined to be for all time to come. Jew against Arab, Arab against Arab as well as the West, the West having a large Jewish population whilst over the years, all but four of the US Presidents could trace their origins back to the United Kingdom. In other words, the English, Scots, Welsh and Irish.

So back in time we go to the period of Abraham, Joseph, Isaac and Isaiah who again are in close touch with God. Just supposing that between them they decide to send, in the distant future, someone spiritual, not of our world but with some sort of USP [in commerce this is the Unique Selling Point] that would make mankind sit up and take notice. Something like a Virgin Birth from a young woman artificially inseminated from above. It is obvious that to send a great warrior would be tantamount to pouring oil onto the fire. No, this one must be benign, wise and most of all He must promote peace and understanding. If the world then followed Him, gradually it would become a beautiful and peaceful land for mankind for ever more.

And so, into the number one hotbed of the world, was born Jesus Christ who was to become our universal saviour and, whilst he quickly acquired many supporters and followers, these were mainly the Gentiles. Neither Jew nor Arab wanted to know. In the great scheme of things this would have been a big setback. Those above, now including Christ and the Virgin Mary, could see that whilst he was gaining support in Europe with the Christianization of Rome, followed by the Holy Roman Empire, with footholds in Gaul and Britain, no headway was being made in the Middle East. And that was the one place where it was intended to happen. The Jews were now embarked on their great migrations into Eastern and Western Europe leaving an embittered, illiterate and unfortunately, indolent Arab people in the now Holy Land. An area that was arid and devoid of any obvious natural resources.

So what could they do? They couldn't pull off another Virgin Birth because then people would disbelieve the first one, but they could do the next best thing which was to find an illiterate Arab peasant in Arabia, with whom the Arabs could identify as being one of their own – not some smart ass from a ruling class - and introduce him to one of the Archangels – Gabriel. This young man, who was called Mohammed, would then have many visits over his life time from Gabriel who would teach him another version of the extension to the Bible which would be called 'The Holy Koran'. Mohammed would then retell the story to the scribes who wrote it down in the form we read today. And so now the Arab people could have a prophet of their own, albeit with the same overall God pulling the strings, whom they must share with Israel and Christendom. The followers of this prophet in the new religion of

Islam could now preach to their own people peace, understanding and forgiving. How they could live in harmony with Jew and Christian and so save mankind from this eternal threat of, and march towards, Armageddon.

At least that was the idea. Simplistic? Maybe, but any more so than the Virgin Birth, Crucifixion, Resurrection and Ascension, followed by visitations from The Archangel Gabriel, the dictating of the Koran to an illiterate peasant who again then ascended into heaven? I don't think so. The birth of Christ was carefully orchestrated, wise men, kings and shepherds turning up from afar, Herod being convinced that the Jews suddenly had a king causing the slaughter of the innocents, the star remaining overhead and the well publicised virgin birth element. There can be no doubt that someone, or thing, wanted the world to know that someone special had arrived amongst the myriad of other Jewish children born at the time. As a marketing exercise, any of the world's leading agencies would have been proud to call it their own. And, now confirmed, if the '*Book of Judas*' story can be relied on in any way, his death had to be equally spectacular. That had to be something with which followers in the years to come could readily identify. A simple cup of poison or a knife in the back would not do, so what could be better than a public crucifixion?

Obviously it didn't work. We were soon into the Crusades with each side wanting to throw out the infidel and that same struggle continues today.

So what went wrong? Where they got it wrong was in the thinking that mankind would change, not so much its habits but its ingrained long held attitudes and personality. The Bible says it often enough that basically man was not a good person and it was surely to change this that both Christ and Mohammed were, as it were, discovered in the right places and at the right times in history. And the Biblical Nephilim made their appearances, but it was not as simple as that, for by far the largest number of people on earth had no contact with the Nephilim. And with those who were of direct descent from the invaders, the blood line was getting weaker every time they married into the indigenous populace that was following Darwin.

Our problem is that man is probably the world's cruellest of animals and that includes us all. We subscribe to the tribal instinct all the time and can so easily be whipped up into a frenzy about something affecting our own tribe. You see proof of this every weekend when football supporters go wild when their team scores a goal. Many a time does this spill over after the match into a full blooded fight with knives and guns in the streets, very often ending in someone being killed. Even a sport like rugby union, played very much in front of an upper class crowd, attracts the same frenzy. I vividly remember seeing the Scotland/England match at Murrayfield where the Scots crowd tried to boo and shout down the playing of 'God Save the Queen'. And this is their own National Anthem.

As Winston Churchill wrote in *'Thoughts and Adventures'*, *"Under sufficient stress – starvation, terror, warlike passion or even cold intellectual frenzy, the modern man we know so well will do the most terrible deeds, and his modern woman will back him up."*

Except for foxes and jackals, the animal world kills to eat and so live. But man kills for fun. Not just with the fox hounds either or out shooting grouse. In many cities of the world it is no longer safe to walk the streets, for they are infested by petty thieves with knives and guns who will not hesitate to kill if necessary, very often for just a few pounds or dollars, or simply just for the fun of it all. On television every night are scenes of young children swaggering through the streets of Baghdad or Kabul, or some central African war zone armed to the teeth and just itching to use their automatic rifles. Nations are just as culpable. The perennial genocide in Africa as one tribe tries to wipe out another is endemic. In Britain one only has to remember Glencoe and Culloden, the Highland clearances and the appalling treatment of the Irish in the 19th century. Slavery is, and always has been, the worst cruelty inflicted by men on men. And it goes on throughout the world today. Despite the occasional posturing of some actress or politician up for re-election, this increases across the globe and is probably at the very bottom of the list of priorities anywhere.

Ethnic cleansing was practiced with enthusiasm in the Balkans after the fall of Yugoslavia and in Iraq in an effort to get rid of the Kurds. The biggest examples of this were Nazi Germany, Stalinist Russia and China under Mao Tze Tung. The stories of Japanese atrocities before and during the Second World War are just too horrific to mention. But, whatever religion is dominant in the country concerned, we should never imagine that it could not happen in Britain or in America today. When you see the average British thug, just imagine him in a Nazi uniform with permission to beat up and kill a few Jews or coloureds. He would relish the idea. As did the Ku Klux Klan in America's Deep South. And again it is not just the thugs and yobs who infest our streets. Many are the noble British families living on vast estates, the pillars of society, who owe their wealth and position to the Slave Trade and/or the exploitation of child labour in the pits and factories.

A hundred years after the American Civil War and the death of Lincoln, it was still acceptable to lynch an unfortunate black person in the Deep South. No, I am afraid that underneath we are all culpable in this respect. Since writing the above piece, Europe has been invaded, for want of a better word, by peoples from the Middle East and Africa seeking refuge from tyranny and/or seeking a new and better life. A few could be absorbed but Europe just cannot cope with millions, for those are the numbers, of illiterate, young, mainly male, unemployable people all arriving over a very short period of time. It is a time bomb waiting to explode. Many of the 'asylum seekers' have an agenda to create Islamist caliphates in the west, at the same time engaging in hostile demands against the host nations and all the time hiding behind the ever growing 'racial intolerance and 'human rights' industries' that silence the west. Sooner or later either the Far Left or the Far Right, or both will rise against these people and then there will be a problem.

So is there an answer to it all? Sadly the answer is a resounding no. Our leaders today, in the same way as the leaders of the past, feel the need to prove their worth as leaders and the easiest way is to pick a fight with someone. Domestic problems at home can be quickly put to one side in a united show of support for the armed services, however flimsy the reason for the current conflict. The loss of thousands of lives is acceptable if it wins the next election.

I repeat the verse from The Book of Enoch 12.7. This more than anything confirms the resignation felt from above when those from wherever they came bred with the only possible Earth evolved animals – Homo sapiens – who were the best available, but only just, *'That on Earth they shall never obtain peace and remission of sin. For they shall not rejoice in their offspring, they shall behold the slaughter of their beloved, shall lament for the destruction of their sons and shall petition forever but shall not obtain mercy or peace.'* If that is not a statement of *'You make your own bed, so lie in it.'* I do not know what is.

One other thought that may be way off course is whether the Nephilim arrived on Earth as a stop off to somewhere else. They needed huge monuments to give others directions, information or whatever and that the crude two legged simple animal that could do the work happened to be Homo sapiens. Unfortunately they bred with the women of that breed and it got out of hand. Too many of them did it and their resulting progeny suddenly became a whole different species that soon got totally out of control. It could think for itself. Maybe not, but an idea none the less.

28

THE NOSE

It was whilst casually glancing at the photograph of a bust of Caesar and then opening a book with another photograph of a statue, this time of Ramesses 11, that the thought came to me. Could that long straight nose with little, if anything, of a bridge but sometimes with a pronounced hook effect, actually be a genetic link between the Romans and the Dynastic Pharaohs? From which, by extension, there must be a further link back until we get to the time of the last of the Nephilim. And, by further extension forward, a link to people alive today? Some have a completely straight nose with no bridge and this is commonly known as 'The Roman Nose'. Others have an equally pronounced one with a hook like bend at the bridge.

Looking at the general wall paintings of ancient Egypt was of little help since it appeared that everyone had the characteristic nose. That is until I began to look more carefully.

Little is available in paintings in the pre-dynastic period from the Pyramid Age and the earliest that I have found is a palette in the British Museum dating from c3150BC which shows a large Egyptian, with the nose, bashing the head in of a smaller opponent who possesses an obviously 'normal' one. From this I discarded all 'run of the mill' pictures of everyday life and concentrated on statues which one would reasonably expect to be somewhere near to life like. Again, if everyone had the nose, then this line must be treated with some doubt and the theory probably dropped as just another good idea at the time.

But this did not happen. Many of the pharaohs had the nose, others did not. Some servants did, some did not. One of the best of these is one of a woman servant with offerings, in the Egyptian Museum, dating from about 1900BC who sports a classic one. Chefren (of the Pyramid) had one, his son or nephew? Mykerinus in the Boston Museum did not. The statue of Seti 1 in the British Museum mirrors exactly the pronounced nose on the

131

mummy in the Cairo Museum. The mummy of Rameses 11 most certainly shows one. Queen Nefertiti also had one but Tutankhamen did not. The last of the Egyptian monarchs to obviously have one was Cleopatra around 50BC. There is a painting in the tomb of Menena, c1395BC, showing agricultural workers and here some have the nose, others did not.

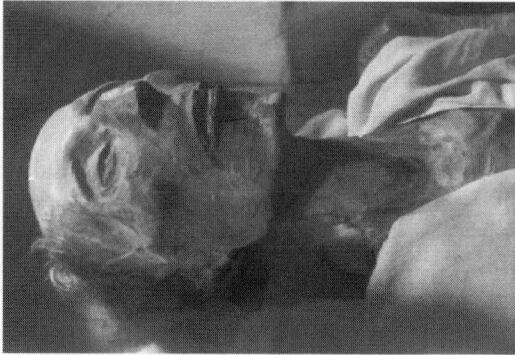

Ramesses 11. It was from a similar mummy of Seti 1 that the idea came.

Away from Egypt, Alexander the Great had a very pronounced one as did the Emperor Augustus of Rome. In more

Isambard Kingdom Brunel

modern times prominent possessors have included Leonardo da Vinci, Napoleon Bonaparte, the Duke of Wellington, Isambard

Kingdom Brunel, J M W Turner, Bernard Berenson [the art historian] and de Gaulle. In the later era, Elvis Presley, the French racing driver Alain Prost and the Australian Daniel Ricciardo, Nicholas Sarkozy and the Welsh rugby international, Jonathon Davies are typical members of what must be a very select club indeed. The actor Tom Cruise has a classic example. Another possessor was Britain's tallest ever man, William Bradley who lived for 33 years in the eighteenth century. He stood 7ft 9inch and came from a family of normal sized people. He had a sister who died at 16 but who was his size. The only American President who appeared to

J.M.W Turner from a contemporary drawing.

be similarly endowed was Thomas Jefferson. At the moment this is only a theory. A logical one yes, but still a theory nonetheless. It needs a DNA analysis to confirm one way or the other.

Some time after I had written the above I was reading the autobiography of the painter, Augustus John. His was a Bohemian lifestyle mixing with an eclectic group of peoples, pre-the First World War, amongst whom were various tribes of Romany Gypsy. They seldom bred outside the clans and so must be considered to have a relatively pure, if incestuous, blood line. They always claimed that they were the direct descendents of the Pharaohs, the reasons given being their prominent facial features.

That is where I would begin with my DNA analysis.

A bust of a 'Priest King' in the Karachi museum, Pakistan taken from Mohenjo Daro. Note once again the straight nose.

But, having said that, just as the book was going to print in August, 2008, a small piece appeared in an English paper about an excavation of a pyramid in Peru where the archaeologists found a rare pre-Inca mummy. It is of the Wari people who were there much earlier. The most significant fact as far as I am concerned is that it included a face mask of a young woman who displays a very

prominent hooked nose, very similar to those on the Egyptians that I have mentioned in this book. Also she was trussed in exactly the same way as the skeletons found in France. Two coincidences? Hmm. Obviously much further research must be done before any conclusions can be arrived at but we must now wait and see what develops.

Other examples of the distinctive nose appear on carvings and paintings throughout Mesoamerica. Zacharia Sitchin remarks on it when describing an obvious one in Mexico that is dated around 1,500BC. But not everyone boasted the feature. On the Gulf coast of Mexico, in what is now Tabasco province, are a series of 17 huge carvings of heads in basalt. They are again dated around the same period, they weigh in at around the 6 – 25 ton region with the only obvious supply of the rock being some sixty miles away across mountains, ravines and dense jungle but, as the picture shows, they most certainly do not boast a Semitic nose. These carvings are in fact of sub-Saharan Africans. In Mexico during the 2nd millennium BC????

29

THE STARS

Like so many others since time began, I have been fascinated by the stars. On a clear night I can look up at both infinity and eternity at the same time. Unfortunately these days, light pollution virtually everywhere on dry land in the civilized world, precludes seeing all but the brightest lights in our sky but, even so, we can see enough to tempt further research. It is quite something to see the light from some of those distant stars so very far away, knowing that the light we see today began its travels before the dinosaurs set foot on this planet. Some even going back to the days of that first amoeba.

Studying the stars is a long established profession in its own right whilst, before the days of the chronometer, sailors relied on them for much of their navigation. But the scientific study of the stars, I would submit, must be extremely difficult without a telescope, pencil, paper, knowledge of and access to, mathematics at all levels, the same for the poles and a zero longitude as reference, a compass, an accurate clock and some method of measuring and recording inclination. All things we take for granted today. And the certain knowledge that the earth was a sphere that rotated on its own axis, and preferably with the thought that it revolved around the sun rather than the opposite being the case. If you were convinced that it was flat then no astronomical observation could possibly make any sense at all.

But it was not always so. If we accept without question the accepted chronology of academia then it was many years after the beginning of the 1st Dynasty before we achieved all this. Not even the Romans had the valuable number zero in their range. Imagine dividing 306 by 42 using Roman numerals and you will see what I mean. The compass came with iron, telescopes with Galileo, the idea that the earth revolved round the Sun, rather than the other way about, from Copernicus, clocks in the 16th century AD, advanced mathematics with Newton, with everything else in between. Longitude was only accurately measured following John Harrison's invention of the chronometer in the 18th century.

Now stars are very much alive and kicking as far as being moveable objects. We begin with our own moon going round the earth at very regular intervals but never on the identical orbit. The earth is spinning with a tangential speed at the equator of 1,000 miles per hour and, at the same time, it rotates around the sun. There is an extra minute rotation plus wobble at the poles that takes about 26,000 years to complete and this is precession.

Add to this that the brightest of our stars, our fellow planets, are also on an orbit of the sun but at totally different times and distances. And everything is slowly moving relative to each other. So when you gaze up into the sky, all these things must be taken into consideration. If you are doing serious research then you can only study one tiny part at once, writing down what you see, since an hour later all will change and you must start again.

And here is my problem. Without the basic equipment listed above, especially pencil and paper – by the time you drew your hieroglyph it would be daylight – and a numerical system that allowed quick reference, I just do not see how both the Egyptians and the Mayans were able to do any calculations at all. Forget the Mayans for the moment and let us, as before, just consider Egypt. For a very long time the Egyptians thought that the world was flat with the sun travelling through the underworld back to the east each night. Even the seamen with Columbus thought that they were going to fall off the edge. Galileo was held under house arrest during his final years by the Inquisition for even suggesting that the world may be round, and that Copernicus was correct. They would be totally ignorant of the magnetic field and therefore the existence of the two poles leaving any astronomic calculations impossible.

I would contend that making any sense at all from this ever changing scene would have been nigh on impossible without the knowledge, and understanding, that the one body most in motion relative to everything else was, in fact, the very ground on which we stood. They would have had to rely entirely on what could be seen with the naked eye and, to get any meaningful observations, would have needed to position the stars at exactly the same time each evening. From this they could plot the movement across the skies, deducing what they could from the result. But to do this they would have needed that accurate clock, the permanent reference point like the north or south poles, the method of measuring inclination, accurately calibrated plus, most of all, somewhere or something with which to easily record it all. But they had none of this. Not one single thing, yet they were supposed to have been aware of precession! Even today, with all the computer guided telescopes and every technical aid you can muster, if you were unaware of the existence of precession, it would be more than a million to one chance of stumbling on some anomaly that may point you in the right direction. And then to work out exactly what was happening, and that it would take 25,920 years to complete the cycle, if you had no mathematical knowledge, I feel is stretching credulity to the absolute limit.

It is here that I have a problem with the Sphinx. Thinking amongst many scholars is that he is facing due east as it would have been at the very end of the Age of Leo some 12,500 years ago even though he was not supposed to be carved out until the time of the pyramids. The evidence for this being that at that time, during the summer solstice, it would have been the last time that the constellation of Leo was on the horizon at dawn. Fine, but was it on the horizon at dawn in the west or the east? I ask this simple question because if it was to the east then no one could see it with the naked eye. When you think of it, it is obvious why. I lived with a clear view over the sea to the horizon in the east and one morning, it being clear and the day of the equinox, I got up early to watch the sunrise. You could still see the stars at 5am when it was pitch dark but twenty minutes later the first light of dawn appeared in the east at which point only stars in the west were visible. By 6am I could see no stars at all, certainly not in the well lit east and just before 7am when the first rays of the sun appeared there was not a star to be seen. In those two hours the earth had rotated by 30 degrees by which time constellations invisible at night would have come into the field of vision, except that now they could not be seen because of the sun light. So who could identify the constellation of Leo, against a rising sun, which the Sphinx is supposed to be facing?

To understand this in layman's terms i.e., mine, it is obvious when you apply some logic. At night half the earth is in the Sun's shadow and its rays are very much behind us. Then we can see clearly through the Earth's atmosphere at the stars beyond. They appear to 'twinkle' because their light is travelling through our atmosphere. As dawn approaches, the Earth has rotated enough, so that the upper reaches of the atmosphere catch the Sun's rays first and reflect it down towards sea level. The moment this happens it becomes impossible to see through the atmosphere to those stars. As the Earth continues its rotation more and more sky is illuminated until the Sun itself emerges. During this period it is difficult to clearly see a Full Moon. The time from first light to full dawn is at least an hour and, sometimes a lot more, depending on your degree of latitude where the observation is taking place. But wherever you are the stars vanish from view, first on the eastern horizon, making the sighting with the naked eye of any stars or constellations just over the horizon impossible. Impossible then, impossible now, with the naked eye. If your horizon is over land then by the time you see the first light of the sun it will have illuminated all the sky to the east. I know this because I have enjoyed 20/20 long term vision for most of my life. I still do not need glasses to drive.

We now know all about it because we have access to advanced mathematics, high powered computers and enormous telescopes but those who carved out the massive structure did not. Or did they? If they did not, then I would say that it could be just a simple coincidence that the Sphinx lies where he does in that position, and that it is all subsequent scholarship, based on present knowledge, which has enabled those concerned to make yet another 'mighty bound' with their deductions. It is my contention that it could not have been set up like that deliberately without advanced knowledge of both mathematics and astronomy, something impossible for Darwinian Stone Age man. Without outside help.

As before with the pyramids, it must be remembered that once they mastered the hieroglyphs and could chop out their little cartouches, there was no holding them. They were at it everywhere. Pictures of them grinding corn, bathing, cooking, bashing in the head of a smaller opponent, grovelling to the pharaoh [there is even one I saw that appeared to be an old man groping a small girl's bottom !] but not one of them dragging a large stone nor gazing at the stars.

Astronomy and astrology should never be confused. I have no problem with astrologers identifying and then putting a name to various constellations such as the Great Bear, Leo, Orion, the Plough, Gemini, Aquarius, Cancer and so on. Or coming up with the names of 'Age of Aquarius' and similar ones. I have no problem of ancient man doing the same either. I could imagine them watching in awe as these vast constellations, obviously even to them, many miles away, slowly making their way across the skies each night. Moving, as they do, relative to other stars. To them it would be the constellations and stars that appeared to be moving relative to a stationery earth, rather than the opposite which is correct. Somehow they had come to the right deduction about the known planets [was this handed down from their extra terrestrial ancestors?] and so would see one night Venus passing Orion. A month later and it would be passing, either faster or slower, another constellation, depending on the relative distances from the earth. And from these simple observations made over a great many years, some method of prophecy was deduced, to be handed down through the generations and still be avidly consulted today. One thought here. Looking up at the night sky with the naked eye, the other planets appear to be merely bright stars. Who, and when, was someone able, again without instruments, to decide that they were inert satellites of the sun whilst still thinking that the earth was a flat plate?

Without that one absolutely essential tool – the ability to write down and accurately record – those people could never have been the great astronomers that they are supposed to have been. They could not have calculated the length of the year, accurately down to several decimal places, simultaneously in Egypt and Mexico, without some outside help and intellect. We must not forget that the blood line from the first Nephilim, those who successfully bred with the indigenous population, would now be getting thin in both Egypt and the Americas. Their descendents, now at least 100 generations on, were making their way north as the Minoans, Greeks and then Romans, leaving in Egypt an

140

incestuous monarchy leading a still backward workforce. And only with a scattering of the more intelligent people left to actually govern. No, you must go back several thousand years to the first of those early colonizers to find the real astronomers. They had to be good if they were ever going to find their own host planet again, and then get back here in one piece. Doesn't Enoch say *'Barkayal taught the observers of stars'?*

Sorry, but another piece of sacred folk law dashed by the use of simple logic.

30

THE BIBLICAL FLOOD

When de Lesseps got to the final cut on the Suez Canal he was very worried. He was in doubt whether or not the levels of the sea in the Indian Ocean would be the same as in the Mediterranean because, if not, rather than a sedate canal, he would have a fast running river on his hands. He had no means in 1869 of measuring the relative sea levels over even a quite short distance. As it turned out his fears were groundless. The Red Sea is only a few inches higher, a variation negligible in the context of tidal flows. This means that the sea, all the way round the enormous African land mass, is obeying one of the absolute basic rules of physics in that liquids will always find their own level. As we saw earlier, the same holds good for the Panama Canal with the level of the Pacific being the same as in the Atlantic, again only the tidal surges being the difference.

From this I think it is safe to assume that anything introduced to raise or lower the sea level at point [a] will have an eventual equal effect at points [b] right down to [z] across the globe. This is what happened when the ice in the north began to melt from its peak in 20,000 BC. From then over the next 12,000 years it gradually melted into the sea which then rose by, or so we are told, 100 metres which is 325ft. The land bridges between Britain, the Continent and Ireland were immersed, the conifer forest on the Dogger Bank went as did the bridges blocking the Bering Sea and the New Guinea/Australia land mass. This left us with more or less what we have today.

Let us consider the topography of 20,000BC in the Mediterranean. The Nile will have been at more or less the level it is today except that in all probability the delta, if any, would have been small. The sea level drops quickly off the North African coast and so, rather than its slow meander of today, it would have been a fast flowing river that tumbled into the sea. This would make navigation on the river difficult towards the mouth, rendering a journey to sea nigh on impossible. As the sea level rose, the low lying land was submerged and river flow slowed down until sea and river were more or less at the same level. And, of course, this was happening simultaneously across the globe.

By 6 – 5,000BC, when the Nephilim [but not necessarily the first Nephilim] were busy with their colonization, sea levels were steady, so where, into all of this, do we fit the floods? Especially the one for which Noah is supposed to have built his Ark? Looking at the chronology for the time, it is difficult to place Noah later than 2,700BC or much earlier than 3,000BC and so it is during this time that he had his flood. And when Egypt was supposed to be building its pyramids. Sitchin thinks that it was somewhat earlier at around 11,000BC. We also have handed down the mythological flood on Haiti, the one that is supposed to have devastated California whilst most of the myths of Central and South America – even at the top of the Andes – all describe one massive flood. There is supposed to have been a meteorite landing in the sea off the coast of Mexico around 11,500BC and that would have created havoc in the Caribbean. But only in the Caribbean. It would not have sent Tsunamis across the Atlantic. One of these in the Atlantic would have devastated the American Eastern Seaboard as well as Portugal, France, Spain and Morocco, but would have petered out as it expanded after going through the Straights of Gibraltar. It certainly will not have been felt in California. Nor, under any circumstances would it have been noticed in the Middle East. The meteorite would have had to land in the Pacific to affect the west coast of America and the Indian Ocean for Sumeria. But tsunamis come and tsunamis go. Once that massive tidal wave has been stopped by dry land, it loses all its momentum. It floods to a depth of 20 to 30ft before immediately returning back to the sea and that is it. Whilst they can create huge tidal waves, they eventually peter out over a distance which is why I was astonished to read one explanation for the flood being an ice flow in the Antarctic falling into the sea and flooding the Mediterranean. And that was in a serious published account!!! Sitchin also believes that this is what happened but he feels that it covered the whole of Iraq right up to Mount Ararat in Armenia. That, I'm afraid is a scientific impossibility. A tidal wave so big would have also devastated much of India, the Indus valley, the Persian Gulf, all of East Africa and much of Australia. There is no written or anecdotal evidence of which I am aware of this happening. No, there was no Antarctic conceived tsunami of that magnitude.

Which leaves us with the problem of how we are supposed to have had selective – or even general – flooding that could drown everybody. If there was one that inundated California – from the sea – then surely the Pacific must have risen in depth by another 100 ft or so. And with water doing what it does, the rest of the world's oceans must have been the same. But they were not. So California's flood must have come from the land. Rapidly melting snows in the Sierra Nevada, accompanied by heavy rains, strong westerly winds and high spring tides could easily engulf the Nappa Valley and other flat, low lying parts. Similar floods can be seen in Europe, the Mississippi and Missouri valleys, the Yangtze in China and regularly in the UK. I cannot see how it can be any other way.

Whether the floods in the Caribbean islands and the rest of the Americas can be explained away so simply, I do not know. It must have been the same for Noah's flood. We can easily account for the rising of the sea level from 16,000 BC onwards by simply working out how much ice there was on land and how much water it would produce when melted. But where did the water come from for Noah? More to the point, where did it go afterwards? If he ended up stranded high on Mount Ararat in Turkey then surely over the period of time he was both building and using the Ark, the sea would have levelled out to this depth. Had it done so then the Nile Valley right up to the Ugandan border would have been under water. Everything drowned or washed away. The sea at the new level would then have swamped everything low lying including the Amazon basin for 2,000 miles inland and hundreds of miles wide. Most of America up to the Rockies would have gone too. An enormous amount of water – far more than from the melting ice – that came, stayed a little, then went away.

This book has revealed some amazing things but this is going too far. Another law of physics is that matter can be neither created nor destroyed in any chemical reaction. What you go in with, whatever you do with it, you come out with the same. There is no difference with water. It begins in the sea which evaporates with the wind and the sun. This makes clouds. Clouds fly over mountains and release the moisture as either rain or snow. The snow melts and joins the rainfall in rivers which flow back out to sea in a never ending eternal cycle. If it remains as a glacier then sea levels fall. When the glacier melts they rise again. There is as much water on earth now as there was at the time of the first amoeba. Only glaciations change the sea levels. It is to this fact that we must look for explanation for the flood questions.

Floods from the sea can only come from tsunamis caused by natural adjustments to the earth or dramatic changes in the weather. Like volcanoes at sea, earthquakes, foreign bodies arriving from space [bear in mind that over 100 tons of space debris hits the earth every single day and always has done] plus tidal surges caused by high tides and storms. Hurricanes and Typhoons do the same. They will devastate a small area of coast for a time but will then quickly return to normal. Noah's flood was not like that. It certainly did not affect Egypt otherwise you would have found them hammering out their cartouches to commemorate the event. There is no contemporary picture of anyone building a massive boat anywhere in the Middle East. No, they didn't even know it was happening and it is not mentioned in the long timeline of the country. Could you have a massive flood in Turkey or Mesopotamia that didn't affect Egypt?? Could you flood Mt Ararat without drowning Sumeria?

I think we must look inland for our explanation of this. Mt Ararat is situated in the far east of Anatolia, modern day Turkey, in an extremely mountainous and barren region near the borders with Iran and Armenia. The Armenian Tourist Board advertises the country as being 'The Land of Noah'. Mt Ararat is 16,695 ft high, which is well over the highest in the Alps, and is nearly 800 miles as the crow flies from Jerusalem. Significant rivers nearby are the Tigris and Euphrates which go on to flow through old Mesopotamia, now modern Iraq. But they are well to the south and away from any possible watershed from the mountain. Due west is a lake, out of which flows a river that skirts the mountain, and drains into the larger Lake Urmia to the south. To the South East is another small lake out of which is another river which flows north around the east side of the mountain, then through Azerbaijan and

Georgia, into the Caspian Sea. The flood lasted 150 days and was 15 cubits – about 26 ft - deep. Hardly deep enough to, as Genesis says, cover the tops of the mountains. It does say that it rained for forty days and forty nights and, even though the area is quite arid, I can believe that. But a major factor with arid places is that they do not have any vegetation, no top soil nor trees and therefore this type of torrential rain will cause landslides, sometimes washing away entire mountain sides. And this is what I think _could_ have happened. That is if it happened at all and, more to the point, happened in that part of the world. As I say, we are talking about a place that is 800 miles from all the action in a very high and inhospitable area where few people live today. To me it is inconceivable that Noah and his family would uproot from Canaan, make their way across the Syrian desert towards a hostile area, devoid of vegetation or cattle, and then settle long enough on the barren wastelands around Ararat to build a massive ship, to save a non-existent animal kingdom, from a catastrophic flood.

Be that as it may, if it did happen and it happened just there, this is what could have happened. I think that there may have been a land slide blocking either one of the rivers. This would have created a massive natural dam behind which the waters would build up. Depending on the topography above the dam, a substantial lake would form, flooding and drowning everything that lived there. Then Noah would sail across his lake for 150 days. Eventually the waters would evaporate and seep through the blockage, even washing it away, as the river gradually returned to normal, leaving Noah and his boat abandoned on the side of a mountain. We must remember that the landslide could be a long way down the valley, possibly far away in an inaccessible part, of which Noah would have no knowledge. He will have begun building his Ark when he got word of the waters gradually creeping back up the valley. To him it would appear that the entire world, from what he could see, was slowly being drowned in these rising waters. Then, 150 days later the pressure became too much, the dam burst and things returned to normal, leaving him wondering why he bothered.

This theory does, however, demand answers to the following questions to which, at the moment, I am unable to even offer a guess.

1. Why were Noah and his family so far away from home in the Holy Land and based in this wild and inhospitable place? If all his family were with him then we must assume that he lived there. Is this where the rest of the Hebrews came from rather than Canaan? If it turned out that the Hebrews did in fact originate from Armenia and the Caucuses, their claim to Palestine as their own 'Promised Land' is somewhat compromised.

2. Who knew in advance – a long time in advance – that there was going to be a flood to be able to warn Noah?

3. Where, like Moses with the Ark of the Covenant in the desert, was Noah able to get enough Gopher Wood, in an area with no trees, to build a 525ft long ship? [So far no one has been able to identify Gopher Wood but it is assumed to be Acacia]. All timbers would have to be planed flat for the shell and steamed into shape for the ribs. Remember again that we are well away from having Bronze and iron, yet we are able to build a boat, in the wilderness, bigger than any attempted in civilization, with no tools, no timbers, no fixings and, most of all, hardly any labour. No, he did not build on the coast and simply float inland. To do this the seas would have had to rise at least 10 – 12,000 thousand feet, and that would certainly have engulfed an enormous area including the whole of Egypt, most of Greece, Crete and large swathes of Northern Europe including the entire British Isles. That, of course, did not happen and so he could not have started at sea level.

4. To put the size of this vessel into context, it was considerably bigger than any World War 11 destroyer, being about the same size as an average cruiser then, or a medium sized cruise ship today. In fact, if she was actually built at all, she would have been the biggest ship ever built right up until Brunel built the Great Eastern in the mid 19th century. She would have displaced about

3,500 tons of water yet she was supposed to be built only by Noah and his sons!!!!

5. Where did he get enough food to feed all the animals for 150 days? How did he stop them eating each other? Who cleaned them out each day?

6. Where did the animals come from in such a desolate area?

The other answer could just be that this is another 'Mighty Bound' story put about to show how angry God was with mankind.

It is my contention that the continual references to the 'world flood' in other books are much exaggerated. That is for the simple reason that they would have needed billions, if not trillions, of gallons of water, which would be still with us today. There is nowhere else for it to have gone. Rain and land generated floods? Yes. Floods caused by an extended increase in sea level and then returning back to the 'status quo' are physically impossible.

So let us go back to the meteorite of 11,500BC, a date that sits comfortably within Sitchin's timeframe, give everyone the benefit of the doubt, and agree that it landed with an almighty splash in the Gulf of Mexico, off the Mexican coast. My first observation which most seemed to have overlooked, is that in 11,500BC we were still very much in the Ice Age with significant quantities still to melt. Since the total rise in sea level was around 325 ft, by this time there would still be at least 100 ft to go. In simple terms, sea levels were still 100 ft below what they are today. Let us agree on that. Next, at that time throughout the world everyone was still in the Stone Age. We are many thousands of years away from the first farming and the first permanent settlements. Any boats built then would be little better than a crude coracle or canoe made from a hollowed out tree trunk, certainly nothing that could cross a sea, never mind an ocean. Again we are a long time before the supposed Polynesian exodus across the Pacific. No one in their right mind would have put to sea in the face of a tidal wave – had they known one was coming.

But there would have been groups living near the water's edge who would have felt the full force of the wave. And only a wave it would be. Tsunamis live in the clear ocean. They need a great depth to give them the volume, after which they need the space to gather momentum, so doing their damage on hitting land. This is not available in the Caribbean.

Let us go through the scenario of that meteorite landing plum in the middle of the Gulf of Mexico. Immediately there would be a leading tidal wave setting off in all directions, those going north, west and south west would soon hit dry land, killing everything on the shore line. But only on the shore line. Even if the hinterland was dead flat, it would run out of steam in a few hundred yards. Those going east and south east would gain momentum before hitting, first the Caymans [a lot bigger than they are now], and then Jamaica. Those going slightly north east would hit Cuba and Hispaniola, the leading edge of which is Haiti, which would explain why they got a flood but others did not. By this time our tidal wave will have lost much of its power, so that when it got to the Florida Keyes and then the islands of the Antilles, it will have been a spent force. Any power left would have been dissipated by the Bahamas so that, by the time it met the Atlantic, there would be nothing there. The same meteorite landing in the Atlantic would have sent a Tsunami across to Europe and Africa.

Once again, if you doubt this, you can find out for yourself with a fun experiment with the kids. Find a rocky river in which there will be many big deep holes and many shallow ones. In a shallow one arrange some big stones to protrude like islands. Then find two other big stones of about the same weight. Toss one into the middle of a deep pond and measure how far the leading ripple spreads. Now toss the other one into the shallow pool and see the difference. It is only a matter of scale, the principal is the same.

I hope that this shows in a simplistic but accurate way, that there was not, and never could have been, a universal catastrophic flood anytime between 11,500BC and 2,500BC for Noah. A minor disturbance, yes. This same meteorite would have sent its debris skywards blotting everything out for a brief time and its ash would be uniformly spread across the world – which it is. But it would not, and could not, have threatened to wipe out mankind and the entire animal kingdom. I feel that those who pin their works on a supposed massive catastrophe, should accept the irrefutable

149

evidence of geology, which tells us that the earth has never been still. The crust is wafer thin compared to the rest of the mass and this must contain forces beyond our imagination, all trying to burst out. The crust is made up of disjointed plates that are permanently rubbing together or trying to ride up over the next one. The continents, whilst now fairly stable in our terms, are still geologically on the move; some of our coast lines are still rising, others are falling into the sea. All is happening naturally and is way beyond the control of man. We can only stand and watch.

There always have been catastrophic shifts in the crust which is why we have mountains; there have always been earthquakes sending tsunamis across the world, as there have always been massive volcanoes sending their ash into the stratosphere. There always will be in the future. There was no major catastrophe around 11,500BC, no universal flood at all. Merely a big pebble in a big pond.

I had put the above to bed with just a few additions to my 2006 thoughts when I came across, in February 2016, the name of Robert Solarion. He hailed from Texas and died in 2011. He had some interesting, to say the least, ideas on the subject.

He discusses the 'Velikovsky Affair' where Dr Immanuel Velikovsky of Princeton University in America, one of the Ivy League campuses, put out a theory about the Earth shifting its axis suddenly by around 30 degrees.. Not in ancient geological time, where the occurrence is not in doubt, but comparatively recently. It was vigorously denied by competing academics from Cornell and Harvard. No change there then! His date is 1587BC when the North Pole moved from mid-Atlantic to its present position with the South Pole moving from Southern Australia at the same time. Just how could it have happened at that time?

So how did this happen, if indeed it did, in such comparatively recent times? Most academics agree that such a shift could only be made by a 'near miss' by a passing huge comet or asteroid causing the huge quantity of water on the surface of our planet plus the molten inner cores to surge due to gravitational forces. The moon does this causing our tides. Apparently there are over 1000 records of a mythical flood at that time and, to a certain extent, that could be the explanation. Would it flood the plains of Mesopotamia right up to Mount Ararat? I don't know. Anyway it could be the answer with the reservation that it must also deluge northern Europe, including the UK as well, but of that there is no mythical, archaeological or anecdotal evidence at all. So it must have only affected the Indian and Pacific Oceans. Possible, but doubtful in my mind. It does, however, leave our previous Great Circle line as now being the Equator.

Robert Solarion's drawings on a large globe showing how Giza was the only place, plus its antipodal equivalent, that remained at the same relative latitude and longitudes when shifting the position of the Poles.

But Solarion goes further by saying that it was not a comet at all but actually the rogue and missing planet Nibiru on its orbital axis attempting to attach itself by electro-magnetic beams to our North Pole.

He enters the Velikovsy debate by agreeing with the argument in '*The Earth Upheaval*' that the Great Pyramid was built and set out in its mathematical precision so that it remained at the exact position of 31 degrees east and 60 degrees south of the North Pole. Its antipodal equivalent in the Pacific does the same. Those are the only places on earth where this happens. As proof he cites that either the corners or the sides of the Great Pyramid always face one or other of the poles.

In June 1999 there was a 'Catastrophist Conference' in The University of Bergamo, Italy where Flavio Barbiero of Capodimonte said that since the earth contained so much water and was the only planet so to do, an exterior flying object would have a cataclysmic effect causing the world's oceans to flood across the globe. I cannot argue with that. He adds that it would cause the poles to shift but with that I cannot comment because I don't know. Alexander Tollman of the University of Vienna thought that it happened much earlier, around 9,500BCE which is more realistic. Mark Bailey of Queen's University in Belfast said that carbon dating of tree rings in Ireland showed Ice in Oak in 3195BC, 2345BC, 1159BC, 207BC and 540AD meaning that at those times there were 'mini' Ice Ages but no evidence of a flood in the area at any time.

A thought on this theme going back to the section on maps. Many show Antarctica in some detail free of ice and the whole of the Americas but, as I commented, they fall short when drawing the British Isles and Scandinavia. None show any sign of Australia which is strange. Then, and now, Australia was a large land mass that would be difficult to miss if looking from above. Could in fact those maps have been drawn when the poles were in the positions Solarion suggests when it would have been the Antipodes and North West Europe under ice and Antarctica free? From this it means that the Ice Age was so because the areas affected were then much nearer the pole. If you study the areas covered with ice during the period and, more to the point, those that were not, this does make a great deal of sense. It would answer why northern Britain was covered in ice but that the Straights of Dover were a sea way. I don't know whether this is feasible but throw in the thought. As this edition goes to press comes the reports from various academic sources that the Dark Planet, or 'Planet X' has been indentified, in our solar system and that it orbits the Sun every 22,000 years. During this orbit at one stage it gets uncomfortably close to us and is due to do so again in 2017. They think that at some stage it came so close as to create the conditions that caused the last two mass extinctions. This could confirm much of what has been described in this book but, if Solarion is correct, we must be ready for one very big tsunami in the not too distant future. If you are reading this after 2018 you will know whether or not it has happened. It is not my theory, me being a simple 'amateur', it is one put out by academic experts.

A further theory put forward by Solarion is that Nibiru actually came to us from none other than the orbit of Sirius which is all of 8.5 light years away. That is a very long distance. Sitchin was amongst those grasping at that idea. It came to us across outer space, complete with inhabitants, orbited our planet and then went off again on its distant journey. Do I buy that one? No I do not.

Think of when we were young and got our first roller skates. We wobbled along and then grabbed the nearest lamp post to stop, nearly wrenching our arm out in the process. Nibiru is on the skates and we are its lamp post. Travelling at the speed of light, since I would have thought that the idea of tele-porting an entire planet, a step too far into science fiction, it would be going at an incredible speed when it got here after those 8.5 years. Light travels at 633.6 million miles per hour which is an incredible speed indeed. Again think of our lamp post. We are it and have granny walking by at around three miles per hour when along comes someone on roller skates at hundreds of miles per hour who puts out his arm and is halted by the post. That, I would suggest, may cause a lot of damage all round. In fact it is a physical impossibility. Anything going at that speed would pass us in seconds with no time for any tidal surge to even begin. If going slower the years mount up making it totally unrealistic to think that anything could live as creatures, rather than deep frozen bugs, in outer space for any length of time at all.

No, I do not accept that at all. I think that a passing asteroid could have caused a tidal surge and that it is a better idea of one landing in either the Caribbean Sea or Indian Ocean. Only time will tell who gets it right. The other point against this is to ask how and why it chose our north pole to act as its lamp post? With bigger planets out there and our sun, surely there were better targets? If it did as suggested, after such a journey through space it would have been attracted to the sun, and only the sun, rather than just one part of one of the minor planets.

31

THE SECOND COMING – BEFORE OR AFTER ARMAGEDDON?

Before we come to the end of this work, we must consider the prospect of a Second Coming of Jesus Christ [already alluded to], plus a second coming in the world of Islam. Here the big questions are 'When', 'Where' and in what form could this happen to have any effect on such a self centred and materialistic world.

First we must ascertain what is needed, as perhaps those Divine beings did, two thousand years ago. Their idea of not one, but two, humble, peace preaching people deposited into the centre of the world's troubles may have been right at the time, but history has proved beyond doubt that it did not work. Would one or two such beings introduced to us in the early twenty first century have any effect at all? Let us see.

Looking at the great leaders, then the great men, of the last century, this is what you get. Like it or not, the greatest leaders of men in the twentieth century were also some of the most evil. Adolf Hitler stands supreme as the man who could get things done. In the short time of just six years he transformed a bankrupt and desolate Germany into an industrial giant capable of taking on the world. And, looking at the films of the time, there is little doubt that the German people were almost 100% behind him. Compare that to the achievements of Blair and Bush, Cameron and Obama or other groups of politicians over a similar period of time seventy years later. Of course the down side is well known now and history will forget the good bits, only remembering the appalling cruelty of the war, the slavery and the Holocaust. Nevertheless, he was an outstanding leader.

Mao Tze Tung was another. His long march through China beginning well before the Second World War, was another triumph of leadership, leading to the overthrow of Chiang Kai Tsheck and the forming of the Communist state out of yet another desolate and backward country. Again it was to end in tears.

In Russia it was the same. A country still basking in the feudal middle ages when along comes Lenin who overthrows a tyrannical Royalist Regime with an even worse communist one. [It was actually Kerensky who did the overthrowing, Lenin set up the communists. He then died leaving the evil Stalin a free hand.] I don't put him in the same league as Hitler or Mao however. Russia was a time bomb waiting to explode. Lenin and his cohorts just happened to be in the right place at the right time.

Who else? Churchill was the man of the hour who inspired the British people as no one else at the time, nor since, has done. But he was voted out as soon as hostilities ended. Thatcher was fortunate to have a minor war thrust upon her enabling her to mount the incredible invasion of the Falklands from so far away. She also achieved something that no one else has since achieved, and that is a decisive and clear cut victory, leaving no loose ends at all. She had the guts to take on the unions but never could be described as a great leader of men. No post WW2 European politician from any country has shown the remotest ability to become a great leader.

In America, most Presidents have been isolationists, only fighting when forced to do so. Even Roosevelt had to wait until Pearl Harbour before entering the Second World War. Unlike the likes of Bush Jnr whose 'gung ho' approach could eventually have catastrophic consequences for the world as a whole, for Europe in particular. I think that Kennedy would have been up there with Lincoln as one of the very great Presidents had he lived, but that we will never know. His nerve and restraint, against all advice at the time of the Cuban missile crisis, plus his determination to end segregation puts him right at the top

All these great leaders of men have the one thing in common. They led in time of war – some of their own making. But what of the others?

Nelson Mandela must be near the top. When he came out of Robin Island he could so easily have precipitated a blood bath across Africa. But he didn't. He preached a peaceful and forgiving message that resulted in the safe transfer of power in South Africa. Only a truly great man could have achieved this. I count the Dalai Lama in this group for his persistent opposition to Beijing, and Ghandi for his passive resistance that freed India from the British rule. Martin Luther King was a very brave Christian leader but sadly I can think of no other leader of any of the great religions, certainly no Pope or Anglican Archbishop, who could possibly be described as a very Great Person.

Of course, most of the greatest people of the last century were the writers, engineers, scientists, architects, medical researchers and electronic geniuses amongst many others, who made their contribution but, here we are only looking to who can make an impact politically on the entire world. In fact, who can the greater powers that be, send this time to save mankind from a hideous Armageddon?

Let us be in no doubt that with all the sabre rattling going on, this is going to happen. And it could happen in the not too distant a future. And that answers our first question of 'When'. As soon as possible is the only answer. 'Where' is the difficult one? Obviously he, or she, must be in a position of enormous influence throughout the world which rather limits things. It may not be in Russia since that country is still recovering from its 70 year stint as a communist regime but, as this second edition is being penned in 2016 that country has risen again due to a ruthless but strong leader. China is more interested in economic development now, its Imperialistic ambitions being restricted to hanging on to what it's got. I can see no leader of any party in the UK with charisma or ability for the job nor do I see it being a European leader of any nationality. In Europe there is no single elected leader over all member states. Having said that the European Union has meant that now for sixty years and as far into the future as we care to look, we have had no Western European war. This, for the first time since the end of the Ice Age, and surely this must point the way to a successful future.

Looking at the trouble spots of the world as this book is being written [2016] we see that they all have the one thing in common. Someone wants to be in charge of their own affairs and someone else is saying 'no'. In each case one person's terrorist is someone else's freedom fighter. Just supposing we had a leader who could persuade Israel to sacrifice those West Bank settlements in Arab lands and then come to a settlement with Syria, Jordan, Lebanon and Egypt. And at the same time, supposing we had an Arab leader, respected by all Islam, who could unite Islam into its original, peaceful and benign form? Stop Sunni killing Shiite, and vice versa, just because they have a slightly different idea of the Koran. And give up the idea of brutal, medieval caliphates across the world whose sole objects are to suppress women and kill non-believers. What would be the consequences of Spain granting a homeland for the Basques, Sri Lanka the same for the Tamils and the two Koreas to unite as one powerful nation as they surely must someday?

And, of course, the Western powers to totally withdraw from the Middle East and leave Islam to sort out its own affairs in peace. Persuading the oil rich Gulf States to share their wealth with the rest of its peoples, across the entire region, instead of keeping it all for just a very small minority. And then for the militant minority of terrorists to accept that others have a right to live, and so abandon their weapons forever. For Islam to accept that the Western world is basically either Christian or secular and would prefer to stay that way. Muslims seeking to live in that world would then accept the status quo rather than trying to inflict their own medieval and barbarous rules on the rest of the population. Or leave and return to the Islamic paradises of their ancestors.

All this leads up to the only two alternatives. One is that the second coming in the world of Islam must be both powerful and persuasive but, most of all, be in a position to get things done. The one and only way to do this is to be in charge. To be President of Iran, Saudi Arabia or Egypt. Someone who can and will make things happen. More to the point, want to as well.

And for Christ's second coming it has to be the same. He must be a leader, with influence, of one of the great countries of the

158

west. The only ones with sufficient stature are France, Germany [in 2016], the United Kingdom and the United States. Or possibly even a very strong willed Secretary General of the United Nations, but that, I feel is a long shot. The only nation with sufficient clout is the United States, and it is only from the White House that any person, whether secular or divine, can wield enough worldwide influence to put a stop to the present headlong rush to our universal demise. It most certainly will not be in Canterbury, Rome or Medina. And it should go without saying that all must be in power at the same time.

There must also be a moral crusade by all the world's religions to bring some sort of decency back to life. I am not talking here about Victorian ethics which merely swept everything under the carpet, but a simple return to the basic decencies for which the two great wars were fought. Respect for neighbours and their property, an acknowledgement of the difference between right and wrong, an end to the culture amongst the young to both carry and use knives, an end to the culture of teenage pregnancies that result in either a despicable abortion or a life time of misery and anguish all round. Happy marriage be the accepted norm but respect for those who wish to live their lives in a different way but, in turn, those so doing not to try to make their, and only their way of life to be seen as the 'norm'. And simple tolerance of those who may, in any way at all, be different. Make contraception an accepted part of life so cutting the enormous birth rate amongst peoples unable to feed their children. Only when people both want to, and are seen to, do the 'decent' thing as a matter of course, will we be on our way. We must end this materialistic obsession with having, from a very early age, to have the very latest electronic gadgets, cars, boats and houses, and sometimes just be thankful for what we have. Whether the drug culture can be halted without draconian penalties on those pushing them is a difficult one, but one that must be faced. One solvable problem by simple edict from Rome and the Eastern religions is to halt the massive rise in the Third World populations. Those countries cannot feed their peoples, but should the more responsible peoples in the west always be expected to step in to do so? And to keep on doing so, for ever?

There must be an equal end to the culture of ludicrous salaries and bonuses in the financial districts of the world. By cynical manipulation of everything from interest rates to share prices they can destroy the economies of nations and create instability across the globe. By reckless gambling of other people's money they can bring massive banks to their knees and misery to the masses. This goes on across the world and must be halted as being just as big a menace as all the others listed above.

Again, is this all farfetched and impossible? Not really. Both Christ and Mohammed were placed on this earth at a time in history, and in a form in history, and in a place in history where it was thought they could do some good. Their followers became great religions, something that could never happen again. If there is to be a second coming then the same criteria apply. Only this time the places must vary, as do the problems, and I very much doubt whether we will actually know that it has happened. There will be none of the advance publicity. No child will be born in a mountain hut that would then have the weight of the world's media on its shoulders for the rest of its life. It will be none of these things. This time whoever he/she/they are, they will just emerge as one of us, get on with the job, and then disappear on death back to whence they came. The very last thing they would want is publicity of any type. Certainly not who they really were since this would only hold them up to ridicule. Jesus Himself, when prophesying his Second Coming in Luke 18.8 asks *"Nevertheless when the Son of man cometh, shall he find faith on the earth?"* He anticipated the state of world morality and feelings, especially in the Christian church. He could see that making a difference with the Second Coming would need a totally different approach to the first time. And, if not how I describe it, then how else to make the massive difference required?

160

32
TAILPIECE

I call the period under consideration, which is from the colonization by the last Nephilim, if indeed they did colonize us, up to the fall of the Roman Empire, *THE BIBLICAL AGE OF WORLD ENLIGHTENMENT*. I do this because, during those 8,000 to 10,000 or so years, Homo sapiens escaped from its eternal and desperately slow Darwinian progress of evolution, now millions of years in progress, to become modern, civilized man. This is no more than a blink of the eye in terms of world evolution. This could never have happened by an accidental, random coincidence simultaneously across the globe, but then only in certain small areas. Leaving other parts and peoples to struggle on in their own little 'Stone Ages', even though history has since proved that a significant proportion of those 'Stone Age' peoples were equal in intelligence to any in the 'civilized' world.

Something happened between 8 and 25,000 years ago to halt evolution in its tracks and replace it with something else. Have we identified that?

Only a selective mixing with a more advanced culture could have been the catalyst for such a change, and I hope that this book has shown just how and when that actually *could* have happened. You have seen how the Bulge changes out of all proportion, from the one based on accepted chronology, and the real one showing the sudden worldwide spread of knowledge and technology. This is because in this version I consider **all** the *Ancient Monuments* as one item to be treated collectively rather than in isolation. As soon as you do this, too many similarities emerge which cannot be ignored under any circumstances. It continues to baffle me why extremely capable historians always treat each individual historic site in total isolation, with no suggestion that they just may be part of a very much bigger picture. I try to look at them all from every possible angle before suggesting a conclusion.

My local site, the significant North Yorkshire one at Thornborough Henges, is a very typical example. These are three large earthworks set up in a very deliberate fashion using a large workforce for a deliberate purpose. Almost alongside are three other random tumuli. If the Henges were for a Druid type ceremony and were later than the other three, why not use the originals? If the Henges precede the others, why bother with those any way? Instead the Henges are revered, the others airbrushed away. No one has asked these simple questions until now.

But ignored they are by accepted historians despite all the physical evidence of their existence. In my list of pyramids and other ancient sites, I indicate which monuments seem not to exist to academia, and where you may find them yourselves. This I find to be a travesty of the truth as I see it, not something inconvenient over which we must keep on making a 'Mighty Bound'.

When looking at the section at the end where I give my notes on sources used, it will become apparent that, throughout, one book has been by far the most useful. That book is the Holy Bible in which are so many of the clues – and riddles – that make up this story. Again I am astonished as to the different interpretations that each sect of each religion gives to so many of them. Equally I am astonished how religion as a whole has 'cherry picked' the bits that suit them, airbrushing anything inconvenient from history. More 'Mighty Bounds' as being the most logical explanation.

In answer now to our original question, I feel that the answer must be a resounding 'Yes'. When I began this work following a discussion with a highly respected astronomer back in 2002 I was very much an agnostic who wanted to believe. Now I feel that I can believe in both Christianity and the basic elements of evolution. Not all of either but, yes, basically I believe that both are correct. Along the way many very difficult questions have reared up and, by using simple logic and basic common sense, I think that I have given a possible answer. I may not be right each time, but I invite all those writers who have simply raised the question in the past to now, if they disagree with me, to come up with their own plausible explanations.

Other questions have emerged for which there seems to be no credible explanation. The origin of our seas is just one of them. Just where did that come from? I first raised the question in 2006 when looking across the Mediterranean, this revision is some ten years later and there has been no further theory of any kind. Until that question is answered, once and for all, everything else is open to conflicting ideas. Just how the various enormous inter- group jumps in evolution happened, and when, is another. It is assumed that crustaceans became fish; it is assumed that the fish decided to breathe air and grow legs; it is assumed that the fish became amphibian and then reptile; it is assumed that at some time a reptile became warm blooded and ceased to lay eggs, gathering at the same time a maternal instinct and it is assumed that those first tiny mammals eventually became us. All assumptions and, as I write this, all 'Mighty Bounds'.

I mention my idea of a memory gene. If evolution is as Darwin and all subsequent experts in the field believe it to be, is in fact an accurate explanation, then the memory gene must have been one of the very first to be common to all living things from Day One. Think about it logically and, again, I am trying not to be facetious. If, for argument's sake, in order to evolve into something better, an Angel fish thinks it would be better off as a Guppy. Then what? It has found a need but obviously can do nothing about it and so the idea is passed down to more Angel fish through its own genes. That thought carries on through the genes of the now millions of other Angel fish, hundreds, if not thousands, of years later until one, just one, finds itself growing into a different colour. Slowly its own descendents do the same through their own memory genes until eventually, a million years later we have a new species that is half Angel Fish and half Guppy. Or some of the eggs may accidently interchange and accelerate the process but somewhere down the line that scenario must be the case. Evolution as promulgated could not happen without memory genes. A lizard may want to become a mammal but so what? When it dies that thought dies with it until it reappears in another one, and then another until it happens????? Hmmmmmm!!

Mankind remains the one major unanswered question. If accepted theories are to be believed, and that we are all descended

163

from those few people in Africa some 2,500 generations ago, it is a mystery how we ended up as so many races of different colours and facial identity. And how at the very dawn of the period under discussion, only about 600 generations ago, the first settlers in the Americas could have evolved into all the peoples of those continents, and of many of the South Pacific as well. It just does not add up at all. As we have seen, recorded history began some 5,000 years, or 200 generations, ago and so all the peoples of the Americas and Polynesia had to have evolved in just 400 generations. Is this realistic? Again as this edition goes to press, the above is still the accepted version of man's timeline according to academia. Every TV programme put out by academics states this as a given fact, yet now it is thought that the Aboriginal Australians arrived on the continent at around 75-55,000BCE. From where, no one knows. That man arrived in the Americas in 14,500BC is a 'fact' yet in the next breath we are told that human bones dating to pre-17,000BC have been found in South America. Amazing.

Along the way I have been quite shocked with the volume of irrefutable evidence, freely available and very often published, that has been deliberately suppressed by academia when it cast doubt on their theories. Especially in relation to the WORLD's pyramids, not just those in Egypt. So much of the Egyptian theory goes out of the window when you know that others were building the same things, to the same specification, on the other side of the world, and at the same time. Of this information I was totally ignorant when I began this book. I thought that only Egypt and Mexico had them. When you see the similarities of design and shape you must feel that there is a connection.

I recently saw on television a history of the archaeology of Stonehenge as shown on television over seventy years. It was introduced by a professor who did not seem to be much older than thirty! The variety of different 'definitive' explanations that were laughingly trashed by later 'experts', whose own 'definitive' explanations were similarly trashed *ad infinitum*, was extraordinary. And the practical experiments that they used to justify their theories were beyond a joke. Watching that made me feel much better. After all, I am only an 'amateur'. I just wish that an enterprising TV producer would take them all out to Giza, give them some raw copper, some bronze even, and ask them to cut out a single block of limestone and a single large lump of granite. If they can get it over the First Cataract and onto dry land around Cairo I'll buy them all a large drink. Chris Dunn suggests that but so far I am unaware of anyone taking him up on it.

I would love someone to come up with a competing explanation of why granite was so important, preferably better than that the Pharaoh wanted it in his burial chamber. He would have had no idea of its existence. There has to be a reason why granite was so important to the builders of the great pyramids and, equally so, for those working on Stonehenge and other places across the globe. In all cases the sources were enormous distances away. Equally we have no idea how they were able to identify granite, or any other stone for that matter, and then extract it when all they had to work with was flint, bone, copper or bronze. Yes, I know that using swollen wet wood will separate it but what then? We do not know how they were able to identify tin in its bedrock, smelt it and then mix it with copper to make bronze. And to do this, more or less simultaneously, across the world. The same with iron. I have offered a possible explanation for the identifying of granite and that may hold true for iron as well but that it is a very shaky one, I am the first to admit.

Since the first edition I have gone to a lot of trouble consulting practical real life experts on the working of stone. These are people who make their living doing so in which case I respect their opinions ahead of academic thought on the subject. With regard to identifying the rocks they are unanimous that it is far from easy for people, even with sound geological knowledge, to identify granite, or diorite, against grit stone if they did not know it was there. A consulting mining engineer looked carefully at the extraction in one piece of the limestone and granite blocks used it Giza. He came to the conclusion that today, using modern equipment it could be done but it would not be easy or quick. He doubted that today we could extract seven million of them at all. No 'ifs' or 'buts' about it, today, with the best mining equipment in the world it would be a nigh on impossible task to extract and trim 7 million perfect limestone blocks of the size used. But they are there and were placed there in antiquity. Others in America asked the same question and got the same answer. I have not asked anyone how they either moved or lifted them. The removal, carving and erection of the blocks in South America is another thing that would be incredibly difficult to achieve today. In ancient times it would not have been possible at all. The Thornborough henges, and Silbury Hill each used nearly a quarter of a million tons of gravel and wet earth to build them, but all Stone Age Neolithic man had as a tool was flint. He could use bone as well to extract and move all that material which must have taken a great deal of time. One must ask why?

Since the publication of the first edition I have done much research on 'earth currents' or 'ley lines' in my quest for the use of granite. My thoughts were that several Neolithic circles and monoliths had a granite element and by using this ancient man may have used his powers to tap into those currents. So far I have not found one scrap of evidence, other than that that I have mentioned, to support this theory. Enormous effort was used to transport bluestone shards from South Wales to Wiltshire but equal effort, in other parts of the country, was put into transporting grit stone and sandstone shards from their source to the eventual site. Having studied it for another ten years I am nowhere near to coming close to an answer other than the one I have used in this book.

I was equally shocked to discover that the entire attribution as to a father, his brother or son, or son and grandson as the sole builders of the Giza complex came from Herodotus, effectively a tour guide and local historian during the time of Alexander and Ptolomey. According to Alan Moorhead in 'The White Nile', he had an equally sweeping version of the source of the Nile, even though, at the time, no one had actually penetrated the Sudd. He was a very capable and diligent man to whom we should all be grateful, but he did make a great number of attributions on the material he had to hand, much of which he made up as he went on. He did have access to the library at Alexandria from which he was able to arrive at the names and years on the throne of all pharaohs beginning with the first in 3022BC. This has never been challenged as far as I am aware. This has since remained the absolute rock on which all subsequent Egyptology scholarship is irrevocably stranded. It has never been subsequently confirmed by anyone, yet the real technical work of people like Petrie, Dunn and Legon is summarily dismissed.

In my sources I mention Von Daniken. I knew of his theories having read '*Chariots of the Gods*' some thirty years ago, but I had completely finished this work when I happened on two somewhat bedraggled 1970 copies. This was interesting because I was now able to compare my original thoughts with his, for he was the first to write anything *widely read* in this genre.

I find his works both interesting and confusing. He is far more obsessed with the South American remains than with Egypt. Little drawings and statues of fat little people supposedly in space suits are the main thrust of his argument. He identifies much of the Biblical references that appear here but, like everyone else, he treats everywhere and everything as a unique, one off, happening that occurred at some indeterminate time in the past. He is guilty of many 'Mighty Bounds' in his story and makes no attempt to answer most of the myriad of questions that he rightfully poses. He does, however, suggest some sort of nuclear capability which again makes me feel somewhat less isolated. That the intruders could then spot Uranium on their way in does, to me, stretch credulity to the limit. But then, he never considered the enigma of granite.

Another writer whom I did not consult in the first edition was Zecharia Sitchin. He is more interested in the Nephilim side of my argument. I was both pleased and astonished to find that he too refers to the '*Book of Enoch*' in detail, something everyone else seems to keep at arm's length, but he also embraces all my nuclear thoughts as well. Good, that made me feel even better.

I have tried to take things that massive step further by putting all the happenings into a collective historical perspective and give each its place in the correct chronological context. I've tried to make this very difficult subject easy to read and the story to unfold as the text flows. Not an easy task and by now my reader will know whether or not I have succeeded.

Throughout I've tried to keep away from anything that could be thought of as being 'sensational' but, try as I may, I just cannot get to grips with some of the stories that have emerged. If, as seems likely, there was an invasion of some sort by a people from another planet, they must have had remarkable powers. Going back to the old chestnut of the granite, Somers Clarke reports that thousands of tons were first excavated and then discarded before they got to a supply of sufficient quality. Quality for what?

The sheer effort required using normal, normal 21st century AD I mean, ways of extraction would be immense for the sizes of blocks being discarded was large. Huge cranes and drills would be needed, plus high explosive as well, but there is no evidence anywhere of this. The only possible explanation does in fact now border on the 'sensational' because it infers that they had strange powers of quarrying and were able to transcend gravity as well.

But if they did have these powers and the technological knowledge that would go with them, would they really need to build such enormous and basically useless monuments to generate their power? Surely they would have the knowledge of much easier methods and if, as seems likely, they were able to fly with ease, why not settle in areas where the raw materials were available in unlimited quantities? Why the plains of the Nile and the mountains of South America when Europe and North America were far more welcoming?

Along with the question about the seas, these questions must be asked as well as why no written evidence has survived. Only when the cuneiform was being scratched into clay blocks did the written word begin. Or was everything they wrote destroyed at Alexandria and by the Spanish in Peru and Mexico? Why no evidence at all of machinery of any sort or did that simply rust away in the damp savannah and wet mountains over many thousands of years?

I raised the question of Armageddon and how the Biblical elders all banged on about it, as did many other religions as well. I suggested that our visitors may have witnessed this for themselves on a distant planet. Now I suggest that they may in fact have witnessed it much nearer to home. In Mohenjo Daro in the Indus valley of Pakistan where there is still a higher than normal level of radio activity, archaeologists found the remains of humans lying in the streets as if struck down as they were at Pompeii. There was no obvious volcanic dust so one must infer that they may have been the subject of a possible nuclear blast. The marks in the Saudi hills suggest that a similar blast may have destroyed Sumeria and even in Scotland there is evidence of vitrified rock that could only come from incredibly intense heat. So was the legend of Armageddon passed down by the survivors of this type of thing?

All through this work the dates of around 15 -10,000BC keep cropping up. If this all happened around that time, there most certainly was time for metal machines to simply rust away as the technology was lost until, in 3022BC it all began again, but this time with the great buildings intact as they had been for so many years and mankind having to learn it all again from scratch.

It is not for me to do this research but for other, younger people. People with an open mind prepared to consider every point of view before coming to a conclusion.

Finally I must say that all through the writing of this book, every time I came to a road block along the way and dried up, something, somewhere gave me the tiniest clue which then opened the floodgates to more information. That again pointed me in yet another direction which then tied everything in. Only as I finished one previous chapter, I simply had no idea how to get, what is a difficult thought, over in a logical way that us simpler souls could understand. Next morning I would rise with it in my mind as clearly as possible and was able to write it out so very easily.

If someone or something has been nudging my elbow then I give my profound thanks. Otherwise I put it down to the strictly secular good night's sleep and an adequate supply of good wine. Something of which all the Biblical elders would have approved.

..........oOo..........

PART 3

APPENDICES

1. THE BULGES

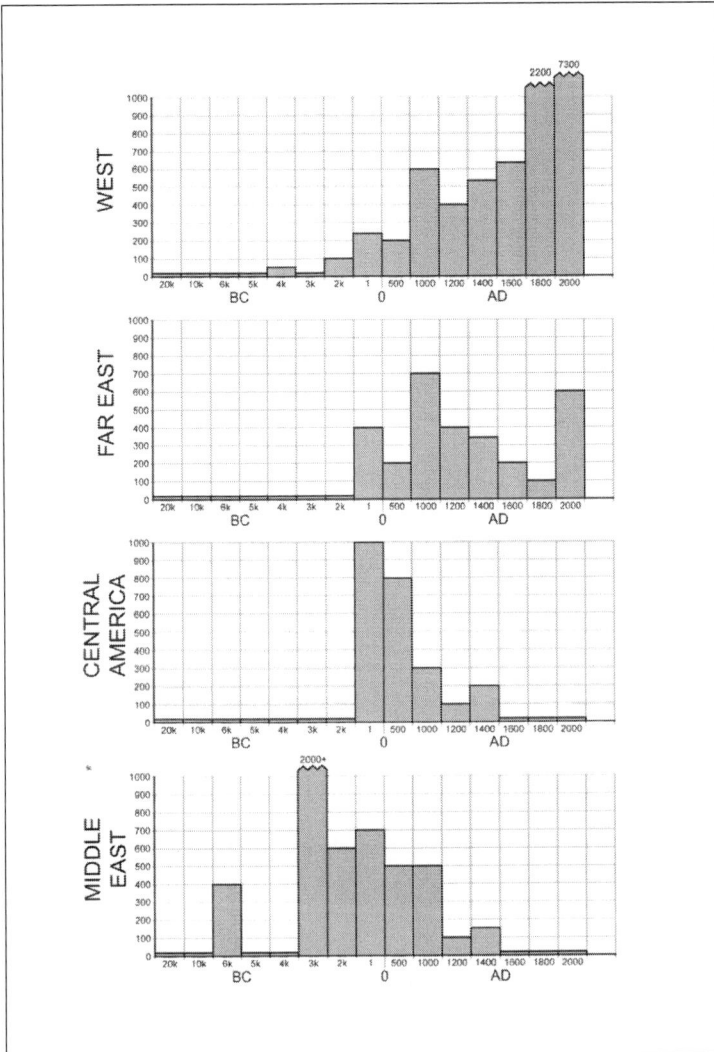

The Bulge according to accepted current thought. The Middle East shows Jericho, the pyramids and the Egyptian Golden Age gradually fading to nothing

2

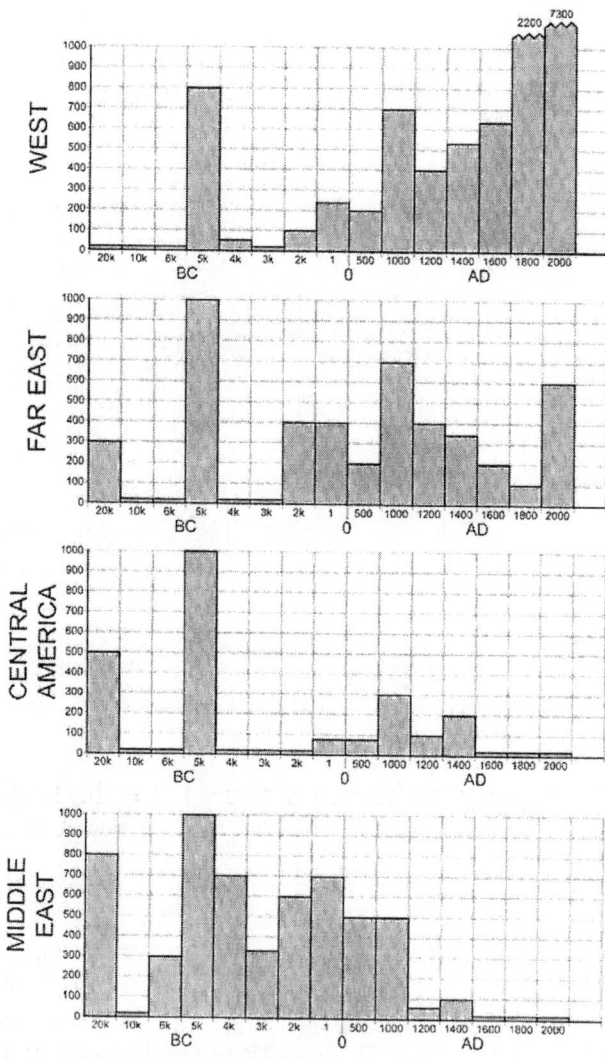

The true Bulge now showing the Middle East beginning so much earlier with the identical developments c5,000BC across the world. No effort has been made to put the various maps into this graph because there is no evidence of their earlier sources.

3

2

LOCATIONS OF THE PRINCIPLE PYRAMIDS AND SIGNIFICANT OTHER SITES IN THE WORLD

Those shown in italics are the ones ignored by academia as a whole, *when looking at the big picture of the history of the world's people,* most putting the beginning only from the first Egyptian Dynasty in 3022BC. I have deliberately not indicated any dates for any of these edifices. Those that have been 'scientifically' dated so far, all fall conveniently into the period from 1st Dynasty Egypt up to the end of the pre – Columbian period in Central America.

AUSTRALIA

There is a pyramid at Gympie, Tin Can Bay, north of Brisbane. It is, or was, 100 ft high but is in a poor shape. Others nearby were bulldozed by the army in the 1950s (Why?). When it was excavated a statue of the Egyptian God 'Thoth' clutching a cross of life was found. According to Aborigine legend, they were built by bronze skinned, fair haired people over 5000 years ago, the people coming from Orion!

There is supposed to be another one twice the height and dimensions to Gympie on the Central New South Wales coast.

BAHAMAS

In 1970 an American scuba diver discovered a submerged pyramid off the coast of Bari Island. It is in about 130 feet (22 fathoms) of water and is 120 ft high although only the top 90ft protrude out of the sand. The stone work is reported to be perfect and it contains at least one accessible chamber in which hangs in the dead centre a red gemstone. In the chamber there has been no attempt made by the coral or anything else to adhere to the walls. A remarkable piece of carved Rock Crystal is said to have been recovered. In it can be seen 4 pyramids, metals magnetise near it whilst it makes any compass spin out of control. I have no idea where it is today, if it exists at all.

BELIZE

Altun-Ha is approx 30 miles north of Belize City, six miles from the sea. Originally it covered 1.8 square miles and had more than 500 structures. 300 jade objects were found here, the largest being 9.75 lbs and is the head of the Mayan Sun God, Kinisch Ahau. It is thought to be the largest Mayan jade carving in the world.

The tallest structure in Belize is at Caracol, south of San Ignacio in the Cayo district. This rises to 140ft and is one of 20 such buildings.

There are three large acropolises at Cerros, on a peninsular in the northern Bay of Chetuma. The Lamanai ruins are overgrown now and lie in an area of 3.5 square miles along the lagoon. There are over 700 structures, one of which is 100 ft high.

Just near the western town of San Ignacio and straddling the border with Guatemala, lies the El Pilar Archaeological Reserve. It spreads to over 100 acres and contains 25 plazas and over a dozen large pyramids.

In the north west is Las Milpas which has over 24 courtyards and 85 structures including pyramids, advanced agriculture and water management schemes.

Again in the north west is Lubaantunis which has a large pyramid made of precision cut blocks that fit together without mortar.

In the Cayo district across the river from the village of San Jose Succotz is a 130ft high pyramid.

BOLIVIA

There is a huge mound constructed of mainly square stone slabs and thought to be designed as an early reservoir at Akapana. Unfortunately the Spanish Conquistadores took much of the original stone to build their cathedral in nearby Tiwanaku. This is still standing and can be seen from Akapana across the Altiplano.

The big site in Bolivia is high in the Andes at 12,000 ft. It is called Tiahuanaco and originally it sat on the banks of Lake Titicaca but now, since the levels dropped, it is some distance away. It is very old indeed and its astronomical alignments suggest a period of around 15,000BC. This makes it contemporary with the Sphinx in Egypt and, possibly, Mohenjo Daro in Pakistan. This site is heavily described and analysed in many other books including 'Fingerprints of the Gods' by Graham Hancock. For more information that is where I would look.

BRAZIL

Satellite photography has identified 12 pyramids in two rows of six side by side deep in the jungle near the Peruvian Andes. Only accessible by helicopter, so far the jungle has defeated all attempts at surveying. A range of pyramids has been identified on the Atlantic coast and, because they are made to a certain extent from sea shells, they were thought to be ancient rubbish dumps! Much material has been plundered for local building work.

Google Earth has now shown evidence of very big settlements and earthworks indicating an advanced civilization along the banks of the Amazon River. So far no attempt has been made to excavate any of these and so they are as yet undated.

CAMBODIA

Anghor Wat is a Buddhist temple in the Cambodian jungle near to Phnom Pen. Since it is clearly on the ancient Great Circle circumnavigation route, there must also have been a much earlier building on the site.

CHINA

The world's largest pyramid is in Xian on the China/Tibet border and is about 1000ft high – twice the height of the Great Pyramid of Giza. First photographed by a World War 11 pilot helping the Chinese, it is now situated in a 'Forbidden Zone' and has never been touched by archaeologists. Apparently there are over a hundred pyramids in the area, most are flat topped and some have small temples on the top. Buddhist records from nearby monasteries say that it was 'very old' some 5000 years ago

A three story pyramid has been found in north China's Inner Mongolia Autonomous region. It is 100 ft long by 50ft wide. Initial excavations have discovered a bone flute, much pottery and wall paintings related to astrology and a full sized stone statue of a Goddess. On an inner wall, with a small stone statue below of a Goddess, is a palm sized stone genital.

In Buhtan Province is the Burma Tibet Pyramid, also known as the 'Pyramid of Gathering'. It is built of bright white limestone, still perfectly preserved, and is said to glow under certain conditions of light. It is stepped, flat topped and equal in size to any in Egypt.

Near the Korean border at Ziban is an almost perfect small stepped pyramid, exactly 102 feet square and 40 ft high. The stone work on the inner chambers is to the same perfection as those in Egypt.

ECUADOR

On a 200 plus acre site at Cochasqui in the northern Andes are fifteen truncated pyramids. These are set in an archaeological park some 45 minutes drive north from Quito via the Pan-American Highway. They seem to be of celestial use mainly and are built from roughly hewn stones although now are mostly covered in grass and vegetation.

EGYPT

As this book has shown, Egypt was at the centre of things from the beginning. To list all the historic sites in the country would fill this book completely, whilst, as with Mexico, they are listed and described in great detail elsewhere. Obviously you must see the Giza complex, Dojer's pyramid and the Bent Pyramid. The Valleys of both the Kings and the Valley of the Queens are a must as is Abu Symbol on Lake Nasser. Luxor will take your breath away and don't ignore Alexandria with its amazing 'Pompey's Pillar' and the Catacombs. Just go and look for yourself.

EL SALVADOR

The Chalchuapa site is nearly 50 miles from San Salvador and is a group of flat topped stepped pyramids in very good condition.

San Andres. Another group of stepped pyramids in the Zapotitan Valley, 21 miles from El Salvador.

Guija Lake. Near the border with Guatemala are many archaeological finds awaiting excavation on the lakeshore.

Cihuatan. 1.5 sq miles of ruined cities.

Joya de Ceren. A settlement 21 miles from San Salvador that was buried by an eruption in 600AD.

Corinto. Two caves with drawings ascribed as pre-historic at 10,000 years BP.

FRANCE

On the Atlantic coast of Brittany lie the remains of the Neolithic site of Carnac. There are nearly 3,000 stones set out generally on a deliberate WSW/ENE alignment on a series of adjoining sites. Now a protected area, it has been much plundered in the past.

GERMANY

There are numerous pyramids, known as 'cairns' spread all over Germany. They are oblong, stepped and formed on the outside by rough cut but easily managed small stones

GREAT BRITAIN

Avebury, near Marlborough in Wiltshire is home to an incredible stone circle, the largest in the world, set inside an ancient earthworks. Nearby is Silbury Hill, a massive man made circular pyramid, 129 ft high and 543 ft in diameter, made entirely of chalk and earth and accepted by history as being in the first place contemporary with Giza and secondly that it was not a burial mound. It has a flat top 100 ft in diameter and was originally stepped but time has now rendered the sides more or less smooth and covered in grass.

Stonehenge

Also in Wiltshire on Salisbury Plain is the huge monolith of Stonehenge, some of the stones for which were originally quarried near Milford Haven in South West Wales – a considerable distance away. This has connotations with the summer solstice and is considered, but not proven, to have Druid origins. The first circle was of timber but the first stones were of a sandstone quarried some miles away in Marlborough. 45 of these made a circle. Then for some inexplicable reason it was discovered that a different type of stone, namely a form of igneous rock called 'bluestone' because of its colour when wet, was needed instead. This was only available 250 miles away in Wales. Why did those people need a form of granite and how were they able to find and recognise it all those years ago?

In Britain are numerous tumuli which are relatively small man made mounds but, nevertheless, enormous civil engineering projects for people yet to discover the wheel or iron. Most, including the three Thornborough Henges in North Yorkshire that mirror the belt of Orion, are only really apparent from the air. These three are significant since the area must have been covered by ice which would have levelled them. Because of this they must date from after the last Ice Age and after the land had dried sufficiently to work it. Joined by the three near Milan they describe a perfect straight line to Giza, which helps us to put a reasonably accurate date on Giza itself. They are enormous and, interestingly, it is thought that they were originally covered in gypsum which is plentiful locally. The gypsum would give them a brilliant white sheen enabling them to be seen from a far distance – from the air. As were some of the Chinese ones.

There are also numerous figures carved by removing the topsoil from hillsides to reveal the bedrock. Most famous of these is in Dorset at Cerne Abbas which has the 'Cerne Giant', a huge representation of mankind leaving nothing to the imagination. In North Yorkshire near the village of Kilburn on the edge of the moors is the 'White Horse of Kilburn', visible from the other side of the Plain of York.

GREECE

The oldest of the sixteen pyramids spread over Greece is at Hellinikon, west of Athens. These are all very small and crudely built rising to about 12ft high. They used individual roughly cut stones of grey limestone and were hollow, having an entrance and a chamber.

GUATEMALA

There is a twin pyramid complex at Tikal in an enclosed courtyard. The pyramids are flat topped, stepped and set on the east/west axis

IRAQ

Near the modern town of Abu Sharain, near the Syrian border, is the ancient city of Eridu where you will find a very early but perfectly preserved large temple. Across the entire country are remains from the very dawn of civilization, some of which are being wantonly destroyed by Islamist militants as this book is being written.

Looted antiquities from the Iraq Museum following the 2003 invasion. Again note the 'nose' on the central bust.

IRELAND

About 27 miles north of Dublin is Drogheda on the east coast where you will find a round earthwork made mainly of pebbles that was once 45 ft high and 262 ft in diameter. The significant thing about this one is that it has a 62ft long horizontal passage above which is a window through which, at dawn on the winter solstice, and only on that day, the sun shines straight in to illuminate the far chamber. The roof of this chamber is of exactly the same design of corbels as the ones in Egypt's Red Pyramid. Most interesting, and so far no one has been able to come up with an answer as to why, is that the long entrance panel is lined with granite. Yes, once again granite, that had to be quarried in the mountains of Co.Wicklow some 50miles to the south of Dublin.

11

ITALY

Only identified from a satellite picture very recently are three overgrown pyramids that mirror Orion's belt. They are in Montevecchia, near Milan, and are built of stone as preliminary excavations have discovered. The biggest is 487 ft high and the construction seems to be similar to that in Egypt.

JAPAN

There is an ancient stone pyramid, only 6ft tall and 12ft across the base but cut from one solid block of grey granite. It is perfect and could easily have been the capstone for one of those at Giza. 100 yards away further up the hill is an identical one followed by another to the north, all set out in some sort of celestial orientation, as yet unidentified.

Also near Ena in Honsu, Japan's largest island, is a perfect flat slab of granite, 8ft x 15 ft with an extremely smooth surface. On this surface are dozens of human and geometric figures together with a linear script. This lies in a rice growing valley of terraced farms of great age, very similar to the terraces found at Machu Pichu in the Andes. On the

opposite side of the valley are two stone pillars that are effectively two granite slabs, 7ft tall and 2ft thick, stuck in the ground vertically with a one inch gap in between. Only at sunrise on the winter solstice does the sun shine precisely through the gap. On one flank is a faint image of the sun.

There are also many small pyramids and other man made structures submerged between some of the islands, most as yet unexcavated.

Off the island of Okinawa, 60 – 100 ft down, lies an enormous under water pyramid complex, some 240ft long. That land was last above sea level around 12,000BC before the ice melted or, being on the Pacific Rim, it could have sunk following an earthquake.

Since there is no knowledge of a society that could have built these ruins off Yonaguni, near Okinawa in Japan, many experts believe that they must have formed naturally.

JAVA

On the island of Java in Indonesia at Candi Sukuh is a remarkable pyramid. Remarkable because it is built to more or less the same design as those in Mexico, Central America and Teneriffe. The site is in good order, not overgrown, but otherwise little is known. As with Mexico, it has a twin headed serpent, the God Quetzalcoatl.

MAGNETIC ISLAND,

There is a pyramid on Magnetic Island off the coast of Queensland in the South Pacific together with a sphinx.

MEXICO

On the Yucatan peninsular facing the Caribbean lie the great pyramids of Mexico. History suggests a period of the immediate pre Columbian era but it is my contention that they are contemporary with Egypt. What cannot be denied is that they are incredible edifices, the ones at Teotihuacan rise to nearly 300 ft and there are 600 of them spread over a vast area. Going back to how they built them, it is interesting to note that at the time the total population of the area varied between 85,000 and 200,000 people. Allowing for women and children there would never have been more than 75,000 men available to do the work. One very interesting and, to me, significant fact about these pyramids is that they contain some very large pieces of Mica, hidden away and therefore of no cosmetic value at all. Now, like the granite in Egypt, Mica is not readily available in Mexico and it is very difficult to quarry being both fragile and flaky. The nearest supply is 2,000 miles away in Brazil and so, again like Egypt, there must have been a very urgent need for its presence. And what is its sole use? It is as an insulator in the electronic and nuclear industries. And nobody has stepped back to wonder why????

There are many more sites in the area, all fully covered in works from the Mexican Tourist Board, most other works in this genre and extensively on the Internet.

NEW GUINEA

Five pyramids, identical to Gympie, have been found in north eastern New Guinea.

14

NORTH AMERICA

Emerald Mound is a large earthwork 35 ft high covering 8 acres and is located in Mississippi alongside the Natchez Trace Parkway.

The largest pyramid in North America is Monk's Mound at Cahokia, 12 miles from St Louis, near the Mississippi river. It covers 16 acres, is 951 ft long and 836 ft wide and 92 ft high. Its bulk of 610,274 cu.metres of earth, not all of which is local, exceeds the largest Egyptian pyramid and it is only surpassed by some in Mexico and the Great White Pyramid of China.

Poverty Point in Louisiana is a vast amphitheatre with a diameter of .75 mile. It is 70ft high, the ridges range from 5 to 10ft and is 800ft long by 700ft deep. Again the cubic capacity of the earth easily outstrips those on Giza. Miamisburg Mound, Ohio is a conical structure 70ft high and 877ft in circumference.

Monks Mound, Illinois.

Etowah Mounds, Cartersville, Georgia are six flat topped earth mounds with a plaza. The highest measures 63ft and they are just starting excavation. They are known to have caves or chambers underneath as do the ones at Giza. Nearby is a Limonite mine. Limonite is an iron bearing rock used as radiation shields extensively in the nuclear industry.

PAKISTAN

In the Indus Valley about 200 miles from the coast lies the remains of the ancient city of Mohejo Daru. Excavations here show the effects of an explosion similar in size and intensity to the one at

Horoshima. The remains are highly radio active. Skeletons were found holding hands in streets with no attempt at burial, many of which contained as much as 50 times natural radio activity. Because of the still high radio-active content, accurate carbon dating has been compromised with site dates varying by as much as 10,000 years. There is radio-active dust at many sites in India dating back 8 – 12,000 years. 10 miles west of Jodpur and also near Ranjasthan there is still dangerous radiation over areas of about 3 sq miles.

PALESTINE

Where accepted chronology and I agree is that Jericho is all of 10,000 years old, the world's oldest walled city. Other sites in the general area known as The Holy Land that should be visited are Petra in Jordan, the town hewn out of solid rock, Damascus with its Biblical 'Street Called Straight' where Paul escaped after his conversion, Baalbeck, the amazing Roman Temple in Syria and, although strictly out of our period, the Crusader castle of the Krak des Chevaliers in Syria. A mixture of Israel and Jordan will take you to the Holy sights where you will see, amongst other things, the remains of Solomon's Temple – the Western or Wailing Wall.

PERU

The principal sites in Peru include Machu Pichu, Cuzco and the NAZCA lines, all of which are more than adequately covered in other works. In fact, just about every other book on the subject describes these in detail. Briefly, Machu Pichu is an ancient city containing incredible stone work, high up in the Andes. No one as yet has dated it with any conviction but it is most certainly pre Inca. As indeed are the amazing NAZCA lines excavated out of the desert landscape high on the tops of the Andes. Only apparent from the air, they would suggest an extra terrestrial connection. Both these lie on the Great Circle line from Easter Island to Giza. There is another group of pyramids some distance away in the jungle, one of which 'sings' like a bird. This is because of the way the wind passes the faces is very much like the sounds made when you blow across the top of a milk bottle.

Machu Picchu in the High Andes. Again look at the incredible stone work on boulders that must have been brought up from the valley below.

SAMOA

On the island of Savai'i there is a 2 tier stepped pyramid 40 ft high with base of 198 x 162 ft. It is now much overgrown but is set exactly on the N/S/E/W meridians.

SUDAN

At Neroe by the 6th Cataract of the Nile are to be found 180 pyramids, all of perfect shape and displaying the identical highly skilled stone work of the one on Tenerife.

TAHITI

James Cook discovered and drew a stepped pyramid not unlike the Mexican ones. It measured a base of 259ft x 80ft with unknown height. Now it is totally destroyed and overgrown.

The Tahiti pyramid as drawn during the expedition of James Cook.

TENERIFE

On Tenerife island is a large pyramid built in the identical style to those in Mexico whilst the stone work, which is highly skilled, matches those to be found in the Sudan.

TURKEY

On Mt Nemrut to the east of Turkey is a 168 ft high artificial cone top surrounded by a large number of Easter Island type heads, some of which display the pronounced nose. The interesting thing here is as to where the material came from to build this not inconsiderable sized edifice. It is stuck on the top of a very barren mountain amongst many square miles of equally barren terrain.

UZBEKISTAN

About 100 miles north of Samarkand, just off the Silk Road to China, the Russians have discovered a series of perfect pyramids with straight sides that are so far unexcavated.

I have tried to include as much information here as I can. I have left the full descriptions and analyses of the more popular sites for others to describe, but this still leaves an incredible number, spread all over the world, of similar works that cannot be ignored by any detailed history of this subject. They are nobody's theory, they are a fact. They are all there. Somebody built them. Why, when and how? These are questions that will be valid just as much tomorrow as they are today. They cannot be airbrushed aside by just taking the Giza or Mexican complexes in isolation and totally out of context with what was going on elsewhere. Yes, it is a can of worms that I have opened, but now I hope that it will not close again until academia accepts that at least some of the points raised must have a grain of truth and possibility in them. When it becomes accepted that the magic date of 3022BC, the start of the 1st Egyptian dynasty, was not the moment when the modern world began. The information above shows that it most certainly was not.

3.

THE MECHANICAL PROBLEMS OF SLIDING A LARGE WEIGHT

I know that some of you still don't believe it, and so now I present to you the simple mechanical and engineering problems that would have been involved in trying to slide a 2.3 ton solid block of stone.

First you must know what forces are acting on the piece at any one time. When stationery it has just the one force (A) which is the total weight, effectively spread over the whole base more or less evenly. Its Centre of Gravity is in the dead centre lengthwise but about one third of the way from the bottom. This force at all times will act in an exact vertical direction when stationery according to the simple laws of inertia and gravity.

Figure 1

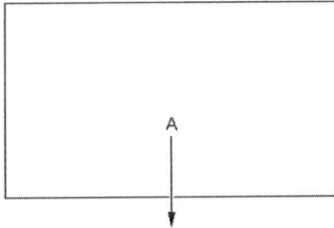

When you attempt to move the piece other forces come into play. The first is the force of friction (B), generally known as 'tractive resistance' and that will vary depending on how smooth each surface is. The second force, which in this case is negligible, is wind resistance (C) and the other force (D) is the one trying to move the object. When a body gathers speed the force at the centre of gravity gradually leaves the vertical and rotates through up to 90 degrees at which point it is going fast enough to fly. It is then that force (C) becomes a problem but, for this exercise, it does not. However you will see that I have shown force (D) at the rear of theblock since the only way that the labourers could have attached suitable ropes would be to wrap them round the block and pull, the point of the force being on that edge. And if they did this, no amount of effort would move the block. The simple reason for this is that by pushing (or pulling) from that point you create a fulcrum at corner (1) which will tend to dig into the ground, your force (D) then is trying to lift the entire weight of the block against its centre of gravity. Only at extreme ground level for your ropes could you have a chance. In context try a little experiment. Put a breeze block into the back of your wheel barrow, lift at the extremity of the handles and see how difficult it is to push the barrow. Especially over a curb.

By pulling from a position forward of the centre of gravity (E) you create a fulcrum at corner (2) and, if the pull is a few degrees above the horizontal, it will have the effect of taking some of the weight off the leading edge. It also, to a small amount, reduces the force of tractive resistance [B].

Figure 2

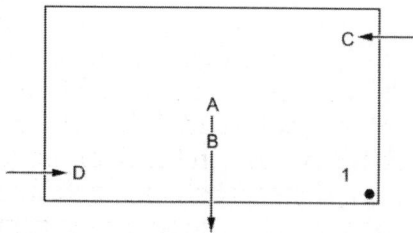

Figure 3

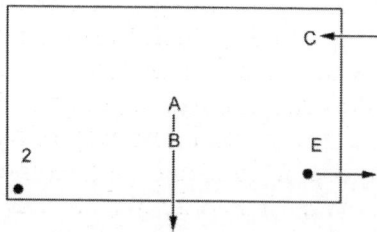

Then the stone will eventually move. But to do this the tractive resistance must be reduced as much as possible and, of course, there must be some method of attaching the ropes near the front of the block. The obvious one would be to drill a hole through and insert a wooden pole (if you could find one strong enough) but this would further weaken an already fragile block and the chances are that the leading corner of the block would break off, especially on the ten mile plus journey to the Red Pyramid. My problem so far is that I have yet to see any evidence of attaching points on any big stone anywhere. Without which they could not be dragged. Back to our little experiment. Now you pull the wheelbarrow backwards and you will see that it easily mounts a small curb. The principal is identical.

'But,' I hear you say, '*surely there is a cartouche showing the large statue being pulled proves you wrong?*' No, it proves me right. Yes I have shown this picture earlier and have studied it carefully. My first point is the reduction of friction, and here they have mounted the statue onto a purpose made sledge. Because of its shape I would guess that it was carved from a very solid piece of wood to get the shape of the front. The statue is carefully tied to the sledge to stop it falling since its centre of gravity would be quite high up, and then the four teams are seen to be pulling from the front in exactly the correct manner. Their pulling force will take sufficient weight off the leading edge which, with its curved face, will now be a relatively easy task to pull over soft sand. Without a curved leading edge, just dragging a vertical face flat on the floor, no matter what it is being pulled over, will act as a snow plough, quickly building up a 'bow wave' for want of a better term. The softer the going, the bigger the bow wave. They must stop every few inches and remove this before it gets too big. Also it would only take one hard outcrop sticking up an inch for the whole thing to come to a dead halt. If they are dragging over limestone (which they would be) then more limestone would not shear it off. The block must gather some momentum and then allow the outcrop to gouge a channel down its length. If they stopped there would be no way of starting again for the outcrop would act as a locating peg, something that has numerous uses up to this day. The only way to start again would be to physically lift the block off the peg and then carry it clear. The only way that a soft limestone block could be slid and remain intact over virtually any distance would be to pull it from the front mounted on a carefully made sledge with a distinctly curved front constructed from either a very hard wood or cast in iron or bronze.

22

And we need 7 million of them. The picture shows with abundant clarity that the statue was in fact being slid on what appear to be timber tracks with some men carrying spares. Above is someone else pouring a lubricant onto those tracks to ease the friction, again proving my point completely.

What about manpower?

We have seen that just to raise this 2.3 ton block off the ground we need 150 men, that is if they could get a purchase on it and could all fit around. Neither is in fact possible. To pull it with little tractive resistance i.e. wheels with rubber tyres on a tarmac road, one man could do it but not very easily. This is the size and weight of a big Mercedes, Bentley or Cadillac. Another simple experiment for you. Park your car on a level piece of smooth road with the handbrake off [obviously with someone left inside to put it on again] and then try to push it on your own. Then see how many people you need to push it up a shallow incline. Remember that you are on a smooth road with hard tyres. Try to put it onto a wooden sledge and then push it along a farm track and you will see what I mean. But, with the tractive resistance that we encounter here, we will need all of those 150 men plus some more if any progress is to be made.

'But', again I hear you say, 'surely the picture proves the point? They will simply have mounted each block onto a cast bronze sledge. Problem solved. Or even a simple wooden one with a curved front'. Yes, it would be except that few of the sledges would last for more than one journey and we need seven million of them, some of which would have survived, buried in the sand, to be found by modern day archaeologists. There is no evidence so far of any massive foundries able to cast bronze in these quantities over such a long time. We need 300 new ones every day, remember, and that is a lot. Just where would the raw materials come from? From where would come the astronomic quantity of wood to fuel the foundries? From where the tin and copper? If of wood, from where did enough come, at the sites of the quarries, to build the sledges? What fastenings did they use? The questions are endless and unanswerable, especially when you consider that in fact all the four big pyramids are supposed to have been built when all they had was copper and gold. The statue would be a 'one off', a special occasion when the boat would be pushed far out with no expense spared. And what about the granite blocks? Here we are not talking about a big Mercedes but a railway engine or two huge juggernaught lorries, all without wheels, to be dragged enormous distances. And loaded onto huge boats at Aswan before unloading again at Giza.

Anyone who now still thinks that they simply dragged them, please come up with the following evidence.

1. The remains of dockyards at two levels on both sides of the Nile near both the Red Pyramid and the Giza complex.
2. The remains of one bronze or wooden sledge.
3. Any block with anchorage points for ropes low down on its leading edges.
4. Evidence of a substantial bronze foundry. (Please discount wood. There would never have been anywhere near enough to make rollers nor to form huge hard planks suitable for this purpose. Also, as mentioned before, rollers, like tyres, need a very solid base to roll on. Again, if in doubt, try to drive out of a seriously muddy field, through thick, soft snow or sand.)
5. Some evidence, either in cartouches or remains on the ground, of how they lifted even the smallest blocks.

If you cannot, then please give my theories some credence.

However, I have been looking at an interesting web site www.forgotten_technology.com and DVD where the author, W T Wallington, demonstrates how he can move huge lumps of concrete by himself. He uses the dead centre as his fulcrum with a system of balanced counterweights that allows the concrete to rock very simply. By transferring counter weights he is able to shift the position of the fulcrum and so help the block to move. Rightly he claims that little in the way of work force is needed but it is my contention that using this as a theory for the building of the pyramids is seriously flawed. For the following reasons:-

1. On soft ground the pivot would simply sink in. For the Red Pyramid the stones would need to move more than 3 miles over soft sand.

2. He still has to both place and remove the blocks from a fragile boat.
3. They still need to be dug out of a quarry somewhere.
4. There are no drawings, paintings or cartouches demonstrating the method.

Looking at the stones actually used on the pyramids, I see no signs of helpful chamfering of one edge to get the initial fulcrum without which the block could not be moved at all. Nor are there small stones let in to provide the fulcrums. If, and only if, the blocks were to be moved over a smooth and solid concrete base, then I would submit that three hardwood rollers using his technology would be infinitely easier. That is assuming that there was an unlimited supply of hardwood available. Which there was not.

I give his theories credence because he is quite happy to demonstrate them using enormous self made blocks of cast concrete. He doesn't just rely on academic theory, but I would like to see him first of all obtain, in one piece, at least one quarried limestone block of the pyramid dimensions and then both move and lift it into position.

Once again I am open to be proved wrong.

4.

LOCATIONS OF THE PRINCIPAL HISTORICAL SITES ACROSS THE GLOBE.

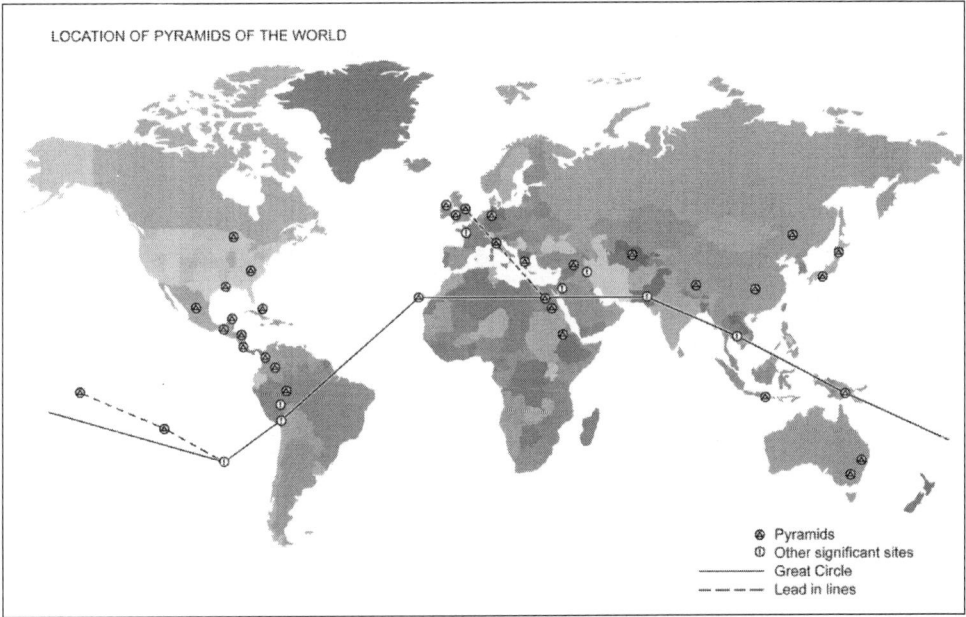

LOCATION OF PYRAMIDS OF THE WORLD

⊕ Pyramids
① Other significant sites
―――― Great Circle
― ― ― Lead in lines

This layout shows clearly the migrating patterns of the early Nephilim. From a base around Central America they went north and south; from the Giza base they went to Britain, into Africa and the Middle East and from Cambodia north and south again.

5.

THE LAST ICE AGE

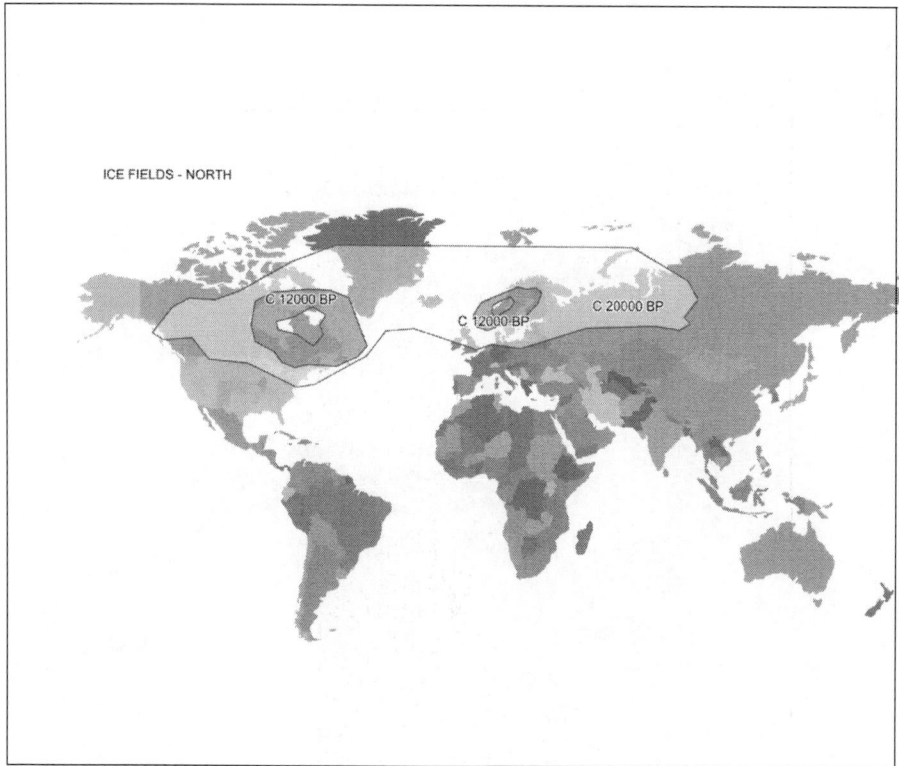

ICE FIELDS - NORTH

C 12000 BP

C 12000 BP

C 20000 BP

The Ice fields clearly show that the northerly sites must be after 18,000BC to be clear of ice. If we switch the poles so that it is South Australia that is the South Pole we have a new North Pole in North America and Antarctica free of ice. And the UK with its top half ice bound. This is the Velekovsky theory backed up by Solarion. It makes some sense but I must ask just what caused the poles to shift, if indeed they did.

6.
THE RELATIVE SIZES OF THE MAIN PYRAMIDS.

Relative Sizes Of The Main Pyramids.

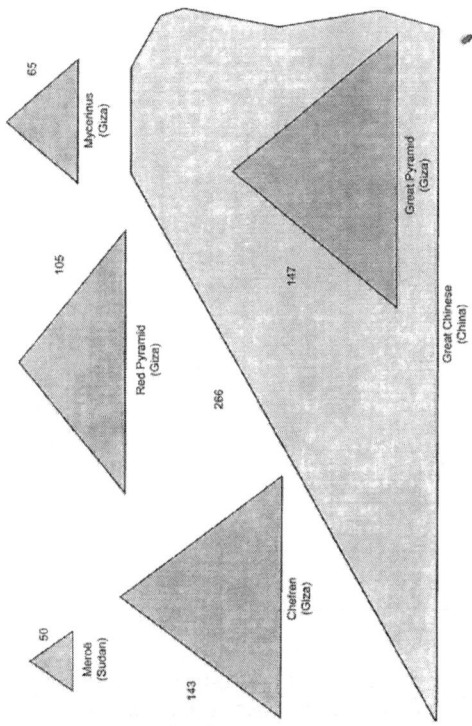

This diagram shows clearly that the Chinese pyramid at Xian was so very much bigger than the rest. There must have been a very good reason to commit all those resources so many years ago.

7.

RELATIVE LAYOUT OF GIZA TO MILAN

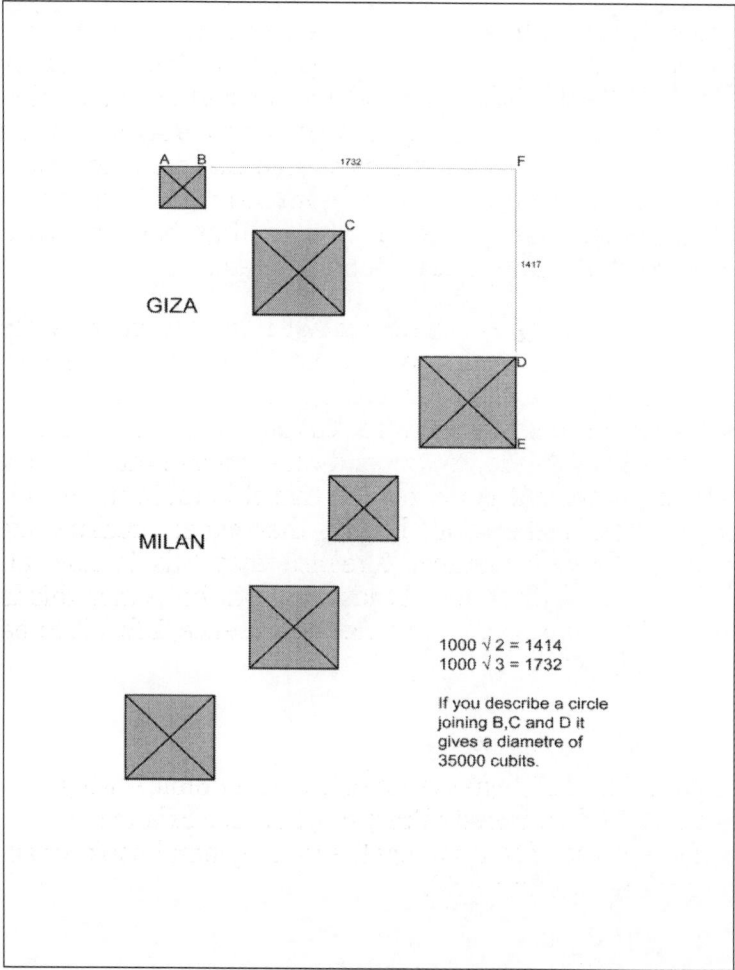

Doing the same exercise with the Milan ones gives a similar result.

I do not show it until a very detailed survey has been done.

Notes on sources.

Since the first edition of this book was published in 2008 the Internet has expanded a great deal, making research for this type of project that much easier. I have used it extensively for both the text and some of the pictures, the rest of which have been taken by myself. This, however, raises the problems of correct attribution since most are posted anonymously and so presumably are in the public domain. All the pictures that I have used that were not taken by me fall into this category – as far as I am aware. If I have used something that should have been attributed, but has not, then please accept my apologies since it is not deliberate.

Most chapters contain an element of information from the Internet but I have also taken on board what I have seen on serious television programmes as well. Where specific books have been consulted I list them in the 'Foreword' chapter and below merely refer to the author only. I do not depend on copious notes to back up these references since it is my feeling that it is more important that the book 'flows' rather than having the reader breaking off repeatedly to check on a source. I realise that this is now an outdated approach for any serious academic work but, since this is intended for a wider, but equally intelligent audience, I feel it to be the correct method.

Foreword.

Here I refer to my early experience of The Holy Bible – King James Edition, Oxford University Press c.1900. Also existing knowledge of the works of Darwin together with general books of all types relating to the ancient world.

Part 1.

1   **In The Beginning.** Again the Bible and Darwin were my early sources added to by reference to the Holy Koran. (I use the normal spelling rather than the more formal

'Qu'ran'). The Tao Ching by Lao Tzu gave an insight into Eastern thinking. I used The Times Atlas of World History for basic chronological information and Koneman's Egypt, Land of the Pharaohs, for the detailed Dynastic information post 3022BC.

2   **The Myths of Creation.** The Bible first then the Crystalinks site on the Internet. The Larousse Encyclopaedia of Mythology, Koneman again for dynastic information.

3   **The Prophets.** Most information came from the Bible. At this point most of my first ideas had been proved doubtful as I carried on seeking some logical explanations.

4   **Darwin or The Creation?** Mostly the Bible and Wikipedia. I refer to the works of Charles Hapgood, Charles Darwin, Albert Einstein and Dr Hugo Ross.

5   **The Chicken or the Egg?** Charles Darwin, Wikipedia.

6   **Scientific Fact or a Mighty Bound?** Wikipedia and my own original thoughts.

7   **Armageddon.** Recent scientific works in the press, television and internet that questioned earlier assumptions.

8   **The Bulge.** As above but mostly my own work. I used the accepted chronology as shown in, amongst many others, the Times Atlas of World History. Julian Janes 'The Origin of Consciousness in the Bicameral Mind'. The rest I deduced for myself and is all original.

9   **Waves.** The whole chapter on waves is my original work. I did see much corroborating evidence on various BBC TV productions.

10 **Do the Numbers Add Up?** For the three construction sites I used mainly the Wikipedia site on the Internet. This gave me

sufficient background to base my argument. The rest is entirely my own original work.

11 **The Giza Pyramids.** Various unattributed sites plus the Crystalinks one located the world's pyramids. I looked at many pictures in published works such as 'Fingerprints of the Gods' by Graham Hancock, 'Genesis Unveiled' by Ian Lawton and Koneman's Egypt. These were carefully analysed before my own original thoughts were revealed. By this period of the book, previously published sources had more or less dried up. Many hours were spent scouring the Internet for any information still available. I consulted the web sites of most of the principal museums of the world.

12 **Pyramids Again.** Tingley Monuments of Nova Scotia published a wonderful account of the working of both marble and granite on their web site. Anyone doubting my thoughts should read this which puts the obviously essential use of granite into some sort of perspective. I consulted the Properties of Pyramids site together with many, but not all, the 139 million ones on nuclear energy. I got my mathematical information from the works of Flinders Petrie and John AR Legon and Astronomical details from the site of 'Map Makers of the Ice Age' by Jean Pierre Lacroix. I read with interest the work of Jean Pierre Houdin and his ideas on how the pyramids were built. The work by Somers Clark on the practical side to the problem was a big help. The deductions are all my own.

13 **Why Granite?** Wikipedia, 'The Old Straight Track' by Alfred Watkins,' The Megalithic Portal' web site, The Handbook of Ancient Artefacts by William Corless, 'Building the

Great Stone Circles of the North' by Colin Richards.

14 **Back to the Pyramids Again**. Flinders Petrie, J. A R Legon, Charles Hapgood.

15 **Awkward Questions.** This is mainly the result of detailed analysis of many published photographs. I refer to the works of Michael Cremo and Richard Thompson, Charles Hapgood, Graham Hancock, Eric Von Daniken, Augustus John, E Keble Chatterton and Wikipedia.

16 **The Ark of the Covenant and The Holy Grail.** The whole chapter is my own original work. The Bible and numerous Internet sites. 'The Holy Grail – Chalice or Manna Machine' by the Fieberg Brothers with George Sassoon and Rodney Dale. They are the first to categorically include as fact an extra terrestrial element.

17 **Why Gold?** Richard Holliday and the site of the Gold Council.

18 **Time**. J.W Dunne ' Serial Universe' and 'An experiment with Time'. All the rest are my own original findings.

PART 2

19 **The Plot So Far.** The Bible and the lost Book of Enoch. Somers Clark, Timothy Goode.

20 **Ships, Pulleys, Tools and Lifting Gear.** Wikipedia, Herodotus, Somers Clark, E Keble Chatterton.

21 **Maps.** Charles Hapgood.

22 **How they Could have Built the Pyramids**. The Bible. 'Human Devolution – A Vedic alternative to Darwin' by Michael Cremo. The Cairo Museum, Somers Clark, Graham Hancock, H.W Brands, Joseph

Jacovits, Konemann. The rest all my original work.

23 **The Extra Terrestrials.** Zecharia Sitchin, The Bible, Alan Moorhead.

24 **Back to the Question of Why?** The Megalithic Portal, Samuel N Kramer.

25 **The Nephilim and Nibiru.** Zecharia Sitchin, The Bible, The Megalthic Portal, Wikkipedia.

26 **Waves, Ghosts and Ghoulies.** The Bible, Alan Moorhead. Michael Cremo. Rest all my original work.

27 **What Has God Got To do With It?** The Bible. The Book of Enoch. Otherwise all my own original work.

28 **The Nose.** Various museums. Otherwise all my own original work.

29 **The Stars.** Robert Solarion. Otherwise all my own original work.

30 **The Floods.** All my own original work.

31 **The Second Coming.** All my own original work.

32 **Tailpiece.**

PART 3

Appendices.

1. **The Bulges.** All my own original work.

2. **Locations of the Principal Historical Sites.** Various sources.

3. **The Mechanical Properties of Moving a Large Object.** All my own original work.

4. **Locations Map.** Various internet sites. The deductions are my own.

5. **The Last Ice Age.** All my own original work.

6. **Relative Sizes of Pyramids.** Various internet sites. The deductions are my own.

7. **Relative layouts of Giza and Milan.** All my own original work.